Innovations in
Bond Portfolio Management:
Duration Analysis and
Immunization

CONTEMPORARY STUDIES IN
ECONOMIC AND FINANCIAL ANALYSIS, VOLUME 41

Editors: Professor Edward I. Altman and Ingo Walter, Associate Dean,
Graduate School of Business Administration, New York University

CONTEMPORARY STUDIES IN ECONOMIC AND FINANCIAL ANALYSIS

An International Series of Monographs

Series Editors: **Edward I. Altman and Ingo Walter**
Graduate School of Business Administration, New York University

Innovations in
Bond Portfolio Management:
Duration Analysis and
Immunization

Edited by   **GEORGE G. KAUFMAN**
Loyola University of Chicago

G. O. BIERWAG
University of Arizona

ALDEN TOEVS
University of Oregon

 **JAI PRESS INC.**

Greenwich, Connecticut   *London, England*

Library of Congress Cataloging in Publication Data
Main entry under title:

Innovations in bond portfolio management.

(Contemporary studies in economic and financial
analysis; v. 41)
Includes bibliographies and index.
1. Bond—Addresses, essays, lectures.   2. Portfolio
management—Addresses, essays, lectures.   I. Kaufman,
George G. II. Series.
HG4651.I56   1983   332.63′23   82-81206
ISBN 0-89232-320-5

Copyright © 1983 JAI PRESS INC.
36 Sherwood Place
Greenwich, Connecticut 06830

JAI PRESS INC.
3 Henrietta Street
London WC2E 8LU
England

ISBN NUMBER: 0-89232-320-5
Library of Congress Catalog Card Number: 82-81206
Manufactured in the United States of America

CONTENTS

PART V.   SUMMARY OF CONFERENCE

PART VI.   APPENDIXES

120349

PREFACE

Papers in this volume were prepared for a conference on "Duration: The State of the Art" in Ashland, Oregon on July 9–10, 1980. The conference was cosponsored by the Center for Capital Market Research at the University of Oregon and the Center for Financial and Policy Studies at Loyola University of Chicago. The conference brought together some 45 leading researchers in bond portfolio management from both academic and financial institutions and a number of bond portfolio managers for a two-day interchange.

Although duration as a statistic was developed by Frederick Macaulay in 1938 and "rediscovered" numerous times since, it did not receive widespread attention until the publication by Professors Larry Fisher and Roman Weil of their seminal article "Coping with the Risk of Interest Rate Fluctuations: Returns to Bondholders from Naive and Optimal Strategies" in the *Journal of Business* in 1971. Thereafter, duration caught the imagination of researchers and practitioners alike in bond portfolio management and has become one of the hottest topics in finance. Indeed, as a single factor explaining bond returns, duration promises to become as widely used as beta is for equities. Because researchers at the Center for Capital Market Research, where all three editors were employed at the time, were involved in research on duration since shortly after the publication of the Fisher-Weil article and have contributed significantly to increasing our understanding of its uses, it was appropriate that the Center sponsor this conference as its final major activity.

This volume contains all but one paper presented at the conference and all but one discussant's comments. The papers review the development of duration, and in particular single factor duration models (SFDMs), examine its theoretical underpinnings, analyze its potential uses and limitations, evaluate the empirical evidence, and discuss how portfolio managers use it. The volume truly reflects the state of the art in duration analysis as of 1980 and should serve as basic reading for all researchers and practitioners in bond portfolio management.

Preparation of the papers for publication was supervised by Ann Fischer and Michelle Taylor of Loyola University. The index was prepared by Ann Fischer and Mary Lisa Meier. Susan Oppenheim was production editor at the JAI Press.

George G. Kaufman
Loyola University of Chicago

PART I

DURATION, BOND PRICING, AND RISK

DURATION, BOND PRICING, AND PORTFOLIO MANAGEMENT

Michael J. Brennan and Eduardo S. Schwartz

I. INTRODUCTION

In this paper we are concerned with a comparison, both theoretical and empirical, between duration theory and the related concept of portfolio immunization on the one hand, and the modern equilibrium theory of the term structure on the other. We argue that the essential feature of both theories from the viewpoint of bond portfolio management lies in the fact that they yield estimates of the variance-covariance matrix of bond returns, and we present evidence on the comparative adequacy of the estimates derived from particular duration and equilibrium models.

The proliferation of, and interest in, different measures of bond duration can be understood only in light of the role of duration as an a priori measure of the responsiveness of bond returns to some index of change in bond yields; its other role, as a summary measure of bond maturity, is without economic significance.[1] It is unfortunate therefore that Macaulay [20], whose main interest was in summary measures of bond maturity, should have been the first to calculate a duration measure, and that it should have been his title which stuck to the

3

concept rather than, for example, Hicks' [16] more cumbrous, but more meaningful, "elasticity of capital value." Despite this accident of no-menclature, the primary significance of duration relates to its elasticity property, in which aspect its function is very similar to that performed by the beta coefficient in common stock portfolio analysis. It is our thesis that duration models may be viewed as simplified portfolio models tailored specifically for the analysis of bond portfolios.[2] It is at first sight ironic in view of the early development of duration and the related concept of the immunization of bond portfolios[3] that bond analysis should have remained for so long a bastion against the advance of modern portfolio theory. The most likely explanation for this is that practical bond portfolio analysis presents serious problems which are not present, or at least are not so apparent, when portfolio theory is applied to common stocks. Modern portfolio theory has until recently lacked a solution to these problems, whereas duration theory has been able to address them, if only in a partial and incomplete fashion.

To be specific, practical portfolio analysis requires that the covariance structure of asset returns either be estimated from historical data or be known a priori. Estimation from historical data presupposes some model of how the covariance matrix changes over time; for example, when portfolio theory was applied to common stocks, it was for a long time, commonplace to estimate either the full Markowitz [22] covariance matrix or the constrained Sharpe [31] diagonal matrix, on the assump-tion that return covariances between stocks in any two particular companies were intertemporally stable. Only subsequently were these covariances permitted to change over time in response to shifts in more basic descriptors.[4]

The obstacle to estimation of a variance-covariance matrix of bond returns from historical data has been that a structure similar to that for common stocks could not reasonably be assumed, and it was unclear what alternative structure should be assumed: it may be acceptable as a first approximation to assume that the covariance between returns on the common stocks of General Foods and General Motors is the same in 1981 as it was in 1971, but such an assumption would be unacceptable for two bond issues due in 1990 and 1982, since casual observation reveals that the variability of bond returns is a function of time to maturity which changes with calendar time for any given bond issue.[5]

A solution which suggests itself to this problem of the everchanging character of the particular bond is to change the unit of observation from the individual bond with a given maturity date to the class of bonds with the same time to maturity; the covariance of returns between bonds in given classes would then be treated as intertemporally stationary. Unfortunately there exist several problems which effectively preclude this solution. First, individual bond classes cannot be treated as homogeneous since they will in general contain bonds with different coupon rates. Secondly, errors will be created by a gross classification of bonds by maturity since maturity is a continuous variable; yet if the maturity classification is made fine, there will be too few contemporaneous observations of returns to permit accurate estimation. Thirdly, bond prices depend upon the level of interest rates, and there is no reason to expect the variance-covariance matrix of bond returns to be independent of the level of interest rates, but unless the dependence can be modeled, the variance-covariance matrix cannot be estimated.

In view of the foregoing estimation problems, it is not surprising that until recently there have been no serious attempts to estimate the covariance structure of bond returns. However, the concept of duration may be viewed as providing a bold and simple solution to the problem of obtaining a (local) variance-covariance matrix of bond returns, and a solution which was particularly suited to the precomputer age in which it was developed since it requires no statistical estimation; by imposing a particular a priori structure on the variance-covariance matrix, the duration model avoids all of the above problems. It recognizes that bonds differ by coupon as well as by maturity, it provides a measure of covariance which varies continuously with time to maturity, and it explicitly allows for dependence of the local covariance matrix on the general level of interest rates.

On the other hand, the duration model is necessarily limited to dealing with but a single source of interest rate uncertainty.[6] This strong assumption about the stochastic process for interest rates imples that the local variance-covariance matrix of bond returns is singular and possesses a particularly simple structure. This structure was exploited by Redington [27] in deriving his immunization policy which is discussed in more detail in Section II.

As Ingersoll, Skelton, and Weil (ISW) [17] and Cox, Ingersoll, and Ross (CIR) [8] have pointed out, a more significant deficiency of traditional duration theory is its neglect of the fact that singularity of the local variance-covariance matrix of bond returns implies restrictions on equilibrium expected returns and therefore on the type of underlying uncertainty that can be assumed. CIR and ISW have discussed the nature of these restrictions.

In this paper we contrast the duration approach to bond portfolio analysis with its single source of interest rate uncertainty with an equilibrium model of bond pricing based upon two sources of uncertainty. This model has been described in previous papers by the authors[7] and is similar to models developed by others.[8] The theoretical bases of the models are discussed in Sections II and III. In Section IV the equilibrium model is estimated using data on U.S. Government bonds, and in Section V the two models are compared in terms of their implied variance covariance matrices of bond returns and their relative success in yielding immunized portfolio strategies. The duration model performs remarkably well by comparison with the more sophisticated equilibrium model, and in view of the computational cost of the latter, the duration model appears to be more useful for practical bond portfolio management if attention is restricted to straight default-free bonds with no option provisions.

II. DURATION AND IMMUNIZATION

Our object in this section is to show that duration and immunization theory are closely related to modern portfolio theory, but that duration theory has inherent conceptual limitations which are overcome in modern equilibrium theories of the term structure: a more extensive analysis of duration in terms of modern term structure theory is to be found in ISW or CIR.

Denote by $B_j(s,t)$ the value of a particular default free bond j at time t when the state of the yield curve is as represented by the state variable s. Duration models generally fail to specify the dynamics of the underlying state variable and for expository purposes it will be helpful initially to take s as a deterministic, continuous, differentiable function of time.[9]

Then the rate of return on a bond may be written[10] as

$$R \equiv \frac{1}{B} \frac{\partial B}{\partial t} + \frac{1}{B} \frac{\partial B}{\partial s} \frac{ds}{dt} \qquad (1)$$

In duration models the term

$$\frac{1}{B} \frac{\partial B}{\partial s}$$

is referred to as the *duration* of the bond. The distinguishing feature of duration models is that this term can always be constructed as an appropriately weighted average of the maturities of the individual payments on the bond so that the duration of a pure discount bond, and therefore the elasticity of its value with respect to the state variable, is equal to its maturity.[11] The particular weighted average which is chosen to represent duration depends upon the definition of the state variable s, since the duration measure and the state variable must be jointly consistent with equation (1).

The simplest duration model, which is described in the first line of Table 1, takes as the state variable the yield to maturity on the bond itself. This definition is consistent with Equation (1), but it has no implications for the relative return behavior of different bonds and therefore no implications for risk or portfolio design[12] unless the rate of change in yield to maturity (ds/dt) is the same for all bonds. ISW have shown that the yield to maturity for arbitrary coupon bonds can change at the same rate only if the yields are initially equal and the yield curve flat. Thus this duration model implicitly presupposes parallel shifts in a flat yield curve. The alternative Macaulay model, described in the second line of Table 1, takes as the state variable a measure of the level of the yield curve and allows for parallel shifts in a not necessarily flat yield curve. The Bierwag [2] model shown in the third line of the table is similar but allows for uniform multiplicative shifts of the yield curve. More complex models have been developed by Bierwag [2] and Khang [18]: the latter allows for a predetermined mixture of shift and rotation in the yield curve; the former allows for both additive and multiplicative shocks. This Bierwag model is in fact a two-state variable model[13] which requires two distinct measures of duration to describe the risk of a bond.

Even in the world of certainty discussed so far, the evolution of the state variable s cannot be arbitrary but must be consistent with security market equilibrium if the duration model is to have any plausibility. Unfortunately, classical duration theorists gave no attention to equilibrium and on occasion appear to have made assumptions about the dynamic behavior of the yield curve which were inconsistent with equilibrium. To illustrate the nature of the restrictions imposed by the equilibrium requirement, suppose, for example, that s is taken as the level of the flat yield curve in the Hicks-Macaulay model of Table 1. Then the equilibrium requirement that under certainty all bonds must have the same rate of return is expressed by

$$\frac{1}{B}\frac{\partial B}{\partial t} + \frac{1}{B}\frac{\partial B}{\partial s}\frac{ds}{dt} = s \qquad (2)$$

Since the first term in the equation is s, when s is the yield to maturity, the equilibrium condition (2) implies that ds/dt = 0 so that the yield curve must remain stationary. For general definitions of the state variable, a given function $g(t) \equiv ds/dt$ which describes the trajectory of the yield curve will imply certain values of $B_j(s,t)$ which are consistent with the equilibrium requirement.[14] These equilibrium bond values

Table 1. Alternative Measures of Duration[a]

Authors	Duration	State Variable
(1) Hicks [16], Macaulay [20], Samuelson [30], Redington [27]	$D(t) = \dfrac{\sum (\tau - t)c(\tau)e^{-y(\tau - t)}}{\sum c(\tau)e^{-y(\tau - t)}}$	$s(t) \equiv y$
(2) Macaulay [20], Fisher and Weil [14]	$D(t) = \dfrac{\sum (\tau - t)c(\tau)q(\tau - t,t)}{\sum c(\tau)q(\tau - t,t)k}$	$s(t) \equiv -\dfrac{1}{\tau - t} \log \dfrac{q(\tau - t,t)}{q(\tau - t,0)}, \quad \forall \tau$
(3) Bierwag [2]	$D(t) = \dfrac{\sum (\tau - t)R(\tau - t,t)c(\tau)\,q(\tau - t,t)}{R(D(t),t) \sum c(\tau)q(\tau - t,t)}$	$s(t) \equiv \dfrac{R(h,t)}{R(h,0)}, \quad \forall h$

[a] Here $c(\tau)$ = payment at time τ; y = yield to maturity; $q(\tau - t,t)$ present value at time t of \$1 receivable at time τ; $R(h,t) = h^{-1} \ln q(h,t)$.

must then be consistent with the state of the yield curve implied by the underlying model and the current value of s. It is apparent that this consistency condition will not be satisfied for arbitrary definitions of s and g(t). ISW and CIR have derived in an uncertainty context the corresponding restrictions on the dynamics of the state variable which are imposed by different duration measures.

Relaxing the assumption of certainty but continuing to assume that the state variable evolves continuously over time,[15] its behavior may be described by an Ito process of the general type

$$ds = \eta(s)\, dt + \sigma(s)\, dz \;, \tag{3}$$

where dz is the increment to a standard Gauss–Wiener process. Then, corresponding to equation (1), the (now stochastic) instantaneous return on a bond is given by

$$\frac{dB}{B} = \alpha_j\, dt + \delta_j\, ds \;, \tag{4}$$

where from Ito's lemma

$$\alpha_j = B^{-1}\left[\frac{\partial B}{\partial t} + \frac{1}{2}\frac{\partial^2 B}{\partial s^2}\,\sigma^2(s)\right]$$

and

$$\delta_j = B^{-1}\frac{\partial B}{\partial s} \;.$$

In a duration model δ_j is the duration of the bond calculated as the appropriately weighted average maturity of the payments on the bond.[16] Note that expression (4) reduces to equation (1) when $\sigma(s) = 0$ and the state variable evolves in a deterministic fashion.

The typical element of the instantaneous variance-covariance matrix of bond returns, Ω, is

$$\Omega_{ij} = \delta_i\delta_j\sigma^2(s) \;, \tag{5}$$

and the different duration modes may be thought of as alternative a priori specifications of the structure of the variance-covariance matrix Ω.[17]

It is a model of bond returns such as is represented by equations (4) and (5) which underlies the Redington [27] theory of immunization. An immunized bond portfolio is one which bears no interest rate risk, and Redington was able to show in the context of the duration model that it was possible, given any portfolio of assets or liabilities, to tailor an offsetting portfolio so that the aggregate portfolio bore no interest rate risk and was, therefore, immunized.[18]

Thus consider a portfolio of bonds represented by the vector of portfolio proportions X. According to the duration model, the instantaneous variance of the portfolio return will be given by $X'\Omega X$. Moreover, in view of the special structure of Ω, this variance will be equal to zero if the portfolio is chosen so that $X'\delta = 0$, the weighted average of the durations of the bonds in the portfolio is equal to zero. It was Redington's insight to see that it was possible to eliminate all interest rate risk by choosing a portfolio whose average duration was equal to zero. The extension to immunizing a given portfolio of assets or liabilities by treating some of the elements of X as fixed is straightforward.

The essential distinction between duration models and modern single-state variable equilibrium approaches to bond analysis may now be stated. Duration theory starts from an a priori definition of the state variable which defines the yield curve and makes (usually implicit) assumptions about its evolution over time. The state variable is chosen so that δ_j may be calculated directly and has the weighted average maturity property of a duration measure. No check is made as to whether the stochastic behavior of the term structure implied by the state variable is consistent with equilibrium. The equilibrium approaches also start from an exogenously specified state variable and its behavior over time; however, the state variable is taken to define only a single point on the yield curve rather than the entire curve. Equilibrium considerations are then adduced to yield a family of bond valuation functions which define a corresponding family of yield curve functions whose parameters depend upon investor tastes. In these equilibrium models $(1/B) \, \partial B/\partial s$, the elasticity of capital value, has typically no weighted average maturity interpretation and cannot be calculated directly but depends upon the parameters of the stochastic process for the state variable as well as upon investor tastes.

From a precomputer viewpoint the duration measure has the decided advantage that it does not require estimation. The price of this is that the a priori specification of the variance-covariance matrix may not fit the facts. The equilibrium approach requires estimation but is far more flexible and is readily extended to incorporate more than one source of uncertainty or state variable: the model described in the following section is based upon two state variables. However, it is an empirical issue whether duration provides a measure of risk which is adequate for practical purposes. Fisher and Weil [14] have cast some light on this, and we shall provide further evidence in Section V by comparing the duration model with the two-state variable equilibrium model.

III. AN EQUILIBRIUM BOND PRICING MODEL

Modern equilibrium theories of the term structure of interest rates assume that the values of default-free bonds of all maturities may be expressed as determinate functions of a small number of state variables which follow continuous diffusion processes. Equilibrium conditions then imply that bond values must satisfy a certain partial differential equation which involves as many unknown (possibly nonconstant) parameters as there are state variables, each of these parameters representing the market price of risk associated with one of the stochastic state variables.

The power of this equilibrium theory depends upon the number of relevant stochastic state variables being reasonably small. As we have seen, the duration model is a (nonequilibrium) model with a single-state variable. Other models with a single-state variable have been studied by Brennan and Schwartz [4]; Cox, Ingersoll, and Ross [7,8]; and Vasicek [32]—all of these authors taking the instantaneously riskless interest rate as the relevant state variable. Two-state variable models, in which the second state variable is the exogenously determined stochastic rate of inflation or the price level, have been developed by Cox, Ingersoll, and Ross [7] and Richard [28]. The CIR model is distinguished from all other work in this area by being set within a general equilibrium framework.

Cox et al. have pointed out that if yields on bonds of different maturities are determinate functions of the underlying state variables, so that if it is possible to invert this system and thereby express the state variables as twice differentiable functions of a vector of interest rates, then the vector of interest rates may be used as instruments for the state variables. In this section we develop an equilibrium bond pricing model in which we take as state variables the yield on an instantaneously maturing bond, r, and the yield on a consol bond, ℓ, and assume that the price of a discount bond promising \$1 at maturity can be expressed as a determinate function of the two state variables and time to maturity τ.[19] This function is written B(r, ℓ, τ). Note that the function B(r, ℓ, τ) defines the whole of the yield curve in terms of its extremities r and ℓ and that values of B(r, ℓ, τ) are present value factors for given values of r and ℓ, so that they may be used to price arbitrary patterns of future payments. As we shall see, the form of the

M. J. BRENNAN and E. S. SCHWARTZ

function $B(r, \ell, \tau)$ depends on the exogenously specified stochastic process for r and ℓ, the condition for equilibrium in security markets, and investor tastes.

Here, r and ℓ are assumed to follow a joint stochastic process of the general type

$$dr = \beta_1(r, \ell, t)\, dt + \eta_1(r, \ell, t)\, dz_1$$

$$d\ell = \beta_2(r, \ell, t)\, dt + \eta_2(r, \ell, t)\, dz_2 , \tag{6}$$

where t denotes calendar time, dz_1 and dz_2 are Wiener processes with $E[dz_1] = E[dz_2] = 0$, $dz_1^2 = dz_2^2 = dt$ and $dz_1 dz_2 = \rho\, dt$.

Applying Ito's lemma, the stochastic process for the price of a discount bond is

$$\frac{dB}{B} = \mu(r, \ell, t)\, dt + s_1(r, \ell, \tau)\, dz_1 + s_2(r, \ell, \tau)\, dz_2 , \tag{7}$$

where $\mu(r, \ell, \tau) = \dfrac{B_1\beta_1 + B_2\beta_2 + (1/2)\,B_{11}\eta_1^2 + (1/2)B_{22}\eta_2^2 + B_{12}\rho\eta_1\eta_2 - B_3}{B}$,

$$s_1(r, \ell, \tau) = \frac{B_1\eta_1}{B},$$

$$s_2(r, \ell, \tau) = \frac{B_2\eta_2}{B},$$

$$B_1 = \frac{\partial B}{\partial r},$$

$$B_2 = \frac{\partial B}{\partial \ell},$$

$$B_3 = \frac{\partial B}{\partial \tau},$$

. . . .

Consider a portfolio of bonds P with proportions x_1, x_2, and x_3 allocated to bonds of maturity τ_1, τ_2, and τ_3. The rate of return on this portfolio is

$$\frac{dP}{P} = [x_1\mu(\tau_1) + x_2\mu(\tau_2) + x_3\mu(\tau_3)]\, dt$$

$$+ [x_1s_1(\tau_1) + x_2s_1(\tau_2) + x_3s_1(\tau_3)]\, dz_1 \tag{8}$$

$$+ [x_1s_2(\tau_1) + x_2s_2(\tau_2) + x_3s_2(\tau_3)]\, dz_2 .$$

The rate of return on the portfolio will be nonstochastic (the portfolio will be "immunized") if the portfolio proportions are chosen so that the coefficients of dz_1 and dz_2 in equation (8) are zero:

$$x_1 s_1(\tau_1) + x_2 s_1(\tau_2) + x_3 s_1(\tau_3) = 0 \tag{9}$$

$$x_1 s_2(\tau_1) + x_2 s_2(\tau_2) + x_3 s_2(\tau_3) = 0 .$$

Capital market equilibrium then requires that the rate of return on the portfolio be equal to the instantaneous riskless interest rate r, so that

$$x_1(\mu(\tau_1) - r) + x_2(\mu(\tau_2) - r) + x_3(\mu(\tau_3) - r) = 0 . \tag{10}$$

Equations (9) and (10) will possess a solution only if there exist functions $\lambda_1(\cdot)$ and $\lambda_2(\cdot)$ which are independent of bond maturity τ, such that

$$\mu(\tau) - r = \lambda_1(r, \ell, t)s_1(\tau) + \lambda_2(r, \ell, t)s_2(\tau) \tag{11}$$

Equation (11) is an equilibrium condition which constrains the relative risk premia on bonds of different maturities. If the expressions for $\mu(\cdot)$, $s_1(\cdot)$, and $s_2(\cdot)$ are substituted in equation (11), the result will be a partial differential equation $B(r, \ell, \tau)$ for the price of a discount bond, which depends upon the parameters of the stochastic process (6) for r and ℓ as well as on the undetermined functions $\lambda_1(\cdot)$ and $\lambda_2(\cdot)$. However, by making use of the fact that ℓ is a function of the value of a traded asset, the consol bond, it can be shown that[20]

$$\lambda_2(r, \ell, t) = -\frac{\eta_2}{\ell} + \frac{\beta_2 - \ell^2 + r\ell}{\eta_2} . \tag{12}$$

Then, use of equation (12) to eliminate $\lambda_2(\cdot)$ in the aforementioned partial differential equation permits us to rewrite the equilibrium condition (11) as the partial differential equation

$$\frac{1}{2} B_{11}\eta_1^2 + B_{12}\rho\eta_1\eta_2 + \frac{1}{2} B_{22}\eta_2^2 + B_1(\beta_1 - \lambda_1\eta_1)$$

$$+ B_2\left(\frac{\eta_2^2}{\ell} + \ell^2 - r\ell\right) - B_3 - Br = 0 . \tag{13}$$

Equation (13) together with the boundary condition specifying the maturity value, $B(r, \ell, 0) = 1$, may be solved to yield the prices of discount bonds of all maturities and hence the whole term structure of interest rates as a function of the current values of r and ℓ.

Once the function $B(r, \ell, \tau)$ has been determined, the instantaneous variance-covariance matrix of bond returns Ω may be computed. For example, Ω_{ij}, the covariance of return between bonds of maturity τ_i and τ_j is given by

$$\Omega_{ij} = s_1(\tau_i)s_1(\tau_j) + \rho s_1(\tau_i)s_2(\tau_j) + \rho s_2(\tau_i)s_1(\tau_j) + s_2(\tau_i)s_2(\tau_j) , \quad (14)$$

where $s_1(\tau) = B_1 \eta_1/B$, etc.

Application of this equilibrium bond pricing model requires that the coefficients of the partial differential equation (13) be estimated. These depend upon the coefficients of the joint stochastic process (6) as well as the undetermined function $\lambda_1(\cdot)$. In the following section we report some estimates derived from U.S. data on government bonds.[21]

IV. ESTIMATION OF THE BOND PRICING MODEL

Implementation of the equilibrium bond pricing model developed in the previous section has two aspects. The stochastic process (6) for the two interest rates must be specified and estimated; and the form of the function $\lambda_1(\cdot)$ must be specified and it also must be estimated.

The Stochastic Process

The specific form of the stochastic process (6) assumed for purposes of estimation was

$$dr = (a_1 + b_1(\ell - r)) \, dt + r\sigma_1 \, dz_1 \qquad (15a)$$

$$d\ell = \ell(a_2 + b_2 r + c_2 \ell) \, dt + \ell \sigma_2 \, dz_2 . \qquad (15b)$$

This formulation presupposes that the instantaneous standard deviaton of each interest rate is proportional to its current level, an assumption which is tested below. The form of the coefficient of dt in equation (15a) was motivated by the consideration that long-term interest rates reflect expectations about future short-term rates so that if these expectations are rational, the short rate will tend to regress toward the current value of the long rate; this would imply that $b_1 > 0$. The corresponding drift term in equation (15b) was obtained by specifying $\lambda_2(\cdot)$ as a linear function of r and ℓ, and then solving equation (12) for $\beta_2(\cdot)$; note that the drift term in equation (15b) does not enter the partial differential equation.

For empirical purposes the system (15) was replaced by the discrete approximation

$$\frac{r_t - r_{t-1}}{r_{t-1}} = \frac{a_1}{r_{t-1}} + b_1\left(\frac{\ell_{t-1}}{r_{t-1}} - 1\right) + \xi_{1t}$$

$$\frac{\ell_t - \ell_{t-1}}{\ell_{t-1}} = a_2 + b_2 r_{t-1} + c_2 \ell_{t-1} + \xi_{2t},$$

(16)

and the system (16) was estimated using monthly data from the CRSP Government Bond File for the period December 1958–December 1979.[22] Furthermore, r was approximated by the annualized yield to maturity on the U.S. Treasury bill whose maturity was closest to 30 days on the last trading day of the month. The consol rate ℓ was approximated by the annualized yield to maturity on the highest yielding[23] U.S. Government bond with a maturity exceeding 20 years. If there was no such bond, then the yield on the highest yielding bond with a maturity of more than 15 years was used instead.

The equations were estimated using an iterative Aitken [1] procedure[24] and the estimates are reported in Table 2 along with some diagnostic statistics. The estimate of σ_2, the only parameter from the consol rate equation used in the differential equation shows reasonable stability, as does σ_1. However, a_1 and b_1 show unwelcome instability, although this was not the case when a similar stochastic process was estimated using Canadian data.[25] In addition, ρ, the estimated correlation between the two stochastic processes, is also much less stable than was the case in Canada.

If the stochastic process (15) is correct, then the error terms from equation (16) should be serially independent. Table 2 reports the serial correlation coefficient and Durbin's h statistic[26] for the two equations. Again, contrary to the Canadian findings, the serial correlation is predominantly negative and is statistically significant for the short rate equation, particularly during the first half of the sample period. This finding of serial correlation in the errors from the stochastic process implies either that the functional form of the stochastic process is misspecified or that the current values of r and ℓ are not sufficient statistics for the joint distribution of future values of r and ℓ, and therefore that if the true stochastic process is to be represented in Markov form as is necessary for the derivation of the partial differential equation, at least one other state variable must be introduced. The practical importance for bond pricing of omitting these state variables (or of misspecifying the stochastic process) is an empirical issue, and

Table 2. Estimation of the Stochastic Process (Standard Errors in Parenthesis)

Period	a_1	b_1	a_2	b_2	c_2	σ_1	σ_2	ρ	$\rho(\xi_{1t}\xi_{1t-1})$	$\rho(\xi_{2t}\xi_{2t-1})$	DH^*	DH_2^*	γ_1	γ_2
Dec 1958– Dec 1979	-.0887 (.0526)	.1102 (.0301)	.00891 (.0069)	.00358 (.0017)	-.0037 (.0020)	.1133	.0298	.2063	-.195	-.064	-3.52	-1.022	-.6269 (.3710)	.7503 (.5711)
Dec 1958– June 1969	-.1809 (.0754)	.1882 (.0480)	.0151 (.0200)	.00468 (.0037)	-.0062 (.0067)	.1286	.0233	.0519	-.239	-.032	-3.183	-.364	-1.9363 (.6704)	3.9373 (1.701)
July 1969– Dec 1979	-0.135 (0.826)	.0377 (.0369)	.0319 (.0221)	.00444 (.00229)	-.0074 (.0039)	.0914	.0349	.3923	-.043	-.067	-.526	-.748	-.2489 (.7837)	-1.1807 (1.6619)
Dec 1958– March 1964	-.4667 (.1594)	.3357 (.0907)	.2142 (.0725)	.00869 (.00567)	.0588 (.0202)	.1619	.0205	.2126	-.160	.018	-1.830	.146	-1.3433 (1.2774)	-8.270 (6.889)
April 1964– June 1969	-.1079 (.0593)	.2729 (.0796)	.00078 (.0252)	.0038 (.0069)	-.0022 (.0087)	.0688	.0248	-.1637	-.104	-.022	-1.066	-.175	-1.3955 (1.9133)	8.656 (2.200)
July 1969– Sept 1974	-.0350 (.1103)	.0551 (.0578)	.1233 (.0614)	.0120 (.0055)	-.0283 (.0129)	.1031	.0415	.3778	-.034	-.040	-.308	-.320	+.2869 (1.110)	-.3579 (3.002)
Oct 1974– Dec 1979	.0361 (.1375)	.0118 (.0525)	.1675 (.0713)	.0089 (.0033)	-.2710 (.0109)	.0777	.0243	.4423	.026	-.032	.231	-.259	-.6625 (1.137)	4.348 (4.286)

Note:
*Durbin's h statistic

16

the empirical adquacy of the bond pricing model will be apparent below.

Finally, to test the assumption of homoscedastic errors in equation (16), the logarithm of the squared error was regressed on the logarithm of the two interest rates, following a procedure suggested by Parks [25]:

$$\ln \xi_{1t}^2 = \delta_1 + \gamma_1 \ln r_{t-1} \tag{17}$$

$$\ln \xi_{2t}^2 = \delta_2 + \gamma_2 \ln \ell_{t-1} .$$

The estimates of γ_1 and γ_2 are reported in Table 2. Under the null hypothesis of homoscedasticity these parameters are zero, and this is not rejected by the data. On the other hand, the signs and magnitudes of the coefficients are similar to those found using Canadian data, suggesting that an alternative assumption about the stochastic process might be appropriate. However, for the balance of this paper we shall use the estimate of the stochastic process derived from the total sample which is presented in the first line of the table, unless otherwise stated.

Estimation of $\lambda_1(\cdot)$

For empirical purposes λ_1 was assumed to be constant and was estimated by an asymptotically maximum likelihood procedure which is described in detail in the Appendix. Briefly, having estimated the parameters of the stochastic process, the valuation equation (13) was solved numerically for selected values of λ_1. The resulting values of $B(r, \ell, \tau; \lambda)$ are the present values of $1 receivable in τ periods when the two interest rates take on the values r and ℓ. For each of the values of λ_1 all taxable bonds on the CRSP Government Bond File which had maturities of less than 10 years were valued each month from December 1958 to December 1979 by applying the present value factors appropriate to the prevailing values of r and ℓ to the promised stream of coupon and principal payments. λ_1 was estimated by minimizing an appropriately weighted sum of the squared price prediction errors.

The estimated value of λ_1 was -0.450 with an asymptotic standard error of 0.028, and this value is employed in calculating the B–S model bond values in the remainder of the paper except when stated otherwise.

V. EMPIRICAL COMPARISON OF DURATION AND EQUILIBRIUM TERM STRUCTURE MODELS

In this section we shall offer some empirical comparisons between the Macaulay duration model described in the second line of Table 1, "the duration model," and the particular equilibrium model of the term structure which was developed in Section III and estimated in Section IV, "the Brennan–Schwartz model," or more succinctly "the B–S model." In comparing these two models our primary concern is with their use in portfolio management.

The Measurement of Duration

The Macaulay–Fisher and Weil measure of duration for a given bond is

$$D_t = \frac{\sum_{\tau=t+1}^{\infty} (\tau - t) \, c(\tau) \, q(\tau - t, t)}{\sum_{\tau=t+1}^{\infty} c(\tau) \, q(\tau - t, t)} \,,$$

where t is the current date, $c(\tau)$ is the payment on the bond at time τ, and $q(\tau - t, t)$ is the present value at time t of \$1 payable at time τ, the "discount function." Application of this duration model presupposes that the discount function is known. In reality since there exist no discount government bonds and the set of coupon bonds available is not complete,[27] the discount function for each period must be estimated. The discount function was therefore estimated for each month of the sample period using data on all taxable government bonds.[28] The function was approximated by a continuously differentiable piecewise quadratic function as suggested by McCulloch (1971) and described in Section B of the Appendix.

The Variance-Covariance Matrix of Bond Returns

As explained in Section III, the significant difference between the duration and the equilibrium model from the viewpoint of portfolio management lies in their different estimates of the variance-covariance matrix of bond returns. As may be seen from equation (4), the duration model with its single source of uncertainty implies that returns on all bonds are perfectly correlated and that the covariance between the returns on any two bonds is given, up to a scale factor, by the product of the durations. According to the B–S model, on the other hand, bond returns are not perfectly correlated because they are determined by two imperfectly correlated factors, and the covariance between any two bonds is given by equation (14).

To illustrate the difference in the covariance matrices yielded by the two models, the covariance matrix for 8 percent coupon bonds with maturities of from 1 to 20 years was calculated using the two models for the interest rates r and ℓ prevailing and the discount function estimated, for the last day of the sample period, December 31, 1979.

For ease of presentation we show in Table 3 the correlation matrix yielded by the B–S model which should be compared with the corresponding matrix of ones for the duration model. It is clear that the correlation matrices yielded by the two models are very similar particularly for bonds with more than five years to maturity. Also shown in Table 3 are the instantaneous standard deviations of return predicted by the two models for bonds of different maturity relative to the 10-year bond.[29] Again the overall similarity of the two models is striking, although the duration model tends to overstate the relative risk of long-term bonds in comparison with the B–S model.

While the evidence of Table 3 suggests that the covariance estimates of the two models are quite similar up to a scale factor, the significance of the differences for portfolio construction cannot be assessed by such comparisons but must be evaluated in the context of specific portfolio policies.[30] We consider this issue below together with the related question of which model provides the better estimate of the variance covariance matrix.

Discount Bond Replication Strategies

Consider an investor who wishes to have a fixed sum of money on a given future date. His objective could be accomplished simply by purchasing a discount bond of the appropriate maturity if such existed. Without such discount bonds the investor must purchase coupon bonds and face the uncertainty associated with the rate at which the coupons

Table 3. Comparative Risk Measures for 8% Coupon Bonds on December 31, 1979

Maturity (years)	Correlation Matrix: B–S Model[1]					
	1	*3*	*5*	*10*	*15*	*20*
1	1.0	0.93	0.83	0.68	0.64	0.61
3		1.0	0.97	0.90	0.87	0.86
5			1.0	0.98	0.96	0.95
10				1.0	1.0	1.0
15					1.0	1.0
20						1.0
Relative Risk[2]:						
Duration Model	2	16	37	100	152	199
B-S Model	8	25	44	100	144	169

Notes:
[1] The corresponding correlations for the Duration Model are all unity.
[2] Standard Deviation of the instantaneous return relative to that of 10 year bond.

can be reinvested. Redington [27] suggested that this risk could be eliminated by following the appropriate immunizaton strategy.

In an important paper Fisher and Weil [14] have provided empirical evidence of the ability of such an immunization strategy to eliminate the reinvestment rate risk. However, individual bond price data were not available to them, and they were forced to rely upon hypothetical bond prices derived from the Durand [12] yield curves; consequently, it is not clear whether the success of their immunization strategy could be achieved using real bond prices.[31]

In this section we compare the results of following a Fisher–Weil-type strategy of immunization based on the duration model with the results of a hedging strategy based on the B–S model. The data for the comparison are the monthly prices and returns on up to 20 basic portfolios of taxable U.S. Government bonds from December 1958 to December 1979. Each of the 20 basic portfolios corresponds to a different number of years to maturity, and the price and return for each basic portfolio is a simple average of the corresponding charac-teristics of all available bonds of that maturity.[32]

The Immunization Strategy.   Under this strategy a portfolio of the 20 basic portfolios[33] is constructed so that its duration is equal to the time to the desired payment; it is then revised monthly[34] to keep the duration equal to the remaining time to the desired maturity. The realized wealth relative from following this strategy is compared with the expected wealth relative.

Our estimate of the expected wealth relative from following this strategy from time t to time T is $q(T - t, t)^{-1}$, the inverse of the empirical discount function whose estimation is described in Section B of the Appendix.[35] The portfolio proportions, $x_{i\tau}(i = 1, \ldots, 20)$, are determined each period $\tau(\tau = t, \ldots, T - 1)$ as the solution to the following portfolio problem:

$$\text{Minimize} \sum_{i=1}^{20} x_{i\tau}^2$$

subject to

$$\sum_{i=1}^{20} x_{i\tau} D_{i\tau} = T - \tau \qquad \sum_{i=1}^{20} x_{i\tau} = 1 \, ,$$

where $D_{i\tau}$ is the duration of basic portfolio i at time τ. The resulting portfolio has the required duration and is also well diversified across the available basic portfolios. The realized wealth relative is calculated by compounding the portfolio returns over the period t to T.

The Hedging Strategy. Under this strategy the portfolio is constructed so that its estimated response to changes in r and ℓ is the same as for a discount bond with the appropriate maturity. It then follows from the B–S model equation (11) that the return on the portfolio must be the same as on the discount bond. Therefore the compound rate of return earned on the strategy is equal to the compound rate of return on the discount bond over its life, and this is in principle known, through in practice it must be estimated.

The specific portfolio problem which is solved each month is the following:

$$\text{Minimize } \sum_{i=1}^{20} x_{i\tau}^2$$

subject to

$$\sum_{i=1}^{20} x_{i\tau} \frac{P_r(i, \tau)}{P(i, \tau)} = \frac{B_r(\tau, T)}{B(\tau, T)}$$

$$\sum_{i=1}^{20} x_{i\tau} \frac{P_\ell(i, \tau)}{P(i, \tau)} = \frac{B_\ell(\tau, T)}{B(\tau, T)}$$

$$\sum_{i=1}^{20} x_{i\tau} = 1 .$$

Here $P(i, \tau)$ is the B–S model prediction of the value of basic portfolio i at time τ; $B(\tau, T)$ is the B–S model prediction of the value at time τ of a discount bond promising \$1 at time T; subscripts denote partial derivatives.

The appropriate measure of the expected wealth relative is the inverse of the price of the relevant discount bond. If the bonds were priced exactly in accord with the B–S model, this would be $B(t, T)^{-1}$. Discrepancies between the model and market prices may be attributable either to model errors or to market inefficiencies; in either case, the expected return to the hedging strategy must depend upon the market prices of bonds. Therefore, to take account of discrepancies between model and market prices, $B(t, T)^{-1}$ was multiplied by the ratio of the model value of the portfolio purchased at time t to its market value in order to obtain the expected wealth ratio. This adjustment would be exactly correct if the discrepancy between market and model prices represented a temporary disequilibrium, which was eliminated instantaneously.

Tables 4 and 5 present the results of replicating the returns to 5- and 10-year discount bonds, respectively, using the two portfolio strategies and starting from different dates. These results are directly comparable with those of Fisher and Weil. Note first that the expected wealth ratios are quite similar whether calculated from the empirical discount function (the immunization strategy) or from the B–S present value factor adjusted for price discrepancies (the hedging strategy).

The root mean square error for the five-year immunization strategy of 1.6 percent may be compared to the 0.26 percent standard deviation of the wealth ratio obtained by Fisher and Weil; our root mean square error for the 10-year strategy is approximately five times as large as their standard deviation. For both 5- and 10-year horizons, the hedging strategy appears to outperform the immunization strategy. While the hedging strategy in this case is derived using model parameters estimated over the same sample period and therefore it does not represent a truly feasible strategy, it will be seen below that similar results obtain when the hedging strategy is based on out-of-sample period parameter estimates.

Table 4.   Replicating 5-year Discount Bonds by
Immunization and Hedging

		Wealth Ratio			
		Immunization		Hedging	
Starting Date		Expected	Realized	Expected	Realized
December	1958*	1.207	1.201	1.204	1.220
	1959	1.265	1.259	1.265	1.271
	1960	1.181	1.176	1.183	1.187
	1961	1.209	1.207	1.211	1.210
	1962	1.187	1.190	1.193	1.196
	1963*	1.214	1.213	1.217	1.215
	1964	1.217	1.208	1.221	1.232
	1965	1.255	1.271	1.259	1.254
	1966	1.257	1.270	1.259	1.249
	1967	1.313	1.310	1.322	1.310
	1968*	1.325	1.337	1.350	1.333
	1969	1.485	1.470	1.467	1.459
	1970	1.343	1.371	1.350	1.342
	1971	1.308	1.356	1.320	1.312
	1972	1.348	1.357	1.355	1.362
	1973*	1.390	1.377	1.394	1.393
	1974	1.420	1.410	1.425	1.421
Root Mean Square Error		0.060		0.008	

Note:
   *non-overlapping observations

Table 5.   Replicating 10-year Discount Bonds by
Immunization and Hedging

	Wealth Ratio			
	Immunization		Hedging	
Starting Date	*Expected*	*Realized*	*Expected*	*Realized*
December 1958*	1.472	1.473	1.464	1.472
1959	1.583	1.594	1.588	1.615
1960	1.443	1.472	1.447	1.447
1961	1.504	1.532	1.506	1.505
1962	1.463	1.455	1.470	1.458
1963	1.504	1.501	1.512	1.498
1964	1.507	1.519	1.527	1.519
1965	1.595	1.628	1.607	1.602
1966	1.584	1.652	1.606	1.598
1967	1.753	1.786	1.782	1.802
1968*	1.895	1.828	1.879	1.869
1969	2.028	2.200	2.129	2.143
Root Mean Square Error	0.060		0.013	

Note:

   *non-overlapping observations

This comparison of the two strategies which is based upon the Fisher–Weil study suffers from limitations arising from the hypothetical nature of the discount bonds whose returns are being replicated. First, the comparison is sensitive to the way in which the expected wealth ratio is estimated. More importantly, it is possible to compare the returns from the two strategies with the corresponding discount bond returns only over a period corresponding to the life of the discount bond. With 21 years of data this means that only two independent observations can be made for the 10-year bond and only one independent observation for longer maturities; this clearly limits the confidence that can be placed in the results. Therefore we shall also make a comparison based on the results of replicating returns to coupon bonds which do exist and for which we have prices.

Coupon Bond Replication Strategies

The ability of the two models to yield portfolio strategies which replicate the monthly rates of return on each of the 20 basic portfolios is evaluated in terms of the standard deviations of the difference between the return on the basic portfolio and the return on the replicating portfolio formed from the remaining basic portfolios. For both strategies diversification of the replicating portfolio is ensured by minimizing the sum of the squared portfolio weights subject to the relevant constraints.

For the immunization strategy the replicating portfolio for basic portfolio j is found in month τ by solving the following problem:

$$\text{Minimize} \sum_{i \neq j} x_{i\tau}^2$$

subject to

$$\sum_{i \neq j} x_{i\tau} D_{i\tau} = D_j\tau \qquad \sum_{i \neq j} x_{i\tau} = 1 .$$

For the hedging strategy the corresponding problem is

$$\text{Minimize} \sum_{i \neq j} x_{i\tau}^2$$

subject to

$$\sum_{i \neq j} x_{i\tau} \frac{P_r(i, \tau)}{P(i, \tau)} = \frac{P_r(j, \tau)}{P(j, \tau)}$$

$$\sum_{i \neq j} x_{i\tau} \frac{P_\ell(i, \tau)}{P(i, \tau)} = \frac{P_\ell(j, \tau)}{P(j, \tau)}$$

$$\sum_{i \neq j} x_{i\tau} = 1 .$$

The standard deviations of the monthly return differences under the two strategies are shown in Table 6: it is apparent that there is little to choose between the results of the two strategies.

Measures of Risk in the Duration and B–S Models

Further insight into the relation between the models may be gained by comparing the measures of risk derived from them. As we have seen, the measure of risk for a bond in the single-state variable duration model is the measure of duration itself; for the two-state variable B–S model, the risk measures are $s_1(\cdot)$ and $s_2(\cdot)$, which are the standard deviations of return attributable to r and ℓ, respectively.[36] If $s_1(\cdot)$ and $s_2(\cdot)$ were proportional to the duration measure for any bond at a particular point in time, then the duration and B–S models would be indistinguishable from the viewpoint of the covariance structure of bond returns,[37] and any portfolio which was riskless according to one

Table 6. Replicating Returns on Coupon Bond Portfolios

Maturity of Replicated Portfolio (years)	Number of Monthly Observations	Standard Deviation of Monthly Return Difference	
		Immunization Strategy	Hedging Strategy
1	252	.00477	.01215
2	252	.00211	.00267
3	252	.00189	.00245
4	252	.00278	.00231
5	252	.00421	.00385
6	239	.00395	.00371
7	225	.00476	.00431
8	104	.00376	.00369
9	98	.00466	.00451
10	100	.00561	.00617
11	44	.00798	.00823
12	48	.00805	.00814
13	41	.01074	.00993
14	49	.00646	.00650
15	51	.00643	.00665
16	20	.00571	.00564
17	18	.01019	.00948
18	18	.00641	.00717
19	26	.01225	.01151
20	35	.00850	.00883

model would also be riskless according to the other. Since the portfolio results for the two strategies were so similar, this possibility was explored.

In Figure 1, $s_1(\cdot)$ and $s_2(\cdot)$ are plotted against duration for 8 percent coupon bonds with maturities from 1 to 20 years for the interest rates prevailing on the last day of the sample period. $s_2(\cdot)$ is indeed almost proportional to duration so that any portfolio with zero duration will be almost perfectly hedged against changes in the consol rate. Furthermore, $s_1(\cdot)$ is not proportional to duration; yet, as may be seen from the figure, short-term rate risk is much less important than consol rate risk for most bonds. Moreover, the linearity of $s_1(\cdot)$ and $s_2(\cdot)$ in duration for values of duration in excess of about 25 months has important implications for the use of duration in designing bond portfolios. For example, the duration model suggests that bond C will have the same risk characteristics as a portfolio of bonds A and B with weights BC/BA and CA/BA. The linearity of the $s_1(\cdot)$ and $s_2(\cdot)$ functions means that in the B–S model also, the bond and the portfolio would have the same risk.

B–S Model Performance Outside Estimation Period

The careful reader may have felt that the foregoing comparisons cast the B–S model in an unduly favorable light, since the parameters of the model were estimated over the same sample period for which the coupon and discount bond replication strategy comparisons were made. Therefore the comparisons were repeated for the second half of the sample period using parameter estimates for the B–S model derived from the first half of the sample period.

Figure 1.   Risk Measures From the Duration and B–S Models.

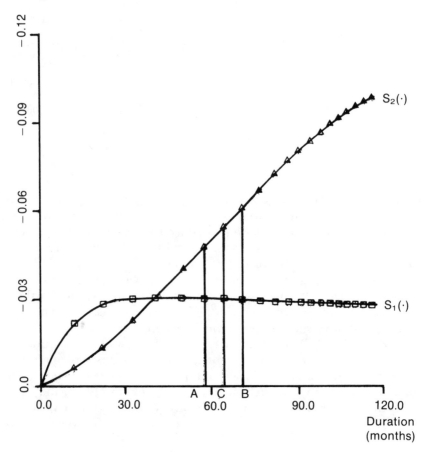

Table 7. Replicating 5-year Discount Bonds by Immunization and Hedging, 1969–1970: B-S Model Estimated over Prior Period

| | Wealth Relatives | | | |
| | Immunization | | Hedging | |
Starting Date	Expected	Realized	Expected	Realized
December 1969	1.485	1.470	1.467	1.453
December 1970	1.343	1.371	1.350	1.336
December 1971	1.308	1.356	1.324	1.318
December 1972	1.348	1.357	1.357	1.367
December 1973	1.390	1.377	1.397	1.396
December 1974	1.420	1.410	1.429	1.414
Root Mean Square Error	0.025		0.011	

Table 8. Replicating Returns on Coupon Bond Portfolios, 1969–78: B-S Model Estimated over Prior Period

| Maturity of Replicated Portfolio (years) | Number of Monthly Observations | Standard Deviation of Monthly Return Difference | |
		Immunization Strategy	Hedging Strategy
1	125	.00595	.02784
2	125	.00276	.00406
3	125	.00233	.00298
4	125	.00327	.00279
5	125	.00523	.00493
6	125	.00492	.00459
7	122	.00565	.00520
8	50	.00506	.00504
9	62	.00574	.00558
10	72	.00644	.00688
11	32	.00834	.00849
12	36	.00887	.00887
13	29	.00951	.00958
14	41	.00690	.00692
15	51	.00643	.00658
16	20	.00571	.00563
17	18	.01019	.00952
18	18	.00641	.00703
19	26	.01225	.01159
20	35	.00850	.00867

Specifically, the B–S model values were based on the estimated coefficients of the stochastic process derived for the period December 1958–June 1969 as reported in Table 2. λ_1 was also estimated by fitting the model to bond prices for this period. The estimated value of λ_1 was -1.185 with a standard error of 0.019. This value is substantially different from that obtained for the whole sample period as are the estimated coefficients of the stochastic process. Despite this the hedging strategy performs just about as well as the immunization strategy over the second half of the sample period, exhibiting a welcome stability. The results of replicating the discount bond and coupon bond portfolio returns outside the B–S model parameter estimation period are given in Tables 7 and 8 which are comparable to Tables 4 and 6. It may be seen that the root mean square error from replicating the five-year discount bond using the hedging strategy is approximately one-half that obtained when the immunization strategy is used, and this is true whether or not the hedging strategy employs B–S model parameters estimates derived within the sample period. Just as striking is the fact that the expected return on the hedging strategy is almost exactly the same whether it is derived from the B–S model estimated over the sample period as in Table 4 or from the B–S model estimated over a prior period as in Table 7. Since this expected return is simply the inverse of the B–S model value B(r, ℓ, 5) it suggests that the model is sufficiently robust to yield reasonable estimates of value outside the sample period.

VI. CONCLUSION

In this paper the relationship between duration theories of the term structure and equilibrium theories of bond pricing have been examined from the viewpoint of bond portfolio management. It was argued that duration theory is most reasonably interpreted as a theory of the covariance matrix of bond returns which rests upon the implicit assumption of a single underlying source of uncertainty. While duration theories have tended to ignore the equilibrium implications of their restrictions on the covariance matrix, modern theories of bond pricing explicitly use the equilibrium conditions in arriving at their estimates of the covariance structure.[38]

A particular two-state variable equilibrium bond pricing model was compared with the duration model in terms of the resulting covariance structure and the implications for bond portfolio management. The duration model yielded results which were close to those of the equilibrium model suggesting that in the current state of the art, the duration model is probably the most appropriate one for practical purposes when the analysis is concerned only with default-free straight bonds which involve options neither for the purchaser nor for the issuer.

On the other hand, the equilibrium model, unlike the duration model, is able to deal with bonds which do contain option provisions. The equilibrium model also provides evidence as to possible mispricing of individual bonds. Whether this feature of the equilibrium model can be profitably exploited remains an open question.

APPENDIX

A. Maximum Likelihood Estimator of λ_1

Solving the differential equation (13) yields values $B(r, \ell, \tau; \lambda)$ which are the present values of 1 in τ periods when the two interest rates are r and ℓ and λ is the appropriate risk aversion parameter. For each of several values of λ_1 a sample of 317 U.S. Government bonds was valued on the last day of each month from December 1958 to December 1979 by applying the appropriate present value factors to the promised stream of coupon and principal payments. The resulting predicted bond values are written $B_{it}(\lambda)$ (i = 1, . . . , 317; t = 1, . . . , 253), and the actual bond value y_{it} may be expressed as

$$y_{it} = B_{it}(\lambda) + u_{it}, \tag{A1}$$

where u_{it} is the valuation error. Consider an estimator of λ, $\lambda(S)$, which minimizes

$$L(\lambda, S) = \sum_t [y_t - B_t(\lambda)]'S[y_t - B_t(\lambda)], \tag{A2}$$

where S is a positive definite matrix and y_t and $B_t(\lambda)$ are vectors. Then $\lambda(S)$ satisfies the necessary conditions for a minimum:

$$H(S, \lambda) = \sum_t Q_t(\lambda)'S[y_t - B_t(\lambda)] = 0 \tag{A3}$$

where $Q_t(\lambda) = \partial B_{it}(\lambda)/\partial\lambda$ is a vector. Starting from a particular value of λ, λ^0, $H(S, \lambda)$ can be approimated by

$$H(S, \lambda) = H(S, \lambda^0) + \frac{\partial H(S, \lambda^0)}{\partial\lambda}(\lambda - \lambda^0) \tag{A4}$$

and setting equation (A4) equal to zero yields $\lambda(S)$. In the present context no analytic expressions are available for $Q_t(\lambda)$ or $\partial H/\partial\lambda$, and therefore $H(S, \lambda^0)$ and its partial derivative were calculated using values of $B_{it}(\lambda)$ obtained from adjacent values of λ.

The estimator $\lambda(S)$ will be a maximum likelihood estimator if the errors in equation (A1) are $N(0, \Omega)$, and $S = \Omega^{-1}$. Since Ω is unknown, an asymptotically MLE is obtained by the following iterative procedure described by Malinvaud (1966):

1. Calculate $\lambda^* = \lambda(I)$ by the above procedure; this is the (nonlinear) OLS estimator.
2. Calculate the residuals $\epsilon_{it} = y_{it} - B_{it}(\lambda^*)$, and their covariance matrix Ω^*.
3. Calculate the estimator $\lambda^{**} = \lambda(\Omega^{*-1})$. This estimator is asymptotically normal with variance

$$\left[\sum_t \left(\frac{\partial B_{it}(\lambda^{**})}{\partial \lambda} \right)' \Omega^{*-1} \left(\frac{\partial B_{it}(\lambda^{**})}{\partial \lambda} \right) \right]^{-1}. \tag{A5}$$

Estimation of the covariance matrix Ω^* requires prior restrictions on the covariance structure of the valuation errors u_{it}. It was assumed that the covariance of the valuation errors of any two bonds depends only on their maturities. Therefore each month the outstanding bonds were assigned to one of 10 basic portfolios ($j = 1, \ldots, 10$)[39] depending on their maturity: the first portfolio consisting of all bonds with maturities of less than one year, the second of all bonds with maturities between one and two years, etc.[40] The valuation error for portfolio j in month t is assumed to be given by

$$u_{jt} = \rho u_{jt-1} + v_{jt} \tag{A6}$$

where $E[v_{jt}] = E[v_{jt} \, v_{jt'}] = 0$ and $E[v_{jt} \, v_{kt}] = \omega_{jk}$, an element of the (10×10) matrix Ω.

The OLS estimator was computed using these portfolio data. Since not all bond maturities were represented each month, matrix S of equations (A2) and (A3) was indexed: $S_t = I_{n_t}$, where n_t is the number of portfolio observations in period t. In addition, to assure that the estimated variance-covariance matrix of portfolio valuation errors, u_{jt} was positive definite, the matrix of residuals from the OLS regression was completed using a procedure suggested by Dagenais [9].[41]

The serial correlation of the errors of each of the 10 portfolios was then estimated using these OLS residuals according to equation (A6). Then to take account of both serial and contemporaneous correlation of the errors, an asymptotically efficient estimator proposed by Parks [26] was developed: the actual and predicted portfolio values were transformed according to

$$\bar{y}_{jt} = y_{jt} - \hat{\rho}_j y_{jt-1} \tag{A7}$$

$$\tilde{B}_{jt}(\lambda) = B_{jt}(\lambda) - \hat{\rho}_j B_{jt}(\lambda) .$$

Equation (A1) can be written as

$$\tilde{y}_{jt} = \tilde{B}_{jt}(\lambda) + \hat{v}_{jt} \tag{A8}$$

The errors $\hat{v}_{jt}$, now serially uncorrelated, were used to estimate Ω^*, and the MLE was computed by minimizing

$$L(\lambda, \hat{\Omega}^{*-1}) = \sum_t [\hat{y}_{jt} - \tilde{B}_{jt}(\lambda)]' \hat{\Omega}_t^{*-1} (\hat{y}_{jt} - \tilde{B}_{jt}(\lambda)) , \tag{A9}$$

where Ω_t^* is the relevant submatrix of Ω^* taking account of missing observations. Table 3 reports the MLE together with the asymptotic standard error computed from expression (A5).

B. Estimation of the Discount Function: q(τ − t, t)

$q(\tau - t, t)$ is the present value at time t of \$1 due at time τ as estimated from the yield curve. Following McCulloch [23] let the discount function at time t, $\delta(m)$, be defined by

$$\delta(m) \equiv q(m, t) . \tag{B1}$$

Assuming continuous coupon payments, the price of bond i at time t can be written as

$$P_i = 100\, \delta(m_i) + c_i \int_0^{m_i} \delta(m)\, dm + e_i \tag{B2}$$

where m_i and c_i are the maturity and coupon of the bond and e_i is an error term. The discount function is assumed to be expressible as the sum of k continuously differentiable functions $f_j(m)$ so that

$$\delta(m) = 1 + \sum_{j=1}^{k} a_j f_j(m) \tag{B3}$$

Substituting for $\delta(m)$ in equation (B2) and rearranging yields

$$P_i - 100 - m_i c_i = \sum_{j=1}^{k} a_j [100\, f_j(m_i) + c_i F_j(m_i)] + e_j \tag{B4}$$

where $F_j(m_i) = \int_0^{m_i} f_j(m)\, dm$.

Given the functions $f_j(m)$ the coefficients a_j can be estimated from equation (B4) using a sample of bonds with different maturities. The estimated discount function is then calculated from equation (B3).

In the present application $\delta(m)$ was approximated by a continuously differentiable piecewise quadratic function so that

$$
f_1(m) = \begin{cases} m - \dfrac{1}{2d_2}\, m^2 & 0 \le m \le d_2 \\[2ex] \dfrac{1}{2d_2} & d_2 < m \le m \end{cases}
$$

$$
f_j(m) = \begin{cases} 0 & 0 \le m \le d_{j-1} \\[2ex] \dfrac{(m - d_{j-1})^2}{2(d_j - d_{j-1})} & d_{j-1} < m \le d_j \\[2ex] \dfrac{1}{2(d_j - d_{j-1})} + (m - d_j) - \dfrac{(m - d_j)^2}{2(d_{j+1} - d_j)} & \begin{array}{l} d_j < m \le d_{j+1} \\ d_{j+1} < m \le m_n \end{array} \\[2ex] \dfrac{1}{2(d_{j+1} - d_{j-1})} & j = 2, \ldots, k-1 \end{cases}
$$

$$
f_k(m) = \begin{cases} 0 & 0 \le m \le d_{k-1} \\[2ex] \dfrac{(m - d_{k-1})^2}{2(m_n - d_{k-1})} & d_{k-1} < m \le m_n \end{cases}
$$

where k is the integer closest to the square root of the number of bonds in the sample and the breakpoints d_j are chosen so that there are equal numbers of bonds maturing within each maturity interval.

ACKNOWLEDGMENTS

This paper has developed from a broader study of the pricing of U.S. Government bonds supported by the Institute for Quantitative Research in Finance. The research on duration was sponsored by the Center for Capital Market Research, Univeristy of Oregon.

We thank Bruce Dietrich-Campbell for computer programming assistance.

NOTES

1. Bierwag and associates [3] have suggested three uses of duration measures: as a summary measure of maturity, as an index of responsiveness of capital values to changes in interest rates, and as an input to portfolio immunization strategies. It will become apparent that the last two are closely related.

2. Grove [15] has attempted a formal integration of portfolio theory and duration theory. We use *bond* here as a generic term for any financial asset or liability whose payments are certain.

3. Redington [27].

4. Rosenberg and Marathe [29].

5. This is not the case for a consol bond, but there can exist only one economically distinct consol bond for any given currency.

6. Cox et al. [8] seem to imply that their measure of duration is also applicable when there are multiple sources of uncertainty; this does not seem to be true in general.

7. Brennan and Schwartz [6,7].

8. See, for example, Richard [28], Vasicek [32], Cox et al. [7], Dothan [11], and Langetieg [19].

9. Recall that duration models were developed some 30 years before the stochastic calculus was applied to problems in finance. Cf. Merton [24].

10. The subscript j is omitted where the context permits. Strictly speaking, equation (1) holds only between coupon dates. The condition that no arbitrage be possible on the coupon date provides a boundary condition for this equation; we ignore such technicalities here.

11. An exception is provided by the CIR definition of duration which is not equivalent to $(1/B)\ \partial B/\partial s$, and does not correspond to a weighted average maturity. It is therefore outside the mainstream of the duration literature and the usefulness of this definition remains unclear. It will not be considered here.

12. We speak loosely here since no risk has yet been explicitly introduced.

13. It is therefore closer in spirit to the model described in the following section; however, Bierwag's is not an equilibrium model.

14. This will take the form of equation (2) except that the right-hand side will be replaced by r(s), the equilibrium return on all bonds, and ds/dt by g(t). Bond values are obtained as the solution to the ordinary differential equation obtained by substituting the appropriate function of time for s.

15. ISW show that except for special cases, discontinuous shifts in the yield curve are inconsistent with equilibrium.

16. This is not true in the nonclassical CIR model; see note 11.

17. The legacy of Macaulay has been so strong that any new measure of duration (except that of CIR) had to retain the weighted average maturity property of the first. This imposes restrictions on the class of variance-covariance matrices which can be represented by duration measures in addition to those resulting from the assumption of a single source of uncertainty.

18. Strictly speaking, Redington's policy only guaranteed a minimum rate of return on the immunized portfolio; but he was contemplating discrete shifts in the rate structure which ISW have shown to be incompatible with equilibrium except in special cases. If interest rates follow continuous sample paths as implied by equations (3) and (4), then immunization eliminates all risk.

19. A more detailed development of this model is to be found in Brennan and Schwartz [6].

20. See Brennan and Schwartz [6], Appendix A1.

21. Estimates of a similar model using Canadian data are reported in Brennan and Schwartz [6,7].

22. Initial estimates obtained using weekly data from *The Wall Street Journal* were found to be inferior on account of the coarseness of the yield quotes (to the nearest basis point) compared to the size of weekly changes in ℓ.

23.   The highest yielding bond was chosen to avoid the problem posed by flower bonds whose yields are distorted (bid down) on account of the privilege they offer of redemption at par for payment of estate duty.

24.   The iterative Aitken estimator has been shown by Dhrymes (1971) to be a maximum likelihood estimator.

25.   Brennan and Schwartz [7].

26.   See Durbin [13]; for large samples this statistic is normally distributed.

27.   A complete set of coupon bonds would be said to exist if one bond matured each period in the future up to the horizon.

28.   Excluding "flower bonds."

29.   We do not deal with the issue of how the models compare in their predictions of absolute levels of risk since it is unclear how the variance of the state variable should be measured for the duration model.

30.   Although we might guess that for "well-diversified" portfolios the two models will yield similar results.

31.   The smoothly fitted Durand yield curves may satisfy the implicit dynamics underlying the duration model better than do actual bond prices.

32.   Flower bonds were excluded. Only 10 portfolios had been used for estimation of λ_1 because of the large number of missing observations for the longer maturities. They cause no difficulties in this context. See the Appendix for further discussion of the basic portfolio.

33.   Or fewer in months in which some maturities are lacking.

34.   Fisher and Weil assumed only annual revision.

35.   If $T - t$ exceeds the maturity of the longest bond used in estimating the discount function in a given month, then the yield to maturity is assumed to be the same for all discount bonds with maturities greater than or equal to that of the longest available coupon bond.

36.   See equation (7).

37.   Compare expressions (5) and (14).

38.   We are not suggesting that estimation of the covariance structure is the primary objective of these theories.

39.   There were insufficient observations to include bonds with maturities over 10 years.

40.   Each portfolio characteristic was a simple average of the corresponding characteristic of the bonds in the portfolio; this corresponds to a portfolio policy of buying an equal number of each bond.

41.   An estimator was also derived which used a variance-covariance matrix estimate obtained using only observations for those months for which data were available on all of the 10 portfolios. The resulting estimate was almost identical to the one obtained by the procedure described above.

REFERENCES

1.   Aitken, A. C., 1935, "On Least Squares and Linear Combinations of Observations," *Proceedings of the Royal Society of Edinburgh*, Vol. 55, 42–48.

2.   Bierwag, G. O., 1977, "Immunization, Duration, and the Term Structure of Interest Rates, *Journal of Financial and Quantitative Analysis* (12), 725–742.

3.   Bierwag, G. O., George Kaufman, and Chulsoon Khang, 1978, "Duration and Bond Portfolio Analysis: An Overview," *Journal of Financial and Quantitative Analysis* (13), 671–681.

4. Brennan, M. J. and E. Schwartz, 1977, "Savings Bonds, Retractable Bonds and Callable Bonds," *Journal of Financial Economics* (5), 67–88.

5. ——, 1979, "A Continuous Time Approach to the Pricing of Bonds," *Journal of Banking and Finance* (3), 133–155.

6. ——, 1980, "Conditional Predictions of Bond Prices and Returns," *Journal of Finance* (35), 405–417.

7. Cox, J. C., J. E. Ingersoll, and S. A. Ross, 1978, "A Theory of the Term Structure of Interest Rates," Research Paper No. 468, Stanford University.

8. ——, 1979, "Duration and the Measurement of Basis Risk," *Journal of Business* (52), 51–61.

9. Dagenais, M. G., 1973, "The Use of Incomplete Observations in Multiple Regression Analysis: A Generalized Least Squares Approach," *Journal of Econometrics* (1), 317–328.

10. Dhrymes, P. J., 1971, "Equivalence of Iterative Aitken and Maximum Likelihood Estimators for a System of Regression Equations," *Australian Economic Papers*, (19), 20–24.

11. Dothan, U. L., 1978, "On the Term Structure of Interest Rates," *Journal of Financial Economics* (6), 59–69.

12. Durand, D., 1942, Basic Yields of Corporate Bonds 1900–42, National Bureau of Economic Research, New York.

13. Durbin, J., 1970, "Testing for Serial Correlation in Least-Squares Regression When Some of the Regressors are Lagged Dependent Variables," *Econometrica* (38), 410–421.

14. Fisher, L. and R. L. Weil, 1971, "Coping with the Risk of Interest Rate Fluctuations: Returns to Bondholders from Naive and Optimal Strategies," *Journal of Business* (44), 408–431.

15. Grove, Myron A., 1974, "On Duration and the Optimal Maturity Structure of the Balance Sheet," *Bell Journal of Economics* (5), 696–709.

16. Hicks, J. R., 1939, *Value and Capital*, Oxford: Clarendon Press.

17. Ingersoll, J., J. Skelton, and R. Weil, 1978, "Duration Forty Years Later," *Journal of Financial and Quantitative Analysis*, (13), 627–650.

18. Khang, C., 1977, Bond Immunization When Short-Term Rates Fluctuate More than Long Term Rates, Working Paper, University of Oregon.

19. Langetieg, T. C., 1980, "A Multivariate Model of the Term Structure," *Journal of Finance* (35), 71–98.

20. Macaulay, Frederick R., 1938, *Some Theoretical Problems Suggested by the Movements of Interest Rates, Bond Yields, and Stock Prices in the United States since 1856*, Columbia University Press (New York).

21. Malinvaud, E., 1966, *Statistical Methods of Econometrics* (North Holland, Amsterdam).

22. Markowitz, H., 1952, "Portfolio Selection," Journal of Finance (7), 77–91.

23. McCulloch, J. H., 1971, "Measuring the Term Structure of Interest Rates," *Journal of Business*, (44), 19–31.

24. Merton, R. C., 1969, "Lifetime Portfolio Selection under Uncertainty: the Continuous Time Case," *Review of Economics and Statistics*, (51), 247–257.

25. Parks, R. E., 1966, "Estimation with Heteroscedastic Error Terms," *Econometrica* (34), 888.

26. Parks, R. W., 1967, "Efficient Estimation of a System of Regression Equations when Disturbances are both Serially and Contemporaneously Correlated," *Journal of the American Statistical Association*, 500–509.

27. Redington, F. M., 1952, "Review of the Principles of Life-Office Valuations," *Journal of the Institute of Actuaries* (18), 286–315.

28. Richard, S. F., 1978, "An Arbitrage Model of the Term Structure of Interest Rates," *Journal of Financial Economics* (6), 33–57.
29. Rosenberg, B. and V. Marathe, 1976, "Common Factors in Security Returns: Microeconomic Determinants and Macroeconomic Correlates," Working Paper No. 44, University of California, Berkeley.
30. Samuelson, P. A., 1945, "The Effect of Interest Rate Increases on the Banking System," *American Economic Review* (35), 16–27.
31. Sharpe, W. F., 1963, "A Simplified Model of Portfolio Analysis," *Management Science* (9), 277–293.
32. Vasicek, O., 1977, "An Equilibrium Characterization of the Term Structure," *Journal of Financial Economics* (5), 177–188.

COMMENTS

Terence C. Langetieg

In recent years, the concept of *duration* has fallen from academic favor as more sophisticated equilibrium models of the term structure were introduced by Brennan and Schwartz [2], Cox, Ingersoll, and Ross [3], and others. Indeed, the usefulness of duration seemed increasingly dubious after Ingersoll, Skelton, and Weil [4] pointed out the highly restrictive assumptions needed to validate the notion of duration. However, this paper by Brennan and Schwartz may put new life into duration. Brennan and Schwartz demonstrate quite clearly that in practical portfolio applications, the simple concept of duration performs as well as a highly technical equilibrium bond pricing model. Brennan and Schwartz compare the degree of portfolio immunization and bond replication obtained by using duration and by using risk measures derived from a two-factor equilibrium model. Overall portfolio strategies based on the equilibrium model perform somewhat better (as judged by the mean square error), but duration-based strategies perform almost as well. Since duration strategies are extremely simple to apply, it can be argued that duration methods are parsimoniously preferred. However, before concluding that sophisticated equilibrium approaches to portfolio management be abandoned, several comments are in order concerning the Brennan–Schwartz methodology, and the Brennan–Schwartz (B–S) equilibrium model.

1.   The equilibrium model utilized by Brennan and Schwartz must be regarded as only one of many possible equilibrium models. Hence, the inability of the B–S equilibrium model to exhibit superior perform-ance does not preclude the possibility of another equilibrium model with superior performance. Furthermore, Bierwag, Kaufman, and Khang [1] propose several alternative measures of duration that share the attribute of simplicity in portfolio applications. It is possible that one of these alternative measures might even outperform the B–S model. A somewhat more robust test would be the comparison of portfolio strategies pitting the "best" duration measure against the "best" equilibrium model. In this perspective, the Brennan–Schwartz paper should be regarded as a preliminary bout with interesting results, but not necessarily reflective of the ultimate outcome of this contest.

2.   Unlike duration, the equilibrium model requires coefficient es-timation. Subperiod estimates indicate considerable variation of esti-mates across subperiods. The unstable coefficient estimates could in-dicate an improper specification of the functional form of the stochastic process (discussed further in comment 5) or nonstationary coefficients, or both. If the coefficients are nonstationary, then the Brennan–Schwartz assumption of stationarity from 1958 through 1979 will bias tests against the equilibrium model. One way to control for nonstation-arity would be to run the comparison tests over different subperiods in which the stationarity assumption is reasonable. If perfect foresight is assumed, then both coefficient estimates and portfolio tests would be based on the same subperiod data. Alternatively, a more realistic test would use "adaptive" estimates based only on historical data. While a perfect foresight estimation should improve the performance of the equilibrium model, an adaptive estimation may even worsen perform-ance.

3.   Brennan and Schwartz examine portfolio immunization and bond replication from 1958 to 1979. However, it may be far more interesting to focus on certain subperiods where differences between the equilib-rium model and duration model are a priori largest. There are two ways to characterize such a subperiod. First, it is well known that duration is a good measure of risk when the term structure experiences a shape-preserving shift, and the general rise of interest rates from 1958 to 1979 is roughly shape preserving. One potential advantage of a two factor model is in explaining term structure movements during

specially chosen subperiods characterized by a nonproportional change or a twisting change. Second, recalling that the simple random walk underlies the duration concept, we would expect differences between the equilibrium model and the duration model only in subperiods where the stochastic process of the equilibrium model departs from a random walk. In the last section of the paper, Brennan and Schwartz report the curious result that "consol risk" is essentially proportional to duration. Hence, performance differences, if any, must come from "short-term interest rate risk." However, from 1958 to 1979, the short-term rate follows a process that is close to a random walk (i.e., $b_1 = 0.11 \approx 0$). If coefficients are nonstationary, it would be interesting to examine subperiods where b_1 differs greatly from zero, since performance differences can occur only for departures from a random walk. Finally, Brennan and Schwartz note that for longer term bonds, short-term interest rate risk is approximately linear in duration. Hence, immunization or bond replication is the long-term range of the term structure is expected to be similar for the equilibrium model and the duration model. However, by focusing on bonds in the nonlinear range of short-term interest rate risk, it is possible that greater performance differences might be found.

4. Brennan and Schwartz construct portfolios to maximize diversification. However, several other portfolio structures should be examined: Replication with only the shortest and longest term bond, replication with bonds of adjacent maturity, and replication with only shorter term (longer term) bonds. If the duration model and equilibrium model are equivalent in portfolio applications, then duration and equilibrium models should provide a similar degree of replication for all alternative portfolio strategies.

5. The formulation of equilibrium models is critically dependent on the assumed stochastic process of the long- and short-term rates. As mentioned above, the unstable coefficient estimates may indicate specification error. The finding of residual autocorrelation suggests that alternative time series models be examined. For example, inflation rates are often modeled as a moving average process, suggesting a similar form for the short-term nominal interest rate. The restriction that the short-term rate approaches the long-term rate also requires further justification. While the long-term rate may proxy a "normal" long-run level for the short-term rate, there is no justification, that I am aware of, to ensure equal coefficients on the past long-term and short-term rates. The stochastic process for the long-term rate also needs further justification. The long-term rate is an internal rate and also an instru-

mental variable for an unobserved second factor. Suppose pure discount rates had a linear relation to the unobserved factor and the short-term rate and suppose that the unobserved factor and the short-term rate follow stochastic processes as depicted in Brennan–Schwartz equation (15). Then the pure discount rate would follow a stochastic process of similar functional form. However, the internal rate on a coupon bond or a consol is a nonlinear function of pure discount rates and would follow a different type of stochastic process. Hence, it may be desirable to choose as the instrumental variable a pure discount rate rather than an internal rate. Finally, as Brennan and Schwartz acknowledge, error analysis indicates that the residual standard deviations may not be proportional to the state variables.

6.   The consol rate is subjected to double duty. It serves as an instrumental variable and as an estimator of the risk premium for consol risk. Therefore, estimation error of the consol rate is especially critical in the Brennan–Schwartz model. There are at least two potential sources of estimation error. First, the internal rate on a long-term bond is used as a proxy for the consol rate. As Cox, Ingersoll, and Ross [3] show, λ_2 estimated via a coupon bond is not the same as λ_2 estimated via a consol bond. Second, long-term government bonds are typically callable, and the impact of this provision will introduce some bias in periods of time where the probability of future call is positive. Both of these sources of potential bias might be eliminated by choosing as the instrumental variable the empirical estimate of the rate on a long-term pure discount, noncallable bond.

7.   Brennan and Schwartz use different expected wealth relatives for the duration and equilibrium models. Having no reason a priori to prefer one wealth relative over another, it would seem desirable to run tests for each of the different relatives, using the *same* relatives for both the duration and equilibrium models.

In summary, I regard the Brennan and Schwartz paper as providing an econometrically eloquent examination of equilibrium and duration based portfolio strategies. In this preliminary bout the duration concept emerges as the parsimonious portfolio management tool. My comments are primarily "speculations" on alternative methodologies; however, I suggest that the contest between equilibrium and duration-based portfolio strategies has not yet determined a final victor. Finally, as Brennan and Schwartz comment, "the equilibrium model, unlike the duration model, provides evidence as to possible mispricing of bonds," especially risky bonds, callable bonds, convertible bonds, and bonds with special characteristics.

REFERENCES

1. Bierwag, G. O., George Kaufman and Chulsoon Khang, 1978, "Duration and Bond Portfolio Analysis: An Overview," *Journal of Financial and Quantitative Analysis* (13), 671–681.
2. Brennan, Michael J., and Eduardo S. Schwartz, 1978, "A Continuous Time Approach to the Pricing of Bonds," *Journal of Banking and Finance* (3), 133–155.
3. Cox, John C., Jonathan E. Ingersoll, and Stephen A. Ross, 1978, "A Theory of the Term Structure of Interest Rates," Research paper no. 468, Stanford University.
4. Ingersoll, Jonathan E., Jeff Skelton and Roman Weil, 1978, "Duration Forty Years Later," *Journal of Financial and Quantitative Analysis* (13), 627–650.

THE USE OF DURATION IN THE DYNAMIC PROGRAMMING OF INVESTMENTS

Irwin T. Vanderhoof

The concepts of *duration* and *immunization* were developed independently by several individuals working at different disciplines. While the academics in finance are generally familiar with the line that developed from Samuelson, Hicks, Fisher, and Weyl, etc., they are not necessarily so familiar with the separate development by the actuarial profession. (Please note that I have almost resisted the temptation to go into various aquarian analogies, viz., streams, rivers, wellheads, lakes, oceans, etc.)

On occasion, George Kaufman has complained to me that the *Transactions of the Society of Actuaries* has not been easily available to him. George doesn't know how bad it really is. While the *Transactions of the Society of Actuaries* is available in many of the major libraries of the United States, the *Journal of the Institute of Actuaries* has a more limited circulation, being easily available from London to John o' Groats in Northern Britain. On the other hand, the *Transactions of the Faculty of Actuaries* can be generally obtained anywhere from Edinburgh to the Outer Hebrides. Now that is a difficult-to-obtain journal. The difficulties in obtaining the *Transactions of the International Congress of Actuaries* are probably more severe, since its distribution is mostly limited to participants.

Granted, the actuarial sources are more difficult to consult; nevertheless, I believe it is important for both academics and practitioners to make the effort to consult them. Let me explain why. Life insurance companies have about $400 billion in assets, mostly invested in fixed-dollar instruments like bonds and mortgages. Property and casualty companies have about $200 billion of similar investments, and trusteed pension funds have about another $330 billion. Banks of all types have about $1.5 trillion. I doubt that bond mutual funds have total assets of more than $100 billion. All of the financial intermediaries have the same fundamental kinds of problems in the matching of assets and liabilities because they are intermediaries, and that is the essence of the actuarial approach to handling of fixed assets. The problems of intermediaries are, then, essentially the problems of the actuaries in determining the proper handling of the assets purchased to back guarantees implicit in the contracts they sell to the general public.

But what is the size of the bond market? I guess a little over a trillion dollars in total value. Therefore, when you are talking about the fixed-dollar assets of funds that are concerned with the actuarial problem of the intermediary, you are talking about the bond markets. When you are using mutual-fund kinds of techniques, you are catering to the pigmy of the capital markets rather than the giants. I submit to you that there is more good to be done, more glory to be achieved, and more grants to be obtained by educating the giants than the pigmies.

While I may not have convinced you to take subscriptions to all of the actuarial journals, I hope that I have convinced you that an occasional investigation into these arcane tombs might be of value. To be entirely fair about the subject, the actuaries in this country have not always been so very sophisticated on this subject. Up until 1975, there were occasional sparks of interest in immunization, which I fanned as hard as I could. Mostly though, the attitude was that, even if such techniques worked, their use would prevent the achieving of the profits available from the correct prediction of interest rate changes. Since those profits never seem to be actually available, that criticism has not come up recently. Until about 1975, the required education for actuaries for the exams included material on money and banking and some selections of readings on the practices of insurance company investment written by practitioners about 20 years earlier.

In 1975, I was asked to provide recommendations for a revision of the syllabus for the investment part of the exams. My recommendations were accepted, so that all actuaries subsequently taking the exam were required to study not only macroeconomics and security analysis but also a study note, which I prepared, on immunization and related techniques. In recent years, therefore, all new actuaries have studied this basic material in their training, and the topic of immunization is on the program at almost every meeting of the society.

Additional evidence of the importance being placed on these techniques by the profession is the fact that the international award for research in the field was presented last year to Phelim Boyle, present at this meeting, for his paper on immunization of insurance contracts and assets under the assumption of stochastic changes in the term structure of interest rates—where short-term rates vary more widely than long-term rates, as postulated by Cox, Ingersoll, and Ross [2].

In addition, committees of the Society of Actuaries are meeting to establish methods of evaluating the needs for surplus by insurance companies caused by the mismatching of assets and liabilities. While no conclusions have yet been reached, it seems likely to me that within a year, there will be some recommendation that the actuaries of companies should be required to submit, along with their certification of the reserves of the company, a statement that there is a reasonable relationship between the maturity structures of the assets and the liabilities of the company. While this will probably not mean anything like strict matching of durations and will probably be a rather loose and qualitative approach for the first several years, this step toward following the practice of the British companies certainly highlights the importance of these techniques to the actuarial profession and those institutions that look to actuaries for their solvency, viz., insurance companies and pension funds. As we have seen, these are the institutions that dominate the bond markets.

There are a series of techniques that actuaries have developed to keep reasonable relationships between maturities of assets and liabilities. Since they were devised by actuaries for the problems of actuarial funds (insurance and pension), I call them *actuarial investment management systems*. I also call them that because it leads to such a nice acronym: AIMS. The acronym is meaningful, because these AIMS techniques are different in kind and purpose from the currently popular modern portfolio theory and capital asset pricing model paradigms.

There are many differences between the two approaches. I think that the reason for the differences may be laid to the different clienteles that they are aimed at. Well knowing that I will get some reaction from the MPT people, I will still suggest that MPT is really designed for the mutual-fund owner or the individual investor. The techniques are designed for short time periods, and there is the assumption that there is no serial correlation of the returns on the investments.

In contrast, AIMS works with very highly leveraged funds. Insurance companies tend to be leveraged at between 10 and 20 to 1 for life companies and 4 or 5 to 1 for casualty companies. Pension funds are probably more leveraged than insurance companies, but if the margins in their calculations are eliminated, there is the prospect of getting additional funding from the sponsor. The point of this distinction is that a small change in the value of the assets compared to the liabilities can bankrupt these funds, and therefore, losses of as little as 10 percent compared to the liabilities cannot be tolerated. The managers are not managing for their own accounts, where they might tolerate small losses, but are managing as intermediaries where a small loss in the account not only makes the fund insolvent but gets the manager fired. The risk characteristics demand that effort should be expended in minimizing the possibilities of even small losses. However, the losses can only be measured with respect to the liabilities, and if both assets and liabilities change by the same amount, no losses have been experienced.

AIMS techniques are intended to be applicable over long periods of time. While mutual fund techniques are measured a success or failure over a period of days or months, the liabilities of actuarial funds stretch out for forty and fifty years. An individual buying a life insurance policy today can turn the policy in for an annuity when he is 65 and continue receiving payments until he is 90 or 100. There are individuals now making purchases who will be depending upon guarantees made by insurance companies for payments to them until the middle of the twenty-first century.

Finally, there is the fact that, generally, AIMS depends on a negative serial correlation of security returns. Basically, this means that, if we take a loss in one period, that loss must sometime be made up in terms of the maturity of the security. AIMS and insurance companies are concerned with the use of fixed-dollar assets, like bonds, as opposed to MPT techniques that are concerned with the management of stocks.

The earliest of these AIMS is the system of absolute matching developed by Haynes and Kirton and described in volume 21 of the *Transactions of the Faculty of Actuaries* [3]. My friends tell me that it is becoming extremely popular today under the soubriquet of "dedicated portfolio." The idea is simple. If a pension plan sponsor can isolate a group of lives already collecting pension benefits, the actuary of the fund can plot out the amounts that have to be paid to the surviving individuals each year for the next 50 or so years. Actuarial calculations of this kind are not perfectly accurate but are very good if the group of lives is large enough. Having the schedule of benefit payments, the investment manager need only choose securities such that the maturities plus the coupon payments in each year will match the payment schedule for the retirees described above.

If absolute matching is possible, and it may be, then all questions of changes in reinvestment rates and risks become almost entirely inapplicable to the plan. If inflation erodes the benefits, the plan sponsor may have to provide an ad hoc increase; but additonal funding from regular purposes should no longer be necessary. While absolute matching may not reduce the total cost of the plan, it certainly can reduce the prospective variance in those costs. I believe that most dedicated portfolios are now set up as a linear programming problem, where the cost of the portfolio is to be minimized subject to there being adequate funds for each payment. Anyone can do the program, but there is some difference in the extent to which companies are set up to provide a maximum choice of the securities needed for particular payments. The completeness of the universe of bonds can be an important factor in the success of matching. There will also frequently be some disarticulation in the matching, so that there is a residual risk of changes in the short-term interest rates. This is, however, a small factor compared to the risks in the funding prior to the absolute matching step.

The second development of AIMS is the very subject we are addressing in this text. While everyone is familiar with Redington's paper, it may not be so generally known that the paper went onto the syllabus for the Institute of Actuaries immediately after publication and has remained there. As I mentioned before, its effect was so great that every British actuary is required to certify as part of the demonstration of the solvency of a company that there is a reasonable relationship between the maturity structure of the assets and the liabilities. There have been some failures of British companies, but the problems have been with companies that allowed book value surrenders of deposit assets—the problem of cash flows that vary with interest rates that has not been a part of the immunization strategy.

The third attempt was what I call the control system described in a paper I wrote for the *Transaction* in 1973 [4]. This approach attempts to model the actual assets transactions of a life insurance company or pension fund over a period of 20 years simulating the effects of differing investment strategies using a variety of economic scenarios. The objective was not only to find the best investment strategy, considering all of the different possibilities, but also to establish what kind of an assured rate of interest earnings could be achieved independent of the future economic environment.

The fourth attempt in this direction was made by me for the

International Congress of Actuaries in 1976. It was an attempt to integrate inflation into the paradigm and immunize against inflation rather than simple interest rates. Any attempt to immunize against inflation must make some assumption about the relationship between interest rates and inflation. In that paper I made what has been described as an heroic assumption, viz., that inflation enters exactly and immediately into all interest rates for all maturities.

I spent the next several years trying to justify a pattern for the way in which inflation actually affects interest rates but was unable to find any consistent set of equations. I believe that this is probably the state of reality. Inflation enters into interest rates for all maturities but with unstable weights and lags; also, the real rate of interest has been drifting. The assumption of immediate and full reflection may still be heroic, but it no longer seems to me that a better assumption is available. Over the very long term (all that actuaries really care about: after all, in the long term everybody's dead, and that's our business), I believe that the assumption has been correct. Despite the remarks that the academics make about the unlikelihood of substantial parallel shifts in the yield curve, that is what has taken place.

The dominant force in the change in interest rates in recent years has been the effect of inflation. The effect of inflation has been to make a massive parallel shift in the yield curve, and that shift has generally reflected inflation completely. I, therefore, now believe that the assumption I made in 1976 was as good as any assumption that can be made. If we accept that assumption, then there is an inflation rate j and a real interest rate i which together produce a nominal interest rate k, where

$$1 + k = (1 + i)(1 + j)$$

If we further define the A's as the asset flows from maturity and coupons and use a subscript prefix f if the asset is a fixed dollar and x if the item is perfectly indexed to inflation, and if we represent by B's the cash flows from business operations with the same prefixes, then the 1976 paper shows that if we wish to immunize against inflation, we must have the condition

$$\frac{\sum t_f A_t w^t}{\sum {}_f A_t w^t + \sum {}_x A_t v^t} = \frac{\sum t_f B_t w^t}{\sum {}_f B_t w^t + \sum {}_x B_t v^t}$$

where $v = 1/(1 + i)$ and $w = 1/(1 + k)$.

Despite any of the reservations that can be held about the assumption as to how inflation enters into interest rates, this formula carries some useful intuitive insights. If all benefits are indexed against inflation, then obviously all investments must be similarly indexed. However, the equation implies that, if an insurance company has some fixed-dollar liabilities of long duration, a substantial portfolio of fixed-dollar assets may produce an acceptable overall result. As with many other aspects of immunization theory, even if the theory itself is subject to criticism, it still gives good answers. The next step in this approach would be to investigate the effects of selling futures on the durations. Obviously, going short on some long-term investments would allow greater inflation sensitivity in the benefits.

The fifth strategic development was the one for which Phelim Boyle received the award alluded to earlier. In his paper in the *Journal of the Institute of Actuaries* [1] in London, he developed the immunization conditions in an environment where both long- and short-term interest rates were the result of stochastic processes and where short-term rates varied more than long-term rates. Using the tools of the stochastic calculus (Ito's dilemma always comes up, doesn't it?), Mr. Boyle showed that, even though duration now has a new and far more complex definition, immunization by the matching of durations is still possible. He extended this in a paper to the International Congress of Actuaries in 1980 to include inflation as a variable.

Over the last several years, James Tilley published in the *Transactions of the Society of Actuaries* two papers that described a more complete scenario method for describing the cash flows to and from an actuarial fund. his approach demands a construction of a set of scenarios of economic conditions that could be experienced over the next period of years and then relate to each of them a set of cash flows that would correspond to each different economic scenario. In this case, however, the cash flows were for both the assets and the liabilities. As I mentioned before, there were failures among the British companies because policyholders had the right to withdraw their deposits with a book-value guarantee. The actuaries did not include in their calculations that, if interest rates became high enough, there would be a radical increase in the number of individuals who would make that election and who would thereby force the sale of securities below cost.

Tilley's approach should reduce this problem. The technique uses modern computer technology to solve the problem in the form of linear programming. All of the scenarios and their cash flows are considered at once, and the computer attempts to determine the current strategy for investments that allow all of the scenarios to be successfully realized by determining the set of all feasible solutions to the problem. Variants solve the problem with the least maximum cost or with a largest expected profit.

However useful this approach may be, it is not a final solution to the problem of cash flows that vary with the steps in the economic scenario. While this approach can establish a pattern of investments that, along with a particular reinvestment assumption, proves a set of scenarios for the future feasible, it can be shown that there are additional feasible futures that are rejected by this technique. A simple calculation will show that if we do the calculation stepped one year into the future, then some scenario that was originally not feasible, that could not be accommodated, is now acceptable.

The reason for this is that when we have stepped one year into the future, we know what happened in the first year. We have, therefore, eliminated all the possible scenarios for the first year that did not actually occur. We are now faced with a severely limited set of possibilities for the future, and they can accommodate paths of the economy that could not be covered in the first year.

It is reasonably easy to construct examples that correspond to the situation described above. The approach described will always produce initial infeasible paths of future interest rates and cash flows that can be accommodated when we consider the problem dynamically knowing how we will make decisions in the future.

I had realized this possible improvement at about the time I was asked if I would make a presentation for this meeting. My subject seemed obvious and easy. I would develop the problem of immunization under varying cash flows by using the dynamic programming method and, hopefully, make a contribution to the current most serious problem of insurance companies and pension funds.

Dynamic programming seemed an easy approach. If we are looking at a 10-year horizon, then we first consider what our actions will be in the ninth year looking at a one-year horizon. We can plot all the different interest rates that could be in effect in the ninth year and consider all the changes that could take place to bring us into the tenth year. We would decide upon our strategy for ninth-year investments so that we would always reach our tenth-year objective. Then, we would look at our eighth-year situation and find the strategies that would get us to the desired position for the ninth year, etc.

Unfortunately, there is a problem. If we assume that interest rates are 10 percent in the ninth year, they could have reached that value following many different paths. Unfortunately, the cash flows associated with increases and decreases in interest rates are not necessarily sym-metrical. If interest rates are well above the rate we are crediting to clients, they may surrender their policies, and an irreversible change has taken place in all the cash flows for the future. While we can, at least in principle, formulate behavioral equations that represent the extent to which clients will take such actions, even knowing the effects on our cash flows complicates the problem.

We are no longer dealing with a simple two-dimensional dynamic programming problem. The cash position at the end of any period is now the third dimension to the problem (the other two are time and interest rate). The problem has now become far more difficult to solve. If interest rates can only go up or down by a fixed amount or stay the same at the end of one year, we have three possible interest rates. At the end of the second year, there are only five possible interest rates in the environment, but there were nine paths to reach them. In the third year there were 27 paths to reach seven possible interest rates. The number of paths that have to be evaluated using behavioral equations to describe the cash flows increases as a power of 3. If the horizon is 10 years, the number of paths is approaching 100,000, and for periods of normal concern to the actuary, 20 years or more, the number of paths gets into the billions. Even modern computers cannot handle problems where the number of calculations increases exponentially. This problem is the bane of the dynamic programming approach to investment.

It seemed to me, when I realized that this was the problem with the use of duration in the dynamic programming of investments, that maybe my presentation would be indefinitely delayed. However, there remained the possibility of a special structure. In dynamic programming there is frequently no practical direct method of solution. It becomes necessary to cheat by finding something about the problem that will allow a solution—a special structure of the problem.

The obvious direction to look in was immunization itself. The standard immunization problem that has been used by actuaries for years and has been sold in the form of a bullet maturity by Manufacturers Hanover can be formulated as a dynamic programming problem, and it is almost as difficult to solve as the one described above. However, in the immunization problem with predictable cash flows, there is a special structure. If you start any period with a portfolio of the immunizing duration, you know in advance that whatever happens you will be able to make a decision at the end of the period, rebalancing the portfolio so that you can go on correctly to the next duration. The matching of durations at the beginning of the problem provides you with an automatic computer that guarantees there is always a correct decision that can be made, whatever the level of interest rates in the next period. Since you know how to start out correctly and you know that once correctly started there is always a way to get satisfactorily to the next year of the problem, it is not necessary to actually go through each year of the solution.

The successful dynamic programming of investments, then, requires that we find a way of assuring ourselves that our current investment structure is such that, if interest rates change and cash flows are thereby affected, the value of the assets after the change will still be consistent with the needed asset values after the cash flows. Since the whole theoretical development of immunization comes from the calculus and since Redington started the whole thing off with a Taylor's series, that would seem like a good place to start.

If f( ) is the present value of the obligation at a given interest rate i, then the expansion is

$$f(i + \alpha) = f(i) + \frac{\alpha}{1} f'(i) + \frac{\alpha^2}{2} f''(i) + \cdots .$$

In this case, the function f not only includes the change in value because of a change in the interest rate but also includes the change on account of the cash flow. Obviously, if we are concerned about only three possible interest rates, then α in the above equation takes on values of 0, plus and minus, while the varying cash flows are introduced because of their effects on the necessary present values from the investments.

If f is a present-value function, then we can solve for the necessary present value for any point in the problem and the way that the present value must change if there is a change in interest rate. This is exactly like immunization except that the curve of asset value in relation to liability value has been forced to take on a specific shape and pass through specific points.

Now

$$f'( ) = -vD_1 f( )$$

and

$$f''( ) = v^2(D_1 + D_2)f( ),$$

where $v = 1/(1 + i)$ and D_1 and D_2 are defined as follows:

The following formula for D_1 is that of Macaulay, to whom I have referred previously; it applies to many types of insurance company investments:

$$\frac{\sum tA_t v^t}{\sum A_t v^t} = D_1 = \frac{R}{R - 1} - \frac{QR + n(1 + Q - QR)}{R^n - 1 - Q + QR},$$

where   F = "face" value of the bond in dollars, that is, the "principal" sum in dollars;

I = number of dollars paid periodically, that is, number of dollars called for by one coupon;

P = number of dollars paid for the bond, that is, the "price" in dollars;

n = number of periods the bond has to run, that is, number of periods to maturity;

R = periodic rate of "yield" (e.g., if the bond is selling to yield 4 percent per annum, R = 1.02 [under the semiannual convention bond tables]);

Q = ratio of the face value of the bond to a coupon payment, that is, Q = F/I;

D_1 = "duration" of the bond in periods.

The following is the corresponding formula for D_2 where PV is the present value of the obligation:

$$\frac{\sum t^2 A_t v^t}{\sum A_t v^t} = D_2 = \frac{1}{R^n(PV)} \left\{ \frac{I}{(R-1)^3} [R^{n+2} + R^{n+1} - (n+1)^2 R^2 + (2n^2 + 2n - 1)R - n^2] + n^2 F \right\}.$$

Thus, for a given set of values for the liabilities after the changes in cash flow, we can calculate values of the derivatives and, therefore, of the D_1 and D_2.

In my 1972 paper, "The Interest Rate Assumption and The Maturity Structure Of The Assets Of A Life Insurance Company" [4], I included a table of these D's for various assets. Using these values or the formulas, it should be possible to identify a set of assets that provides the necessary values to support the varying cash flow contract. Since this is possible, there is an analogue of immunization that applies for contracts for varying cash flows, and the solution of the dynamic programming problem of interest guarantees with varying cash flows can be investigated in terms of assuring ourselves that each future possible change in interest rates can be accommodated by a possible asset structure. The many thousands of calculations are no longer necessary, only the smaller number of calculations that correspond to the different points in the interest rate paths. Perhaps, an example of the calculation will make this argument clearer.

The following example illustrates the immunization of a $1000 maturity contract in 10 years. The going-in interest rate is 6%. If interest rates at the end of one year are 7%, there will be a cash withdrawal of $50. Similarly, if interest rates move down to 5%, there will be a cash inflow of $30. Since we are going to rebalance the portfolio at the end of each year, different cash-flow statements can be made at the end of each year depending on the interest rate environment and years to maturity.

Assuming we could find an asset or group of assets yielding 6%, the initial portfolio would be funded at $558.39. At the end of one year, there are three possibilities: interest rates stay the same, move up to 7%, or down to 5%.

If interest rates remain the same, the portfolio's value in one year will be $591.90. On the other hand, if the interest rates are 7% or 5%, we must take into account the cash outflow or inflow.

At 7%, $50 will be withdrawn. This amount, accumulated nine years at 6%, is subtracted from the maturity amount. The present value of the difference at 7%, $497.97, is the required portfolio value at the end of one year. Therefore, before deduction, the required value, if interest rates move to 7%, is $547.99.

At 5%, $30 will flow into the fund. This amount, accumulated for nine years at 6%, is added to the maturity amount. The assets required at the end of one year in this situation are $677.28 after the inflow and $647.28 before. Hence, to repeat, the three possible asset values at the end of the year are $591.90, $547.99, and $647.28 if interest rates are 6, 7, and 5 percent, respectively.

For each interest rate scenario we have the asset values at the end of one year as $A_1(i_0, \Delta i; p)$, where i_0 is the initial interest rate, Δi is the incremental change, and p is the required portfolio. Expanding A_1 in a Taylor's series, we get

$$A_1(i_0, \Delta i) = A_1(i_0) + \frac{A_1'(i_0)\ \Delta i}{1!} + \frac{A_1''(i_0)\ \Delta i^2}{2!} + \cdots.$$

Assuming the value of the assets can be approximated by the first three terms of the series, we have $A_1(i_0, \Delta i)$ such that

$$A_1(0.06, 0) = 591.90 = A_1(0.06) + A_1'(0.06)$$
$$\times\ 0 + A_1''(0.06) \times 0$$
$$A_1(0.06, 0.01) = 547.99 = A_1(0.06) + A_1'(0.06)$$
$$\times\ 0.01 + A_1''(0.06)\ \frac{(0.01)^2}{2}$$
$$A_1(0.06, -0.01) = 647.28 = A_1(0.06) + A_1'(0.06)(-0.01)$$
$$+ A_1''(0.06)\ \frac{(-0.01)^2}{2}$$

or

$$591.90 = A_1(0.06)$$

$$547.99 = A_1(0.06) + 0.01A_1'(0.06) + 0.00005A_1''(0.06)$$

$$647.27 = A_1(0.06) - 0.01A_1'(0.06) + 0.00005A_1''(0.06).$$

The solution to this system of equations is

$$A_1'(0.06) = -4964.5 \qquad A_1''(0.06) = 114700.$$

The corresponding first and second moments, that is, duration D_1 and second moment D_2, are 9.42 and 221.38, respectively.

Next, we seek that set of assets that combine to give these values of D_1 and D_2. Since, in general, the D_1's and D_2's combine linearly, we have

$$1 = x_1 + x_2 + x_3$$

$$9.42 = D_1 = x_1D_{1A} + x_2D_{1B} + x_3D_{1C}$$

$$221.38 = D_2 = x_1D_{2A} + x_2D_{2B} + x_3D_{2C},$$

where x_i is the fraction of the present value of asset i ($= A, B, C$) out of the present value of the total portfolio.

At this point, we choose three assets whose weighted D_1's or D_2's would give the total value. Using values from the paper, "The Interest Rate Assumption and the Maturity Structure of the Assets of a Life Insurance Company" [4], we select as possible candidates:

a. $486.82 of a 20-year bond, 5-year call, at 3% coupon, $D_1 = 13.8$ and $D_2 = 240.99$.
b. $488.08 of a 50-year bond, no call, at 3% coupon, $D_1 = 17.94$, and $D_2 = 562.09$.
c. Treasury Bond at 6%, $D_1 = 1$ and $D_2 = 1$.

Using these factors, we get

$$1 = x_1 + x_2 + x_3$$

$$9.42 = 13.8x_1 + 17.94x_2 + x_3$$

$$221.38 = 240.99x_1 + 562.09x_2 + x_3$$

and the solution

$$x_1 = 0.31803, \qquad x_2 = 0.25674, \qquad x_3 = 0.42523.$$

Allocation of the initial portfolio value of $558.39 yields

   a. $177.58
   b. $143.36
   c. $237.45

Since we used the first three terms of the Taylor's series to approximate the value in one year of the portfolio, we can now determine how close the present value of the required amounts in each interest rate scenario differ from the allocated portfolio values at each interest rate using the approximation.

At 7%, the present value of $547.99 one year hence at 6% is $516.97. The present values of the assets at this rate are (a) $155.73, (b) $121.79, (c) $237.45, for a total of $514.97. The truncated Taylor's series underestimates the total value required by $2.00 in this case.

At 5%, the present value of $647.28 at 6% is $610.64. The assets present values are (a) $203.59, (b) $172.75, and (c) $237.45, for a total of $613.79. There is an overestimate of $3.15.

Thus, the portfolio is underfunded given an increase in interest rates and overfunded given a decrease in interest rates at the end of one year. However, in this example, the difference is small and is less than 1% in each case.

It should be remembered, however, that the portfolio will be rebalanced at the end of the year for the interest rate existing at the end of the first year and the three possible interest rate scenarios expected at that time.

To answer a few questions that can come up:

1. This technique does not solve the problem. It only says that a solution is possible if we know the way the cash flows will change with interest rates.
2. Like the original Macauley work, this presumes that there is a parallel shift in interest rates in all durations; in fact, the major changes in interest rates are such parallel shifts—generally caused by inflation.
3. Since rebalancing can be done at any time, we can work with much larger changes in interest rates if we assume that the rebalancing has been done for each small step.
4. There is no reason that the techniques cannot be extended to more complex patterns or that greater accuracy in the results should not be able to be achieved by increasing the number of terms used in the Taylor's series.

5. The usefulness of such techniques will depend upon the company's having a sufficiently liquid portfolio.
6. The extension of immunization to varying cash flows should have considerable value in the management of assets of insurance companies in periods of varying interest rates.

As a final comment, I would like to point out how very robust these kinds of techniques are despite the heavy pressure that some of us put on them.

REFERENCES

1. Boyle, Phelim, "Immunization under Stochastic Models of the Term Structure," *Journal of the Institute of Actuaries* (UK), Vol. 105.
2. Cox, J. C., J. E. Ingersoll, and S. A. Ross, 1978, "A Theory of the Term Structure of Interest Rates," Working Paper No. 468, Stanford University, August.
3. Haynes and Kirton, *Transactions of the Faculty of Actuaries*, Volume 21.
4. Vanderhoof, Irwin T., 1972, "The Interest Rate Assumption and the Maturity Structure of the Assets of a Life Insurance Company," *Transactions of the Society of Actuaries*, Volume 24.

PART II

DURATION AND IMMUNIZATION

THE DYNAMICS OF THE TERM STRUCTURE AND ALTERNATIVE PORTFOLIO IMMUNIZATION STRATEGIES

Jeffrey Nelson and Stephen Schaefer

ABSTRACT

An *immunization* strategy is one in which a portfolio of (*component*) bonds is managed so that its value is always as close as possible to the value of another asset: the *target*. The idea and the term *immunization* were introduced by Redington, an actuary, who proposed it as a means for life insurance companies to mitigate the effects of interest rate changes on their net worth. The essence of Redington's strategy is to set the *duration* of the assets and liabilities equal.

This paper has two parts. First, it generalizes Redington's model to accommodate return generating processes in which (1) there is more than one "factor" and (2) the sensitivity of a bond's return to a given factor is other than unity. Second, empirical evidence is presented on the performance of a number of alternative immunization strategies. These include the strategy proposed by Redington and a number of others which are in the spirit of recent contributions to the term structure literature.

61

I. INTRODUCTION

An *immunization* strategy is one in which a portfolio of (*component*) bonds is managed so that its value is always as close as possible to the value of another asset: the *target*. The idea, and the term immunization, were introduced by Redington [15], an actuary who proposed it as a means for life insurance companies to mitigate the effects of interest rate changes on their net worth. The essence of Redington's strategy is to set the *duration* of the assets and liabilities equal. The concept of duration had been introduced earlier by MacCaulay [13].

The literature on immunization is remarkable for the paucity of empirical work. The most extensive study to date is by Fisher and Weil [9] who tested an immunization strategy against some simpler alternatives. However, because no better data were available, Fisher and Weil used the Durand yield curve data [8] to estimate rates of return on bonds. The availability of more extensive and reliable data makes a reexamination of this topic appropriate.

While it might appear that the relevance of immunization is limited to bond portfolio management, it actually has a wider significance. As several authors (Ingersoll, Skelton, and Weil [11] and Boyle [3,4]) have pointed out, an immunized portfolio is constructed in exactly the same way as a "hedged portfolio" in option pricing theory. Thus the problem of immunization is precisely the problem of asset replication which is central to much of the modern theory of contingent claims valuation.

Our paper extends the existing literature in two ways. First, we provide a generalization of the immunization concept to more than one factor and to cases where the sensitivity of the term structure to changes in the factor is not, as Redington's approach assumes, unity for all maturities. Second, we present empirical evidence on the performance of a number of alternative immunization strategies based on one- and two-factor models. These include the strategy proposed by Redington (we shall call this *conventional immunization*) and a number of models in the spirit of the recent literature on the term structure [5, 6, 7, 17]. Our data for these tests are taken from a file of price quotations on Treasury securities, covering the period 1925–1979, produced by the Center for Research in Security Prices at the University of Chicago (CRSP).

The paper is organized as follows. Section II outlines a general K-factor model of the term structure and derives the corresponding immunization policy. Section III describes the price data we employ and also the estimates of the term structure. Section IV presents an analysis of some time series properties of the long and short rates. In

Section V we report estimates of the sensitivity of the term structure to changes in the factors we employ; these, like the estimates of the term structure, are necessary for the calculation of immunizing portfolios. The main results are given in Section VI which reports the performance of several immunization strategies based on "single-factor" models of the term structure, and one strategy based on a two-factor model. In the spirit of the recent literature on the term structure, we use interest rates of particular maturities as "factors." Following Vasicek [18], Cox, Ingersol, and Ross [7], and others we examine a single-factor model based on the short rate. Next we test a two-factor model, similar to that developed by Brennan and Schwartz [5], but based on a long rate and an intermediate rate. (The reason why we used an intermediate rate, rather than the short rate as Brennan and Schwartz did, is explained in Section V). We also test a single-factor model based on a long rate, a conventional (Redington) immunization strategy, and as a benchmark, following Fisher and Weil, a naive strategy based on maturity. Section VII gives our conclusions and a summary of the results.

II. THEORY

Assume that the price at time t of a default-free pure discount bond promising \$1 on maturity at date τ is a function of K factors, f_1, f_2, ..., f_K:

$$p(t, \tau) = p(t, \tau, f_1, \ldots, f_K). \tag{1a}$$

The factors are assumed to follow a multivariate diffusion:

$$df_k = \mu_k(\ ) \, dt + \sigma_k \, dz_k, \qquad k = 1, \ldots, K, \tag{2}$$

where $\mu_k(\ )$ is the drift component of factor k, σ_k^2 is the instantaneous variance rate of factor k, and the dz_k are correlated standard Brownian motions. Thus,

$$E(dz_j \, dz_k) = \begin{cases} dt & j = k, \\ \rho_{jk} dt & j \neq k. \end{cases}$$

Equation (1a) may be rewritten as:

$$p(t, \tau) = \exp[-(\tau - t)R(t, \tau, f_1, \ldots, f_K)], \tag{1b}$$

where $R(t, \tau, f_1, \ldots, f_K)$ is the $\tau - t$ period zero coupon yield (or *spot rate*) at time t. Using Ito's lemma, we may write the local change in price as

$$dp(t, \tau) = \mu_p(\ ) \, dt - (\tau - t)p(t, \tau) \sum_{k=1}^{K} \frac{\partial R(t, \tau)}{\partial f_k} \sigma_k \, dz_k. \tag{3}$$

In equation (3) the drift component of price, $\mu_p(\ )$, involves both the drift rates of the f_k processes and second-order terms which depend on the covariance matrix of the f_k's. As we are interested only in constructing immunizing (or hedged) portfolios, we may suppress the full functional form of the $\mu_p(\ )$ term.

Equation (3) applies to a discount bond. A coupon-bearing bond making J payments $a_j, j = 1, \ldots, J$ at times $\tau_j, j = 1, \ldots, J$, is simply a portfolio of discount bonds, with price at time t:

$$P = \sum_{j=1}^{J} a_j p(t, \tau_j). \tag{4}$$

Using equation (3), it follows immediately that

$$dP = \sum_{j=1}^{J} a_j \mu_p(t, \tau_j) dt - \sum_{j=1}^{J} a_j(\tau_j - t) p(t, \tau_j) \sum_{k=1}^{K} \frac{\partial R(t, \tau_j)}{\partial f_k} \sigma_k \, dz_k. \tag{5}$$

Dividing through by the price P, equation (5) may be written as

$$\frac{dP}{P} = \frac{1}{P} \mu_p(\ ) \, dt + \sum_{k=1}^{K} \eta_k \sigma_k \, dz_k \tag{6}$$

where

$$\mu_p(\ ) \equiv \sum_{j=1}^{J} a_j \mu_p(t, \tau_j), \tag{7a}$$

$$\eta_k(\ ) \equiv -\frac{1}{P} \sum_{j=1}^{J} a_j(\tau_j - t) p(t, \tau_j) \frac{\partial R(t, \tau_j)}{\partial f_k}. \tag{7b}$$

The parameter η_k, which measures the sensitivity of the bond's rate of return to factor k, represents a generalization of conventional duration. While the functional form of the expression closely resembles duration, there are three important differences. First, there are K parameters, one for each factor, rather than just one. Second, there is an extra term, $\partial R(t, \tau_j)/\partial f_k$, which measures the sensitivity of the spot rate for maturity $\tau_j - t$ to factor k. Thirdly, the discount factor $p(t, \tau_j)$ is based on zero coupon yields (the true term structure) rather than on yield to maturity. In this it corresponds to McCaulay's [13] definition of duration rather than Redington's.

In our model we have assumed that both assets and liabilities are default free. By including additional factors, e.g., the value of the firm in the case of risky debt it is possible, in principle, to relax this assumption. However, to do so in a way which would also take into account the involved nature of realistic capital structures would complicate the analysis considerably. Our paper is therefore mainly concerned with the default-free case, although in Section VII, we briefly discuss some possible applications to equity portfolios.

Perfect immunization would be achieved if it were possible to manage the asset portfolio in such a way that, at each instant, it's value was precisely equal to that of the liabilities. Under the conditions we have assumed of continuous trading, diffusion processes and frictionless markets, we know that perfect immunization is feasible (see Harrison and Kreps [10]).[1] The portfolio policy which achieves it is analogous to the well known hedging strategy of option theory. At each instant the following conditions must be met:

1. The portfolio must be fully invested.
2. The sensitivity of the target's rate of return to each factor must equal the sensitivity of the portfolio's rate of return to the same factor.

Thus, in general, if there are K factors, the immunizing portfolio must contain $K + 1$ bonds. Let x_i be the fraction of the portfolio invested in bond i; then the portfolio satisfies

$$\sum_{i=1}^{K+1} x_i = 1 \tag{8a}$$

and

$$\sum_{i=1}^{K+1} x_i \eta_{ik} = \eta_{0k}, \qquad k = 1, \ldots, K, \tag{8b}$$

where η_{ik} is the sensitivity of component bond i's rate of return to factor k, and η_{0k} is the sensitivity of the target asset's rate of return to factor k.

One of the deficiencies of the immunization literature is the absence of a convincing explanation of *why* investors should wish to immunize. It is almost entirely a "how-to-do-it" literature. In the case of a consumer, immunization would be optimal only if he displayed zero risk tolerance. But most investors who have shown an interest in immunization are intermediaries rather than consumers, and in this case no simple inferences appear possible, either on the basis of risk aversion or on other considerations.[2]

An immunization strategy is sometimes used by intermediaries to "manufacture" long-term pure discount bonds from existing coupon-bearing bonds. These are then sold (for example, as guaranteed investment contracts) to consumers or, indeed, to still other intermediaries such as pension funds. But if the purpose of immunization is to construct long-term pure discount bonds (or, more generally, claims with currently unavailable cash flow patterns), another puzzle is raised. It is to ask why primary issuers or intermediaries do not attack this problem directly. If investors want to buy long-term pure discount bonds, why do corporations not issue them or intermediaries create them by issuing appropriate claims against a *fixed* portfolio, rather than committing themselves to a complicated *dynamic* portfolio strategy? We have no answers to these questions and, for the remainder of the paper, take the objective of immunization as a given.[3]

III. DATA: BOND PRICES AND TERM STRUCTURE ESTIMATES

The main source of data for our study is the CRSP Government Bond Tape. This contains prices and other information on essentially all U.S. Treasury issues from December 1925 onward. The most recent data employed in this study was for December 1979. As the study is concerned mainly with longer maturities data on Treasury bills were eliminated, leaving a sample of approximately 500 notes and bonds.

Equations (8a) and (8b) show that an immunizing portfolio policy is defined by a set of $K \times (K + 1)$ parameters for the component assets (the η_{ik}) and K parameters for the target asset (the η_{0k}). To calculate the η's requires five data items for each asset: (1) its price; (2) the vector of cash flows produced by the asset; (3) the dates on which the cash flows occur (the "payment dates"); (4) the value of the discount function for each payment date; and (5) the sensitivity of the spot rate for each payment date to each factor k $(k = 1, \ldots, K)$. Of these five items the first three are readily obtained from the CRSP tape. We used techniques which are described in detail elsewhere to estimate the term structure; these are discussed briefly below. The estimation of interest rate sensitivities is described in Section V.

Two sets of term structure estimates were employed. First, we used the method described in Schaefer [16] to obtain estimates for the entire period covered by the CRSP data, (December 1925–December 1979). Second, we had access to estimates obtained using McCulloch's method (see Ref. 14), for the period from December 1946 to November 1971. The methods used in these two cases differ in some important respects. To accommodate the tax dependence of portfolio choice, Schaefer's method uses linear programming and, in effect, fits to the extreme points of the data. McCulloch's method uses a least-squares criterion and estimates both an "effective tax rate" and an estimate of the term structure. The estimates from Schaefer's method were specific to a zero tax bracket. The data used in conjunction with Schaefer's method were the 500 notes and bonds mentioned above. (Wherever possible, the mean of the bid and asked prices was used.)

To control, to some extent, for the possible influence of estimation method on the results, both sets of data were used in analyzing the dynamics of the long and short rates (Section IV). On the whole they gave similar results. In computing the η sensitivities, and from these the portfolio proportions, only the Schaefer estimates were used because of the limited period covered by the McCulloch estimates. Some summary statistics on the two sets of term structure estimates are given in Appendix A.

IV. THE DYNAMICS OF THE LONG AND SHORT RATES

As mentioned in Section I, the analysis which follows uses both the long and short rates as "factors." To estimate the sensitivity of the term structure to these rates, their *unexpected* changes or "innovations" are required. At a minimum it is necessary to know whether the innovations are well approximated by simple first differences.

Ayres and Barry's [1,2] model of the term structure, which is based on the long rate and the spread between the long and short rates, involves three main assumptions: (1) that the long rate follows a random walk, (2) that the spread between the short and long rates is autoregressive, and (3) that the innovations in the long rate and the innovations in the spread (between the long and short rates) are orthogonal.[4] Using U.S. data for the period 1966–1974, Ayres and Barry find that these assumptions are generally upheld.

Brennan and Schwartz [5,6] develop a model based on the long and short rates and, using Canadian data for the period 1969–1977, report estimates of the stochastic process generating these two variables. They find that the long rate is close to a random walk and that the short rate displays some mean reversion. It is interesting to note (see Schaefer [17]) that their estimated process also is consistent with Ayres and Barry's assumption (3), namely, that innovations in the spread and innovations in the long rate are orthogonal.

Panel A of Table 1 reports regressions of the change in the short (one-year) rate from $t - 1$ to t on the level of the short rate at time $t - 1$. Results are given both for the term structure estimates obtained

Table 1. The Time Series Behaviour of the Long and Short Rates. The Table Shows the Results of Regressions Which Measure the Degree of Mean Reversion in (i) the Short Rate, R1 (Panel A), (ii) the Spread Between the Long Rate and Short Rate, S (Panel B) and (iii) the Long Rate, R13 (Panel C).

PERIOD	DATA	a	b	t(b)	s.e.(e)	D.W.	R-SQUARED
		REGRESSION STATISTICS					
A. Dynamics of the Short Rate: DR1 = a + b*R1 (−1) + e							
1930–1979	CRSP	0.01	0.00	0.67	0.42	2.21	0.00
1946–1971	McCULLOCH	0.06	−0.01	1.60	0.28	1.60	0.01
1930–1939	CRSP	0.07	−0.10	3.14	0.41	2.15	0.08
1940–1949	CRSP	0.02	−0.02	1.02	0.07	1.80	0.01
1950–1959	CRSP	0.12	−0.03	1.09	0.34	2.12	0.01
1950–1959	McCULLOCH	0.05	−0.01	0.32	0.25	1.47	0.00
1960–1969	CRSP	−0.05	0.02	0.89	0.27	2.03	0.01
1960–1969	McCULLOCH	−0.01	0.01	0.44	0.27	1.82	0.00
1970–1979	CRSP	0.24	−0.03	0.78	0.71	2.20	0.01
B. Dynamics of the Spread: DS = a + b*S (−1) + e							
1930–1979	CRSP	0.05	−0.05	3.77	0.37	2.35	0.02
1946–1971	McCULLOCH	0.04	−0.07	3.20	0.22	1.83	0.03
1930–1939	CRSP	0.29	−0.13	3.84	0.34	2.21	0.11

Period	Source						
1940–1949	CRSP	0.02		0.94	0.07	1.68	0.01
1950–1959	CRSP	0.08	−0.02	2.92	0.30	2.34	0.07
1950–1959	McCULLOCH	0.02	−0.15	1.81	0.20	1.82	0.02
1960–1969	CRSP	0.01	−0.05	1.68	0.24	2.37	0.02
1960–1969	McCULLOCH	0.02	−0.06	1.73	0.22	1.84	0.03
1970–1979	CRSP	0.03	−0.10	2.23	0.61	2.27	0.04

C. Dynamics of the Long Rate: $DR13 = a + b*R13(-1) + e$

Period	Source						
1930–1979	CRSP	−0.00	0.00	1.05	0.19	2.40	0.00
1946–1971	CRSP	0.03	−0.01	0.83	0.16	2.10	0.00
1930–1939	McCULLOCH	0.08	−0.03	1.19	0.15	2.07	0.01
1940–1949	CRSP	0.35	0.15	3.05	0.05	1.92	0.08
1950–1959	CRSP	0.04	−0.01	0.33	0.12	1.81	0.00
1950–1959	McCULLOCH	0.05	−0.01	0.47	0.13	2.04	0.00
1960–1969	CRSP	−0.08	0.02	1.11	0.18	2.60	0.01
1960–1969	McCULLOCH	−0.05	0.01	0.87	0.15	2.49	0.01
1970–1979	CRSP	0.16	−0.02	0.59	0.32	2.46	0.00

Note:
(-1) denotes a one-month lag and D denotes the one-month change.

from the CRSP data (using Schaefer's method) and for McCulloch's estimates. The slope coefficient b can be interpreted as minus the degree of mean reversion.

For the 50-year period 1930–1979, b is almost zero and insignificant. For subperiods, b is usually negative (as we would expect if there is indeed mean reversion) and, while still generally insignificant, somewhat larger in absolute magnitude than in the 50-year period. Brennan and Schwartz's results suggest why the coefficients for the subperiods may be larger. If, as their results imply, the short rate actually reverts toward the long rate, rather than towards a fixed mean, then the mean-reversion coefficient is better determined over shorter periods. This is because the mean of the process (the long rate) is close to a random walk and is thus more stable over shorter periods.

To investigate this more directly, we estimated a regression of the same form as in panel A but with the short rate replaced by the spread between the long rate (the 13-year spot rate) and the short rate.[5] Panel B reports the results. In contrast to the previous results the estimated mean reversion coefficient for the 50-year period is highly significant, as it is for the 25-year sample using McCulloch's data. The estimates for all but one of the subperiods are larger and have higher t values than in the previous regression. The exception is the period 1940–1949 which was characterized, as the standard errors of the residuals show, by much less variable interest rates than any other decade covered by the study. The average estimated mean-reversion coefficient, taken over the CRSP estimates for the five 10-year subperiods, is approximately 0.09. This estimate is of the same order as those reported by Brennan and Schwartz and by Ayres and Barry.[6]

Panel C reports results of the same analysis performed on the long rate. Here the estimated mean reversion coefficient is, apart from the 1940–1949 subperiod, small and insignificant. Thus, like Ayres and Barry and Brennan and Schwartz, we also find that the long rate is close to a random walk.

A comparison of the results derived from the two sets of term structure estimates is most conveniently made for the decades 1950–1959 and 1960–1969. Table 1 shows that for the second of these periods the results are quite similar, but for 1950–1959 they are less so. While it is not possible to give a firm reason for this discrepancy, it does appear that the estimates obtained using Schaefer's method may be somewhat "noisier" than McCulloch's.[7] The frequency of Durbin-Watson statistics greater than two in the case of Schaefer's method provides some evidence for this. Given that tax-induced bias in the estimated level of rates is not crucial here, this might suggest using McCulloch's method in preference to Schaefer's in subsequent studies.

Examination of the residual standard errors reveals some marked differences between subperiods. The extremes are the decade 1940–1949 where, as already mentioned, both long and short rates displayed low variability, and the decade 1970–1979 when interest rates were highly volatile. These differences suggest that the t statistics for the 50-year period are upward biased since they are based on an assumption of homoskedasticity. They also raise the possibility of within subperiod heteroskedasticity. We have not tested for this and the issue needs further investigation.

Thus Table 1 suggests that the process for the long rate L and the spread S between the long and short rates is adequately approximated by

$$\Delta L_t = \mu_L + \epsilon_{L,t} \tag{9}$$

$$\Delta S_t = \alpha(\mu_S - S_{t-1}) + \epsilon_{S,t}.$$

In equation (9), μ_L and μ_S are the means of the spread and long rate processes, respectively, α is the coefficient of mean reversion of the spread process, $\epsilon_{L,t}$ and $\epsilon_{S,t}$ are the innovations in the processes at time t, and Δ denotes the change in a rate from time $t - 1$ to t. Ayres and Barry's orthogonality proposition implies that $\epsilon_{L,t}$ and $\epsilon_{S,t}$ are uncorrelated. Some evidence on this issue is described below.

Table 2 reports the simple correlation coefficient between the change in the long rate and the change in (a) the short rate and (b) the spread between the long and the short rates. Because the long rate is close to a random walk, first differences are approximately equal to the innovations plus the mean. However, we claim that the spread does not follow a random walk, and therefore, the innovations are not given simply by the first differences. While this is true, the R^2 values in panel B are so small that we find the correlation between ΔL and ΔS is essentially the same as that between ΔL and ϵ_S. The same applies to the short rate series, and we therefore display in Table 2 only the correlations between first differences.

The results are striking. While the correlation coefficient between ΔL and ΔR_1 is usually of the order of 0.5, the correlation between ΔL and ΔS is quite close to zero. (Again the period 1940–1949 provides an exception.) Thus Ayres and Barry's suggestion seems to be fairly well upheld. While we know of no compelling theoretical reason why these processes should be orthogonal, the evidence in favor of the proposition

Table 2. Ayres and Barry's Orthogonality Proposition. The Table
Shows, for the Entire 50-year Period and for Various Sub-Periods,
the Simple Correlation Coefficient Between (i) the Change in the
Long Rate (DL) and the Change in the Short Rate (D1) and (ii) the
Change in the Long Rate (DL) and the Change in the Spread
Between the Long Rate and the Short Rate (DS)

| Period | Data | Correlations Between | |
		DL, D1	DL, DS
1930–1979	CRSP	0.47	−0.04
1946–1971	McCULLOCH	0.62	−0.10
1930–1939	CRSP	0.56	−0.25
1940–1949	CRSP	0.48	0.45
1950–1959	CRSP	0.37	−0.02
1950–1959	McCULLOCH	0.57	−0.06
1960–1969	CRSP	0.50	0.18
1960–1969	McCULLOCH	0.56	−0.01
1970–1979	CRSP	0.48	−0.04

is persuasive. This result is interesting in its own right, and we shall
find it particularly helpful in interpreting some of the interest rate
sensitivities reported in the next section.

V. ESTIMATION OF TERM-STRUCTURE SENSITIVITIES

It was observed earlier that portfolio proportions necessary for immunization are a function of the rate of return sensitivities, the η's defined
in equation (7b). These in turn require several inputs, and two of these
must be estimated: the term structure of interest rates and the sensitivity
of the term structure to changes in each factor. Section III outlined
how estimates of the term structure were obtained; this section describes
the estimation of term structure sensitivities.

Conventional immunization contains two ad hoc assumptions. First,
it assumes that there is only one factor, and secondly, that the sensitivity
of the term structure to shifts in this factor is unity for all maturities.
One of the objectives of the paper is to determine whether it is possible
to achieve more precise asset replication when these assumptions are
relaxed. Maintaining the single-factor assumption, models using as
factors (a) the short rate and (b) the long rate are tested but in both
cases the sensitivity of the term structure to the factor employed is
estimated from the data. (Because the single-factor assumption is rather

poor in practice, the choice of factors is important. If shifts in the term structure were completely described by one factor, then the choice of which rate to use as "the factor" would, of course, be immaterial.) Next the single-factor assumption is relaxed and a two-factor model is tested using the long rate and one other rate. The manner in which the second rate was chosen is described below.

Using the definition of the spot rate given in equation (2), we may interpret (3) as a multiple regression equation with $dR(t, \tau)$ as dependent variable, the factor innovations $\sigma_k dz_k$, $k = 1, \ldots, K$ as independent variables and the term structure sensitivities $\partial R(t, \tau)/\partial f_k$ as coefficients. This is the method employed to estimate the required sensitivities. For example, in a one-factor model based on the short rate, the sensitivity of the j-period rate to changes in the short rate is estimated as the slope coefficient B_j in the simple regression:

$$\Delta R_{jt} = A_j + B_j \Delta R_{1t} + \epsilon_{jt}. \tag{10}$$

In equation (10), ΔR_{jt} denotes the change in the j-period rate from $t - 1$ to t, ϵ_{jt} is the residual and the short rate is taken as the one-period rate R_{1t}.

This procedure is employed because it is simple and its results are readily interpreted. However it has at least two drawbacks of which one is particularly important. This is that there is no reason *a priori* to expect the interest rate sensitivities, or equivalently, the variances and covariances involved in the regression to remain constant. Both the local covariance between $dR(t, \tau)$ and df_k, and the local covariance matrix of df_k may themselves be the functions of the state variables; without imposing further restrictions, they cannot be assumed constant. A second, though probably less important, problem is that even if the interest rate sensitivities were constant, the discrete time regression described provides only first-order approximation to the true values. However, there is some evidence (see Ref. 17) that such approximations may be quite adequate in this context.

The issue of whether interest rate sensitivities are sufficiently stable to allow them to be estimated in this way is important because there are different ways in which the problem of asset replication could be approached. One alternative is to formulate the model in terms of the sensitivity of one bond's return to the *return* on another security, rather than to changes in an interest rate. Which method should be preferred depends on the empirical issue of parameter stability. Consider a single-factor model. The instantaneous returns ρ_u and ρ_v on two coupon-bearing bonds u and v are [from equation (6)]

$$\rho_u = m_u \, dt + \eta_u \sigma dz, \tag{11a}$$

$$\rho_v = m_v dt + \eta_v \sigma d_z. \tag{11b}$$

In equations (11a) and (11b), m_u and m_v are the expected returns on the two bonds and, interpreting the factor as a short rate r,

$$\eta_u \equiv \frac{1}{P_u} \sum_{j=1}^{J} a_{uj}(\tau_j - t)p(t, \tau_j) \frac{\partial R(t, \tau_j)}{\partial r} \tag{12}$$

Here P_u is the price of bond u and a_{uj} is the payment from bond u at the time τ_j. (The definition of η_v is exactly parallel.) As suggested above, the return on bond u may be expressed in terms of the return on bond v:

$$\rho_u = \left(m_u - \frac{\eta_u}{\eta_v} m_v\right) dt + \upsilon_{u,v}\rho_v. \tag{13}$$

In principle it would be possible to estimate the "rate of return sensitivity" $\upsilon_{u,v}$ using regression in the same way as the interest rate sensitivity is estimated in equation (10). However, if the term structure sensitivities $\partial R(\ )/\partial r$ are *stable* over time, then in general the rate of return sensitivity $\upsilon_{u,v}$ is *unstable*, and vice versa.

To see this, note that if $\partial R(\ )/\partial r$ is constant for a given maturity, then η_u, because it depends on $p(t, \tau)$, must be a function of the state variable r. Thus, if bonds u and v have different cash-flow patterns, the ratio $\eta u / \eta v$, that is, the rate of return sensitivity $\upsilon_{u,v}$, will also, in general, depend on r. The converse is also true: if the ratio $\eta u / \eta v$ is constant, then $\partial R(\ )/\partial r$ will vary.

It is an empirical question as to which of these two hypotheses—constant $\partial R/\partial r$ or constant $\upsilon_{u,v}$—is better. Because this paper is concerned with models which are in the spirit of conventional immunization, it is *assumed* that interest rate sensitivities, as distinct from rate-of-return sensitivities, are constant. Further empirical evidence on this issue would clearly be desirable.

Tables 3A to 3D report regression estimates of the sensitivity to some alternative factors of spot rates for between 1 and 13 years. In each case the estimates of interest rate sensitivity are given by the slope coefficients. The tables also report intercept terms and the R^2's. The R^2's are important because one of the issues of interest is the adequacy of a given factor (or set of factors) as a descriptor of movements in the term structure as a whole. All the regressions use term structure estimates derived from the CRSP data using Schaefer's method. (Results using McCulloch's estimates were broadly similar but are not shown for

Table 3A. Estimation of the Sensitivity of the Term Structure to Changes in the Short Rate. The Table Shows the Results of Simple Regressions Using One-Month Changes in Spot Rates of Between Two and Thirteen Years Maturity as Dependent Variable. In the Equation Estimated, Shown Below, ΔR_{jt} is the One Month Change in the j-year Spot Rate up to Month t and ϵ_{jt} is the Corresponding Residual.

$$\Delta R_{jt} = A_j + B_j \, \Delta R_{1t} + \epsilon_{jt}$$

	DR2	DR3	DR4	DR5	DR6	DR7	DR8	DR9	DR10	DR11	DR12	DR13
						Dependent Variable						
1930–1979	0.0026	0.0049	0.0068	0.0083	0.0093	0.0098	0.0101	0.0100	0.0098	0.0095	0.0092	0.0091
						A_j						
1930–1939	−0.0024	−0.0042	−0.0051	−0.0053	−0.0049	−0.0042	−0.0033	−0.0024	−0.0017	−0.0012	−0.0011	−0.0012
1940–1949	0.0011	0.0016	0.0015	0.0012	0.0008	0.0003	−0.0001	−0.0005	−0.0008	−0.0009	−0.0011	−0.0011
1950–1959	0.0093	0.0147	0.0175	0.0187	0.0190	0.0188	0.0182	0.0175	0.0169	0.0162	0.0154	0.0147
1960–1969	0.0012	0.0021	0.0028	0.0035	0.0041	0.0049	0.0059	0.0071	0.0086	0.0103	0.0119	0.0134
1970–1979	0.0013	0.0031	0.0051	0.0069	0.0086	0.0101	0.0114	0.0126	0.0137	0.0151	0.0166	0.0184
						B_j						
1930–1979	0.767	0.585	0.449	0.355	0.294	0.258	0.240	0.233	0.230	0.227	0.220	0.208
1930–1939	0.750	0.532	0.359	0.236	0.157	0.117	0.106	0.115	0.136	0.161	0.184	0.199
1940–1949	0.817	0.640	0.488	0.367	0.276	0.208	0.159	0.123	0.096	0.076	0.060	0.047
1950–1959	0.700	0.513	0.398	0.327	0.282	0.248	0.222	0.197	0.176	0.157	0.143	0.136
1960–1969	0.906	0.813	0.729	0.656	0.595	0.545	0.503	0.469	0.431	0.397	0.362	0.325
1970–1979	0.766	0.582	0.446	0.353	0.295	0.264	0.250	0.247	0.246	0.242	0.232	0.213
						R-SQUARED						
1930–1979	0.889	0.673	0.482	0.353	0.278	0.243	0.233	0.236	0.242	0.243	0.237	0.223
1930–1939	0.865	0.575	0.311	0.152	0.076	0.049	0.047	0.067	0.112	0.180	0.257	0.318
1940–1949	0.854	0.595	0.320	0.218	0.130	0.082	0.056	0.040	0.031	0.024	0.017	0.011
1950–1959	0.867	0.628	0.459	0.365	0.315	0.281	0.250	0.217	0.186	0.160	0.144	0.143
1960–1969	0.890	0.763	0.682	0.627	0.578	0.529	0.476	0.422	0.370	0.324	0.286	0.254
1970–1979	0.909	0.717	0.537	0.414	0.346	0.318	0.312	0.312	0.306	0.291	0.265	0.230

reasons of space.) Results are presented for the 50-year period 1930–1979 and for five 10-year subperiods. As in Section IV, the interval over which interest rate changes are computed is one month.

Table 3A gives the results of the regression equation (10) which uses the change in the one-year rate as independent variable. For the 50-year period the regression coefficient B_j, which gives an estimate of the sensitivity of the j-year spot rate to changes in the one-year spot rate, declines from 0.767 for a two-year maturity to 0.208 at 13 years. The coefficient declines rapidly with maturity at first and then more slowly. Although the individual estimates differ between subperiods, the overall pattern is quite consistent.

The third panel of Table 3A gives the R^2 for each regression. Two points in particular are of interest. First, the R^2 values for regressions of the change in the 13-year rate on the change in the one-year rate are mainly in the range 0.1 to 0.3; these values are substantially below unity, the value implied by some single state-variable models of the term structure.[8] Second, note that for a given regression, the R^2 is very roughly equal to B_j. In fact, if Ayres and Barry's conjecture holds in the sense that ΔR_j and $\Delta(R_1 - R_j)$ are orthogonal, then it is simple to show that the expected values of R^2 and B_j are equal.

Table 3B reports the results of regressions using the change in the 13 year rate as independent variable. Here the estimates of interest rate sensitivities show an entirely different pattern. Instead of decreasing with maturity, as in Table 3A, the sensitivity is approximately unity for each maturity. There are some anomalies, for example, the estimates for the early maturities in 1930–1939 and 1940–1949, but overall, as in Table 3A, the results show a consistent pattern. Again, it is interesting to note that if Ayres and Barry's conjecture holds, this time in the sense that ΔR_{13} is orthogonal to $\Delta(R_j - R_{13})$, then the expected value of B_j is precisely unity.

Tables 3C and 3D report results of similar regressions for two-factor models. The first (Table 3C) is based on the 13-year rate and the one-year rate. Instead of using the change in the one-year rate as the independent variable, the change in the *spread* between the 13-year rate and the one-year rate is used. The independent variables are then approximately orthogonal (see Table 2), and thus the estimated coefficient associated with the change in the 13-year rate will be approximately the same as in Table 3B. The coefficients associated with the change in the spread now decline from unity (by construction) at one-year maturity, to zero (again by construction) at 13 years. The items of most interest here are the R^2 values.

Even with changes in both the long and short rates as explanatory

Table 3B. Estimation of the Sensitivity of the Term Structure to Changes in the Long Rate. The Equation Estimated is Given Below; for Other Details see Table 3A.

$$\Delta R_{jt} = A_j + B_j \Delta R_{13t} + \epsilon_{jt}$$

	DR1	DR2	DR3	DR4	DR5	DR6	DR7	DR8	DR9	DR10	DR11	DR12
						A_j						
1930–1979	0.0006	0.0007	0.0016	0.0027	0.0035	0.0040	0.0039	0.0034	0.0026	0.0017	0.0008	0.0002
1930–1939	−0.0255	−0.0201	−0.0152	−0.0109	−0.0072	−0.0041	−0.0017	−0.0001	0.0009	0.0014	0.0013	0.0008
1940–1949	0.0066	0.0069	0.0064	0.0055	0.0045	0.0035	0.0026	0.0018	0.0012	0.0007	0.0004	0.0001
1950–1959	0.0128	0.0114	0.0105	0.0097	0.0088	0.0078	0.0066	0.0051	0.0035	0.0021	0.0010	0.0001
1960–1969	0.0106	0.0083	0.0063	0.0044	0.0025	0.0008	−0.0007	−0.0019	−0.0029	−0.0029	−0.0024	−0.0014
1970–1979	0.0117	0.0053	0.0019	0.0007	0.0004	0.0007	0.0010	0.0011	0.0002	0.0002	−0.0003	−0.0005
						B_j						
1930–1979	1.072	1.020	0.937	0.857	0.801	0.779	0.790	0.829	0.884	0.942	0.990	1.012
1930–1939	1.594	1.355	1.125	0.945	0.829	0.776	0.774	0.810	0.865	0.925	0.975	1.003
1940–1949	0.235	0.614	0.877	1.032	1.103	1.115	1.091	1.056	1.021	0.998	0.990	0.994
1950–1959	1.053	1.091	1.099	1.092	1.078	1.068	1.063	1.065	1.070	1.073	1.067	1.045
1960–1969	0.780	0.816	0.832	0.843	0.860	0.889	0.928	0.972	1.014	1.045	1.056	1.042
1970–1979	1.075	1.009	0.901	0.793	0.715	0.679	0.687	0.734	0.806	0.886	0.957	0.999
						R-SQUARED						
1930–1979	0.223	0.304	0.335	0.340	0.348	0.379	0.441	0.538	0.659	0.787	0.898	0.973
1930–1939	0.318	0.354	0.322	0.270	0.235	0.232	0.267	0.346	0.476	0.649	0.828	0.957
1940–1949	0.011	0.097	0.225	0.332	0.396	0.428	0.454	0.494	0.562	0.672	0.817	0.949
1950–1959	0.143	0.271	0.372	0.444	0.511	0.583	0.662	0.744	0.823	0.892	0.947	0.985
1960–1969	0.254	0.301	0.333	0.381	0.449	0.538	0.639	0.742	0.834	0.906	0.958	0.989
1970–1979	0.232	0.316	0.342	0.337	0.337	0.363	0.429	0.534	0.662	0.791	0.899	0.973

Table 3C. Estimation of the Sensitivity of the Term Structure to Changes in the Long Rate and the Short Rate. The Table Shows the Results of Multiple Regressions Using One-Month Changes in the Spread Between the Thirteen Year Rate and the One-year Rate and in the Thirteen-year Rate as Independent Variables. The Equation Estimated is Shown Below; for Other Details see Table 3A.

$$\Delta R_{jt} = A_j + B_j\,\Delta(R_{13t} - R_{1t}) + C_j\,\Delta R_{13t} + \epsilon_{jt}.$$

	DR1	DR2	DR3	DR4	DR5	DR6	DR7	DR8	DR9	DR10	DR11	DR12
						Dependent Variable						
						A_j						
1930–1979	0.0000	0.0003	0.0013	0.0025	0.0034	0.0039	0.0039	0.0034	0.0026	0.0017	0.0008	0.0002
1930–1939	0.0000	−0.0022	−0.0037	−0.0045	−0.0045	−0.0040	−0.0031	−0.0021	−0.0012	−0.0005	0.0000	0.0002
1940–1949	0.0000	0.0016	0.0024	0.0026	0.0024	0.0020	0.0015	0.0010	0.0007	0.0004	0.0002	0.0001
1950–1959	0.0000	0.0032	0.0051	0.0060	0.0062	0.0058	0.0050	0.0040	0.0028	0.0017	0.0008	0.0001
1960–1969	0.0000	−0.0007	−0.0014	−0.0021	−0.0028	−0.0036	−0.0042	−0.0046	−0.0046	−0.0041	−0.0032	0.0017
1970–1979	0.0000	−0.0031	−0.0035	−0.0024	−0.0011	0.0000	0.0004	0.0004	−0.0003	−0.0011	−0.0015	−0.0013
						B_j						
1930–1979	−1.000	−0.715	−0.502	−0.349	−0.242	−0.170	−0.121	−0.088	−0.063	−0.044	−0.027	−0.012
1930–1939	−1.000	−0.703	−0.450	−0.250	−0.103	−0.004	0.055	0.082	0.084	0.071	0.049	0.024

						C_j						
1940–1949	-0.131	-0.030	-0.050	-0.076	-0.110	-0.158	-0.225	-0.319	-0.444	-0.605	-0.796	-1.000
1950–1959	-0.002	-0.015	-0.035	-0.061	-0.090	-0.122	-0.166	-0.211	-0.292	-0.424	-0.644	-1.000
1960–1969	-0.030	-0.072	-0.122	-0.182	-0.250	-0.326	-0.410	-0.504	-0.609	-0.727	-0.858	-1.000
1970–1979	-0.024	-0.049	-0.073	-0.097	-0.121	-0.152	-0.195	-0.260	-0.359	-0.506	-0.715	-1.000
1930–1979	1.011	0.988	0.940	0.880	0.823	0.781	0.767	0.784	0.832	0.901	0.968	1.000
1930–1939	1.017	1.004	0.967	0.915	0.858	0.806	0.774	0.768	0.796	0.858	0.938	1.000
1940–1949	1.004	1.013	1.036	1.079	1.140	1.212	1.287	1.347	1.372	1.340	1.223	1.000
1950–1959	1.045	1.066	1.071	1.067	1.060	1.057	1.060	1.067	1.076	1.076	1.057	1.000
1960–1969	1.048	1.072	1.072	1.054	1.027	0.999	0.979	0.971	0.977	0.992	1.004	1.000
1970–1979	0.997	0.953	0.881	0.799	0.725	0.675	0.664	0.695	0.766	0.863	0.956	1.000
						R-SQUARED						
1930–1979	0.973	0.900	0.794	0.673	0.562	0.483	0.451	0.476	0.566	0.720	0.904	1.000
1930–1939	0.960	0.840	0.670	0.501	0.365	0.274	0.232	0.255	0.373	0.604	0.872	1.000
1940–1949	0.950	0.820	0.680	0.577	0.521	0.501	0.501	0.558	0.634	0.751	0.901	1.000
1950–1959	0.985	0.948	0.898	0.840	0.780	0.720	0.670	0.641	0.655	0.740	0.900	1.000
1960–1969	0.991	0.965	0.928	0.882	0.830	0.780	0.743	0.726	0.736	0.788	0.897	1.000
1970–1979	0.975	0.908	0.811	0.699	0.590	0.510	0.480	0.510	0.605	0.758	0.922	1.000

Table 3D. Estimation of the Sensitivity of the Term Structure to Changes in the Five-year rate and in the Long Rate. The Equation Estimated is Given Below; for Other Details see Tables 3A and 3C.

$$\Delta R_{jt} = A_j + B_j \Delta(R_{13t} - R_{5t}) + C_j \Delta R_{13t} + \epsilon_{jt}.$$

	DR1	DR2	DR3	DR4	DR5	DR6	DR7	DR8	DR9	DR10	DR11	DR12
						Dependent Variable						
						A_j						
1930–1979	−0.0023	−0.0027	−0.0021	−0.0011	0.0000	0.0008	0.0013	0.0014	0.0011	−0.0007	0.0003	0.0000
1930–1939	−0.0237	−0.0154	−0.0088	−0.0037	0.0000	0.0025	0.0039	0.0045	0.0043	0.0037	0.0026	0.0014
1940–1949	0.0028	0.0027	0.0019	0.0009	0.0000	−0.0006	−0.0010	−0.0010	−0.0009	−0.0006	−0.0003	−0.0001
1950–1959	0.0016	0.0005	−0.0001	−0.0002	0.0000	0.0005	0.0009	0.0011	−0.0011	0.0010	0.0006	0.0002
1960–1969	0.0081	0.0055	0.0033	0.0015	0.0000	−0.0014	−0.0024	−0.0032	−0.0036	−0.0034	−0.0027	−0.0015
1970–1979	−0.0113	0.0048	0.0014	0.0002	0.0000	0.0003	0.0007	0.0008	0.0006	0.0001	−0.0004	−0.0005
						B_j						
1930–1979	−0.810	−0.974	−1.055	−1.060	−1.000	−0.890	−0.748	−0.589	−0.430	−0.282	−0.157	−0.062
1930–1939	−0.251	−0.654	−0.896	−1.002	−1.000	−0.992	−0.793	−0.639	−0.477	−0.323	−0.188	−0.079
1940–1949	−0.843	−0.925	−0.999	−1.029	−1.000	−0.913	−0.779	−0.617	−0.448	−0.288	−0.157	−0.059

1950–1959	−0.007	−0.037	−0.130	−0.271	−0.447	−0.641	−0.833	−1.000	−1.126	−1.202	−1.236	−1.262
1960–1969	−0.410	−0.116	−0.223	−0.358	−0.515	−0.684	−0.850	−1.000	−1.112	−1.166	−1.136	−0.995
1970–1979	−0.063	−0.157	−0.278	−0.422	−0.577	−0.734	−0.879	−1.000	−1.084	−1.119	−1.093	−1.000

C_j

1930–1979	1.025	1.021	0.999	0.970	0.946	0.938	0.956	1.000	1.067	1.147	1.213	1.253
1930–1939	1.016	1.007	0.980	0.947	0.919	0.909	0.933	1.000	1.116	1.279	1.467	1.637
1940–1949	0.988	0.974	0.968	0.975	0.992	1.011	1.020	1.000	0.926	0.774	0.518	0.148
1950–1959	1.045	1.064	1.063	1.049	1.030	1.013	1.003	1.000	1.003	1.004	0.994	0.954
1960–1969	1.048	1.072	1.076	1.064	1.044	1.023	1.001	1.000	0.999	0.995	0.975	0.919
1970–1979	1.017	1.001	0.966	0.926	0.898	0.896	0.929	1.000	1.102	1.220	1.321	1.360

R-SQUARED

1930–1979	0.977	0.925	0.871	0.846	0.864	0.916	0.973	1.000	0.964	0.845	0.637	0.375
1930–1939	0.970	0.897	0.826	0.800	0.829	0.895	0.965	1.000	0.949	0.780	0.538	0.336
1940–1949	0.955	0.855	0.777	0.763	0.808	0.885	0.963	1.000	0.946	0.767	0.507	0.277
1950–1959	0.985	0.948	0.907	0.882	0.890	0.930	0.978	1.000	0.971	0.867	0.659	0.371
1960–1969	0.990	0.968	0.943	0.928	0.931	0.954	0.985	1.000	0.981	0.926	0.830	0.628
1970–1979	0.977	0.924	0.870	0.845	0.866	0.922	0.971	1.000	0.972	0.874	0.690	0.434

Table 4. Summary of Estimates of Interest Rate Sensitivities. The Reported Coefficients are Simple Averages of the Corresponding Estimates for the Five Ten-year Sub-Periods Given in Tables 3A, 3B and 3D. The η Coefficients, Used in Section VI to Compute the Proportions for Immunizing Portfolios, are Calculated Using Interest Rate Sensitivities Derived by Interpolating Linearly From These Data. (Note DRJ Denotes the Month to Month Change in the J-year Spot Rate).

Independent Variable	Dependent Variable												
	DR1	DR2	DR3	DR4	DR5	DR6	DR7	DR8	DR9	DR10	DR11	DR12	DR13
A: SINGLE FACTOR MODEL BASED ON ONE YEAR-RATE													
DR1	1.000*	0.788	0.616	0.484	0.388	0.321	0.276	0.248	0.230	0.217	0.207	0.196	0.184
B: SINGLE FACTOR MODEL BASED ON THIRTEEN-YEAR RATE													
DR13	0.947	0.976	0.967	0.940	0.917	0.906	0.909	0.927	0.955	0.985	1.009	1.017	1.000*
C: TWO-FACTOR MODEL BASED ON FIVE-YEAR RATE AND THIRTEEN-YEAR RATE													
DR5	0.870	1.007	1.076	1.071	1.000*	0.893	0.726	0.559	0.395	0.248	0.131	0.050	0.000*
DR13	1.004	1.005	1.054	1.029	1.000*	0.977	0.970	0.977	0.992	1.011	1.024	1.023	1.000*

Note:
Value determined by construction.

variables, the R^2's for intermediate maturities are only of the order of 0.5. The fact that they are not higher may be due in part to estimation error in the term structure: the data for the regression. But it seems unlikely that this could account for a residual variance which is typically almost half the variance of intermediate rates. Instead it appears, as Brennan and Schwartz [6] found, that a two-factor model based on the long and short rates does not account for substantially all the variation in the term structure.

As an attempt to capture some of the independent variation of intermediate rates, Table 3D reports the corresponding results for a model based on the long rate and an intermediate (five-year) rate. As might be expected, this gives a better overall fit except at the very short end. Apart from the results for one- and two-year maturities, the R^2 are mainly in excess of 0.80. For this reason, the model is used in Section VI in preference to the model based on the long and short rates.

One of the remaining problems is to decide exactly which estimates of interest rate sensitivities are to be used in calculating η's. One possibility is to use the estimates for the entire 50-year period, but because the variance of interest rate changes was much higher in the 1970–1979 decade than earlier (see Table 1), the 50-year results are somewhat biased toward the more recent data. Another possibility would be a "rolling" estimate, based on data immediately prior to the date for which the estimate is used. This would be appropriate if there were some evidence of serial correlation in the interest rate sensitivities, but inspection of the estimates in Tables 3A to 3D does not suggest that this is the case. In the event estimates for the five 10-year subperiods were averaged; this gives an estimate of the average for the entire period which is perhaps less influenced by changes in variance than the 50-year point estimate. These simple averages are reported in Table 4.

VI. TESTS OF ALTERNATIVE STRATEGIES

Test Design

In broad outline our tests follow Fisher and Weil [9]; that is, we examine the precision with which alternative strategies replicate a given target asset. However, our approach differs in several important ways, and to avoid confusion, it is described here in some detail.

Fisher and Weil attempt to replicate single payments of 5, 10, and 20 years maturity. This is an interesting approach because it tests the extent to which immunization can "create" assets which are not currently traded. As pointed out earlier, this is an aspect of immunization which is also of practical importance. However, their approach has the drawback that the present value of the single payment is observable only at maturity. Fisher and Weil estimate its value at the beginning of the contract but not at intermediate points. As a result, their summary statistics on the performance of strategies are based on substantially overlapping samples. For example, in their replication of a 20-year single payment, the 40 years of data available actually result in only two *independent* observations of the error associated with a given strategy.

One solution would be to use estimates of the term structure to calculate the present value of the single payment each period, but this would rely heavily on the estimates' precision. An alternative is to choose an existing bond as the target asset; this is the approach we have adopted. Because the prices of these bonds are observable, it is possible to measure the difference in value between the target bond and the immunizing portfolio each period. This should lead to more reliable measures of the error associated with different strategies.

It should be emphasised that the assets we attempt to immunize in our tests are chosen simply because their prices are easily observable. We do not regard them, nor the lump sum payments used in the Fisher and Weil tests, as necessarily characteristic of the assets an investor would wish to immunize in practice. Rather, we have in mind Redding-ton's original idea that an intermediary might wish to immunize his specific set of liabilities and hopefully our attempts to immunize bonds will shed some light on the ability of intermediaries to do this. But the specific portfolios we construct are as unrepresentative of the actual portfolios intermediaries would wish to hold, as are the cash flows from bonds of their actual liability cash flows.

In making comparisons between strategies it is important that, as far as possible, other influences are held constant. For example, while the *portfolio proportions* are determined according to the different immunization strategies, the *bonds included* in the portfolio should be the same. If not, then one rule might appear to be superior to another simply because its portfolio contained a bond which was, say, closer in maturity to the target bond.

Ensuring that the set of bonds used for each strategy remains constant is straightforward when the *number* of bonds to be include (K + 1) is the same. For example, all strategies based on one-factor models have two-bond portfolios, and it is simple to ensure that within any period, each portfolio contains the same two bonds. However two-factor strategies require three-bond portfolios. Two of the bonds would be the same as in the corresponding two-bond portfolios, but the question arises as to how to choose the third bond if useful comparisons between one-factor and two-factor models are to be made. Because bonds of close maturities are typically close substitutes, it was decided that the third bond should be no closer in maturity to the target than either of the other two component bonds.

In the spirit of Fisher and Weil we used target bonds of 5, 10, and 15 years maturity. For single-factor strategies, the immunizing portfolio for the five-year target bond contained component bonds with maturities of two and eight years, for the 10-year target bond the maturities were 5 and 15 years, and for the 15-year target they were 10 and 20 years.

This choice of component bonds ensures that for single-factor models, the portfolio proportions which satisfy equations (8a) and (8b) are almost always nonnegative. The same is not true for two-factor models, and this raises the issue of whether short selling is to be permitted.

In our view it should not. If it were, asset replication could be best achieved by replicating *cash-flows*, rather than by following the type of dynamic portfolio strategy described in this paper. It appears to us that the motivation for the latter approach is greatly diminished if investors are able to short securities. We therefore impose a no short-selling restriction and test the immunizing portfolios, computed as the solution to equations (8a) and (8b), accordingly. If they violate the restriction, the return on the portfolio for that period is set equal to the return from the single-factor model based on the long rate. This strategy violates the restriction on only very few occasions, and when it does, the return on the portfolio is set equal to the return on the single-component bond closest in maturity to the target.

The no short-selling restriction is violated most frequently in the case of the two-factor model. As explained above, it was felt necessary, in the case of three bond portfolios (1) to include the two bonds which were used for single-factor models and (2) to ensure that the third bond was no closer in maturity to the target than either of the other two. With these constraints it was found impossible in the case of the 5- and 15-year target bonds to select the third bond so that the portfolio proportions were nonnegative in any significant fraction of cases. Our only success came with the 10-year target bond, where it was found that by including a two-year bond together with the 5- and 15-year bonds, nonnegative portfolio proportions were obtained roughly two-thirds of the time. For this reason results on the two-factor model are given for the case of the 10-year target bond only.

Table 5. Summary of Composition of Immunizing Portfolios. An "x" Indicates That a Bond is Included.

Maturity of Component Bonds (Years)	Single Factor Models Maturity of Target Bonds (Years)			Two-Factor Model Maturity of Target Bond (Years)
	5	10	15	10
"Short" 2	x			x
5		x		x
10			x	
"Long" 8	x			
15		x		x
20			x	

86

Table 5 summarizes the composition of immunizing portfolios, and Appendix B describes in more detail the method used to select target and component bonds.

An important difference between our method and Fisher and Weil's is that we *reselect* both target and component bonds each period so that their maturities remain approximately constant. This means that our calculations do not, as Fisher and Weil's did, follow an immunization strategy from inception to maturity. Rather, we are concerned with the holding period returns on target assets and immunizing portfolios of roughly *constant* maturity.

It may be useful at this stage to summarize the main steps in our procedure: For illustration we assume a single-factor model and a 10-year target maturity. Using data for month t − 1,

1. Choose a target bond with 10-year maturity and component bonds with maturities of 5 and 15 years. (See Appendix B.)
2. Using prices and cash-flow data from the CRSP tape, term structure estimates and interest rate sensitivities (summarized in Table 4) compute the η's for the target and component bonds according to equation (7b).
3. Using the η's calculated in step 2, compute portfolio proportions for the immunizing portfolio as the solution to equations (8a) and (8b).
4. Check that the portfolio proportions are nonnegative; if so, proceed to step 5. If not, set the return on the immunizing portfolio equal to either (a) the return from the single-factor long-rate strategy (if this has no negative portfolio proportions) or (if it does) (b) the return on the single component bond which is closest in maturity to the target. Proceed to step 6.
5. From the CRSP data, read the returns (from month t − 1 to month t) on the target and component bonds. Using the portfolio proportions computed in steps 3 and 4, calculate the return on the immunizing portfolio over the same period and also the difference in return between the target bond and the immunizing portfolio.
6. Use data for month t and return to step 1.

In the results presented below it was found necessary to amend this procedure slightly. For some periods, the difference in return, computed in step 5, displayed substantial negative serial correlation, and this suggested that part of the return difference was, in fact, measurement error in the rates of return. To investigate this, we amended the procedure so that, while portfolio reallocation was still carried out monthly, the target and component bonds were changed only at six-month intervals. Within these six-month periods, errors in measured rates of return would then "cancel out." Incorporating this change, it was found that the estimated variance of the return difference was typically only 50 percent of that estimated originally. Our empirical results use the amended procedure, and a comparison with the original results is given at the end of this section.

Definition of Strategies

Five alternative strategies are tested: The first four involve two-bond portfolios and the last, based on a two-factor model, involves a three-bond portfolio. The strategies are as follows:

1. *Maturity strategy*—The portfolio is constructed so that its weighted average maturity equals that of the target.
2. *Conventional immunization*—The weighted average (Redington) duration of the portfolio is set equal to the duration of the target.
3. *Short rate*—A single-factor strategy in which the η's are calculated using the interest rate sensitivities with respect to the short rate (reported in Table 4). The portfolio proportions are then given by the solution to (8a) and (8b) with $K = 1$.
4. *Long rate*—As in strategy 3, but using the interest rate sensitivities with respect to the long rate.
5. *Long rate/spread*—A two-factor strategy based on the long rate and the spread between the long rate and the five-year rate. As in strategies 3 and 4 the η's use the appropriate sensitivities from Table 4. To obtain the portfolio proportions, equations (8a) and (8b) are solved with $K = 2$.

Each strategy, except the last, is used to replicate target bonds of each of the three maturities. As explained earlier, the two-factor strategy is used only in the case of the 10-year target bond. The naive maturity strategy is included as a benchmark.

Empirical Results

The main results are contained in Tables 6A, 6B, and 6C, which report summary statistics on alternative strategies for target bonds of 5, 10, and 15 years maturity, respectively. Results are given for the 50-year period 1930–1979 and for three subperiods. Each table gives the mean return on the target bond, the mean return on the immunizing

Table 6A. The Results of Alternative Immunization Strategies for a Target Bond With an Approximately Constant Maturity of 5 Years. The First Two Columns Show the Mean Annual Return on the Target Bond and on the Immunizing Portfolio, and Columns Three and Four Show the Mean and Standard Deviation of the Difference Between These Returns. A Six-Month Holding Period was Used to Measure Returns and the Bonds Selected for the Calculations Were Changed Only at the Same Intervals. This has the Effect of Diminishing the Influence of Noise in the Price Data on the Estimated Variance of Returns. The Final Column Gives the Variance of the Difference in Return Between the Target Bond and the Immunizing Portfolio, Expressed as a Percentage of the Variance of the Target Bond's Return.

| Strategy | Mean Returns (Percent Per Annum) | | | Standard Deviation of Difference (Percent P.A.) | Percentage of Target Variance Remaining |
	Target Bond	Immunizing Portfolio	DIFF.		
		1930–1979			
MATURITY	3.253	3.106	0.147	1.321	11.50
DURATION	3.253	3.072	0.181	1.271	10.65
SHORT RATE	3.253	3.270	−0.017	1.674	18.47
LONG RATE	3.253	3.097	0.156	1.277	10.75
		1930–1946			
MATURITY	2.648	2.137	0.511	0.780	11.36
DURATION	2.648	2.187	0.461	0.757	10.71
SHORT RATE	2.648	3.159	−0.511	0.930	16.16
LONG RATE	2.648	2.169	0.479	0.769	11.04
		1946–1963			
MATURITY	2.298	2.243	0.055	0.928	10.23
DURATION	2.298	2.197	0.100	0.932	10.30
SHORT RATE	2.298	2.343	−0.046	1.220	17.66
LONG RATE	2.298	2.235	0.062	0.925	10.15
		1963–1979			
MATURITY	4.854	4.992	−0.138	1.757	13.91
DURATION	4.854	4.886	−0.033	1.658	12.39
SHORT RATE	4.854	4.371	0.482	2.162	21.07
LONG RATE	4.854	4.939	−0.085	1.676	12.67

Table 6B. The Results of Alternative Immunization Strategies for a Target Bond With an Approximately Constant Maturity of 10 Years. The First Two Columns Show the Mean Annual Return on the Target Bond and on the Immunizing Portfolio, and Columns Three and Four Show the Mean and Standard Deviation of the Difference Between These Returns. A Six-Month Holding Period was Used to Measure Returns and the Bonds Selected for the Calculations Were Changed Only at the Same Intervals. This has the Effect of Diminishing the Influence of Noise in the Price Data on the Estimated Variance of Returns. The Final Column Gives the Variance of the Difference in Return Between the Target Bond and the Immunizing Portfolio, Expressed as a Percentage of the Variance of the Target Bond's Return.

| Strategy | Mean Returns (Percent Per Annum) | | | Standard Deviation of Difference (Percent P.A.) | Percentage of Target Variance Remaining |
	Target Bond	Immunizing Portfolio	Difference		
		1930–1979			
MATURITY	3.495	3.351	0.144	1.791	11.76
DURATION	3.495	3.327	0.168	1.640	9.85
SHORT RATE	3.495	3.270	0.225	1.854	12.59
LONG RATE	3.495	3.324	0.171	1.660	10.10
LONG/SPRD.	3.495	3.324	0.171	1.668	10.20
		1930–1946			
MATURITY	3.807	3.639	0.168	0.998	14.41
DURATION	3.807	3.680	0.127	1.024	15.19
SHORT RATE	3.807	3.173	0.634	1.146	19.03
LONG RATE	3.807	3.662	0.145	1.025	15.22
LONG/SPRD.	3.807	3.659	0.148	1.032	15.42
		1946–1963			
MATURITY	2.303	2.099	0.204	1.203	8.27
DURATION	2.303	2.078	0.225	1.130	7.29
SHORT RATE	2.303	2.127	0.176	1.491	12.70
LONG RATE	2.303	2.079	0.224	1.146	7.50
LONG/SPRD.	2.303	2.074	0.229	1.171	7.83
		1963–1979			
MATURITY	4.443	4.387	0.057	2.448	14.63
DURATION	4.443	4.296	0.148	2.206	11.88
SHORT RATE	4.443	4.584	−0.140	2.294	12.84
LONG RATE	4.443	4.300	0.143	2.234	12.18
LONG/SPRD.	4.443	4.308	0.135	2.250	12.35

Table 6C. The Results of Alternative Immunization Strategies for a Target Bond With an Approximately Constant Maturity of 15 Years. The First Two Columns Show the Mean Annual Return on the Target Bond and on the Immunizing Portfolio, and Columns Three and Four Show the Mean and Standard Deviation of the Difference Between These Returns. A Six-Month Holding Period was Used to Measure Returns and the Bonds Selected for the Calculations Were Changed Only at the Same Intervals. This has the Effect of Diminishing the Influence of Noise in the Price Data on the Estimated Variance of Returns. The Final Column Gives the Variance of the Difference in Return Between the Target Bond and the Immunizing Portfolio, Expressed as a Percentage of the Variance of the Target Bond's Return.

| Strategy | Mean Returns (Percent Per Annum) | | | Standard Deviation of Difference (Percent P.A.) | Percentage of Target Variance Remaining |
	Target Bond	Immunizing Portfolio	Difference		
		1930–1979			
MATURITY	3.088	3.320	−0.232	1.971	12.36
DURATION	3.088	3.287	−0.199	1.971	12.36
SHORT RATE	3.088	3.393	−0.304	2.059	13.49
LONG RATE	3.088	3.338	−0.250	1.975	12.40
		1930–1946			
MATURITY	4.021	3.826	0.194	0.923	8.11
DURATION	4.021	3.867	0.153	0.913	7.93
SHORT RATE	4.021	3.779	0.241	0.926	8.15
LONG RATE	4.021	3.893	0.128	0.920	8.04
		1946–1963			
MATURITY	1.997	2.076	−0.079	1.009	5.32
DURATION	1.997	2.035	−0.038	0.981	5.03
SHORT RATE	1.997	2.276	−0.280	1.072	6.00
LONG RATE	1.997	2.188	−0.191	1.008	5.31
		1963–1979			
MATURITY	3.279	4.166	−0.886	2.625	15.04
DURATION	3.279	4.065	−0.786	2.702	15.93
SHORT RATE	3.279	4.228	−0.949	2.773	16.77
LONG RATE	3.279	4.039	−0.760	2.650	15.33

portfolio and the difference in these means. The fourth column reports the standard error of the return difference; this is the main measure of relative performance and, as mentioned above, is computed using six-month holding periods. The fifth column reports the variance of the difference, expressed as a percentage of the variance of the target bond's return.

Taking a broad perspective, it is simple to summarize the results: there is very little difference between the performance of any of the strategies except that of the short rate, which almost always has the poorest performance. Over the 50-year period the short-rate strategy performs worst for all three target maturities. In the nine subperiod/target maturity combinations, the short-rate strategy had the highest variance in all but one case, where it had the next to the highest. That the short-rate strategy usually performs less well than even a naive maturity strategy is surprising. The results must raise some doubts about the usefulness of pricing models, based on the short rate, which implicitly assume that a portfolio strategy, of the type we have tested, can achieve perfect replication.

The similarity between the performance of conventional immunization and the long-rate strategy is not surprising. Because interest rate sensitivities with respect to the long rate are close to unity for all maturities, the main difference between η for this case and conventional duration is the different definition of the present value factors. As the results demonstrate, this has only a small effect on portfolio performance. It should be noted, however, that such difference as there is between these strategies usually favors conventional immunization. We have no good explanation for this.

The performance of the long-rate/spread strategy (see Table 6B) is disappointing: its error variance is usually slightly higher than that of the *single-factor* long-rate strategy. This result may be surprising in view of the much better performance of two-factor models in explaining term structure movements (see Section IV). Part of the solution to this puzzle is to be found in Table 7, which provides summary statistics on the portfolio proportions for the various strategies. Table 7 shows that the mean porportions for the duration and long-rate strategies are, for the reasons given earlier, very similar. The surprising result is that the proportions for the long-rate/spread strategy are also very similar to those of the duration and long-rate strategies.[9] On average, the only difference between the long-rate/spread and duration strategies is that in the former, between 1 and 2 percent of the portfolio is transferred from the 5- and 15-year bonds to the two-year bond. This small adjustment has a corresponding small influence on performance

Table 7. Summary Statistics on Portfolio Proportions for Alternative Immunization Strategies. The Table Shows the Means and Standard Deviations of the Proportions for a Target Bond With an Approximately Constant Maturity of 10 Years. The Target and Component Bonds Were Changed Only at Six-Month Intervals.

| | *Mean Portfolio Proportions (Standard Deviation In Parentheses)* | | | | |
| | | | *Portfolio Strategies* | | |
Component Bond Maturity	*Maturity*	*Duration*	*Short Rate*	*Long Rate*	*Long and Spread*
		1930–1979			
2 YEAR					1.33
					(4.20)
5 YEAR	54.94	49.97	75.88	51.22	49.36
	(10.08)	(10.50)	(14.31)	(10.96)	(12.18)
15 YEAR	45.06	50.03	24.12	48.78	49.31
	(10.03)	(10.50)	(14.31)	(10.96)	(11.10)
		1930–1946			
2 YEAR					1.47
					(3.02)
5 YEAR	53.38	49.39	73.34	50.85	48.60
	(10.36)	(11.22)	(18.89)	(11.31)	(11.09)
15 YEAR	46.62	50.61	26.66	49.15	49.93
	(10.36)	(11.22)	(18.89)	(11.31)	(11.08)
		1946–1963			
2 YEAR					1.72
					(6.07)
5 YEAR	54.80	48.64	75.65	50.27	48.13
	(10.68)	(10.21)	(12.33)	(10.81)	(12.52)
15 YEAR	45.20	51.36	24.35	49.73	50.14
	(10.68)	(10.21)	(12.33)	(10.81)	(10.91)
		1963–1979			
2 YEAR					0.79
					(2.54)
5 YEAR	56.35	51.60	78.10	52.30	51.10
	(9.34)	(10.22)	(11.23)	(10.96)	(12.90)
15 YEAR	43.65	48.40	21.90	47.70	48.11
	(9.34)	(10.22)	(11.23)	(10.96)	(11.50)

93

(though, as in the case of the duration and long rate strategies, the influence is not only small but usually perverse).

Effect of the Holding Period on Estimated Variances

Finally, we return to the issue of the effect of the holding period on the estimated variance of return differences. For each of the strategies and a 10-year target bond, Table 8 reports the standard deviation and

Table 8. The Effect of the Holding Period on the Estimated Variance of the Difference in Return Between the Target Bond and the Immunizing Portfolio. The Table Shows the Standard Deviation of the Difference (Expressed as Percent Per Annum) and the Variance (Expressed as a Percentage of the Variance of the Target Bond's Return) for Six-Month Holding Periods, as in Tables 6A–C, and Also for Monthly Holding Periods. The Table Gives Results for a Target Bond With an Approximately Constant Maturity of Ten Years and Shows That the Six-Monthly Variance is Consistently Lower. This Suggests That the Monthly Results May be Influenced by Noise in the Price Data.†

| | Holding Period | | | |
| | Six-Months | | One-Month | |
Strategy	Standard Deviation of Difference	Percent of Target Variance Remaining	Standard Deviation of Difference	Percent of Target Variance Remaining
	1930–1979			
MATURITY	1.791	11.76	2.373	21.76
DURATION	1.640	9.85	2.286	20.19
SHORT RATE	1.854	12.59	2.503	24.21
LONG RATE	1.660	10.10	2.301	20.46
LONG/SPRD.	1.668	10.20	2.307	20.57
	1930–1946			
MATURITY	0.998	14.41	1.556	17.62
DURATION	1.024	15.19	1.531	17.08
SHORT RATE	1.146	19.03	1.868	25.42
LONG RATE	1.025	15.22	1.537	17.21
LONG/SPRD.	1.032	15.42	1.528	17.00

†*Note*: The square of the ratio of standard deviations in the table will not be precisely equal to the ratio of the columns headed "percentage of variance remaining". This is because the six-month returns are calculated as the product of (one plus) one month returns. The variance of the six-monthly returns on the target asset will therefore not be precisely equal to six times the variance of one month returns, even if there were no noise in the price data.

	Holding Period			
	Six-Months		One-Month	
Strategy	Standard Deviation of Difference	Percent of Target Variance Remaining	Standard Deviation of Difference	Percent of Target Variance Remaining
		1946–1963		
MATURITY		8.27	1.723	17.55
DURATION	1.203	7.29	1.693	16.95
SHORT RATE	1.130	12.70	1.925	21.92
LONG RATE	1.491	7.50	1.700	17.10
LONG/SPRD.	1.171	7.83	1.724	17.58
		1963–1979		
MATURITY	2.448	14.63	3.391	24.57
DURATION	2.206	11.88	3.234	22.35
SHORT RATE	2.294	12.84	3.400	24.71
LONG RATE	2.234	12.18	3.259	22.70
LONG/SPRD.	2.250	12.35	3.263	22.76

variance of the return difference for six-month and one-month holding periods. The results for six-month holding periods are given in the first two columns and these are simply reproduced from Table 6B. The third and fourth columms give the corresponding results for one-month holding periods.

Comparing the results it can be seen that, except for the 1930–1946 subperiod, the estimated variance measured over six-month holding periods is substantially lower. For the 50-year period the reduction in variance is of the order of 50 percent. As suggested earlier, the most likely explanation is error in the measured rate of return, deriving from noise in the price quotations on the CRSP tape. Because the returns are highly (positively) correlated, any error in the price will have a large proportional effect on the variance of the difference. By measuring returns over a longer holding period, the variance of the return difference is increased, while the variance attributable to the noise is, hopefully, constant.

VII. SUMMARY AND CONCLUSIONS

The strategies considered in this paper generalize conventional immunization in two ways. First, they admit an arbitrary number of "factors," rather than being restricted to one; second, they allow the sensitivity of the term structure to these factors to be other than unity. In this approach there is a durationlike sensitivity, η, for *each* of the K factors, and the proportions of the immunizing portfolio are calculated as the solution to $K + 1$ simultaneous linear equations which involve only η's as coefficients.

Section IV analyzed the time series properties of the long and short rates and confirmed Ayres and Barry's three suggestions that (1) innovations in the long rate and the spread between the long and short rates are orthogonal, (2) the process for the long rate is close to a random walk, and (3) the process for the spread is autogressive.

Section V estimated the sensitivity of the term structure to a variety of factors. There were three main findings. Firstly, the sensitivity to changes in the short rate declines from unity (by construction) for short maturities, to approximately 0.2 for long maturities. Secondly, the sensitivity to changes in the long rate is close to unity for all maturities. This finding is consistent with Ayres and Barry's suggestion concerning orthogonality. Thirdly, changes in the short and long rates together explain, approximately, only 50 percent of the variation in intermediate rates. However changes in the five-year and long rates together explain 80 percent or more of the variation for all maturities greater than two years.

The tests of alternative strategies in Section VI produced the surprising result that conventional immunization seems to perform as well as, indeed, slightly better than, its more sophisticated rivals. The explanation for this result is twofold. First, because of the unit sensitivity of the term structure to the long rate, there is almost no difference between conventional immunization and a strategy derived from a single-factor model based on the long rate. Second, with the component bonds which were used, there was again very little difference in the portfolios implied by conventional immunization and by a two-factor model based on the long and intermediate rates. In sum, these three different strategies (conventional immunization, the long-rate strategy and the long-rate-intermediate-rate strategy) all lead to essentially the same portfolio.

There are many areas in which this study could be extended. First, it would be interesting to use principal components analysis to identify the factors determining term structure shifts. Second, there is considerable scope for refining the data: both the term structure estimates and the sensitivities derived from them. Third, it would also be useful to apply more formal statistical tests to the measures of performance described in Section VI.

It also seems feasible that our approach could be applied to securities other than default-free bonds. One example is the equity market where, using a dividend discount model, Lanstein and Sharpe [12] have found that the difference in duration between stocks is negatively related to the correlation of their extramarket returns.

APPENDIX A:
SUMMARY STATISTICS ON TERM STRUCTURE ESTIMATES

Tables A1 and A2 provide some summary statistics on the term structure estimates obtained using McCulloch's and Schaefer's methods. Table A1 compares the standard deviation of changes in spot rates. In general the estimates using Schaefer's method are somewhat more variable: the standard deviations being typically 5 to 10 percent higher. Given the differences between the methods and, in particular, the fact that Schaefer's method fits to extremes, this probably means that Schaefer's estimates are "noisier."

Table A2 reports the mean and standard deviation of the differences between Schaefer's and McCulloch's estimates. It is worth noting that all the means are positive, that is, Schaefer's estimates are, on average, higher. Again this is to be expected from the differences between the methods and may indicate a tax bias in McCulloch's method. The table shows that the standard deviation of the difference between spot rates is typically of the order of 10 to 15 basis points.

Table A1. Standard Deviations of Monthly Changes in Spot Rates Estimated Using McCulloch's Method and Schaefer's Method (CRSP).

| | | *Standard Deviation of Monthly Change in Spot Rate (Percent p.a)* | | | |
| | | *Maturity (Years)* | | | |
Data Source	*Period*	*1*	*5*	*10*	*13*
CRSP	1946–71	0.335	0.233	0.189	0.166
McCulloch	"	0.282	0.219	0.178	0.156
CRSP	1949–59	0.337	0.183	0.137	0.121
McCulloch	"	0.246	0.170	0.148	0.129
CRSP	1959–69	0.272	0.226	0.192	0.176
McCulloch	"	0.271	0.218	0.175	0.150

Table A2. Mean and Standard Deviation of Difference Between Spot Rates Estimated Using McCulloch's and Schaefer's Method.

		Summary Statistics on Differences in Estimated Spot Rates (Percent p.a)			
			Maturity (Years)		
Period		1	5	10	13
1946–71	Mean	0.150	0.125	0.065	0.044
	S.D.	0.179	0.105	0.132	0.118
1949–59	Mean	0.118	0.099	0.057	0.036
	S.D.	0.187	0.071	0.089	0.088
1959–69	Mean	0.155	0.130	0.017	0.008
	S.D.	0.119	0.088	0.123	0.131

APPENDIX B:
OUTLINE OF METHOD USED TO SELECT TARGET AND COMPONENT BONDS

Excluding Treasury bills, the CRSP tape contains data on approximately 500 Treasury notes, bonds, and similar obligations. From these, a few issues with low aggregate market value were eliminated, on the basis that these were probably of poor marketability and that their prices might be consequently unreliable. Also, a number of other securities with unusual provisions (for example, quarterly coupon payments) were excluded, and this resulted in a sample of 490 securities.

The bonds to be selected fall into three groups: (1) target bonds, (2) component bonds with maturities longer than the corresponding target bond, and (3) component bonds with shorter maturities than the target. The target bonds were selected to have maturities as close as possible to the desired maturities of 5, 10, or 15 years. The component bonds with maturities *longer* than the target had maturities which were as close as possible to but *no shorter* than the desired maturity. Where this was not possible the longest bond was chosen. The last group, component bonds with maturities *shorter* than the target, had maturities as close as possible but *no longer* than the desired maturity. When this was not possible, the shortest bond was chosen. The effect of this procedure is to select component bonds which are, whenever possible, no closer in maturity to the target than the ideal component bonds would be.

After classifying the population of available bonds according to maturity, callability, and flower bond status, it became clear that removal of either callable bonds or flower bonds from the sample was not feasible. For some periods this would have eliminated almost all bonds over 10 years maturity. Even when these categories were included, there were insufficient bonds to obtain useful results for the period 1925–1929, and this period is therefore excluded from the analysis.

For callable bonds with prices higher than par value, the maturity date assumed in the calculations was the first call date. This is a common but obviously ad hoc adjustment.

No allowance was made for flower bond status. While, as mentioned above, it would not be feasible to eliminate all issues with this characteristic, it seems possible that some issues (particularly those with the lowest prices) are much more influenced by this feature than others. Screening the sample along these lines might be helpful but, in the present analysis, the flower bond provision is ignored.

ACKNOWLEDGMENTS

We are grateful both to the conference sponsors, the Center for Capital Market Research at the University of Oregon and to the Stanford Program in Finance for financial support.

We are also grateful for comments received at finance workshops at Columbia University and the London Business School, and at the Fall 1981 seminar of the Institute for Quantitative Research in Finance. The comments of John Y. Barry, Ian Cooper, and Stewart Hodges were particularly helpful.

This paper was largely completed while both authors were at the Graduate School of Business, Stanford University.

NOTES

1. The diffusion process–continuous trading assumptions are invoked here largely as a matter of convenience. As pointed out in the text, these assumptions imply that immunization is feasible and they also lead to a linear return generating model for bond prices [equation (6)]. But alternative assumptions are clearly possible. For example, equation (6) or its discrete-time analogue, could be assumed directly, but then the functional form of the η sensitivities would be lost. Probably more important than the continuous time apparatus are the assumptions which are made regarding the intertemporal stability of particular parameters. The analysis in Section II allows almost all the parameters to be smooth (nonanticipating) functions of the state variables but, in the empirical work, particular parameters are assumed constant. Section V discusses the implications of alternative assumptions.

2. It is obvious that in a perfect market the portfolio policy of an intermediary would be irrelevant because any decisions could be offset by consumers on their own account. However it is also obvious that in a perfect market, there would be no motivation for intermediaries to exist at all.

3. We have recently seen a number of zero or very low coupon issues from U.S. corporationss. However, these may have rather more to do with opportunities created by the provisions of the U.S. tax code rather than with a demand for new cash-flow patterns.

4. Ayres and Barry report that, while the spread for a *constant maturity* was autoregressive, the spread for a *given instrument*—i.e., allowing the maturity to decrease by the interval between observations—was a random walk.

5. The 13-year rate was chosen because this was the longest maturity for which an uninterrupted series was available in the McCulloch data.

6. For example, Brennan and Schwartz [5] report a (continuous time) coefficient of approximately 0.065 for Canadian data over the period January 1964–December 1976. Ayres and Barry's results imply a coefficient of approximately 0.06 for U.S. data over the period July 1966–August 1978. (From Table 1 note that our estimate for 1960–1969 is 0.06 and that for 1970–1979 is 0.10.)

7. See Appendix A.

8. The R^2 should be unity for those single state-variable models which imply that $\partial R(\ )/\partial r$ is constant. It is interesting to note that Vasicek's model [17] and the Cox, Ingersoll, and Ross [7] "square root" model have this property.

9. Over much of the relevant range "spread duration" is almost linearly related to conventional load "long rate" duration. For this reason the matrix of η's in equations (8a) and (8b) is, in the case of the long rate/spread strategy, nearly singular.

REFERENCES

1. Ayres, H. R. and J. Y. Barry, 1979, "The Equilibrium Yield Curve for Government Securities," *Financial Analysts Journal* (May/June), 31–39.

2. ———, 1980, "A Theory of the U.S. Treasury Market Equilibrium," *Management Science* Vol. 26, No. 6 (June), 539–569.

3. Boyle, P., "Immunization under Stochastic Models of the Term Structure," *Journal of the Institute of Actuaries* (UK), Vol. 105.

4. ———, "Recent Models of the Term Structure of Interest Rates with Actuarial Applications," *Proceedings of the 1980 International Actuarial Conference*, Zurich, Switzerland.

5. Brennan, M. J. and E. S. Schwartz, 1979, "A Continuous Time Approach to the Pricing of Bonds," *Journal of Banking and Finance*, Vol. 3, 133–155.

6. ———, 1980, "Conditional Predictions of Bond Prices and Returns," *Journal of Finance*, Vol. 35, No. 2 (May), 405–416.

7. Cox, J. C., J. E. Ingersoll, and S. A. Ross, "A Theory of the Term Structure of Interest Rates," Working Paper No. 468, Stanford University, August 1978.

8. Durand, D., 1942, *Basic Yields of Corporate Bonds 1900–1942*, Technical Paper No. 3, New York: National Bureau of Economic Research.

9. Fisher, L. and R. L. Weil, 1971, "Coping With the Risk of Interest Rate Fluctuations: Returns to Bondholders from Naive and Optimal Strategies," *Journal of Business*, Vol. 44, No. 4 (Oct.).

10. Harrison, J. M. and D. M. Kreps, 1979, "Martingales and Arbitrage in Multiperiod Securities Markets," *Journal of Economic Theory*, Vol. 20, 381–408.

11. Ingersoll, J. E., J. Skelton, and R. L. Weil, 1978, "Duration Forty Years Later," *Journal of Financial and Quantitative Analysis*, Vol. 13, No. 4 (Nov.), 627–650.

12. Lanstein, R. and W. F. Sharpe, 1978, "Duration and Security Risk," *Journal of Financial and Quantitative Analysis*, Vol. 13, No. 4 (Nov.), 653–668.

13. Macaulay, F. R., 1938, *Some Theoretical Problems Suggested by the Movements of Interest Rates, Bond Yields and Stock Prices in the United States since 1856,* New York, National Bureau of Economic Research.
14. McCulloch, J. H., 1975, "The Tax Adjusted Yield Curve," *Journal of Finance,* Vol. 30, (June), 811–830.
15. Redington, F. M., 1952, "Review of the Principles of Life Office Evaluation," *Journal of the Institute of Actuaries,* Vol. 78, 286–315.
16. Schaefer, S. M., 1981, "Measuring a Tax Specific Term Structure of Interest Rates in the Market for British Government Securities," *Economic Journal,* Vol. 91 (June), 415–438.
17. ———, 1980, "Discussion," *Journal of Finance,* Vol. 35, No. 2 (May), 417–419.
18. Vasicek, O. A., 1977, "An Equilibrium Characterization of the Term Structure," *Journal of Financial Economics,* Vol. 5, No. 2 (Nov.), 177–188.

COMMENTS

Charles W. Haley

The theme of this conference is the contribution of the concepts of duration and immunization to the management of financial assets given uncertain future interest rates. I can identify two types of problems faced by different investors:

1. *Funding*—How can a set of known future liabilities be funded so as to immunize the investor from interest rate risk?
2. *Intermediation*—What is the optimal strategy for an investor (individual or firm) that can issue liabilities as well as acquire assets? The intermediary's liabilities may be subject to unpredictable withdrawals.

Funding is the primary problem addressed in the duration literature and by this paper, although the results have implications for the more interesting and difficult intermediary problem as well. Nelson and Schaefer evaluate the ability of multiple asset portfolios to match the returns of individual "target" securities that can be considered as liabilities to be funded by the portfolios. A perfect match for a given portfolio strategy would imply that this strategy can be used to immunize an investor with such liabilities from interest rate risk. Any strategy that provides returns that exceed those of the target is a possible candidate for use by an intermediary issuing such liabilities at its discretion, subject to an analysis of the risk of that strategy.

The authors' empirical results for targets with 5 and 10 years maturity (Tables 6A and 6B of the preceding chapter) suggest that duration-based portfolio strategies can provide such excess returns, but with significant risk. The standard deviations of the excess returns (S.D. of Diff.) are approximately 10 times the mean excess returns (Diff.). Since there are about 100 observations over the entire sample period, the standard deviations of the mean excess returns are of the same size as the means.

Although the focus of the paper is the performance of alternative portfolio strategies, there is much more here than a large performance study. The authors begin by developing a theoretical model of the term structure that provides for multiple factors affecting it. They show the conditions that apply to an immunizing portfolio in this multifactor world. The model is based implicitly on a frictionless, efficient market. In such markets the funding problem is uninteresting. Perfect matching is possible for any given liability stream at known spot prices for dollars to be delivered at any future date. Moreover, there is no scope for an intermediary in these markets since no strategy can offer risk-free returns in excess of those provided by the existing term structure. Thus the authors' evaluation of alternative strategies (some of which are based on their model) is, in part, a test of how well the model applies in the actual market place. Unfortunately, the results here are at best inconclusive and somewhat negative. The strategies based on their model tend not to work as well as those that are not based on the model, but the dispersion in the results is too large to permit firm conclusions.

There is still more to the paper. The section on the dynamics of the term structure contains much of interest to researchers concerned with the stochastic behavior of interest rates. Nelson and Schaefer have provided us with the most comprehensive empirical study in this area since the Fisher and Weil paper a decade ago. It may be another 10 years before the work here is fully digested.

RECENT DEVELOPMENTS IN BOND PORTFOLIO IMMUNIZATION STRATEGIES

G. O. Bierwag, George G. Kaufman, and
Alden Toevs

I. INTRODUCTION

In the last 10 years, a considerable amount of research has been undertaken on bond portfolio strategies that are appropriate for planning horizons of given length. Much of this work focuses on the merits of active and passive strategies for attaining investment objectives with default-free, option-free, fixed coupon bonds. Active strategies permit a portfolio manager to exercise discretion in the selection of bonds to be included in a portfolio, and the success of these strategies depends considerably on the accuracy of the forecasted course of future bond prices and interest rates. Passive strategies are designed to "lock in" specific rates of return over a planning horizon regardless of the course of future bond prices and interest rates. Passive strategies are designed so as to exploit the offsetting impacts of interest rate changes.

When interest rates rise (fall), bond prices fall (rise), thus reducing (increasing) the value of an investment fund; but if the stochastic nature of interest rate fluctuations is gauged correctly, the increase (decrease) in interest rates implies that the periodic inflows from investments can be reinvested at higher (lower) rates so as to offset the initial fall (rise) in the value of an investment fund. A successful passive strategy is thus immune from interest rate changes and is called an *immunization strategy*.

Immunization as a concept has a history that dates from the work of Redington [40], Wallas [45], and others, but it was not until after the publication of the seminal work of Fisher and Weil in 1971, that the underlying nature of interest rate changes and its impact on the appropriate design of immunization strategies were studied rigorously. New technical approaches have been advanced, and new insights into the nature and performance of these strategies have obtained. An immunization strategy is a hedging strategy based on particular stochastic processes governing interest rate changes. In other branches of financial theory the stochastic processes governing the prices of assets have been explored within various frameworks of complete and incomplete markets. Immunization strategies can be considered and discussed within these frameworks also. Immunization cannot be regarded as a curious phenomenon lingering in the backwaters of modern financial theory. It now rests on a solid foundation in the mainstream of modern theory.

In this introductory section, we survey major developments on immunization theory and the attendent empirical research. The emphasis is on research undertaken since the seminal work of Fisher and Weil [17]. Not all of the research on this subject is surveyed in this chapter, but it is hoped that most of the major developments have been noted, at least. Some new and previously unpublished work is also contained in this chapter. In particular, we do the following:

1. Distinguish between *weak* and *strong* form immunization in Section IV; this is a distinction that is of significance for financial organizations that may not be able to estimate accurately their cash flows over time.
2. Discuss the problem of immunizing multiple liability outflows over time and the problem of minimizing "stochastic process" risk.
3. Introduce a new approach to immunization over multiple period horizons; this approach, in a discrete analytical framework, allows for complete markets and for a rich class of stochastic processes for term structures, not previously considered.

The empirical work reported in Section VIII suggests that this last immunization procedure may be a practical addition to the techniques for bond portfolio immunization.

II. EARLY WORK

Redington [40] discussed the immunization concept in an actuarial context. As shown in Appendix A, Redington suggested that a stream of liabilities could be immunized provided assets were chosen so that their "mean term" matched the mean term of the liabilities, provided certain second-order conditions were maintained. Redington, in fact, coined the word *immunization*. The measure *mean term* used by Redington is simply a weighted average of the dates that the flows received on an asset are promised. It is exactly the same measure invented earlier by Macaulay [37] as a measure of the mean maturity of life of an asset that promised a stream of income as opposed to a single flow on a particular date. Macaulay used the word *duration* to denote this average. Hicks [23], who studied the properties of income streams that made the ratio of their values invariant with respect to changes in interest rates, called the same measure the *average maturity*. Samuelson [42], who was studying the postwar impact of an increase in interest rates on the banking system as a whole, called it the *average time period* of the flows. Although these measures, independently devised by different scholars at different times, are equivalent, the word *duration* has become the commonly used term today.

Duration, used by these authors, is technically defined as

$$D = \sum_1^N tw_t, \qquad w_t \geq 0, \qquad \sum_1^N w_t = 1, \qquad (1)$$

where

$$w_t = \frac{s(t)}{V(1 + r)^t} \qquad (2)$$

and $s(t)$ is the flow at time t, r is the discount rate, N is the date at which all flows terminate, and V is the present value of the asset.

Redington assumed that the term structure was "flat" so that the discount rate r applied to all the flows $s(t)$ of the asset held and the entire term structure moved up or down in a parallel fashion.[1] He then showed that if the duration of the assets equaled the duration of the liabilities (and the second order conditions were satisfied), then changes in interest rates over time would affect the value of the liabilities in exactly the same way as it would affect the value of the assets. If immunization is a feasible strategy, it consists of selecting the assets and/or liabilities so as to satisfy the immunization conditions. If immunization is successful, the net worth of the firm will not be reduced by changes in interest rates.

III.   THE FISHER–WEIL RESULT

Fisher and Weil modified Redington's approach in two major ways. First, they focused on the immunization requirements when the liability consists of a single known outflow to occur at a single known future date. The time up to this future date was designated as the planning period or planning horizon. Given a current term structure applicable to zero coupon (or pure discount) default-free bonds, one can calculate a rate of return over the planning period, and this rate of return was called the *target* or promised rate of return for the planning period. Under conditions of certainty in all financial markets, this would be the rate of return that would, in fact, obtain regardless of the investment strategy pursued. (The liability outflow could then be regarded as a *target* value, the present discounted value of which was calculated using the promised rate of return.) If there is uncertainty as to what future interest rates will be, different investment strategies can have different outcomes. Fisher and Weil state that performance should be measured relative to the "promised" rate of return and any deviation from that promised rate of return would be the consequence of the strategy used and of the uncertainty prevailing in financial markets.

Second, Fisher and Weil assume a form of the "expectations hypothesis" of the term structure of interest rates in their proof of the immunization theorem. Under the expectations hypothesis, as formulated by Hicks [23], Meiselman [39], and many others, a forward rate derived from the current term structure for some particular future time period is the market's expectation of the actual rate to prevail over that time period. Thus, if the term structure is specified as [h(0,1), h(0,2), . . . , h(0,N)], where h(0,t) is the current rate of return on a pure discount default-free bond for t periods, then the forward rate spanning the future interval $[\tau,t]$ $(\tau < t)$, and denoted as h(τ,t), is defined implicitly by the formula[2]

$$[1 + h(0,t)]^t = [1 + h(\tau,t)]^{t-\tau}[1 + h(0,\tau)]^\tau . \qquad (3)$$

Under conditions of certainty in competitive markets, the forward rate h(τ,t) will become the actual equilibrium $(t - \tau)$ period rate at data τ. To see this, let an investor spend \$1 on a τ-period bond. His investment accumulates to $[1 + h(0,\tau)]^\tau$ dollars after τ periods. After reinvestment of this amount in a $(t - \tau)$ period bond at the prevailing rate of $h^*(\tau,t)$ his investment then accumulates to $[1 + h(0,\tau)]^\tau [1 + h^*(\tau,t)]^{t-\tau}$ dollars at date t, but this would have been exactly his accumulated earnings from an initial investment of \$1 in a t-period bond, if $h^*(\tau,t) = h(\tau,t)$. Allowing for arbitrage and short selling, it follows that $h^*(\tau,t) = h(\tau,t)$ is an equilibrium condition. Under the expectations hypothesis, $h(\tau,t)$ is the expected value of $h^*(\tau,t)$. If expectations are realized, the term structure will shift through time in a specific way. If initially the structure is specified as

$$[h(0,1), h(0,2), h(0,3), \ldots, h(0,N)] ,$$

then one period later it becomes

$$[h(1,2), h(1,3), h(1,4), \ldots, h(1,N)] ,$$

and one period after that it becomes

$$[h(2,3), h(2,4), h(2,5), \ldots, h(2,N)] ,$$

and so forth. The changes in the one-year rates are $h(1,2) - h(0,1)$, $h(2,3) - h(1,2), \ldots$, and changes in the two-year rates are $h(1,3) - h(0,2)$, $h(2,4) - h(1,3), \ldots$, and so forth. If expectations are realized, as under the conditions of certainty, these changes will be non-zero for at least some rates provided the initial term structure is not flat. If expectations are *not* realized over time, one can view the actual change in rates as decomposed into two parts—an expected and an unexpected change. For example, if $h^*(1,2)$ is the actual one-period rate, one period from now, then the expected change is

$$h(1,2) - h(0,1)$$

and the unexpected change is

$$h^*(1,2) - h(1,2)$$

so that the sum of the two changes is the actual change $h^*(1,2) - h(0,1)$. Fisher and Weil implicitly assume that only the unexpected portion of the change is subject to a specified random variation over the planning period. In particular, Fisher and Weil assumed that the initial term structure shifted instantly after an investor acquired a bond. This shift was assumed to be a random additive shift. The forward rates in the new shifted curve then became the future rates. If there was no shift in the term structure the actual change in rates would be the expected change in rates.

The Fisher–Weil immunization condition is a simple one and Appendix B provides a concise derivation. The investor allocates his or her investment fund so that its duration equals the length of the planning period.[3] However, given the term structure and the implicit expectations hypothesis, the measure of duration that they devised was quite different from that used in earlier work. In discrete terms, their duration is

$$D = \frac{\sum_{1}^{N} s(t) \, t[1 + h(0,t)]^{-t}}{V} . \tag{4}$$

It differs from the Macaulay duration by the substitution of $h(0,t)$ for r, the yield to maturity. To distinguish their duration measure from Macaulay's Fisher and Weil called theirs *expected duration*.

IV.   EXTENSIONS OF THE FISHER–WEIL THEOREM

Alternative Stochastic Processes

Fisher and Weil assumed that the term structure randomly shifted in an additive fashion. That is, if $\langle h(0,t), t = 1, 2, \ldots, N \rangle$ is the initial term structure, then after a random shift in an amount λ, it becomes $\langle h(0,t) + \lambda, t = 1, 2, \ldots, N \rangle$.[4] Suppose the term structure shifted randomly in some other way. Would the Fisher–Weil immunization theorem still hold? Bierwag [2] and Khang [28] consider some different stochastic processes. Bierwag [2] shows that some alternative stochastic processes will permit immunization and some will not. In cases where immunization can occur, the formulas for calculating the appropriate duration of an asset are different depending upon the stochastic process. The expression *immunizing duration* provides convenient nomenclature to indicate a duration that is appropriate for immunizing a specific stochastic process. To show this, consider the impact of the multiplicative stochastic process under continuous compounding. The initial value of the income stream can be expressed as

$$W_0 = \int_0^N s(t) e^{-h(0,t)t} \, dt . \tag{5}$$

Instantly after the stream $s(t)$, $0 \le t \le N$, is acquired, the term structure shifts randomly so that the initial value of the investment changes. To reflect this, we can write

$$W_0(\lambda) = \int_0^N s(t) e^{-\lambda h(0,t)t} \, dt , \tag{6}$$

where λ is the multiplicative shock. If q is the length of the planning period, at date q, the amount $W_0(\lambda)$ will accumulate to

$$W_q(\lambda) = e^{h(0,q)\lambda q} W_0(\lambda) . \tag{7}$$

If the flow s(t) is not totally concentrated on date N, one can show that $W_q''(\lambda) > 0$. That is, $W_q(\lambda)$ is a strictly convex function of λ. Thus, $W_q(\lambda)$ has a minimum at the point where $\lambda = 1$ provided $W_q'(1) = 0$. The equation $W_q'(1) = 0$ can be solved so as to write

$$h(0,q)q = \frac{1}{W_0} \int_0^N s(t)h(0,t)te^{-h(0,t)t} \, dt = h(0,D)D \tag{8}$$

where D is the immunizing duration implied by this process. If the additive stochastic process were used instead, then the immunizing duration can be expressed

$$D = \frac{1}{W_0} \int_0^N s(t)te^{-h(0,t)t} \, dt \tag{9}$$

—clearly a different formula. Moreover, the formulas for calculating the durations of portfolios of assets are also different. Under the multiplicative stochastic process that gives rise to the duration in equation (8), if D_1 and D_2 are the durations of two assets that are combined in the proportions (β_1, β_2), the duration of the combined portfolio will be given implicitly by

$$h(0,D)D = \beta_1 h(0,D_1)D_1 + \beta_2 h(0,D_2)D_2 . \tag{10}$$

On the other hand, under the additive stochastic process for which (9) gives the duration formula, the duration of the portfolio so combined would be

$$D = \beta_1 D_1 + \beta_2 D_2 \tag{11}$$

Khang [28] introduced a stochastic process in which the instant short rate change could be made larger in absolute value than the instant long rate change. Letting $h*(0,t)$ be the new term structure after the instant random shift, Khang (for the continuous additive case) defined

$$h*(0,t) = \frac{\lambda \ln (1 + \alpha t)}{\alpha t} + h(0,t) \tag{12}$$

where α is a parameter. Following the same procedure, as above, the immunizing duration for this stochastic process is given implicitly by

$$\ln (1 + \alpha q) = \ln (1 + \alpha D) = \int_0^N s(t) \ln (1 + \alpha t)e^{-h(0,t)t} \, dt . \tag{13}$$

This formula for duration is different from those in equations (8) and (9). Generally the Khang duration is less than the durations derived for additive or multiplicative processes. The Khang durations also decrease as the value of the parameter α increases. Appendix C contains a table of the continuous and discrete stochastic processes that have been considered and their durations.[5]

There are some stochastic processes for which an immunization strategy does not exist. As a general proposition suppose that the stochastic process is given as

$$h^*(0,t) = h(0,t) + \phi(\lambda) \qquad (14)$$

where ϕ is a differentiable function of λ. It follows that the terminal value of an investment fund then is

$$W_q(\lambda) = \int_0^N s(t)e^{h(0,1)q - h(0,t)t + \phi(\lambda)(q-t)} dt \qquad (15)$$

The second derivative of this function may be positive or negative depending on the properties that $\phi(\lambda)$ is assumed to have. For immunization to be possible, we require that $W_q(\lambda)$ have a minimum at some value of λ, say λ_0, and that $W_q(\lambda) \geq W_q(\lambda_0) \geq W_0 e^{h(0,q)q}$ for all permissible values of λ. If $\phi(\lambda)$ does not have the appropriate properties, then an immunization strategy may not exist. Bierwag [2] shows that one may not be able to immunize for some discrete additive stochastic processes because as the term structure instantly shifts up or down, it is possible for some "forward" term structures embedded in the current term structure to twist in a manner which makes it impossible to design an immunization strategy.

Weak- and Strong-Form Immunization

In the Redington and Fisher–Weil renditions of the immunization theorem, the future date at which each outflow is to be discharged is given ex ante and with certainty. Redington stressed that a duration matching strategy would protect the net worth of the financial organization, and Fisher and Weil stressed that this strategy would earn at least the ex ante promised rate of return for each asset or liability claim. These two points of view are equivalent if all liability outflows are discharged as scheduled using funds generated by the invested assets. The duration matching strategy is a hedging strategy that protects net worth because the asset returns will be sufficient regardless of the movement in interest rates to discharge every obligation at its associated initially promised rate of return.

However, suppose that the dates of discharge are not known with certainty at the time the funds are invested and that some or all of the liabilities are discharged earlier or later than initially schedule, e.g., as for a life insurance company. Will net worth still be protected, and will the liability claims still earn the initially promised rates of return? The answer cannot be found in the extant literature. Yet, a simple example easily illustrates that the promised rate of return cannot be guaranteed. Let a single liability outflow of x dollars be scheduled for date q, and suppose the amount $xe^{-h(0,q)q} = v$ is invested in a zero coupon bond of maturity q. If there is no random shift in the term structure during the investment period, the value of the asset and the liability claim will be $ve^{h(0,t_0)t_0}$ at date t_0 ($<q$), so that the earned rate of return to that date is the a priori promised rate $h(0,t_0)$. If the term structure shifts to $h(0,t) + \lambda$ immediately after the investment of v dollars, its value at date t_0 changes to $xe^{-h(0,q)q-\lambda q}(e^{h(0,t_0)t_0+\lambda t_0} = ve^{h(0,t_0)t_0-\lambda(q-t_0)}$ so that the realized rate of return up to date t_0 becomes

$$r(0,t_0) = h(0,t_0) - \frac{\lambda(q - t_0)}{t_0}$$

and

$$r(0,t_0) \underset{<}{\overset{>}{-}} h(0,t_0) \qquad \text{according as } \lambda \underset{>}{\overset{<}{-}} 0 .$$

The realized rate of return may be greater or less than that promised. However, although the promised return may not be realized, it is easy to see that net worth is protected because the value of the assets and the liabilities have changed by the same amount as a result of the shift in the term structure.

In general, the duration matching strategy protects net worth regardless of the dates at which the liabilities are discharged provided the liabilities are discharged at market values. Let L(t) and A(t) be the initially scheduled liability and asset flows. Assuming these flows have the same present value, then

$$N = \int [A(t) - L(t)]e^{-h(0,t)t} \, dt = 0 . \tag{16}$$

If there is a random additive shift in the term structure, the difference in the value of the two streams becomes

$$N(\lambda) = \int [A(t) - L(t)]e^{-h(0,t)t - \lambda t} \, dt . \tag{17}$$

If A(t) is chosen, given L(t), such that the durations are matched, it follows that

$$N'(0) = 0 , \tag{18}$$

and, if further, Redington's second-order condition holds (as shown in Appendix A), then $N''(0) > 0$, and any change in interest rates in the neighborhood of $\lambda = 0$ causes the difference to increase.[6] Net worth is protected by the duration matching strategy. The market value of the assets will always be sufficient to cover the market value of the liabilities.

These results can be summarized by distinguishing two forms of the duration matching strategy.

- *Strong-form immunization*: If liabilities are discharged on exactly the dates originally scheduled, net worth is protected and every liability claim earns its promised rate of return.
- *Weak-form immunization*: If liabilities are discharged at market value on dates that were not originally scheduled, net worth is protected but the liability claims may not earn the promised rate of return over the period that they are extant.

The implementation of either form of the duration matching strategy requires an initial specification of the flows and their dates of discharge. Using the term structure and traditional discounting procedures the specified flows and their discharge dates must be known in order to determine present market values and the appropriate durations. However, once durations have been matched (and second-order conditions established), early (or late) discharges of liability obligations will not threaten net worth.

In previous work the planning period is identified as the time up to the date a liability is discharged. If the discharges occur earlier (later) than the dates used in calculating the durations, then the planning period may differ from the matched asset and liability durations. This suggests an alternative definition of weak- and strong-form immunization:

$$\text{Weak form:} \quad D_A = D_L \neq q .$$

$$\text{Strong form:} \quad D_A = D_L = q .$$

Some financial organizations may be unable or prefer not to pursue strong form immunization. For example, if managerial performance is to be judged on an annual or short-term basis, a policy of setting $D_A = D_L \neq q$, where q is now the performance period, would not measure performance correctly. Another case where weak-form immunization may occur is when the expected dates used in the a priori calculations of the duration of the liabilities are known to differ from the dates at which the liabilities will be actually discharged. Strong-form immunization may not be achievable, but by using weak-form immunization, the solvency of the financial organization may still be assured regardless of actual inflow and outflow dates.

Redington stressed that immunization protected net worth. The development of weak-form immunization is thus a logical extension of his immunization conditions. The weak-form strategy does not require that the actual dates of the liability discharge be the same as those used to calculate the immunization conditions. Fisher and Weil stressed that immunization would guarantee the promised rate of return over a planning period of given length. They thus stressed the implications of the strong form strategy.

For many financial organizations, contractual arrangements with the holders of liability claims may complicate or make impossible the achievement of either form of immunization. Depository institutions, for example, often accept deposits that grow at some contracted rate for indefinite periods. No explicit maturity dates on many of these liability claims is specified. The depositor can withdraw invested funds on any date, and, more importantly these withdrawals include the original deposit plus interest accumulated at the contracted rates whether or not there have been unexpected changes in market interest rates, i.e., the withdrawals are at par rather than market value. If the withdrawal dates are correctly anticipated, the depository institutions can achieve strong-form immunization, but if not, neither strong nor weak form can be possible.

Immunization Is a Minimax Strategy

The developments in Section IV, Alternative Stochastic Processes, indicate that an immunization strategy and its performance depends on the particular process governing fluctuations in interest rates. Given a stochastic process and a specific investment strategy, at the end of the planning period, one can express the value of an investment fund in terms of the random shocks. For many stochastic processes and strategies the future value of the investment fund has a minimal value that corresponds to some specific value of the random shock to the term structure. Formally, suppose one utilizes investment strategy s and that, given s, the terminal value of the investment at the end of q periods can be expressed as $W_q(\lambda;s)$, where λ is a value of the random shock.

Suppose that $W_q(\lambda;s)$ reaches a minimum at $\lambda_0(s)$. Then, we can write

$$W_q(\lambda_0(s);s) = \min_{\lambda} W_q(\lambda;s) , \qquad (19)$$

where formally the minimal value of λ_0 may depend on the strategy s that is specified. Bierwag and Khang [11] show for a discrete multiplicative process that an immunization strategy is that strategy s* for which

$$W_q(\lambda_0(s^*),s^*) = \max_{s} \{\min_{\lambda} W_q(\lambda;s)\} . \qquad (20)$$

That is, an immunization strategy is a maximin strategy. Appendix D contains a new proof of the maximin theorem. This proof is simpler than that originally presented by Bierwag and Khang.

The notion of immunization as a maximin strategy can be viewed graphically as in Figure 1. Two density functions over the rate of return over q periods are described there. The immunization strategy maximizes the minimal rate of return that can occur with some positive value of the probability density. In the diagram, $f(r;s)$ and $f(r;s^*)$ are probability density functions over the return r corresponding to strategies s and s*, respectively. If s* is the immunization strategy, then no other strategy can have a minimal return r_s that exceeds r_{s^*},—the minimal return corresponding to the immunization strategy.

There are other ways to describe the immunization strategy as a maximin strategy of the type shown here. For example, the Fishburn measure defined as

$$H(s;s^*,\alpha) = \int_0^{r_{s^*}} (r - r_{s^*})^\alpha f(r;s) \, dr, \qquad \alpha > 0 , \qquad (21)$$

can be used to compare any two strategies s and s*. Then, s* is an

Figure 1.

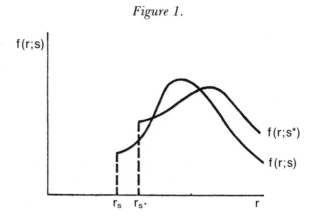

immunization strategy if $H(s;s^*,\alpha) \geq 0$ for all other strategies s considered. As in Fishburn [16], we can regard $H(s;s^*,\alpha)$ as a measure of the "downside" risk associated with the strategy s. In this context, one can view the immunization strategy as a riskless strategy. In a more general context, Fishburn showed that a ranking of strategies on the basis of expected return and the risk measured as $H(s,s^*;\alpha)$ is consistent with first-, second-, and third-order stochastic dominance for various values of α. Bawa and Lindenberg [1] in a one-period setting, show that the downside measures of risk are consistent with the CAPM model.

Marshall and Yawitz [38] point out that the minimum return (or the highest lower bound to the return) from a bond portfolio strategy may impart information about the risk associated with the strategy. In Figure 1, for example, if r_s is reasonably close to r_s^*, the risk borne by such an active strategy may be tolerable to many investors. Leibowitz and Weinberger [35] utilize this idea in the form of "contingent immunization," i.e., an active bond portfolio strategy that is riskier than ordinary immunization, but this risk allows for higher probable returns at a cost of possibly achieving only a lower acceptable return. In pursuing contingent immunization, an arbitrary but acceptable lower bound to the portfolio return is specified in advance. This lower bound is less than that promised by the immunization strategy. The portfolio manager then pursues an active strategy, but if the active strategy begins to fail sufficiently, the manager shifts to an immunization strategy at the point in time where it is still possible to earn the lower acceptable return for the planning period. A more complete discussion of the use of duration in an active bond portfolio strategy is given in Section IX.

Multiple Random Shocks During the Planning Period

The above developments of the immunization strategies are based on the occurrence of a single random shock to the term structure during the planning period. However, no loss in generality results for more than one shock provided the stochastic process governing interest rate changes does not change over the planning period. Figure 2 nicely illustrates this point. Let $W_0(0)$ be the initial level of the investment fund. If there are no shifts in the term structure during the planning period, $W_0(0)$ will accumulate to $W_q(0) = e^{h(0,q)q} W_0(0)$. Now suppose an additive shock λ_0 occurs instantly after $W_0(0)$ has been allocated. Assuming $\lambda_0 < 0$, so that the term structure falls, $W_0(0)$ rises to $W_0(\lambda_0)$. Since the growth rate is now less than before, if there are no further shocks to the term structure, $W_0(\lambda_0)$ grows at a lower rate to $W_q(\lambda_0)$, which is above $W_q(0)$ provided the immunization strategy is continuously

Figure 2.

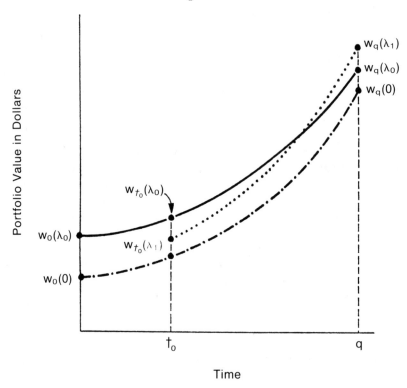

Time

pursued. Now suppose that another shock λ_1 occurs at time t_0. Assume $\lambda_1 > 0$ so that the term structure increases, this forces the value of $W_{t_0}(\lambda_0)$ down to $W_{t_0}(\lambda_1)$. If the immunization strategy is continuously pursued for the remainder of the period, $W_{t_0}(\lambda_1)$ rises to $W_q(\lambda_1)$ which will exceed $W_q(\lambda_0)$. In this way, the shocks to the term structure have a ratcheting effect on the terminal value of the investment fund at time q. Initially, $W_q(0)$ was the prospective future value of the investment at time q. After the first shock, $W_q(\lambda_0)$ became the prospective terminal value of the investment, and after the second shock, $W_q(\lambda_1)$ became the prospective future value of the investment. Each time there was a shock the prospective terminal value rises. Khang [29] shows this result to be generally the case for an immunization strategy if the stochastic process is known. Bierwag [3] showed that the terminal value of the investment fund will not in general be a convex function of all of the shocks occurring during the planning period, but the ratcheting effect still occurs.

This feature of the immunization strategy is sometimes not well understood. Any portfolio of bonds will decrease in value, if interest rates rise. Suppose that the length of time to the end of the planning period is very short and that interest rates rise. Is it not conceivable that the fall in the value of the investment fund could be so severe that a reinvestment of the fund over the short remaining period cannot make up for this loss? The answer is no. The immunization strategy always balances the prospective losses from an increase in interest rates with the prospective gain from reinvestment. As the time to the end of the planning period shortens, so also will the duration of the investment fund under the immunization strategy. This shortening of the duration decreases the impact on the value of the fund resulting from a change in interest rates. In general the loss can never be so severe that it cannot be recovered by reinvestment. The losses and what can be recovered from an increase in interest rates are functionally related. In the last day or hour of the planning period the investment fund will be so liquid that changes in interest rates will have negligible effects on its value.

Multiperiod Immunization

If there are many liability outflows scheduled for many different future dates, an immunization strategy will protect the net worth of the financial organization whether outflows occur on the expected dates or not. This means, in effect, that if the liabilities are initially fully funded then they will remain so over the course of time, provided immunization is undertaken against the stochastic process generating unexpected changes in interest rates.

In the context of the Fisher–Weil approach one can give immunization of multiple outflows a more detailed interpretation. Each of the liability outflows can be regarded as a single outflow and the time to its date of occurrence can be regarded as a planning period. If a separate immunized portfolio is maintained for each of the outflows and they occur as scheduled then the outcome for each planning period is identical to the results already obtained and discussed above. In particular a "promised" rate of return can be associated with each of these portfolios and it is this rate of return that immunization guarantees as the minimal possible rate for the specified planning period, given the stochastic process is correctly gauged. To obtain this result, however, there is a portfolio of assets corresponding to each outflow. For large organizations having a large structure of scheduled outflows, the separate management of many such portfolios can be costly.

In order to reduce portfolio management costs and to produce simple principles of management so as to achieve some form of overall immunization, Bierwag, Kaufman, and Toevs (BKT) [8] and Fong and Vasicek [18] have proposed rules to guide the design of a portfolio of assets that immunizes for multiple planning periods. In the former paper, BKT take the view that a single asset (or portfolio of them) can generate flows that can be applied to several different liability outflows so that unlike the prior approach, no specific portfolio of assets is associated uniquely with any specifically scheduled liability outflow. Immunization of the set of outflows only implies that the assets are chosen so that each outflow can be discharged with certainty. One can regard any future outflow as having a current value, and this current value represents a "claim" on the assets of the organization (whether or not that claim is embodied in a specific portfolio of assets). The value of the claim grows through time as the earnings on the assets accrue through time. If the liability is discharged on schedule, one can regard the claim as having earned the rate initially promised over its life. If a liability is discharged at market value on a date other than that for which it was initially scheduled, it may not earn the promised rate initially associated with the scheduled date of outflow; but weak-form immunization will be in effect so that at least the net worth of the organization is protected.

BKT show that immunization for multiple outflows can be achieved by the management of a single portfolio. As in Redington's earlier analysis, immunization requires that the duration of this portfolio be equal to the duration of the liabilities. There are, however, other conditions that must be satisfied. These conditions are second-order conditions that are easily stated, as Redington did in his special context, but the design of rules for portfolio construction that will satisfy these conditions is another matter. In one of the most simple rules to apply BKT specify that the flows of the assets be divided into two parts having market values of A_1 and A_2, where $A_1 + A_2 = A$, the total market value of the assets. The flows having values A_1 and A_2 need not correspond to any particular portfolio of assets. That is, some assets may have some of their flows incorporated into A_1 and some into A_2. Each of these contrived assets has a duration denoted as D_1 and D_2, respectively, if the discrete multiplicative stochastic process is in effect.[7] The duration of the assets is then $(A_1/A)D_1 + (A_2/A)D_2 = D_A$. Let D_L

be the duration of the liability outflows, and let t_m and t_u be the dates of the earliest and latest outflows, respectively. Immunization is then achieved if the assets are chosen so that

Strong Form	*Weak Form*
1. $D_A = D_L$ and all liabilities are discharged at their expected date. 2. $D_1 \leq t_m$ and $D_2 \geq t_u$.	1. $D_A = D_L$. 2. $D_1 \leq t_m$ and $D_2 \geq t_u$.

A more complicated, but also more general procedure, is to partition the asset and liability flows into m separate sets. Let $A_i = L_i$ be the values of the flows in these sets, $i = 1, 2, \ldots, m$. One can then consider the ith set separately and apply the above rules to determine the allocation of assets having value A_i, $i = 1, 2, \ldots, m$. BKT call these the m-level immunizing portfolios.

Fong and Vasicek [18] approach the problem of multiperiod immunization in a different way. In the process they develop a term called M^2. This term has two functions. The first comes in the formation of the second-order conditions needed for one asset portfolio to immunize against multiple liability outflows. The second use of M^2 is in limiting exposure of the immunized portfolio to "stochastic process risk," i.e., the risk of misidentifying the correct stochastic process.

The terminal value of an immunized investment fund will depend on the changes in the term structure over time. Fong and Vasicek assume that the multiplicative discrete stochastic process is governing interest rate movments. On this assumption the portfolio is chosen so that the Fisher-Weil duration measure of the assets equals that of the liabilities. Fong and Vasicek approximate the net terminal value of the investment fund by expanding it in a Taylor's series around the specified duration. A coefficient in the second term of the expansion is the M^2 term referred to above. More specifically, it is

$$M^2 = \sum_{j=1}^{m} \frac{(t_j - D)^2 A_j P_0(t_j)}{I_0} - \sum_{i=1}^{n} \frac{(s_i - D)^2 C_i P_0(s_i)}{I_0} = M_A - M_L ,$$

where t_j and s_i are the respective dates at which the inflows and outflows occur, A_j is the inflow at date t_j, C_i is the outflow at date s_i, $P_0(t_j)$ is the present value of a dollar received at date t_j, D is the Fisher–Weil duration of both the assets and the liabilities, and I_0 is the fully funding present value of the assets. The M^2 term behaves very much like a variance (actually a difference of variances) and, as we shall see, can be used as a measure of risk.[8]

The asset portfolio needed to immunize multiple liability outflows must meet the following necessary and sufficient conditions:

1. $D_A = D_L$.
2. $M^2 \geq 0$ or $M_A^2 \geq M_L^2$.

It should be stressed that these conditions are correct only for the multiplicative discrete stochastic process. (Fong and Vasicek assume strong-form immunization as all liability withdrawals take place on the initially anticipated dates.) The second, and sufficient, condition requires a "spreading" of asset flows relative to the liability flows.

Fong and Vasicek use these first- and second-order conditions as constraints, in addition to the constraint that the liabilities be fully funded, in a linear programming problem. Sets of assets and liabilities can be given to a computer program and the problem is one of selecting a set of assets such that all the constraints are met. Because many sets of assets may fulfill these constraints, Fong and Vasicek impose an additional constraint that M_A^2 be driven as close to M_L^2 as possible, i.e., $M^2 > 0$ be minimized.

Fong and Vasicek approximate the total change in the terminal value of the investment fund stemming from an interest rate shock by the product $\Delta S M^2 T$, where ΔS measures the assumed change in interest rates (and is equivalent to a particular stochastic process) and T is simply the terminal value of the investment fund if there is no unexpected interest rate shock. If M^2 can be reduced to zero, as with a perfect matching of asset and liability flows, the resulting portfolio will immunize regardless of the stochastic process. Thus, M^2 can be thought of as a measure of exposure to stochastic process risk. Since stochastic process risk is found to be a real danger in empirical work on immunization, the linear programming constraint that M^2 be minimized becomes clear. If M^2 is minimized at a value greater than zero and the assumed stochastic process (assumed ΔS) errs substantially from the actual process (actual ΔS), then there may be an adverse change in the terminal value that could have been mitigated or eliminated by correctly accounting for the stochastic process. Thus, while the Fong–Vasicek approach is a useful first step in addressing the stochastic process risk issue, it is still one that is specific to a particular stochastic process. Measuring and assessing stochastic process risk are important theoretical and empirical issues yet to be fully examined [9].

The Immunization Strategy and Other Properties of Financial Instruments

Most of the research on immunization strategies has concentrated on the use of default-free, option-free, fixed coupon bonds. The only properties of these bonds that affect their durations are the coupon rates, the maturity dates, and the underlying zero coupon bond equivalent term structure used to price the bonds. No or little consideration has been given to call features, sinking fund provisions, default risk, tax implications, or other features of these instruments. Recently, however, the implications of some of these features have been considered.

Reilly and Sidhu [41] attempt to adjust the duration of financial instruments to reflect call features and sinking fund provisions. Weinstein [46] considers the effect a positive default probability might have on the duration of a bond. He finds that the direction the duration changes as default risk increases is ambiguous. Hessel and Huffman [22] have pointed out that it is the after-tax term structure that is relevant to an individual investor. In considering an income tax and a capital-gains tax, they show that the principle of immunization remains unaltered provided the after-tax term structure is subject to the stochastic processes previously considered. Bierwag, Kaufman, and Toevs [7] and Bierwag and Toevs [12] consider immunization when liabilities are required to be marked and paid at book value while assets are not. This analysis is devoted to understanding how banks and savings and loan institutions must structure their assets and liabilities to minimize the exposure of their net worth to changes in interest rates.

V. DURATION ANALYSIS AND MODERN PORTFOLIO THEORY

An immunization strategy can be successful over a multiple-period planning horizon if the returns from the reinvested flows and changes in the values of bonds held tend to offset one another so that the terminal return is not less than the originally promised return. These two changes may not be offsetting if a nonimmunization strategy is pursued. An assessment of the risk of pursuing any investment strategy must thus relate these changes over a multiple period planning horizon. Kaufman [26] outlines some of these relative changes for individual bonds. He notes that a bond, with given characteristics, has a risk that varies with the length of the planning period. If planning periods vary among investors, the riskiness of any given bond may be perceived differently by different investors. In a simple example, Bierwag, Kaufman, and Toevs [10] for a given planning period, show that duration may be used explicitly to assess the risk and expected return on a bond portfolio. This example is described in the last section of this paper.

The duration, which is found to be important in immunization models over a multiple-period planning horizon, has also been shown to be important in assessing the risks in the traditional one-period models.[9] Lanstein and Sharpe [30] (LS) consider a period of analysis so short that no reinvestment of flow occurs within the period. Bond returns over the period are completely described, then, in terms of the changes in bond prices which are in turn functions of the bond durations. LS show that the traditional CAPM beta for any bond is a function of the duration of that bond. Moreover, the covariances of the excess market returns on any two securities will be a function of these durations. In an application of this model to common stocks, LS show that the correlation of excess returns on any two securities decreases significantly with an increase in the difference of the durations on the two securities. LS have thus shown empirically that duration is a factor that may affect bond returns.

Bierwag and Kaufman [5] (BK) extend the Lanstein–Sharpe analysis to the case where the entire planning horizon is regarded as the single period of analysis. The period of analysis is now sufficiently long for reinvestment to occur within the period. BK approximate the terminal value of the investment as a linear function of a single random shock occurring during the period. Again the covariance of the returns (or excess returns) between any two bonds is a function of the durations. Now, however, the beta for any bond depends on the duration of the "market" portfolio and on the length of the planning period. Different investors with different planning period lengths may thus regard the same bond as having a different degree of risk.[10]

Several other papers have noted that a CAPM beta may depend on bond durations. Boquist, Racette, and Schlarbaum [13] were the first to note this. Their procedure simply consisted of taking the formula for the traditional beta, namely,

$$\beta_j = \frac{\text{cov}(R_j, R_m)}{\text{var}(R_m)},$$

where R_j and R_m are the returns respectively for the jth bond and the market return, and substituting values for the returns on R_j based upon a change in bond value expressed as a linear function of duration. In a more detailed analysis, Kaufman [27] approximates the returns so as to show that β additionally depends on the planning period length and on the duration of the market portfolio. Livingston [36], in a paper with different objectives, also shows that beta depends on the duration of the market portfolio. Kaufman notes that there is considerably more variation among the durations on bonds than among the durations on equities. Given the sensitivity of risk measures to these durations, an analysis of the risk-return characteristics for bonds poses a difficulty not shared with an analysis of equities.

VI. DURATION AND BOND PRICE VOLATILITY

Long before duration was found useful for immunization, its relation to bond prices was developed by Hicks in 1946 [23]. Later Hopewell and Kaufman [24] derived Macaulay's duration by taking the first derivative of bond price with respect to the yield to maturity. If

$$P = \sum s(t) [1 + h(0,t)]^{-t} = \sum s(t)(1 + i)^{-t},$$

then

$$\frac{dP}{P} = -D \frac{di}{1 + i}$$

or

$$\frac{\Delta P}{P} = -D \frac{\Delta i}{1 + i},$$

which may be approximated by

$$\frac{\Delta P}{P} \cong -D \Delta i.$$

Thus, duration serves as a measure of the bond price volatility of a bond for a given basis point change, or of basis risk. This use of duration has been widely accepted by bond market practitioners and duration volatility tables have recently been published by the Financial Publishing Company.

However, numerous authors have argued that this formulation holds only if the term structure were flat and the stochastic process restricted interest rate movements to parallel changes.[11] This, of course, is a well-known limitation of the yield to maturity as a measure of the holding period return and is sometimes referred to as the *coupon bias*. But this does not reduce the usefulness of duration as a measure of bond price volatility. Rather, just as for immunization, the correct duration formula for basis risk must incorporate allowance for the correct stochastic process of interest rate changes. This may be easily done for the same "reasonable" stochastic processes developed earlier. Thus, for discrete interest rate changes, we have

- Additive stochastic process:

$$\frac{dP}{P} = -\frac{D}{1 + h(0,D)} d\lambda$$

- Multiplicative stochastic process:

$$\frac{dP}{P} = -D \, d\lambda$$

- Khang multiplicative stochastic process:

$$\frac{dP}{P} = -\frac{\ln(1 + \alpha D)}{\alpha} d\lambda$$

- Khang additive stochastic process:

$$\frac{dP}{P} = -\frac{\ln(1 + \alpha D)}{\alpha[1 + h(0,D)]} d\lambda$$

where D refers to the IDs developed earlier and reported in Appendix C. Of course, if the duration selected to measure basis risk is not consistent with the actual stochastic process, bond price volatility will be misestimated. The usefulness of duration as a measure of basis risk as well as a tool for immunization then is an empirical question and a matter of cost effectiveness relative to alternative more complex formulations.

VII. IMMUNIZATION STRATEGIES, COVEXITY, AND ARBITRAGE

Ingersoll, Skelton, and Weil [25] have pointed out that, given some of the stochastic processes assumed above, profitable and riskless arbitrage opportunities may exist among bonds with coupons of differing magnitudes and pure discount bonds, if the latter are available or can be created from combinations of available assets. As such, these stochastic processes are then inconsistent with the existence of equilibrium in competitive bond markets. This result can occur because the terminal value of the investment fund will be no smaller than the promised return and may be larger if there are random shocks to the term structure during the planning period—and the lower the coupon rates, the larger the terminal values. If $\lambda = (\lambda_0, \lambda_1, \ldots, \lambda_{q-1})$ represents a series of random shocks to the term structures which occur at the beginning of each period during the planning horizon, and if $\lambda = 0$ corresponds to the case where there are no unexpected shocks, then the terminal value of the investment fund $W_q(\lambda)$ satisfies the inequality $W_q(\lambda) \geq W_q(0)$ for the stochastic processes described in previous sections. If pure discount bonds are available, the certain return $W_q(0)$ can be achieved by an investment in them. Consequently, by selling pure discount bonds short or by issuing them and buying the immunized portfolio, one can earn the riskless arbitrage profit, $W_q(\lambda) - W_q(0) \geq 0$. The stochastic process generating $W_q(\lambda)$ is thus inconsistent with a competitive equilibrium in these circumstances.

Of course, if markets are incomplete because the pure discount bonds are unavailable and cannot be created and if bonds of the same maturity all have the same coupon rates, the arbitrage operation just described cannot be undertaken.[12] In that event the stochastic processes used may be consistent with a competitive equilibrium and the issue as to whether they are appropriate processes is an empirical one.

On the other hand, there exist stochastic processes that preclude profitable and riskless arbitrage under competitive conditions. Most of these processes have been specified in the form of stochastic differential equations. These processes, as developed in Vasicek [44], Cox, Ingersoll, and Ross [15], Brennan and Schwartz [14], and Richard [45], are designed to show how bond prices behave over time as a consequence of an underlying process describing interest rate fluctuations. Immunization in this framework is comparable to a perfect hedge continuously undertaken so that a certain rate of return on investment can be calculated for every period in the planning horizon. In effect, markets are assumed to be complete, and the prices of all securities are related to a single underlying stochastic process having properties that rule out profitable and riskless arbitrage.

Bierwag [4] has recently undertaken a similar approach in a discrete framework. In this framework, the possible future term structures are generated by a finite number of possible probability distributions. Thus, if state s_j occurs, $j = 1, 2, \ldots, K$, in a K-state model, the term structure corresponding to that state is generated by a particular probability distribution unique to that state. In this model the markets are complete if one can identify K securities having independent price movements and such that the price behavior of all other securities are identical to the price behavior of portfolios of these K fundamental or primary securities. Assuming that no portfolio of these securities can dominate any other portfolio for all K states, profitable and riskless arbitrage opportunities are ruled out under competitive conditions. Using the stochastic processes implicit in the assumed probability distributions, it is shown that the prices of a bond of duration D will behave like a pure discount bond of maturity D. Thus, even though pure discount bonds are not available, the assumption of complete markets with the specified stochastic process implies that there are bonds having prices that fluctuate in a manner so as to produce the same return as a pure discount bond. An example of such a stochastic process is the generalized additive stochastic process (GASP) which is appropriate for a two-state model. A special case of this process is one in which the discount factor $[1 + h(0,t]^{-t}$, derived from a currently observed term structure, is subject to an additive random shock that is independent of t. If the flows on a portfolio are represented, as s(t), t = 1, 2, 3, . . . , N, the duration of the portfolio is given implicitly by the formula

$$[1 + h(0,D)]^D = \frac{\sum_{2}^{N} s(t)[1 + h(0,t)]^t}{\sum_{1}^{N} s(t)[1 + h(0,t)]^{-t}} , \qquad (22)$$

for D > 1 and when the maturity of the bond is one period the duration is equal to one. A derivation of equation (22) is developed in Appendix E. Virtually any bond having the duration D is equivalent to this one including a zero coupon bond of maturity D. If the stochastic process is one of the GASP variety, then an immunization strategy can proceed in exactly the same way as before, whether or not pure discount bonds exist or can be created.

VIII.   THE EMPIRICAL RESEARCH

The first widely published empirical work on the effectiveness of immunization through duration matching appears in Fisher and Weil [17]. These authors use annual yield curves constructed by Durand from information on "low-risk" coupon corporate bonds for the years 1900–1968. (The first 25 of which are not used by Fisher and Weil because of their purported unreliability.) The Durand yields to maturity are available for maturities of 1, 10, 12, 14, 15, 20, 25, 30, and 40 years until 1960 when the reported yields become those of 1-, 5-, 10-, 15-, 20-, 25-, and 30-year maturities. Intervening year maturities are interpolated by assuming the one-year forward rates between these points are equal.

Fisher and Weil assume that unexpected interest rate changes occur in a discrete multiplicative fashion. Thus, $1 + h*(0,t) = [1 + h(0,t)]\lambda$, where $\lambda > 0$ and $\lambda = 1$ when no unexpected changes in interest rates occur. Fisher and Weil simulate returns for planning periods of 5, 10, and 20 years. The results from the portfolio simulations are compared with that of a maturity matching bond strategy, which locks in the promised rate of return only on the final payment of the bond and has been widely used to immunize by practitioners.

Fisher and Weil note that the yearly readjustment employed to reequate the duration of the assets with the time remaining in the planning period generates larger transactions costs for the immunized portfolios than for the maturity strategy. The relative performances of the two strategies are compared first assuming no transactions costs and then considering transactions costs—of a value per transaction not specified by Fisher and Weil. The conclusions are not noticeably affected by transactions costs.

The immunizing asset portfolio used by Fisher and Weil generally contains two bonds. One important feature of the barbell portfolios is that the short term bond is always a bond that matures at the end of the planning period. The coupon rate of these bonds is set at 4 percent. The period of analysis is from 1925 through 1968. This permits 39 overlapping 5-year planning periods, 34 overlapping 10-year planning periods, and 24 overlapping 20-year planning periods. For the no transactions cost cases, Fisher and Weil find the following:

Table 1.

Planning Period Length	Percent of time $|r_i - r_p| < |r_m - r_p|$	Percent of time $r_i > r_p$
5	77	41
10	82	24
20	96	0

where r_i, r_m, and r_p are the rates of return over the planning period on the immunized portfolio, maturity portfolio and that promised, respectively. Thus, the return on the immunized portfolio tends most often to be closer to the promised return than the maturity strategy.

As is theoretically expected, the successes of immunized portfolios relative to the maturity strategy increases with the length of the planning period. Note that the immunized portfolio frequently fails to equal or to exceed the promised rate of return. In the absence of transactions costs, this can theoretically occur only if the stochastic process governing interest rates is not the discrete multiplicative form assumed.

Bierwag, Kaufman, Schweitzer, and Toevs [6], henceforth BKST, also explore the effectiveness of immunized portfolios relative to the maturity bond portfolio. This work examines several reasonable stochastic processes previously described to see which one appears to be most frequently influencing the yield curves developed by Durand. The period of analysis is now from 1925 through 1978. A summary table of the findings is given in Table 2. This table also shows the results from the newly developed generally additive price stochastic process (GASP), which does not have a convex return function as do the others. The simulations use 10-year planning periods. Barbell portfolios initially consist of a maturity bond and a 20-year bond, both of which carry a 5 percent coupon. Both of these bonds are maintained in the portfolio as time passes. ID1 corresponds to bond portfolios constructed with the Macaulay measure of duration. ID2 and ID3 correspond to the duration formulas used to immunize against a discrete additive and a discrete multiplicative stochastic process, respectively. ID4 crresponds to the duration formula immunizing the Khang discrete multiplicative stochastic process. In this case the nature of the stochastic process depends on the value of α (see Appendix C of this paper). We report the performance of $\alpha = 1.0$ and $\alpha = 0.1$. These values assume, for a typical upward sloping yield curve, one-year rates change 3 times more than 10-year rates and one-year rates change 1.3 times more than 10-year rates, respectively.[13] IDG corresponds to the duration formula for the GASP described in Section VII.

Over the whole time period any of the immunizing portfolios generate returns that on average come closer to that promised than the maturity strategy. The ID1, ID2 and ID3 strategies produce very similar results, generating in each case returns closer to promised than the maturity strategy 86–89 percent of the time. For individual subperiods, the success of these strategies ranges from 80 to 93 percent. ID1, ID2 and ID3 also produce returns that are within 5 basis points of the promised return considerably more often than do those produced by the maturity strategy. The results for ID4 $\alpha = 1.0$ immunizes erratically and, in general, poorly. ID4 $\alpha = 0.1$ performs better but still not as well as the simpler ID1, ID2, or ID3 strategies.

The generalized additive stochastic process simulations produced the best results. The IDG strategy out immunized the maturity strategy 93 percent of the time ove the entire period and within each subperiod as well. The IDG portfolios equaled or exceeded the immunizing performance of ID1 through ID4 in every subperiod. The GASP process has a parameter somewhat like the α value for the Khang stochastic process. Little experimentation on using different parameter values has been conducted at this point. Thus, there is the possibility that specifying other parameter values could improve upon the immunizing characteristics of the IDG.

All immunization strategies frequently fall short of achieving the

Table 2. Promised and Realized Returns for Alternative Portfolio Strategies 10 Year Planning Periods, Durand Data

	Promised Yield	Realized Yield	*(In Percent)* Closer to Promised Than Maturity Strategy	Within 5 Basis Points of Promised	Greater Than Promised
1925–1978[a]					
ID1	3.364	3.288	86	48	9
ID2	3.364	3.289	89	48	9
ID3	3.364	3.289	89	48	9
ID4 α = 1.0	3.364	3.236	52	34	11
ID4 α = 0.1	3.364	3.270	82	27	2
IDG	3.364	3.298	93	50	34
ID4*	3.364	3.307	86	52	7
ID3*	3.364	3.029	20	16	9
Maturity	3.364	3.296	—	16	41
1925–1949[a]					
ID1	3.697	3.552	93	13	0
ID2	3.697	3.555	93	13	0
ID3	3.697	3.555	93	13	0
ID4 α = 1.0	3.697	3.668	93	53	27
ID4 α = 0.1	3.697	3.595	93	20	0
IDG	3.697	3.524	93	13	0
ID4*	3.697	3.642	100	60	20
ID3*	3.697	3.016	0	0	0
Maturity	3.697	3.447	—	0	0
1940–1963[a]					
ID1	2.257	2.214	79	50	14
ID2	2.257	2.214	86	50	14
ID3	2.257	2.214	86	50	14
ID4 α = 1.0	2.257	2.212	64	50	7
ID4 α = 0.1	2.257	2.214	86	50	7
IDG	2.257	2.210	93	50	21
ID4*	2.257	2.209	71	43	0
ID3*	2.257	2.161	21	36	21
Maturity	2.257	2.192	—	36	29
1954–1978[a]					
ID1	4.064	4.026	87	80	13
ID2	4.064	4.027	87	80	13
ID3	4.064	4.027	87	80	13
ID4 α = 1.0	4.064	3.759	0	0	0
ID4 α = 0.1	4.064	3.930	67	13	0
IDG	4.064	4.086	93	87	80
ID4*	4.064	3.999	87	53	0
ID3*	4.064	3.851	40	13	7
Maturity	4.064	4.177	—	13	93

Notes:
[a] The last portfolio is purchased 10 years before the last year in the period.
[b] 10 year yield to maturity at date of purchase.

131

promised rate of return. This suggests that the stochastic process(es) governing fluctuations in interest rates—at least those broadly reflected in the Durand data—are not fully consistent with the stochastic processes for which immunizing durations have been developed.

The immunization duration formula for the Khang discrete multiplicative stochastic process (ID4) when $\alpha = 0$ reduces to ID3. Because, for "reasonable" term structures, the durations of a bond measured by ID1, ID2, and ID3 appear very close in value, the use of ID4 with the correct α at each point in time should provide an indirect test for the relevance the family of stochastic processes for which duration formulas have been devised has with the Durand data. (IDG, the immunizing duration of the gasp, stands apart from the analysis at this point.) Each adjoining annual pair of term structures given by the Durand data from 1925 through 1978 was examined statistically to determine the α value most closely associated with the stochastic process actually governing unexpected interest rate changes.[14] The results of using the computed value of α at the appropriate time in portfolio simulations is given in the ID4* rows of Table 2. As expected, the results improve relative to ID4 for either fixed value of α. Thus, given these results and those for IDG, it appears as though the stochastic process(es) are not fully described by processes for which immunization duration formulas have been computed.

Rows ID3* in Table 2 report the results for portfolios immunized against the discrete multiplicative stochastic process. These results differ from those reported for ID3 because a different maturity composition has been used in the construction of an immunizing barbell portfolio. ID3* uses a one-year bond that is rolled over each year rather than the maturity bond held throughout the planning period in the barbells associated with the ID3 rows in Table 2. The results for ID3* are substantially poorer than those for ID3. This suggests that the maturity composition of the apparently immunized bond portfolio is important if the stochastic process is not correctly identified.[15] The relevance of portfolio composition and the risk of misidentifying the true stochastic process will be discussed later.

Thomas Hackett [21] has examined the performance of immunized portfolios using both the Durand data and the Salomon Brothers interest rate index data for U.S. government securities. Only the discrete multiplicative and the discrete Khang additive stochastic processes with $\alpha = 1$ are employed. His findings for the Durand data are consistent with the two previously cited studies: Portfolio returns are more often than not below promised return, the relative performance betters the maturity bond strategy, and the barbell portfolios constructed with a maturity and a long-term bond immunizes better than barbells where the short bond matures every year. Table 3 gives Hackett's results for the Salomon Brothers data over the 1955–1976 time period. ID3 once again immunizes the discrete multiplicative stochastic process and IDK is the discrete Khang additive immunizing duration. The findings for the Salomon Brothers data set are comparable to those reported for the Durand data.

Martin Liebowitz [34] reports bond portfolio simulations based on unpublished Salomon Brothers U.S. Treasury yield curves for the period January 1958 through December 1979. Almost all of the reported simulations are conducted for five-year planning periods. The one 10-year simulation indicates that longer holding periods generate results qualitatively comparable to those of the five-year planning periods. In the simulations, a new holding period experiment is begun each month; the portfolios, however, are rebalanced to maintain the equality of duration and time remaining in the planning period at the end of 12-month intervals.

Liebowitz assumes that the current yield curve will shift only in a parallel fashion. Furthermore, as time passes and given no interest rate shock, the original yield curve is assumed to remain in its beginning position. That is, one "rolls" down the original yield curve over the course of the planning period in the no interest rate shock case. Leibowitz compares the historical performances of immnized portfolios based on their maturity compositions. He finds that the worst performer for the five-year planning periods is a barbell constructed with 1- and 30-year bonds. The next worst is either a bullet portfolio or a broad (many maturity) laddered portfolio. The barbell consisting of a bond maturing at the end of the planning period and on an initially 30-year bond ranks next. The best performance reported by Leibowitz was from a short-ladder portfolio. Using this short ladder, which is not greatly different in maturity composition than the surprisingly inferior bullet barbell, the target is equaled or exceeded 59 percent of the time and the realized rate of return falls within ±8 basis points 92 percent of the time. The latter results are similar to simulations reported above, although Leibowitz's methodological approach is quite different.

The empirical results of Fisher and Weil, BKST, Hackett, and Leibowitz indicate that the stochastic process is apt to be misidentified. Under these conditions of stochastic process risk, the maturity composition of the bonds in the apparently immunized portfolio can be quite important. Fong and Vasicek [18] and Bierwag, Kaufman, and Toevs [9] have begun to explore avenues for minimizing exposure to stochastic process risk. The methodological approaches of these studies are given in Section IV, Multiperiod Immunization.

These studies suggest that the stochastic process risk minimizing is

Table 3.   Rate of Returns Obtained by Hackett Using Salomon Brothers Date 1955–1976

	Average Promised Yield	Average Maturity Bond Yield	Average Immunized Portfolio Yields				Frequency Return Exceeds Promised				
			1	2	3	4	Maturity	1	2	3	4
5 Year PPL*	4.43	4.45	4.27	4.42	4.08	4.38	12/18	6/18	6/18	1/18	1/18
10 Year PPL	3.80	3.93	3.72	3.81	3.14	3.64	12/13	3/13	8/13	0/13	0/13
20 Year PPL	2.96	3.38	3.14	3.20	2.68	3.02	3/3	3/3	3/3	0/3	3/3

Notes:

* Planning period length

Portfolio 1 assumes the discrete additive stochastic process takes place and uses a barbell consisting of 1 and 10; 20 & 40 year bonds when the PPL is 5, 10 and 20, respectively.

Portfolio 2 assumes the discrete additive stochastic process takes place and uses a barbell consisting of a maturity bond (=PPL) and the same long bond as in Portfolio 1.

Portfolio 3 assumes the Khang discrete additive stochastic process takes place and uses the same bond maturities as Portfolio 1.
Portfolio 4 assumes the Khang discrete stochastic process takes place and uses the same bond maturities as Portfolio 2.

reduced as the barbell, for bonds of like coupons, moves towards the
bullet barbell where the short (long) maturity bond has a duration just
less (greater) than that necessary to immunize.[16]

The importance of maturity composition in minimizing stochastic
process risk is, perhaps, most clearly illustrated in Table 4. These
simulations assume that the discrete additive stochastic process is the
true one. Suppose, however, the investor makes a sizable mistake by
immunizing against the Khang discrete multiplicative stochastic process
with $\alpha = 1.0$. The planning period is five years, and immunization is
attempted using barbells with a maximum term of six years for the
short bond (S), which is shorter than that necessary to immunize against
either one of the two stochastic process at issue here, and a maximum
term of 40 years for the long bond (W). All bonds are assumed to carry
a 5 percent coupon. Both Fong and Vasick and Bierwag, Kaufman,
and Toevs predict that the best barbell to use under these conditions
is the bullet barbell (maturities of six and seven years).

Under the stochastic process assumptions made, the apparently
immunized portfolios will have a true duration that exceeds the length

Table 4. Maximum Losses for Incorrectly Immunized Portfolios[†]
ID4 $\alpha = 1.0$ Used to Form Portfolio

I. Basis Points Below Promised Per Annum

S/W (yrs) (yrs)	7	8	9	10	15	20	30	40
1	−20.1	−30.0	−38.5	−44.6	−79.3	−101.1	−124.5	−133.3
2	−17.9	−25.2	−31.8	−37.9	−62.8	−79.5	−97.7	−104.8
3	−16.1	−21.3	−26.1	−30.5	−48.5	−60.8	−74.3	−79.8
4	−14.5	−17.9	−21.0	−24.0	−35.8	−43.9	−53.0	−56.8
5	−13.0	−14.8	−16.4	−17.9	−24.1	−28.3	−33.2	−35.3
6*	−11.6	−11.9	−12.1	−12.3	−13.2	−13.8	−14.5	−14.8

II. Maximum Loss as a Percent of Promised Rate of Return

S/W (yrs) (yrs)	7	8	9	10	15	20	30	40
1	−3.4	−5.1	−6.5	−7.9	−13.4	−17.1	−21.1	−22.6
2	−3.0	−4.3	−5.4	−6.4	−10.6	−13.4	−16.5	−17.7
3	−2.7	−3.6	−4.4	−5.2	−8.2	−10.3	−12.6	−13.5
4	−2.5	−3.0	−3.6	−4.1	−6.1	−7.4	−9.0	−9.6
5	−2.2	−2.5	−2.8	−3.0	−4.1	−4.8	−5.6	−6.0
6*	−2.0	−2.0	−2.0	−2.1	−2.2	−2.3	−2.4	−2.5

Notes:
* A six-year bond has an ID4 duration for $\alpha = 1.0$ of 4.90 at the time the shock occurs.
† The true stochastic process is the discrete additive.
Source: Bierwag, Kaufman and Toevs [1980b, Table 8].

of the planning period. Thus the portfolios will fail to return at least the promised rate of return if interest rates rise unexpectedly. If interest rates rise by 180 basis points at the beginning of the planning period, the average annual return falls below promised by the number of basis points indicated in the table. (The annual promised rate of return from the initial assumed term structure is 5.9 percent.) The annual loss is maximized with the widest barbell, which yields an annual rate of return 23 percent below promised. The loss for the bullet barbell is only 2 percent of promised. Note that employing a maturity bond as the short bond, regardless of the length of the long bond is quite beneficial compared to the use of even shorter term bonds.

IX. ACTIVE PORTFOLIO STRATEGIES

The empirical section of this paper suggests that an immunization strategy may be useful in hedging interest rate risk if the stochastic process is identified correctly. Immunization, which as Section IV points out is a maximin strategy, is not a desired strategy for every investor. If an investor has expectations of interest rate movements that run counter to market predictions, then following an immunization strategy precludes the opportunity of realizing higher returns. An investor may well maximize expected utility by following more active portfolio strategies. These strategies involve constructing portfolios whose durations are either greater than or less than that required to immunize. It is as a tool for measuring and managing interest rate risk that the full potential of duration analysis is realized. It is, therefore, appropriate that this section concludes the paper.

The expected return and risk on a default-free bond portfolio are functionally related to (1) the cash flow of the portfolio as reflected in the duration of the portfolio, (2) the conditions in the market place as reflected in the stochastic process governing interest rate movements, (3) the investor's planning period, and (4) the probability distribution associated with an investor's assessment of what the direction and size of interest rate changes are relative to the market expectation. In the following analysis, which is based on work by Kaufman [26] and Bierwag, Kaufman, and Toevs (BKT) [10], we will ignore stochastic process risk (2, above) and the risk of misspecifying the probability distribution on interest rate changes (4, above). Thus, the determinants of the expected rate of return E and the appropriate measure of risk R may be written as

$$E = E(D_t, v_t) \qquad \text{for all } t < q$$
$$R = R(D_t, v_t) \qquad \text{for all } t < q,$$

where D_t is the duration of the portfolio given the stochastic process at time t, q is the planning period length, and v is the time remaining in the planning period.

If the investigator immunizes, then $E \geq q$ and $R = R_I$, where p is the promised rate of return.[17] If the investor constructs a portfolio for which $D_t \neq v_t$ at any $t < q$, then $E \geq p$ and $R > R_I$. The greater $| D_t - v_t |$, the more active the portfolio. Thus, duration can be used not only to hedge interest rates, but also to measure the risk-return trade-offs adopted by investors pursuing active strategies.

To demonstrate the risk-return frontier following BKT [10], assume an investor with an eight-year planning period has correctly specified the stochastic process. Furthermore, for the sake of simplicity, assume the investor believes that there will be only one shock during the current period and that it is of the discrete additive type. The shock size is fixed in absolute value but not in its direction. The risk (standard deviation)–expected return frontiers for various probability distributions for a shock size of ± 100 basis points are shown in Figure 3. Each frontier is linear. This linearity is attributable to the Bernoulli (two-state) process governing interest rate changes. Multi-nomial processes give curved frontiers.

If the investor places the probability of a $+100$-basis-point shock at 90 percent (Pr = 0.9) and a -100-basis-point shock at 10 percent, then the expected frontier would be the line AB in Figure 3. If Pr = 0.6, then the frontier is given as line AC.[18] The duration of the portfolio, given q and Pr, fixes the position on the frontier. For example, suppose Pr = 0.9 and D = 6. The expected return would exceed the promised rate of 4.43 percent by 20 basis points. Also, the risk of the portfolio would be 16 basis points, which compares to the very small risk value for the immunized portfolio.

Notice that as the investor becomes more certain that interest rates will increase (Pr goes up), the same duration strategy implies a larger expected rate of return and a smaller risk value. When Pr < 0.5 and D < q (t = 0 being the time the shock occurs), the portfolio has a negative expected excess return. No rational investor would choose this outcome over that from either an immunized or long (D > q) strategy. Intuitively, these results are expected. In general as the investor's probability of a positive interest rate shock increases, a higher expected return for a fixed level of risk may be obtained by decreasing the duration of the portfolio so as to take a more active position. Figure 4 shows comparable results for instances when the probability of a positive interest rate shock is less than 50 percent. As Pr decreases the investor can adopt longer and longer duration strategies relative to that which immunizes and keeps the initial risk level fixed.

Figure 3.

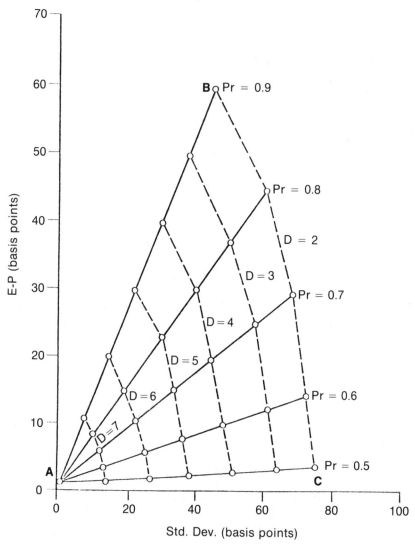

Source: Bierwag, Kaufman, and Toevs [10, p. 22]. (Bullet barbells: Additive stochastic process.)

The strategy adopted by an investor depends not only on the risk-return frontiers as depicted in Figures 3 and 4, but also the investor's subjective attitude towards risk. The risk neutral or risk loving investor will clearly pursue the shortest strategy possible for Pr > 0.5 and the longest strategy possible for Pr < 0.5. Risk-averse investors may or may not adopt active strategies. The form of the utility function in the risk-expected return space will determine how much, if any, extra return given any Pr that will be pursued for an active strategy given the associated risks. Remember, however, that all of this abstracts from the investor's attitude toward the risks associated with misidentifying

Figure 4.

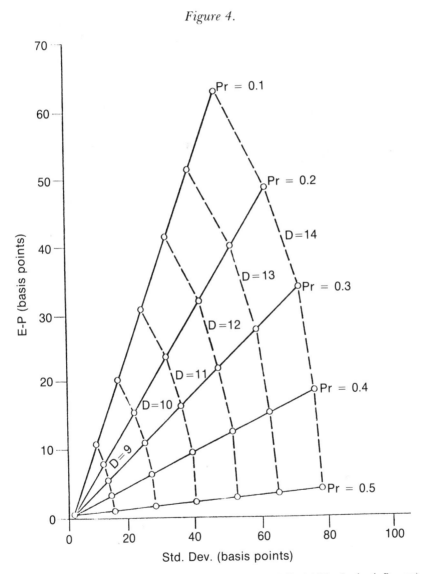

Source: Bierwag, Kaufman, and Toevs [10, p. 23]. (Bullet barbells: Additive Stochastic Process.)

the stochastic process and the probability distribution of interest rate changes.

Recently Leibowitz and Weinberger [35] have integrated active and passive strategies into a new approach called contingent immunization. The investor sets an acceptable rate of return over the planning period below that obtainable from an immunization strategy. The investor then pursues an active strategy based upon the direction in which he believes interest rates will move. If the investor can out predict the market, the active strategy will be successful and the portfolio return over the planning period will exceed that of the immunization strategy. If the active strategy begins to fail, the investor is automatically switched to an immunization strategy at the point where it is still possible to earn the acceptable rate of return over the planning period. This "dynamic" portfolio strategy enables investors to exercise their active management skills, but it limits the losses that can thereby be incurred. The immunization strategy is thus contingent upon experiencing an opportunity loss of a predetermined amount that is regarded as acceptable. By pursuing this strategy, the investor gains the opportunity to acquire the rewards of active management at the possible cost of a limited loss.

Figure 5 provides a graphical elaboration on these points. Assume the initially promised rate for a 5 year planning period is 12 percent. This can be obtained by immunizing the portfolio. Suppose further

Figure 5. Potential Rate of Return on Original Investment for the Entire Planning Period if the Portfolio is Immunized Over the Time Remaining in the Planning Period.

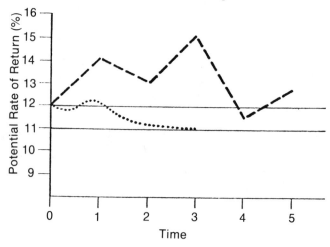

that an 11 percent return is acceptable to the investor over the same period, as a trade-off for a possible return higher than the immunization return. The manager is allowed to adopt an active strategy at each point in time so long as immunization at this time would create a portfolio value at the end of the planning period that returns at least 11 percent on the initial investment. The dashed line indicates the execution of successful active management. Immunization for a two-year period after three years of active management would have returned 15 percent on the original investment, far greater than the 12.5 percent that actually took place over five years of active management. The 15 percent need not be obtained because the rules of play allow the successful manager to lose these past gains. (There is of course no obligation for the successful manager to follow active strategies continuously. If the manager or the investor thinks active strategies in any year to be too risky, he can voluntarily immunize.) Indeed, under Leibowitz's rules immunization (for one year) need not be undertaken at year 4. The dotted line shows the course of an unsuccessful active manager. At year 3 at the current yields and at the current market value of the portfolio only 11 percent can be obtained for the initial portfolio over a five-year period. The manager is forced to immunize for the remainder of the planning period.

One might ask whether or not an immunized portfolio can be changed back into an active strategy. The unsuccessful manager cannot reinstate an active strategy during the planning period. A successful manager, who may have immunized to lock in past gains in the face of growing uncertainty in his interest rate predictions, has the potential to reinstate an active strategy at some future date during the planning period. But it should be stressed that once one voluntarily initiates an immunized portfolio, it may be impossible to switch back to an active strategy under the rules of contingent immunization. Interest rate movements could be such that at points other than at the end of the immunized period the portfolio value may be below that necessary at current interest rates to generate the minimum acceptable return on the initial investment.

Leibowitz reports simulations indicating the chance that an active strategy might have to be immunized after one shock can be surprisingly small even for quite active strategies. For example, suppose that the promised rate over a five-year planning period is 12 percent and an 11 percent rate of return is acceptable over a period from four to six years. No single change in yields can take place at the beginning of the planning period that will drive an active strategy using anything from a 4.5- to a 20-year bond's expected rate below 11 percent (the immunizing bond has approximately a seven-year term). For a ± 400-basis-point shock the portfolio could be in anything from 3.5-year bonds to 23-year bonds.

The approaches to active strategies of BKT [10], Marshall and Yawitz [38], and Leibowitz and Weinberger [35] can easily be integrated. Contingent immunization at least initially allows managers the opportunity to use active strategies. As they do so they need to decide how much risk they should adopt given the strength of their convictions about future movements in interest rates. The analytical framework proposed by BKT is useful in comparing the manager's or investor's subjective risk-return trade-off against that expected from a probabilistic assessment of interest rate changes.

APPENDIX A: REDINGTON'S THEORY

Redington considers an insurance company that has projected liability outflows L(t) at time t in the future and anticipated inflows of A(t) at time t in the future. If r is an appropriate discount rate so that $(1 + r)^{-1}$ = v is a discount factor we can evaluate these streams as

$$V_A = \sum V^t A(t) = \sum v^t L(t) = V_L , \qquad (A1)$$

where it is assumed that $V_A = V_L$. Any excess assets which equal net worth are regarded as "free" funds to be separately invested. If interest rates change to $(r + \Delta r)$, we can evaluate the resulting difference in $V_A - V_L$ as

$$\Delta(V_A - V_L) = (V_A - V_L) + \Delta r \frac{d(V_A - V_L)}{dr}$$

$$+ \frac{(\Delta r)^2}{2!} \frac{d^2(V_A - V_L)}{dr^2} + \cdots , \qquad (A2)$$

using a Taylor's expansion around Δr. Redington points out that the main effect of the change Δr occurs in the second term if Δr is small, and that a second-order condition for $\Delta(V_A - V_L)$ to be positive is that the third term be positive. Thus, two conditions for immunization are advanced:

$$\frac{d(V_A - V_L)}{dr} = 0 \qquad (A3)$$

$$\frac{d^2(V_A - V_L)}{dr^2} > 0 . \qquad (A4)$$

The first condition is interpreted as an equality of the "mean terms" of the assets and liability flows. The second condition is interpreted as meaning that the "spread" of the asset flows should exceed the liability flows. The first condition is the same as equating the Macaulay durations, and the second has been subsequently interpreted as a measure of risk by Fong and Vasicek [1980] and as a measure of the "inertia" of the portfolio or as the degree to which terminal wealth is a local convex function of Δr by Bierwag [1977, 1979].

APPENDIX B: FISHER AND WEIL'S THEOREM

As noted in the text, Fisher and Weil [1971] utilized a term structure given as h,t), $t \geq 0$ to evaluate asset flows. Thus, the value of the assets can be expressed as

$$V_A = \int_0^N A(t)e^{-h(0,t)t} \, dt \, . \tag{B1}$$

This approach differs from Redington's in that $h(0,t)$ is allowed to vary with t. The target value of the investment can be expressed as $V_A e^{h(0,q)q}$, where q is the length of the planning period and it is the value to which V_A will accumulate if there is no unexpected change in the term structure during the planning period. After the initial allocation of assets, suppose that the term structure shifts to $h(0,t) + \lambda$, where λ is an additive shift. The value of the assets immediately becomes

$$V_A(\lambda) = \int_0^N A(t)e^{-h(0,t)-\lambda t} \, dt \, , \tag{B2}$$

and if there is no futher shift in the term structure $V_A(\lambda)$ accumulates to

$$V_A(\lambda)e^{h(0,q)+\lambda q} = e^{h(0,q)q} \int_0^N A(t)e^{-h(0,t)t-\lambda(t-q)} \, dt \, . \tag{B3}$$

The difference between the initially projected terminal returns and the actual is then

$$\varphi(\lambda) = e^{h(0,q)q} V_A(\lambda)e^{\lambda q} V_A \tag{B4}$$

$$= e^{h(0,q)q} \left[\int_0^N A(t)e^{-h(0,t)t-\lambda(t-q)} \, dt - V_A \right] \, .$$

The first two derivatives of this difference are

$$\varphi'(\lambda) = e^{h(0,q)q} \int_0^N A(t)(q-t)e^{-h(0,t)t-\lambda(t-q)} \, dt \tag{B5}$$

and

$$\varphi''(\lambda) = e^{h(0,q)q} \int_0^N A(t)(q - t)^2 e^{-h(0,t)t - \lambda(t-q)} \, dt \, . \qquad (B6)$$

Immediately it is observed that $\varphi''(\lambda) > 0$, i.e., $\varphi(\lambda)$ is a strictly convex function of the shock. Thus, if $A(t)$ is chosen to satisfy equation (B1) and in such a manner that $\varphi'(0) = 0$, then $\varphi(0)$ will be the minimal difference to be anticipated. Now, $\varphi'(0) = 0$ implies that

$$\frac{\int_0^N A(t)(q - t)e^{-h(0,t)t} \, dt}{V_A} = q - D = 0 \qquad (B7)$$

or that duration D be equal to the planning period length q, where

$$D = \frac{\int_0^N A(t)te^{-h(0,t)t} \, dt}{V_A} \qquad (B8)$$

and D is a weighted average of t, but the weights are a function of $h(0,t)$ and not the yield to maturity as in the Redington Version. It may be noticed, also, that q is the duration of a single liability outflow that may be specified as the amount $V_a e^{h(0,q)q}$ to occur at date q. That is, immunization is achieved by equating the duration of the assets to the duration of the liabilities, but the liabilities have this special specification of being a single outflow.

APPENDIX C: RANDOM SHOCKS AND DURATION CALCULATIONS

Discrete shocks (Annual Compounding)	Instantaneous Random Shifts; $h^*(0, t)$ is New Term Structure; $h(0, t)$ is Old Term Structure	Duration Calculation of Bond of Maturity n, Coupon Rate c, Face Value $1, and Price $p(c, n)$
Multiplicative	$1 + h^*(0, t) = \lambda[1 + h(0, t)]$	$$D = \frac{c\sum_1^n t[1 + h(0, t)]^{-t} + n[1 + h(0, n)]^{-n}}{p(c, n)}$$ $$\frac{D}{1 + h(0, D)} = \frac{c\sum_1^n t[1 + h(0, t)]^{-t-1} + n[1 + h(0, n)]^{-n-1}}{p(c, n)}$$
Additive	$h^*(0, t) = h(0, t) + \lambda$	
Multiplicative Maturity Dependent (Khang)	$1 + h^*(0, t)$ $= \left[1 + \dfrac{\lambda \ln(1 + \alpha t)}{\alpha t}\right][1 + h(0, t)]$	$$\ln(1 + \alpha D) = c\sum_1^n \ln(1 + \alpha t)[1 + h(0, t)]^{-t}$$ $$\frac{\ln(1 + \alpha D)}{1 + h(0, D)} = c\sum_1^n \ln(1 + \alpha t)[1 + h(0, t)]^{-t-1}$$ $$+ \frac{\ln(1 + \alpha n)[1 + h(0, n)]^{-n}}{p(c, n)}$$
Additive Maturity Dependent (Khang)	$h^*(0, t) = h(0, t) + \dfrac{\lambda \ln(1 + \alpha t)}{\alpha t}$	$$\frac{\ln(1 + \alpha D)}{1 + h(0, D)} = c\sum_1^n \ln(1 + \alpha t)[1 + h(0, t)]^{-t-1}$$ $$+ \frac{\ln(1 + \alpha n)[1 + h(0, n)]^{-n-1}}{p(c, n)}$$

(Continued)

145

APPENDIX C: (Continued)

Continuous Shocks (Continual Compounding)	Instantaneous Random Shifts; $h^*(0, t)$ is New Term Structure; $h(0, t)$ is Old Term Structure	Duration Calculation for Bond of Maturity n, Coupon Rate c, Face Value \$1, and Price $p(c, n)$
Multiplicative	$h^*(0, t) = \lambda h(0, t)$	$h(0, D) \cdot D = \dfrac{c\int th(0, t)e^{-h(0, t)t}dt + nh(0, n)e^{-h(0, n)n}}{p(c, n)}$
Additive (Fisher-Weil)	$h^*(0, t) = h(0, t) + \lambda$	$D = \dfrac{c\int te^{-h(0, t)t}dt + ne^{-h(0, n)n}}{p(c, n)}$
Multiplicative Maturity Dependent (Khang)	$h^*(0, t) = \left[1 + \dfrac{\lambda \ln(1 + \alpha t)}{\alpha t}\right] h(0, t)$	$h(0, D) \ln(1 + \alpha D) = c\int \ln(1 + \alpha t)h(0, t)e^{-h(0, t)t}dt$ $+ \dfrac{h(0, n) \ln(1 + \alpha n)e^{-h(0, n)n}}{p(c, n)}$
Addtivie Maturity Dependent (Khang)	$h^*(0, t) = h(0, t) + \dfrac{\lambda \ln(1 + \alpha t)}{\alpha t}$	$\ln(1 + \alpha D) = c\int \ln(1 + \alpha t)e^{-h(0, t)t}dt$ $+ \dfrac{\ln(1 + \alpha n)e^{-h(0, n)n}}{p(c, n)}$

Portfolio Formation

Below, β_1 is the proportion of an investment allocated to the first asset, and $1 - \beta_1$ is the proportion of an investment allocated to the second asset. Also, D_1 and D_2 are the respective durations of the two assets, and D is the duration of the portfolio of the two assets.

Discrete Shocks

Multiplicative

$$D = \beta_1 D_1 + (1 - \beta_1) D_2$$

Additive

$$\frac{D}{1 + h(0, D)} = \frac{\beta_1 D_1}{1 + h(0, D_1)} + \frac{(1 - \beta_1) D_2}{1 + h(0, D_2)}$$

Multiplicative Maturity Dependent

$$\ln(1 + \alpha D) = \beta_1 \ln(1 + \alpha D_1) + (1 - \beta_1) \ln(1 + \alpha D_2)$$

Additive Maturity Dependent

$$\frac{\ln(1 + \alpha D)}{1 + h(0, D)} = \frac{\beta_1 \ln(1 + \alpha D_1)}{1 + h(0, D_1)} + \frac{(1 - \beta_1) \ln(1 + \alpha D_2)}{1 + h(0, D_2)}$$

Continuous Shocks

Multiplicative

$$D \cdot h(0, D) = \beta_1 D_1 h(0, D_1) + (1 - \beta_1) D_2 h(0, D_2)$$

Additive

$$D = \beta_1 D_1 + (1 - \beta_1) D_2$$

Multiplicative Maturity Dependent

$$h(0, D) \ln(1 + \alpha D) = \beta_1 h(0, D_1) \ln(1 + \alpha D_1) + (1 - \beta_1) h(0, D_2) \ln(1 + \alpha D_2)$$

Additive Maturity Dependent

$$\ln(1 + \alpha D) = \beta_1 \ln(1 + \alpha D_1) + (1 - \beta_1) \ln(1 + \alpha D_2)$$

APPENDIX D: THE MAXIMIN THEOREM

A new proof of the maximin theorem is presented here under the condition that there is an additive shock to the term structure when there is continuous discounting, as in the Fisher-Weil case. Let the flows on the assets be given as $s(t)$, $t \geq 0$, and let the term structure be given as $h(0,t)t$, $t \geq 0$. Let V_0 be the initial value of the flows, so that

$$V_0 = \int_0^N s(t)e^{-h(0,t)t}\, dt \, . \tag{D1}$$

After an initial shock to the term structure of an additive amount λ, the value of the flows, $s(t)$, $t \geq 0$, changes to

$$V_0(\lambda) = \int_0^N s(t)e^{-h(0,t)t - \lambda t}\, dt \, . \tag{D2}$$

If there are no further shocks to the term structure, the terminal value of the investment fund will be

$$W(\lambda) = e^{h(0,q)q} \int_0^N s(t)e^{-h(0,t)t - (t-q)\lambda}\, dt \tag{D3}$$

where q is the length of the planning period. Bierwag and Khang [1979] define a *quasi-duration* as

$$D(\lambda) = \frac{\int_0^N s(t)\, t\, e^{-h(0,t)t - \lambda t}\, dt}{V_0(\lambda)} \tag{D4}$$

which is the duration of the income stream immediately after the shock λ. Using equation (D4), one can show that

$$W'(\lambda) = e^{-h(0,q)q + \lambda q}\, V_0(\lambda)\, [D(\lambda) - q] \, . \tag{D5}$$

Consequently,

$$W'(\lambda) \gtrless 0 \qquad \text{as} \qquad D(\lambda) \gtrless q \, . \tag{D6}$$

Using the definition of $D(\lambda)$ in (D4), it follows that

$$V_0'(\lambda)D(\lambda) + V_0(\lambda)D'(\lambda) = -V_0''(\lambda) \, , \tag{D7}$$

or

$$D'(\lambda) = \frac{-V_0''(\lambda)}{V_0(\lambda)} + D^2(\lambda) \, . \tag{D8}$$

One can define the weights in the calculation of $D(\lambda)$ as

$$w(t;\lambda) = \frac{s(t)e^{-h(0,t)t-\lambda t}}{V_0(\lambda)} \geq 0 \qquad (D9)$$

so that

$$\int_0^N w(t;\lambda)\, dt = 1 . \qquad (D10)$$

Using these weights in the calculation of the terms in equation (D8), one has

$$D'(\lambda) = -\int_0^N t^2 w(t;\lambda)\, dt + \left[\int_0^N tw(t;\lambda)\, dt\right]^2$$

$$= -\int_0^N (t - D(\lambda))^2 w(t;\lambda)\, dt < 0 \qquad (D11)$$

reflecting the fact that quasi-duration decreases with increases in the term structure when $s(t)$, $t \geq 0$, is not a flow pattern that is concentrated on q ($<N$), the length of the planning period.

Regardless of how $s(t)$ is chosen (or assets calculated) $W(0) = V_0 e^{h(0,q)q}$. If an investor chooses his assets so that $D(\lambda_0) = q$ for $\lambda_0 > 0$, it must follow that $D(0) > q$ because $D'(\lambda) < 0$. Thus, $W'(0) > 0$ using equation (D5), and so there are values of $\lambda(<0)$ such that $W(\lambda) < W(0)$ for such an asset allocation. If an investor chooses his assets so that $D(\lambda_0) = q$ for $\lambda_0 < 0$, it must follow that $D(0) < q$, using equation (D11). Then $W'(0) < 0$, using equation (D5), and there must be λ (>0) at which $W(\lambda) < W(0)$. On the other hand, if assets are immunized so that $D(0) = q$, then $W'(0) = 0$, and because of convexity, $W(\lambda) > W(0)$ for all $\lambda \neq 0$. Consequently, the immunization strategy is a maximin strategy.

As a maximin strategy, one can therefore, claim that Prob $[W(\lambda) \geq W(0)] = 1$ for an immunization strategy but this is not true for a nonimmunization strategy. To some extent the word *maximin* is not very descriptive because for some strategies there may be no minimal return at finite interest rates. For example, a zero coupon bond of maturity t tends in value to zero at date q for $t > q$ as λ tends to infinity. The immunization strategy might better be described as a strategy that maximizes Prob $[W(\lambda) - W(0)]$ with respect to the asset allocations.

APPENDIX E: A GENERALIZED ADDITIVE TWO-STATE STOCHASTIC PROCESS

If there are only two states that represent the outcome of any investment strategy, then in complete markets all investments will produce a return that is equivalent to some portfolio of only two securities. For convenience, let the two securities be zero coupon bonds having one- and two-period maturities. The methodology pursued is similar to that for other stochastic processes. An investment is initially made and then the term structure shifts unexpectedly to one of two possible positions, $h_1^*(0,t)$ or $h_2^*(0,t)$, which correspond to the two uncertain states. Thereafter, no unexpected shocks to the term structure are assumed to occur. Consequently, we need only to calculate the uncertain possible returns after one period because with certainty prevailing thereafter, we simply multiply the one period return by $[1 + h_j^*(1,q)]^{q-1}$ ($j = 1, 2$) to find the return after q periods. After one period, the return per dollar on an investment in one period securities is $1 + h(0,1)$ for $j = 1, 2$, so that this is a certain return. The return for a two-period security is

$$\frac{[1 + h_j^*(1,2)]^{-1}}{[1 + h(0,2)]^{-2}} = [1 + h(0,1)] \frac{F_j^*(1,2)}{F(1,2)}, \qquad j = 1, 2, \quad (E1)$$

where $F_j^*(1,2) = [1 + h_j^*(1,2)]^{-1}, j = 1, 2$, is the price of a one-period security one period hence, and $F(1,2) = [1 + h(1,2)]^{-1}$ is the current one-period forward price of the same security. The one-period return on a t-period ($t > 2$) zero coupon bond is analogously

$$\frac{[1 + h_j^*(1,t)]^{-(t-1)}}{[1 + h(0,t)]^{-t}} = [1 + h(0,1)] \frac{F_j^*(1,t)}{F(1,t)}, \qquad j = 1, 2. \quad (E2)$$

If markets are complete, the return on a t-period security ($t > 2$) is a linear combination of the returns on the one and two period securities so that one can write

$$[1 + h(0,1)] \frac{F_j^*(1,t)}{F(1,t)}$$

$$= [1 + h(0,1)] \left\{ \beta_t + (1 - \beta_t) \frac{F_j^*(1,2)}{F(1,2)} \right\}, \qquad j = 1, 2, \quad (E3)$$

for some appropriate value of β_t.

Now consider an instrument having flows $s(t) > 0, t = 1, 2, 3, \ldots,$ N. The present value of this instrument is

$$V_0 = \sum_1^N s(t)[1 + h(0,t)]^{-t}. \quad (E4)$$

One period hence the value of this security will be

$$V_{1j} = s(1) + \sum_{2}^{N} s(t) [1 + h_j^*(1,t)]^{-(t-1)}$$

$$= s(1) + \sum_{2}^{N} s(t)F_j^*(1,t) , \qquad j = 1, 2 .$$

(E5)

Substituting from equation (E3) this becomes

$$V_{1j} = s(1) + \sum_{3}^{N} s(t)\beta_t F(1,t)$$

$$+ \frac{F_j^*(1,2)}{F(1,2)} \left\{ s(2)F(1,2) + \sum_{3}^{N} (1 - \beta_t)s(t)F(1,t) \right\} .$$

(E6)

The return on this instrument must also be a linear combination of the two primary securities indicated if markets are complete. This implies that there exists B such that

$$\frac{V_{1j}}{V_0} = [1 + h(0,1)] \left\{ B + (1 - B) \frac{F_j^*(1,2)}{F(1,2)} \right\} , \qquad j = 1, 2 . \quad \text{(E7)}$$

From equations (E6) and (E7) one can calculate B as

$$B = \frac{s(1) + \sum_{3}^{N} s(t)\beta_t F(1,t)}{V_0[1 + h(0,1)]}$$

$$= \frac{s(1) [1 + h(0,1)]^{-1} + \sum_{3}^{N} s(t)\beta_t[1 + h(0,t)]^{-t}}{V_0}$$

(E8)

and all bonds for which B is the same number, regardless of the time profile of s(t), will behave in the same way. This is the key to a new duration formulation for the problem.

For a special case of the generalized additive stochastic process, we define $F_j^*(1,t) = F(1,t) + \lambda_j, j = 1, 2$, where $\lambda_j (\neq 0)$ is an additive shock to the forward price (some restrictions are required on λ_j so as to preclude the dominance of one bond by another). In equation (E3) this implies that

$$\frac{F_j^*(1,t)}{F(1,t)} = \beta_t + (1 - \beta_t)\left(1 + \frac{\lambda_j}{F(1,2)}\right)$$

$$= 1 + \frac{(1 - \beta_t)\lambda_j}{F(1,2)}, \qquad j = 1, 2 .$$

(E9)

or

$$1 + \frac{\lambda_j}{(F(1,t)} = 1 + \frac{(1 - \beta_t)\lambda_j}{F(1,2)}, \qquad j = 1, 2 , \qquad \text{(E10)}$$

so that

$$\beta_t = 1 - \frac{F(1,2)}{F(1,t)} = 1 - \frac{1}{F(2,t)} . \qquad \text{(E11)}$$

Thus, every security or portfolio for which β_t and $1 - \beta_t$ are the respective proportions invested in one and two period securities will have a return exactly like a zero coupon bond of maturity t. Substitution of equation (E11) into (E8) implies that

$$B = \frac{s(1)[1 + h(0,1)]^{-1} + \sum_3^N s(t)[1 - F(1,2)/F(1,t)][1 + h(0,t)]^{-t}}{V_0}$$

(E12)

$$= \frac{V_0 - s(2)[1 + h(0,2)]^{-2} - \sum_3^N s(t)[1 + h(2,t)]^{t-2}[1 + h(0,t)]^{-t}}{V_0}$$

If this security behaves like a zero coupon bond having maturity D (where D is an integer and D > 2), then

$$B = 1 - \frac{1}{F(2,D)} . \qquad \text{(E13)}$$

From equation (E12), this implies that

$$\frac{1}{F(2,D)} = \frac{s(2)[1 + h(0,2)]^{-2} + \sum_3^N s(t)[1 + h(2,t)]^{t-2}[1 + h(0,t)]^{-t}}{V_0}$$

(E14)

for D > 2. Multiplying both sides of equation (E14) by $[1 + h(0.2)]^2$

implies that

$$[1 + h(0,D)]^D = \frac{s(2) + \sum_{3}^{N} s(t)[1 + h(0,t)]^t[1 + h(0,t)]^{-t}}{V_0} \qquad (E15)$$

$$= \frac{\sum_{2}^{N} s(t)}{V_0}, \qquad D \geq 2,$$

or if we let $w_t = s(t)[1 + h(0,t)]^{-t}/V_0$, so that $\sum_{1}^{N} w_t = 1$, it follows that

$$[1 + h(0,D)]^D = \sum_{2}^{N} w_t[1 + h(0,t)]^t, \qquad D \geq 1. \qquad (E16)$$

Interpreting D as a measure of duration for a portfolio, the maturity of a zero coupon bond equals its duration and any other portfolio having D as its duration, as measured by equation (E16) will behave in the same way as a zero coupon bond of the same maturity. {If $\sum_{2}^{N} w_t[1 + h(0,t)]^t = 0$, then $D = 1$ because in that case $w_1 = 1$, and $w_t = 0$ for $t > 1$.} if

$$[1 + h(0,D - 1)]^{D-1} < \sum_{2}^{N} w_t[1 + h(0,t)]^t$$

$$< [1 + h(0,D)]^D \quad \text{for some D},$$

then the portfolio behaves like a mixture of two zero coupon bonds, one with maturity D and the other with maturity $D - 1$. As shown in Bierwag [1981], this result can be further generalized.

NOTES

1. Grove [19,20] extended Redington's analysis by specifying the discount rate at $r(t)$, a function of t. Then, by allowing additive shifts of a random amount h to $r(t)$, he was able to derive Redington's result, but the measure of duration varied because r in equation (22) was expressed as a function of time. Grove also expanded the terminal value of the investment fund in a Taylor's series to show that the expected return and risk of an investment strategy could be expressed as a function of the mean and variance of h if only the first two terms of the Taylor's expansion were used.

2. The symbol $h(0,t)$ is used here largely to distinguish a zero coupon yield from a yield to maturity calculated for non-zero coupon bonds. Under conditions of certainty, the yield, $h(0,t)$, is the yield per period gained from *holding* a t-period zero coupon bond until maturity.

3.   In Redington's analysis, the length of the planning period is the same as the duration of the liability, given the liability is a single outflow on a single future date. The Fisher–Weil restatement is not basically different in that regard.

4.   An additive random shift to the term structure h(0,t) under continuous compounding is analogous to a multiplicative shift of 1 + h(0,t) if there is discrete compounding. A multiplicative random shift in h(0,t) under continuous compounding is analogous to an additive shift to h(0,t) under discrete compounding. Bierwag [2] derives these relationships.

5.   The Khang durations combine differently than do those in equations (8) and (9) for formulating the duration of a portfolio. Thus, the manner in which the durations combine depends generally on the stochastic process.

6.   Bierwag, Kaufman, and Toevs [8], as described in the section on multiperiod immunization, show that there are second-order conditions in a discrete framework that make the result hold generally and not just in the neighborhood of $\lambda = 0$.

7.   The immunization rules do not depend on the particular process, but then the rules for calculating the durations and for forming the portfolios would have to change as is clear from the table in Appendix C.

8.   A similar measure was devised by Bierwag [3] and called *inertia*; it was shown there that the portfolio had to behave over time such that the inertia decreased in order to be assured of dynamic convergence of the immunization result. A similar condition was devised by Redington [40], but neither of these writers perceived it as a measure of risk.

9.   The multiple-period planning model reduces to a single-period problem for purposes of risk-return assessments if the investor's utility function exhibits the appropriate "myopic" conditions. Also, for purposes of analysis one can often regard the planning horizon as the single period of analysis.

10.   The beta derived here is not a general equilibrium beta in the traditional sense. It is a beta appropriate for measuring risk relative to the market for a given planning period. For example, a zero coupon bond of maturity q will be risky for investors having planning periods not equal to q but will be riskless for investors having a planning period equal to q.

11.   See, for example, Cox, Ingersoll, and Ross [15] and Ingersoll, Skelton, and Weil [25].

12.   In most bond markets the opportunity to sell short or engage in futures operations so as to create hedges comparable to that of selling pure discount bonds short is restricted to short-term government securities.

13.   The returns for the Khang Discrete additive stochastic process are so close to the Khang discrete multiplicative process with the same α that they are not reported here.

14.   The criterion used to establish the best α was the minimization of the computed mean absolute deviation summed over term lengths to 20 years. Further details are available from the authors upon request.

15.   Theoretically it can be shown that wide barbells exceed in final return narrow barbells when the stochastic processes like those associated with 1D1–4 are correctly immunized. Thus, again there is indirect evidence that the true stochastic process is unlike that against which interest rate risk protection is sought.

16.   Bierwag, Kaufman, and Toevs limit the analysis to barbell portfolios and single-length planning periods. Laddered portfolios are weighted averages of barbell portfolios. Thus, for single planning periods, laddered portfolios should have higher stochastic process risk than the bullet barbell. Fong and Vasicek's measure of exposure to stochastic process risk is general to single-bond, barbell, and laddered immunizing portfolios. It associates the least risk with a single-bond immunizing portfolio.

17. There are many measures of risk. The standard deviation of the rate of return around the promised rate will be greater than zero for immunized portfolios when the stochastic process is strictly convex in its return functions. In these instances, R will be at a minimum—but positive—value when investors immunize. If risk is associated only with realized returns that are below that promised, then risk from immunized portfolios under even strictly convex stochastic processes equals zero. Such risk measures would include the semivariance and Fishburn's measures.

18. For strictly convex stochastic processes point A is actually a series of closely related points. Each one corresponds to a different Pr for the immunized portfolio. The bullet barbell is used to construct *all* portfolios in Figures 3 and 4. Changes in the maturity composition of the portfolios does not noticeably change the findings for the strictly convex stochastic processes and cannot affect the findings for the new generalized additive stochastic process.

REFERENCES

1. Bawa, Vijay, S., and Eric B. Lindenberg, 1977, "Capital Market Equilibrium in a Mean-Lower Partial Moment Framework," *Journal of Financial Economics*, Vol. 5, No. 2, 189–200.
2. Bierwag, G. O., 1977, "Immunization, Duration and the Term Structure of Interest Rates," *Journal of Financial and Quantitative Analysis*, December.
3. ———, 1979, "Dynamic Immunization Portfolio Policies," *Journal of Banking and Finance*, April.
4. ———, 1981, "Bond Portfolio Strategies in a Discrete Framework and the Term Structure of Interest Rates," Working Paper, University of Oregon, February.
5. Bierwag, G. O., and George G. Kaufman, 1979, "CAPM Betas in a Multi-Period Framework," Center for Capital Market Research, University of Oregon, September.
6. Bierwag, G. O., George Kaufman, R. Schweitzer, and Alden Toevs, 1981, "The Art of Risk Management in Bond Portfolios," *The Journal of Portfolio Management*, Spring, 27–36.
7. Bierwag, G. O., George G. Kaufman, and Alden Toevs, 1979, "Management Strategies for Savings and Loan Associations to Reduce Interest Rate Risk," *New Sources of Capital for the Savings and Loan Industry*, Proceedings for the Fifth Annual Conference, San Francisco Home Loan Bank Board.
8. ———, 1980, "Immunizing for Multiple Planning Periods," Working Paper, Center for Capital Market Research, University of Oregon.
9. ———, 1981, "Bond Portfolio Immunization and Stochastic Process Risk," Working Paper, Center for Capital Market Research, University of Oregon, Revised July.
10. ———, 1980, "Duration Analysis and Active Bond Portfolio Management," Working Paper, Center for Capital Market Research, University of Oregon, October.
11. Bierwag, G. O. and Chulsoon, Khang, 1979, "An Immunization Strategy is a Mini-Max Strategy," *Journal of Finance*, May.
12. Bierwag, G. O. and Alden, Toevs, 1981, "Immunization of Interest Rate Risk for Commercial Banks and Savings and Loan Associations," Working Paper, University of Oregon.
13. Boquist, John A., George A. Racette, and Gary G. Schlarbaum, 1975, "Duration and Risk Assessment for Bonds and Common Stocks," *Journal of Finance*, December, 1360–65.
14. Brennan, Michael J. and Eduardo S. Schwartz, 1979, *Savings Bonds: Theory and Empirical Evidence*, Monograph 1979–4, Salomon Brothers, Center for the Study of Financial Institutions, New York University.

15. Cox, John C., Jonathan E. Ingersoll, and Stephen A. Ross, 1979, "Duration and Measurement of Basis Risk." *Journal of Business*, January, 51–61.
16. Fishburn, Peter C., 1977, "Mean-Risk Analysis with Risk Associated with Below-Target Returns," *American Economic Review*, March, Vol. 67, No. 2, 116–126.
17. Fisher, Lawrence and Roman Weil, 1971, "Coping with the Risk of Interest Rate Fluctuations Returns to Bondholders from Naive and Optimal Strategies," *Journal of Business*, October.
18. Fong, Gifford, and Oldrich Vasicek, 1980, "A Risk Minimizing Strategy for Multiple Liability Immunization," Working Paper, September, 15.
19. Grove, M. A., 1966, "A Model of the Maturity Profile of the Balanced Sheet," *Metroeconomica*, Vol. 18, April, 40–55.
20. Grove, M. A., 1974, "On 'Duration' and the Optimal Maturity Structure of the Balance Sheet," *The Bell Journal of Economics and Management Science*, Autumn, Vol. 5, No. 2, 696–709.
21. Hackett, T., 1978, *A Simulation Analysis of Immunization Strategies Applied to Bond Portfolios*, Doctoral Dissertation, Department of Economics, University of Oregon.
22. Hessel, Christopher A., and Lucy Huffman, 1980, "The Effect of Taxation on Immunization and Duration Estimation," Working Paper, Baruch College, City University of New York.
23. Hicks, John R., 1946, *Value and Capital*, 2nd ed. The Clarendon Press, Oxford.
24. Hopewell, Michael and George G. Kaufman, 1973, "Bond Price Volatility and Years to Maturity," *American Economic Review*, September, 749–753.
25. Ingersoll, Jonathan E., Jr., Jeffrey Skelton, and Roman Weil, 1978, "Duration Forty Years, Later," *Journal of Financial and Quantitative Analysis*, November.
26. Kaufman, George G., 1978, "Measuring Risk and Return for Bonds: A New Approach," *Journal of Bank Research*, Summer, 82–90.
27. ———, 1980, "Duration, Planning Period, and Tests of the Capital Asset Pricing Model," *Journal of Financial Research*, Spring, Vol. III, No. 1, 1–9.
28. Khang, Chulsoon, 1979, "Bond Immunization When Short-Term Rates Fluctuate More Than Long-Term Rates," *Journal of Financial and Quantitative Analysis*, December.
29. Khang, Chulsoon, 1980, "A Dynamic Global Portfolio Immunization Strategy in the World of Multiple Interest Rate Changes," Working Paper, Department of Economics, University of Oregon.
30. Lanstein, Ronald, and William F. Sharpe, 1978, "Duration and Security Risk," *Journal of Financial and Quantitative Analysis*, November, 653–668.
31. Leibowitz, Martin L., 1980, "Bond Immunization: A Procedure for Realizing Target Levels of Return," Appendix F in *Pros and Cons of Immunization*, Salomon Brothers.
32. ———, 1980, "Bond Immunization—Part II: Portfolio Rebalancing," Appendix G in *Pros and Cons of Immunization*, Salomon Brothers.
33. ———, 1980, "Bond Immunization—Part III: The Yield Curve Case," Appendix H in *Pros and Cons of Immunization*, Salomon Brothers.
34. ———, 1980, "Theory and Practice," *Pros and Cons of Immunization*, Salomon Brothers.
35. Leibowitz, Martin L. and Alfred Weinberger, 1981, "Contingent Immunization: A New Procedure for Structured Active Management," Salomon Brothers memorandum.
36. Livingston, Miles, 1978, "Duration and Risk Assessment for Bonds and Common Stocks: A Note." *Journal of Finance*, March, 293–295.
37. Macaulay, F. R., 1938, *Some Theoretical Problems Suggested by the Movements of Interest Rates, Bond Yields, and Stock Prices in the U.S. Since 1856*, New York: National Bureau of Economic Research.

38. Marshall, William J. and Jess B. Yawitz, 1979, "Fixed Income Portfolios: Lower Bounds on Performance Throughout the Intended Holding Period," Working Paper, Washington University.

39. Meiselman, David, 1962, *The Term Structure of Interest Rates*, Englewood Cliffs, N.J.: Prentice-Hall.

40. Redington, F. M., 1952, "Review of the Principle of Life Office Valuations," *Journal of the Institute of Actuaries*, Vol. 18, 286–340.

41. Reilly, Frank K. and Rupinder S. Sidhu, 1980, "The Many Uses of Bond Duration," *Financial Analysts Journal*, July–August, 58–72.

42. Richard, Scott F., 1978, "An Arbitrage Model of the Term Structure of Interest Rates," *Journal of Financial Economics*, March, 33–57.

43. Samuelson, P. A., 1945, "The Effect of Interest Rate Increases on the Banking System," *American Economic Review*, March, 16–27.

44. Vasicek, O., 1977, "An Equilibrium Characterization by the Term Structure," *Journal of Financial Economics*, November.

45. Wallas, G. E., 1959, "Immunization," *Journal of the Institute of Actuaries Students' Society*, Vol. 15, 345–57.

46. Weinstein, M., 1980, 1981, "The Systematic Risk of Corporate Bonds," Working Paper, University of Chicago, *Journal of Financial and Quantitative Analysis*.

COMMENTS

William Sharpe

Bierwag, Kaufman, and Toevs [1] have admirably summarized the literature on bond portfolio immunization. Not inappropriately, many of their references are to their own work. Bierwag and Kaufman, especially, have made major contributions to this literature, and this paper adds to that enviable record.

Since the paper is broad in its coverage, it seems appropriate to take a similar approach in discussing it. I will concentrate on the role of the immunization literature and, in particular, on its relationship to the type of portfolio theory utilized frequently in discussions of stock risk and return. Many of my comments are covered in the paper by Brennan and Schwartz [2] and are undoubtedly dealt with in some of the other papers presented here. A few of the ideas were also covered in a paper by Ronald Lanstein and William F. Sharpe [3] that may set an all-time record for lack of impact on a field (based on the evidence from the papers presented here).

159

A key issue concerns the concept of a *yield curve*, whether presented as a set of spot rates, a set of forward rates, or (even more offensive) a set of rates on various coupon bonds. Such a representation seems at best a circuitous way to describe a set of prices. In other domains we find it convenient to express all prices in terms of *present certain* dollars. The analagous way to describe the "term structure" is with a *discount function* (or *valuation function*) which indicates the present value (price) of a dollar one period hence, the present value of a dollar two periods hence, etc. Such a function can be used to infer forward discount rates (assuming sufficient spanning of the space of alternative cash flows and the usual arbitrage conditions) and, if one considers expectations theories appropriate, to infer expected future discount functions. More importantly, the return on any instrument over a given holding period will depend in a direct and simple way on the relationship between the beginning and ending discount functions.

A yield curve is, of course, a transformation of a (more fundamental) discount function. But such a transformation tends to mislead and obfuscate rather than to clarify. Thus the specification of a stochastic process for yields that is inconsistent with simple no-arbitrage conditions would undoubtedly have been avoided had the process been stated directly in terms of discount functions.

This can be simply stated in a discrete framework. Let V(0) be the discount function (vector) at time zero and V(1,s) the function at time one if states. A simple equilibrium condition requires that there be no *self-financing strategy* that provides a positive cash flow in one or more states and a negative cash flow in no state. While this condition might be violated in an incomplete market (in which the available instruments do not allow spanning of the time periods), I, for one, am uncomfortable with a characterization of the world via a stochastic process that violates this condition.

The tradition of assuming a specific stochastic process, *ex cathedra*, for the time series behavior of yields and thus, by implication, for the discount function seems decidedly inappropriate now (as others have indicated). Since at last we have adequate data on individual bond prices, empirical evidence can be utilized to estimate the nature of the actual process. The limited empirical work done prior to the last year or two suffers from reliance on the Durand data. Since Durand fitted his curves with 9 (later 7) degrees of freedom, it must be the case that a nine- (later seven-) factor model perfectly describes all the associated variation in the discount function. Actual bond returns presumably require more factors for a complete description. The relevant question, of course, concerns the minimum number of factors that can describe "most" of the variation and their identification. As discussed in other papers here, this question can best be addressed directly with the data now available.

A serious aspect of the immunization literature is its basic premise. In most cases the approach is consistent with the maximization of a utility function having as an argument the net worth of an organization or individual at a single time (the end of the "planning period"). Moreover, this utility function in effect exhibits zero risk tolerance (infinite risk aversion). As the authors point out, the immunization approach is consistent with a maximin strategy. In a sense it finds one point on an efficient frontier in risk-return space (the point appropriate for someone with zero risk tolerance) and ignores the task of finding other points. The utility foundations of immunization theory are thus radically different from those of portfolio theory. One might be excused for wondering about the appropriateness of these very strong, and very limiting, assumptions.

To indicate the usefulness of a focus on the discount function, let me suggest a simple approach to the multiperiod immunization problem. Take as given the objective of arranging a portfolio of assets so that a given stream of liabilities can be paid with certainty. Assume also that it is impossible to simply match the assets' cash flows to those of the liabilities. A sufficient condition for meeting the objective is that the market value of the assets be greater than or equal to the market value of the liabilities at each time. Now consider the one-period allocation problem. The goal is to select a set of assets such that for all possible states of the world the market value of assets one period hence will be greater than or equal to the market value of the liabilities. If the stochastic behavior of the changes in the components of the discount function can be represented completely by a linear equation in M factors, then a sufficient condition for this sort of "one-period immunization" is that the sensitivity of net worth to each of the M factors be zero. This can be accomplished by selecting a set of assets with a vector of sensitivities equal to that of the liabilities. A sufficient condition for the solution of a multiperiod immunization problem is the solution of a one-period problem in each period.

If changes in the discount function cannot be completely expressed as a linear function of M factors, complete immunization may be impossible, and one might then choose to minimize the residual variance. But this suggestion makes more obvious the limiting assumption of zero risk tolerance and raises again the larger question: Why not consider other points on the efficient frontier? Of course this involves the selection of one or more measures of risk as part of the definition of efficiency, but this is no different than the problem addressed (although hardly solved) in the portfolio theory and capital asset pricing literature.

As the papers presented here indicate, the somewhat narrow views represented by the "old" immunization and duration literature are being augmented (if not entirely replaced) by "new" and more general approaches characterized by more attention to empirical data, the use of equilibrium conditions in capital markets, and consistency with sensible objective functions for individuals and institutions. Bierwag, Kaufman, and Toevs have provided an excellent summary of their own and others' pioneering work and a bridge to the newer approaches. Moreover, at this conference they have brought together major contributors in both traditions. As more a consumer than a producer of material in this area, I feel especially qualified to thank them on behalf of the many people trying to understand how to approach the task of investing in these complicated but important instruments.

REFERENCES

1. Bierwag, G. O., G. G. Kaufman, and A. Toevs, "Recent Developments in Bond Portfolio Immunization Strategies." (Paper in this volume, 1983.)
2. Brennan, M. and E. Schwartz, "Duration, Bond Pricing and Portfolio Management." (Paper in this volume, 1983.)
3. Lanstein, R. and W. F. Sharpe, 1978, "Duration and Security Risk," Journal of Financial and Quantitative Analysis (November).

IS IMMUNIZATION FEASIBLE?
EVIDENCE FROM THE CRSP DATA

Jonathan E. Ingersoll, Jr.

I. INTRODUCTION

The old adage that "life begans at forty" may be very appropriate in the case of bond portfolio immunization. Macaulay [8] first defined duration and used it in analyzing bonds in 1938. At almost the same time Koopmans [7] explained that to reduce the interest rate risk faced by an intermediary, the maturity dates of the securities chosen for its investment portfolio should be governed by the anticipated payments of claims.

Thirty years ago, Redington [10] combined these two notions when he proved that the profits of an insurance company could not be reduced by interest rate fluctuations if the duration of the asset and liability streams were equal. He was also the first to employ the term *immunization* in this context.

The first definitive study of this result is now just 10 years old. Fisher and Weil [3] concluded that the reduction in risk afforded by a duration matching strategy is "so dramatic that . . . a properly chosen portfolio of long-term bonds is essentially riskless."

In the last decade the amount of money under management by financial institutions and intermediaries has increased substantially. At the same time interest rates and their volatilities have reached record highs. For the last five years, at least, interest in practical methods of immunization has been high among fiduciaries holding fixed income securities.

During this same interval academic research in this area has multiplied many fold. Most of it has been concerned with correcting or replacing Macaulay's measure to fine tune a portfolio manager's ability to immunize. There have not, however, been any published tests of these new models. Indeed even the Fisher and Weil test has not been independently confirmed.

In this paper, we review the Fisher–Weil findings and report substantially different findings when a similar test is performed on the quoted bond prices in the CRSP Government Bond File. In Sections III and V we discuss the differences between index based tests such as that of Fisher and Weil and price based tests such as ours. In the final section we show how immunization may be improved if there are multiple factors affecting bond returns.

II.   THE FISHER–WEIL TEST: A SUMMARY

In their 1971 study Fisher and Weil [3] examined the risk characteristics of three portfolio strategies over the period 1926–1968. Their "naive" portfolio consisted of a single 20-year bond purchased at the beginning of each year and sold at its end. The sale proceeds and coupons were then reinvested in a new 20-year bond. Their "maturity" portfolio also consisted of a single bond. Chosen in this case was the bond which matured at the end of the holding period under consideration. All coupons were reinvested in the same bond. Their "duration" portfolio included two or more bonds chosen so that the duration of the portfolio was equal to the remainder of the holding period at each annual rebalancing date. The two bonds most commonly used were the one in the maturity portfolio and the bond with the longest term to maturity.

They compared the return realized on each of these portfolios with the return expected, ex ante, on a pure discount bond with maturity equal to the holding period. A summary of their results is presented in Table 1. Their conclusion was that the "maturity strategy removes most of the uncertainty that exists when one simply rolls over a portfolio of long-term bonds. Most [sic] of the remaining uncertainty is removed when the duration rather than the maturity strategy is followed."

Taking this statement at face value could easily lead one to infer that the duration strategy substantially outperformed the maturity strategy.

Table 1. Root Mean Squared Deviation of Difference Between
Expected and Realized Wealth Relatives in The Fisher-Weil Study
(in percentage points)

Holding Period	Naive	Strategy Maturity	Duration
5 years	11.5	0.31	0.26
10 years	17.4	1.70	1.20
20 years	18.2	7.60	2.90

Source: L. Fisher and R. Weil, "Coping with the Risk of Interest-Rate Fluctuations," *Journal of Business* (January 1971).

This inference is open to question.[1] For five-year holding periods, a commonly adopted standard, the maturity strategy eliminated 97 percent of the risk found in the naive portfolio, but the duration strategy removed only 16 percent of the remainder. Only for the 20-year period test was the risk of the duration portfolio less than half of that on the maturity portfolio. Nevertheless, in terms of average risk reduction, duration matching outperformed maturity matching for each holding period length. One of the primary purposes of this paper is to reexamine Fisher and Weil's results and answer this question of improved performance.

In certain respects the Fisher–Weil study was a simulation rather than an empirical test since all of their results were based on artificial bond prices calculated from indices of bond yields and not on actual market prices. In their portfolio strategy simulations they used Durand's "basic yields on corporate bonds." Fisher and Weil dismissed this difference stating:

> Durand himself has adequately pointed out that the way he constructed them makes his basic-yield figures rather unreliable for testing many hypotheses about the behavior of forward interest rates. It seemed to us [Fisher and Weil] that, given the method of constructing the basic-yield data, even more violence would be done to the assumption required for immunization than would be found from analyzing better, but not yet constructed data. Thus, it appears likely to us that we have overestimated the true risk from following a duration strategy over the period 1925–68.

The "better data" that Fisher and Weil desired is now available. The Center for Research in Security Prices at the University of Chicago (CRSP) has recently made available a U.S. Government bond file which has monthly price data on virtually every issue of the U.S. Treasury outstanding at any time since 1925. With this file it is possible to perform true empirical tests, as distinct from simulations.

III. TESTS WITH PRICE AND INDEX DATA: A COMPARISON

There are a number of procedural problems which arise when actual prices are used in tests of duration in place of prices computed from yield indices. Because of these difficulties there is no unarguably correct way to replicate the Fisher–Weil tests. The major difficulties are discussed below.

Government bonds are not actively traded on any organized exchange so closing transaction prices are not available. Instead CRSP uses final bid and ask quotes from various sources. Ideally such quotes would permit us to gauge the trading costs in addition to the risk reducing benefits of various different strategies. Unfortunately, for certain institutional and historical reasons, these bid ask spreads are not representative of the true inside trading spreads. Using these spreads in trading studies substantially overstates the true costs of trading to large active traders.

Because neither the bid nor ask quotes can be assumed accurate, we have simply used their mean as a representative price. If these representative prices are inaccurate, the measurement error will cause the risk of portfolios with substantial rebalancing (duration and naive) to be overstated relative to that on portfolios requiring little rebalancing (maturity). On the other hand, ignoring the spread cost should bias the results in favor of duration strategies.

Ideally government bonds are all identical apart from different coupons and maturities. In actuality some are callable and some, the so-called flower bonds, are redeemable at par to pay federal estate taxes. To keep the sample uniform, all flower bonds and bonds callable within ten years were excluded. This restriction created a 15-year period from the late 1950s to the early 1970s during which there were no available bonds with durations in excess of eight years. We were therefore forced to examine only shorter holding periods or to permit short sales. We chose the former.[2]

A bond's or portfolio's duration is the weighted average of the times at which payments are received

$$D = \frac{\sum_{t=1}^{\tau} tP(t)X(t)}{\sum_{t=1}^{\tau} P(t)X(t)}, \qquad (1)$$

where $X(t)$ is the cash flow at time t and $P(t)$ is the present value of $1 at time t. With indices of spot yields $R(t)$ these present values are computed simply as

$$P(t) = \exp[-R(t)t] . \qquad (2)$$

When spot yields to all maturities are unavailable, however, it is common practice to compute the duration of a given bond using its own yield

Table 2. Coupon Rates Required on Bonds of Five to Twenty-five Year Maturities for Them To Be Priced at Par (Yields Constructed from CRSP Data Assuming Semi-Annual Payments.)

	Coupon Rates				
	Maturity (years)				
	5	10	15	20	25
1950	1.65	1.61	1.68	1.94	2.08
1951	1.83	1.88	1.96	2.14	2.25
1952	2.18	2.36	2.39	2.54	2.62
1953	2.27	2.30	2.30	2.58	2.74
1954	2.09	2.17	2.30	2.48	2.58
1955	2.06	2.38	2.48	2.59	2.64
1956	2.85	2.79	2.83	2.85	2.86
1957	3.60	3.36	3.54	3.41	3.32
1958	2.72	2.90	3.11	3.14	3.16
1959	3.86	3.85	3.87	3.85	3.84
1960	4.94	4.72	4.67	4.55	4.47
1961	3.33	3.66	3.77	3.78	3.78
1962	3.90	4.12	4.18	4.19	4.19
1963	3.52	3.81	3.87	3.89	3.90
1964	4.06	4.15	4.29	4.19	4.18
1965	4.09	4.18	4.19	4.17	4.16
1966	4.91	4.73	4.67	4.53	4.44
1967	4.78	4.68	4.62	4.58	4.55
1968	5.71	5.72	5.72	5.58	5.50
1969	6.27	6.19	6.14	6.06	6.03
1970	8.26	7.62	7.39	7.06	6.86
1971	6.07	6.58	6.59	6.52	6.47
1972	5.52	5.93	6.27	6.48	6.60
1973	6.30	6.55	6.25	6.00	5.85
1974	6.93	6.89	7.32	7.37	7.40
1975	7.37	7.33	7.62	7.94	8.10
1976	7.51	7.81	7.99	8.07	8.12
1977	6.30	6.98	7.15	7.29	7.39
1978	7.67	7.93	7.98	8.08	8.15
1979	9.59	9.38	9.22	9.18	9.15
1980	10.64	10.60	10.57	10.40	10.29

to maturity y, i.e., to approximate

$$P(t) \approx \exp[-yt] \,. \tag{3}$$

Also required is the benchmark or expected holding period return. With an index this is just R(T). Without an index, it must be estimated from bond prices. One choice is to use the yield to maturity on a bond whose duration or maturity matches the original length of the holding

Table 3A.   Durations of Par Bonds in Table 2 Computed from Macaulay's Formula (Equations 1 and 2.)

	Duration (using present value)				
			Maturity (years)		
	5	10	15	20	25
1950	4.82	9.28	13.33	16.63	19.47
1951	4.80	9.17	13.07	16.33	19.14
1952	4.77	8.97	12.69	15.77	18.40
1953	4.76	9.00	12.78	15.70	18.10
1954	4.77	9.04	12.76	15.83	18.44
1955	4.78	8.95	12.59	15.69	18.35
1956	4.70	8.80	12.33	15.39	18.04
1957	4.62	8.59	11.77	14.71	17.28
1958	4.71	8.75	12.08	14.95	17.40
1959	4.60	8.40	11.53	14.16	16.35
1960	4.50	8.11	11.01	13.47	15.51
1961	4.65	8.46	11.57	14.18	16.35
1962	4.59	8.30	11.29	13.74	15.73
1963	4.63	8.41	11.51	14.07	16.17
1964	4.58	8.30	11.29	13.76	15.79
1965	4.58	8.29	11.31	13.80	15.84
1966	4.50	8.11	11.02	13.50	15.58
1967	4.51	8.12	11.04	13.41	15.33
1968	4.43	7.78	10.32	12.42	14.09
1969	4.38	7.64	10.09	11.98	13.43
1970	4.21	7.25	9.48	11.38	12.90
1971	4.39	7.48	9.74	11.49	12.80
1972	4.44	7.68	9.87	11.30	12.25
1973	4.37	7.50	10.02	12.13	13.83
1974	4.32	7.42	9.32	10.70	11.64
1975	4.28	7.30	9.20	10.21	10.78
1976	4.26	7.13	8.98	10.19	10.98
1977	4.37	7.33	9.37	10.68	11.50
1978	4.25	7.10	9.03	10.24	10.99
1979	4.11	6.78	8.59	9.75	10.54
1980	4.03	6.49	7.99	9.06	9.80

period. Alternatively, the appropriate spot yield may be imputed from the bonds' prices.

To measure the magnitude of the effects of these potential problems, the CRSP data file was first used to construct indices of spot yields. The method employed consists of finding a single smooth function P(t) which best describes all the observed bond prices. A thorough description is beyond the scope of this paper. The method was closely modeled on that used by Houglet [4].

Table 3B. Durations of Par Bonds in Table 2 Computed from Approximation Formula (Equations 1 and 3.)

	Duration (using yield-to-maturity)				
			Maturity (years)		
	5	10	15	20	25
1950	4.82	9.28	13.33	16.69	19.63
1951	4.80	9.17	13.08	16.39	19.28
1952	4.77	8.97	12.71	15.83	18.52
1953	4.76	9.00	12.78	15.77	18.29
1954	4.78	9.05	12.78	15.91	18.61
1955	4.78	8.96	12.63	15.76	18.48
1956	4.70	8.80	12.34	15.41	18.06
1957	4.62	8.59	11.79	14.70	17.22
1958	4.71	8.76	12.12	15.03	17.51
1959	4.60	8.41	11.55	14.17	16.35
1960	4.50	8.10	10.99	13.40	15.37
1961	4.65	8.48	11.62	14.26	16.44
1962	4.59	8.31	11.32	13.79	15.79
1963	4.63	8.42	11.55	14.12	16.24
1964	4.58	8.30	11.31	13.79	15.81
1965	4.58	8.29	11.32	13.80	15.84
1966	4.50	8.10	10.99	13.42	15.41
1967	4.51	8.12	11.02	13.36	15.25
1968	4.43	7.78	10.32	12.36	13.96
1969	4.38	7.63	10.07	11.92	13.32
1970	4.21	7.21	9.38	11.10	12.40
1971	4.39	7.51	9.81	11.54	12.82
1972	4.44	7.71	9.99	11.57	12.68
1973	4.37	7.52	10.00	11.98	13.53
1974	4.32	7.42	9.41	10.86	11.87
1975	4.28	7.30	9.26	10.45	11.22
1976	4.27	7.16	9.08	10.35	11.21
1977	4.38	7.40	9.50	10.92	11.87
1978	4.26	7.13	9.08	10.35	11.18
1979	4.10	6.75	8.51	9.63	10.36
1980	4.02	6.46	7.95	8.93	9.56

Using these present value functions we next constructed time series of par bonds of different maturities. Table 2 gives the coupon rates which were required at the start of each year for bonds of different maturities to be priced at par.

Tables 3A and 3B give the Macaulay durations of these bonds and the approximate durations computed using the bond's own yield to maturity. Table 4 presents the percentage error in the approximation. For the longest maturity bonds this error is sizable at times particularly

Table 4. Percentage Error in Durations Calculated Using The Yield-to-maturity Approximation on Bonds in *Table 2*

	Percent Error				
			Maturity (years)		
	5	10	15	20	25
1950	0.00	−0.00	0.04	0.37	0.82
1951	−0.00	0.02	0.08	0.35	0.70
1952	0.01	0.05	0.09	0.35	0.66
1953	0.00	0.02	0.02	0.47	1.08
1954	0.02	0.07	0.19	0.53	0.92
1955	0.03	0.14	0.27	0.49	0.73
1956	0.01	0.00	0.04	0.09	0.13
1957	−0.01	−0.07	0.14	−0.08	−0.37
1958	0.00	0.09	0.35	0.51	0.64
1959	0.06	0.09	0.12	0.09	0.04
1960	0.00	−0.11	−0.21	−0.56	−0.95
1961	0.05	0.22	0.42	0.51	0.57
1962	0.05	0.18	0.30	0.36	0.41
1963	0.03	0.18	0.30	0.40	0.48
1964	0.02	0.07	0.16	0.16	0.14
1965	0.01	0.05	0.08	0.05	0.00
1966	−0.02	−0.13	−0.25	−0.65	−1.08
1967	−0.02	−0.08	−0.19	−0.34	−0.49
1968	−0.02	−0.04	−0.05	−0.47	−0.95
1969	−0.03	−0.10	−0.22	−0.50	−0.79
1970	0.00	−0.50	−1.12	−2.47	−3.85
1971	0.09	0.50	0.65	0.42	0.12
1972	0.12	0.42	1.22	2.36	3.51
1973	0.06	0.31	−0.22	−1.17	−2.15
1974	−0.03	−0.01	1.00	1.55	1.98
1975	−0.01	−0.05	0.62	2.31	4.08
1976	0.16	0.47	1.01	1.60	2.11
1977	0.17	0.83	1.44	2.27	3.27
1978	0.09	0.36	0.55	1.06	1.74
1979	−0.17	−0.46	−0.98	−1.30	−1.63
1980	−0.26	−0.40	−0.55	−1.44	−2.46

in the later years. At shorter maturities, however, the error is typically small. As would be expected errors are smaller when the yield curve is nearly flat.

In our tests we employed both methods. Because only five year holding periods were examined, however, our portfolios consisted predominantly of short and intermediate term bonds and there was virtually no difference in results.

Unfortunately, the expected (benchmark) yield approximation was disappointing. In one case the difference between the index computed five-year expected annual yield and the yield to maturity on a bond with a duration of five years was 113 basis points. While the next biggest discrepancy was less than 30 basis points, the difference was as large as 20 basis points eight times in the 30 years since 1950.

To allow for possible errors we used both the index and yield-to-maturity benchmarks in our tests. Both results are potentially interesting despite the divergence of the two benchmarks since, as a practical matter, it is useful to know what guarantees could be made even if the one actually chosen is not the one which is theoretically the best.

IV. TESTS OF IMMUNIZATION USING THE CRSP DATA

In our tests we compared six different portfolio formation strategies. Two were naive strategies holding a series of two and ten year bonds. The third was the maturity matching strategy of Fisher and Weil.

We examined three duration strategies. The bullet duration portfolio held the two bonds whose durations were closest to and on either side of the targeted holding period. The barbell duration portfolio also consisted of two bonds. In this case they were the bonds with the longest and shortest (in excess of nine months) durations. The ladder duration portfolio held some of every suitable bond.

The holdings of the two bonds in the bullet and barbell portfolios were weighted so that at the beginning of each year the portfolio's duration matched the remaining holding period. The duration of the ladder portfolio was similarly matched to the holding period. Then given this constraint, the portfolio was diversified as much as possible. Specifically, the portfolio weights were chosen to minimize

$$\sum w_i^2$$

subject to

$$\sum w_i = 1 , \qquad \sum w_i D_i = D^* , \qquad w_i > 0 , \qquad (4)$$

where w_i is the fraction of the portfolio held in bond i, D_i is the duration of bond i, and D^* is the desired duration of the portfolio.

If the duration matching constraint were not included, the solution to equation (4) would be $w_i^* = 1/n$. Thus, this strategy, in addition to matching duration, assures that no single bond will unduly influence the return on the portfolio by keeping each bond's weight in the portfolio to a modest level. We adopted this criterion to achieve a diversified portfolio. Even though idiosyncratic risk is not as important a factor in the bond market as it is in the stock market, diversification should still be useful for reducing risk.

In other respects the test was the same as Fisher and Weil's. The reported figures in Table 5 show the root mean squared deviations (RMSD) on an annualized yield basis between the target return and the realized return, over the period 1950–1979. The first column contains the results for the test using an index imputed expectation and exact durations. The second column gives the results for the approximation test. In the latter test the expected yield is set equal to the initial yield to maturity on a bond of five years duration and each bond's duration is calculated using its own yield to maturity. The theoretical justification for this second test is not sound; however, it does have the practical advantage of requiring no estimation of the term structure. Despite our stated misgivings about this expectations approximation, there is very little difference in results.

Unlike the results presented by Fisher and Weil, here it is difficult to conclude that duration matching outperforms maturity matching in terms of risk reduction. However, the most striking feature of our

Table 5.   Root and Mean Squared Difference (in Basis Points) of Actual Yield and Target Yield for Six Portfolio Strategies Over Five-year Holding Periods from 1950–1979

	Root Mean Squared Difference of Yields (Basis Points)	
	Index Target	Yield-to-Maturity Target
Naive Strategies:		
2 year bonds	58.7	65.0
10 year bonds	97.9	99.6
Maturity Strategy	34.6	36.2
Duration Strategies:		
bullet	35.1	32.3
barbell	39.7	36.2
ladder	28.7	34.8

results when compared to those of Fisher and Weil is how great a portion of the risk actually remains. They reported differences in wealth relatives rather than in terms of yields; so our figures are not directly comparable. However, they also gave year-by-year results from which an annualized yield measure can be calculated. Over the period 1950–1968 their five-year maturity and duration portfolios had RMSDs of only 3.22 and 2.42 basis points.[3]

Other rebalancing intervals were also tested with similar results. No appreciable decrease in risk was realized from semiannual or monthly restructuring of the portfolios. In some instances performance was poorer.

Ten- and 15-year horizons were also examined by including the highest priced flower bonds. The RMSDs in annualized yields were smaller on average, but in no case was any less than 25 basis points.

For the period before 1950 duration matching proved to be even worse at immunization. Over the entire period of CRSP data 1926–1979 the RMSDs in yields for duration matching were greater than 80 basis points for all three strategies. Maturity matching, however, had only a slightly higher RMSD, close to 40 basis points.

V. RECONCILING THE DIFFERENCES: FURTHER TESTS

What possible explanation is there for this discrepancy? Obviously, the returns on bonds as calculated from the CRSP data are substantially more volatile about their yields than are bond returns imputed from Durand's indices. The difference in the results must arise from problems with measuring the true anticipated or target yields, inaccuracy in the CRSP data or the index-constructed prices, or some combination of these.

One way to test immunization theory independently of expectations is to compare the returns on different portfolios which have been immunized for the same holding period. If immunization is possible and duration is the proper measure of risk, then identically immunized portfolios should have realized returns equal to those anticipated and, therefore, equal to each other.

The two best performing duration portfolios were the bullet and ladder with RMSDs of 35.1 (32.3) and 28.7 (34.8) basis points, respectively. The root-mean-squared deviations between realized returns on these two portfolios was 28.2 basis points, almost as large as the RMSDs from the expected yield. It is very unlikely, therefore, that errors in expected returns account for the differences in our results.

The only apparent problem with the CRSP price data is that the mean of the reported bid and ask prices might not be representative of the actual market price. If this were the case, then the measurement error in prices at each trade would introduce noise into the measured return on the portfolio causing the risk to be overstated. This explanation seems unlikely. The maturity-matched portfolio requires very little trading, only reinvestmet of the coupons, but the difference in results between our study and Fisher and Weil's is almost as great here as it is for the duration-matched portfolios.

On the other hand, it may be that the use of index-constructed prices removes too much of the individual bonds' characteristics including, of course, any market inefficiencies in their prices making them all too similar in performance. This is particularly true when the index is constructed, as was Durand's, by fitting a yield curve to the yields to maturity on coupon-bearing bonds. Except when the term structure is flat, yields on coupon bonds of the same maturity can differ. The Durand yield curves average these yields together causing the true forward rates and spot yields to be substantially smoothed.

To determine if the Fisher–Weil results were due to the special smoothing properties of Durand's (or a similarly constructed) index or would be common to tests employing any kind of index-constructed prices, we used Houglet's [4] methodology to compute spot yields for all maturities by fitting a single discount function P(t). This method directly fits the spot yield curve to bond prices and avoids the problem mentioned above. These were next used to reconstruct prices for par bonds with maturities 1 through 10 years. The immunization test was performed a second time on these artificial prices. The root-mean-squared deviation on the ladder duration portfolio decreased from 28.7 to 17.52 basis points. The RMSD on the maturity matched portfolio was even more improved. It fell from 34.6 to 9.86 basis points.

These findings indicate that the use of any index probably understates the amount of risk in a bond portfolio (at least when computed from CRSP data). Further it underscores the fact that indices constructed from yield to maturity yield curves, as is Durand's, likely smooth things to an even greater extent.

To understand why this smoothing is damaging, it is important to know how interest rates of different maturities evolve over time. Using the imputed spot yields, we computed forward rates of various maturities and examined their properties. Forward rates were used instead of spot yields because the latter are averages of the former, and therefore must have some degree of common behavior.

Table 6. Properties of Forward Rates: Annualized Standard Deviations (in Basis Points) and Correlation Matrix of Changes in the Continuously Compounded Forward Rates for Maturities of 1, 3, 5, 7, 10, 15 and 20 Years for the Period 1950–1979

Maturity	Standard Deviation of Changes (Basis Points)	Maturity:	1	3	5	7	10	15
1	205.35		1.00					
3	209.38		0.96	1.00				
5	205.43		0.94	0.95	1.00			
7	212.92		0.88	0.94	0.94	1.00		
10	200.28		0.92	0.96	0.92	0.91	1.00	
15	249.17		0.83	0.87	0.87	0.83	0.87	1.00
20	257.86		0.80	0.86	0.87	0.88	0.85	0.95

Table 6 presents the annualized standard deviations and the correlation matrix of changes in the forward rates of various maturities over the last thirty years. For period out to about ten years, the imputed forward rates all have similar variations and are highly correlated. However, since the correlation is not perfect, spot rates of longer maturities will be less variable then those of shorter maturities.

Because duration measures the elasticity of a bond's price with respect to a uniform shift in the yield curve, this finding indicates that the risk of bonds increases less than proportionately with duration. That is, Macaulay's duration overstates the relative risk of longer bonds. Table 7 confirms this using actual bond returns. Reported there are the

Table 7. Properties of Bond Returns: Annulized Standard Deviations (in Basis Points) and Correlation Matrix of Rates of Return on Bonds With Macaulay Durations of One Through Five Years for the Period 1950–1979

Duration (years)	Standard Deviation	Duration:	1	2	3	4
1	230.36		1.00			
2	264.71		0.85	1.00		
3	334.98		0.67	0.96	1.00	
4	395.50		0.56	0.90	0.99	1.00
5	435.06		0.48	0.86	0.97	0.99

annualized standard deviations and correlation matrix of returns on bond portfolios of different durations. Each portfolio was constructed by combining each month all bonds in the CRSP file with durations within one-half year of the desired duration.

As suggested above, the longer duration bonds did not have proportionately higher standard deviations. The five-year portfolio was not five times as risky but less than twice as risky as the one-year portfolio. In addition, the correlations of returns on bonds of different durations were surprisingly low when compared to the correlations of the imputed forward rates.

The former feature has been reported previously, and its deleterious effect on immunization through duration matching is already appreciated. Since Durand's yield curves and those similarly constructed would tend to smooth out this effect, it could account for the discrepancy between our results and those of Fisher and Weil. But if this explanation is correct, then there is little hope for the practical application of Macaulay's duration in immunization.

Risk measures have been proposed by Cox, Ingersoll, and Ross [2], Ingersoll, Skelton, and Weil [5], and Khang [6] to correct for the reduced variation in the longer term spot yields. Each of these modifications allows for and, in the contest of its own model, properly corrects this problem.

To test for the magnitude of risk bias in Macaulay's duration, the previous immunization test was performed a second time using Khang's measure of duration. Use of the other two schemes requires the estimation of the parameters of the stochastic process of the short-term interest rate, a task which is beyond the scope of this paper.

Khang [6] considered the case when changes in the spot yields of different maturities were related by

$$d\tilde{R}(t) = \frac{\tilde{x}}{1 + \alpha t} \tag{5}$$

and proved that the proper duration measure to insure immunization was

$$D_K = \frac{\exp[\sum X(t)\ln(1 + \alpha t)P(t)/\sum X(t)P(t)] - 1}{\alpha}. \tag{6}$$

Note that Macaulay's duration is the special case $\alpha = 0$ for which all spot rate changes are equal.

The test used various different values for the parameter α. Three different methods of estimating the anticipated yield were employed, the index and yield methods previously discussed as well as the yield to maturity on a bond whose Khang duration D_K was five years. In no case did this method of immunization outperform maturity matching and in the later period (1950–1979) it was never better than the worst of the three duration-matched portfolios.

The Khang [6] as well as the Cox, Ingersoll, and Ross [2] and Ingersoll, Skelton, and Weil [5] modifications to duration allow for the reduced variation in the longer term spot yields, but in each of them changes in all yields are still assumed to be perfectly correlated. Given the low correlations of actual returns reported in Table 7 and the poor performance of Khang's measure, it would appear that this rather than the reduced variation in long yields is the major obstacle to improving immunization.

VI. TESTING A TWO-FACTOR MODEL OF IMMUNIZATION

To examine immunization under the observed less than perfect correlation among bond returns, we must introduce a multiple-factor model.[4] We give below a simple two-factor model of interest rate behavior and test its immunization properties. We are not suggesting that it is the best such model or even an accurate one. We believe, however, that it is useful at least as a starting point for the examination of more complex, and accurate, multiple-factor models.

The two factors in this model are the instantaneous spot rate r_0 and the continuously compounded forward rate r_T at time T. For the purposes of predicting relative interest rate and bond price movements it is assumed that the remaining forward rates evolve according to[5]

$$d\hat{r}(t) \approx \begin{cases} \left(1 - \dfrac{t}{T}\right) dr_0 + \dfrac{t}{T} dr_T & t < T , \\ dr_T & t > T . \end{cases} \tag{7}$$

Since the present value function is related to forward rates by

$$P(t) \equiv \exp\left[-\int_0^t \hat{r}(s) \, ds \right] \tag{8}$$

we have

$$\frac{dP(t)}{P(t)} \approx -[\Delta_0(t) \, dr_0 + \Delta_T(t) \, dr_T] \tag{9}$$

where

$$\Delta_0(t) \equiv -\frac{1}{P(t)}\frac{\partial P(t)}{\partial r_0} \approx \begin{cases} t - \dfrac{t^2}{2T} & t < T, \\ \\ T/2 & t > T, \end{cases} \tag{10a}$$

$$\Delta_T(t) \equiv -\frac{1}{P(t)}\frac{\partial P(t)}{\partial r_T} \approx \begin{cases} \dfrac{t^2}{2T} & t < T, \\ \\ \dfrac{t - T}{2} & t > T. \end{cases} \tag{10b}$$

In this model a bond (or portfolio) has two durations which are

$$D_0 = \frac{\sum X(t)\Delta_0(t)P(t)}{\sum X(t)P(t)}$$

$$D_T = \frac{\sum X(t)\Delta_T(t)P(t)}{\sum X(t)P(t)}. \tag{11}$$

Under the assumptions made, the evolution of bond prices are

$$\frac{dB}{B} \approx -(D_0\, dr_0 + D_T\, dr_T). \tag{12}$$

Thus far no assumptions have been made about the relation between dr_0 and dr_T. Under specific assumptions this model has properties similar to those of previous models.

For example, from equations (10a) and (10b), $\Delta_0(t) + \Delta_T(t) \equiv t$. Therefore, D_0 and D_T sum to give Macaulay's duration. If interest rates move in lock step $dr_0 = dr_T = dr$, then from equation (12)

$$\frac{dB}{B} = -(D_0 + D_T)\, dr = -D\, dr \tag{13}$$

and Macaulay's duration is a sufficient measure of risk. If the movement is proportional $dr_T/\alpha = dr_0 = dr$, then again there is a single measure of risk $D_\alpha = D_0 + \alpha D_T$ which is the weighted average

$$D_\alpha = \frac{\sum X(t)[\Delta_0(t) + \alpha\Delta_T(t)]P(t)}{\sum X(t)P(t)}. \tag{14}$$

The averaged number $\Delta_0 + \alpha\Delta_T$ increases at a decreasing rate with t so that D_α has properties similar to Khang's measure.

In addition this model permits true two-factor behavior when r_0 and r_T are less than perfectly correlated. In this general case, bond portfolios will be (approximately) immunized for the holding period t if both sources of risk are neutralized. To do this, we must set $D_0 = \Delta_0(t)$ and $D_T = \Delta_T(t)$ for the portfolio.

To test this model, the index-reconstructed bond prices from the previous section were used. Laddered portfolios of the 10 bonds were created by solving the following problem:

Minimize

$$\sum w_i^2$$

subject to

$$\sum w_i = 1 , \qquad \sum w_i D_{0i} = D_0^* ,$$

$$\sum w_i D_{Ti} = D_T^* , \qquad w_i > 0 . \quad (15)$$

At the start of the holding period D_0^* and D_T^* were set equal to $\Delta_0(5)$ and $\Delta_T(5)$. After one year, the portfolio was rebalanced with $D_0^* = \Delta_0(4)$ and $D_T^* = \Delta_0(4)$, etc.

Five possible models were tested using break points of $T = 3, 4, 5, 6,$ and 7 years. Over the period 1950–1979, the RMSDs of this immunization strategy were 12.30, 8.65, 7.89, 8.98, and 9.99 basis points, respectively. As reported in the previous section the Macaulay duration matching and the maturity matching strategies had RMSDs of 17.52 and 9.86 basis points. This finding indicates that multiple-factor durations may provide a practical solution to immunization.

Extending this model to more than two factors is straightforward. One simple way to accomplish this is to pick as the $n + 1$ factors the forward rates $\hat{r}_0, \hat{r}_1, \ldots, \hat{r}_n$ corresponding to the points of time $0, t_1, \ldots, t_n$. The other forward rates are then assumed to evolve as

$$dr(t) \approx \begin{cases} \dfrac{(t - t_i) \, dr_i + (t_{i+1} - t) \, dr_{i+1}}{t_{i+1} - t_i} & t_i \leq t \leq t_{i+1} , \\ dr_n & t_n \leq t . \end{cases} \quad (16)$$

Now $n + 1$ durations are computed as in equations (8) through (11). To immunize a portfolio, each of its durations must be set equal to the corresponding duration of a pure discount bond maturing at the end of the holding period.

With a sufficient number of factors, immunizing against a wide variety of shape changing shifts in the yield curve is possible. Furthermore, increasing the number of factors above the limit of one set by all previous immunization models can, in theory, only improve immunization. Apart from this theoretical advantage, this scheme also has a practical advantage over those such as Khang's [6]; it does not require the estimation of any parameters.

There is, however, a hazard in this "free" choice of factors. The more factors that are selected, the more constrained is the immunized portfolio. Consequently, the portfolio manager has less freedom to include potentially attractive bonds. In addition if the no short sales constraints are binding, it may be impossible to immunize against all the factors simultaneously. In this situation the model offers no advice on which factors are the most important.

VII. SUMMARY

In repeating the Fisher–Weil immunization tests on quoted bond prices, we found that immunizing through duration matching did nowhere near as well as they report. On an absolute scale we found the remaining risk to be larger by a factor of 10. On a relative scale we found that duration matching could not consistently beat the more naive scheme of maturity matching. After discussing possible reasons for the discrepancy in our results, we introduced and tested a two-factor model which shows some promise for immunizing portfolios.

ADDENDUM

Brennan and Schwartz [1] and Nelson and Schaefer [9] have independently developed two-factor models and presented them at this conference. The purpose of this additional note is to compare and contrast the three models. The reader is cautioned that this viewpoint cannot be unbiased.

The Brennan and Schwartz model is a continuous-time diffusion model. It has a theoretical advantage over the one here and that presented by Nelson and Schaefer in that it is an equilibrium model and therefore not subject to the criticism in note 5. Its application, however, requires the estimation of the underlying state variables' stochastic processes and complicated numerical methods to compute bonds' risk measures. Their results indicate that such effort is not justified when the objective is to immunize a portfolio of government bonds. On the other hand, when portfolios containing more complex instruments, such as options on bonds or convertible bonds, must be immunized, pricing based methods such as theirs may be required.

The Nelson and Schaefer model is closer in spirit to the one presented here. It is also an ad hoc model subject to the criticism in note 5. The basic difference in the models is that Nelson and Schaefer use linear regression techniques to estimate the relations between interest rate movements while our model derives them from the assumption in equation (7). Both models have, therefore, assumed a possibly incorrect structure. Their required estimation may be bothersome or subject to error. In addition it imposes some stationarity on the assumed relation. On the other hand, by admitting parameters to be estimated they may get a more accurate description of reality with the same number of factors. Instead, fewer factors may be used relaxing some of the potentially problematic portfolio constraints discussed previously.

Of the three models only the one given here seemed to do substantially better than duration matching in the empirical tests. However, our tests of the two-factor model were performed with index data, and this may be partially or completely responsible for this distinction.

NOTES

1. It is difficult to compute significance levels for Fisher and Weil's results (or the results of most duration studies) because most of the n year holding periods in the test overlap with 2n − 1 other holding periods. The separate outcomes, therefore, are far from independent.

2. If short sales are not precluded it would generally be possible to construct portfolios with a single cash flow occurring in almost any year. Such a portfolio is completely free of interest rate risk over its life and solves the immunization problem perfectly.

3. Other recent findings confirm these results. Nelson and Schaefer [9] report RMSDs for wealth relatives of 2.11% on a five-year maturity matched portfolio and 2.08% on a duration matched portfolio. Brennan and Schwartz [1] report a RMSD of 1.60% on a duration matched portfolio. These figures are 6.8, 8.0, and 6.2 times as great as the results presented by Fisher and Weil despite more frequent rebalancing.

4. If the less than perfect correlation in bond returns were due solely to idiosyncratic risks rather than additional factors, then the monotone nature of the correlation matrix in Table 7 would have to be attributed to chance. Furthermore, diversified immunized portfolios, such as the ladder should perform better than specialized ones.

5. The assumption in equation (7) cannot be exactly true for all forward rates without creating arbitrage opportunities. See Ingersoll, Skelton, and Weil [5] for a discussion of this point. This paper is concerned with the applicability of this model to immunization so true behavior need be modeled only approximately.

REFERENCES

1. Brennan, M. J. and E. S. Schwartz, "Duration, Bond Pricing and Portfolio Management." (Paper in this volume, 1983.)
2. Cox, J. C., J. E. Ingersoll, Jr., and S. A. Ross, 1979, "Duration and the Measurement of Basis Risk," *Journal of Business*, Vol. 52, No. 1 (January), 51–61.

3. Fisher, L. and R. L. Weil, 1971, "Coping with the Risk of Interest-Rate Fluctuations," *Journal of Business*, Vol. 44, No. 4 (October), 408–31.

4. Houglet, M. X., 1980, "Estimating the Term Structure of Interest Rates for Nonhomogeneous Bonds," Unpublished Doctoral Dissertation, University of California at Berkeley.

5. J. E. Ingersoll, Jr., J. Skelton, and R. L. Weil, 1978, "Duration Forty Years Later," *Journal of Financial and Quantitative Analysis* (November), 627–50.

6. Khang, C., 1979, "Bond Immunization When Short-Term Rates Fluctuate More Than Long-Term Rates," *Journal of Financial and Quantitative Analysis*, Vol. 14, No. 5 (December), 1085–1090.

7. Koopmans, T. C., 1942, *The Risk of Interest Rate Fluctuations in Life Insurance Companies* (Philadelphia: Penn Mutual Life Insurance Co.).

8. Macaulay, F. R., 1938, *Some Theoretical Problems Suggested by the Movements of Interest Rates, Bond Yields, and Stock Prices in the United States since 1856* (New York: NBER).

9. Nelson, J. and S. Schaefer, "The Dynamics of the Term Structure and Alternative Portfolio Immunization Strategies." (Paper in this volume, 1983.)

10. Redington, F. M., 1952, "Review of the Principles of Life-Office Valuations," *Journal of the Institute of Actuaries*, Vol. 78, No. 3, 286–340.

PART III

DURATION, YIELD CURVES, AND PORTFOLIO MANAGEMENT

EFFECTS OF ALTERNATIVE ANTICIPATIONS OF YIELD-CURVE BEHAVIOR ON THE COMPOSITION OF IMMUNIZED PORTFOLIOS AND ON THEIR TARGET RETURNS

Lawrence Fisher and Martin L. Leibowitz

I. INTRODUCTION

The term structure of interest rates at any particular date and the interactions among term structures at various dates have long been of interest to students of money and capital markets—both academicians and market participants. Many authors have suggested that particular relationships of the current term structure and expected future term structures apply. Others have gone further by attempting to describe how the process by which interest rates change might affect the form of the term structure. Such analysis is likely to require rather special

185

assumptions about what the investor in fixed income securities is attempting to do.

The task of paying out a known lump sum at some particular future date is a well-known problem. If the investor must buy a portfolio of coupon bonds, i.e., bonds that pay interest periodically (typically every six months, but once a year for nearly all of the illustrative discussion in this paper), the problem becomes an interesting one. If the investor bought a bond that matured on the same date as the liability (followed a "maturity strategy"), he or she would have to reinvest the interest income at rates that were uncertain at the time of the initial investment. If future interest rates were equal to or greater than expected, the investor would be successful. But if future rates were lower than expected, the maturity strategy would fail. Such a strategy is risky.

Suppose, however, that the investor bought a bond that matured after the liability was due. Then, if interest rates rose or fell unexpectedly, the price of the bond would fall or rise by an amount that might offset the difference between actual and anticipated income from reinvestment of interest. If the hedge were perfect for changes in interest rates that were "small" (in the mathematical sense of the term), the investor's portfolio would be said to be *immune* to changes in interest rates. The investor who attempts to make his or her portfolio immune to interest rate changes is said to be following an *immunization strategy*. However, as interest rates change and as time passes, the relative sensitivities to further fluctuations in interest rates of both reinvestment income and bond prices change. To offset the change in relative sensitivity, the composition of the portfolio must be changed at intervals over its life if it is to remain immunized.

Under some assumptions about the behavior of interest rates, a portfolio is immunized if *Macaulay's duration* of its assets is kept equal to the time until the liability is due. Macaulay's duration is a weighted average of the *number of years until payment* of the rents (principal and interest) due on an asset or portfolio of assets (or a liability or portfolio of liabilities). Each "number of years" receives a weight that is proportional to the present value of its associated rent. Keeping the duration of the assets equal to the duration of the liability (or liabilities) defines a *duration strategy*.

It is fairly well known that whether a duration strategy is, in fact, also an immunization strategy depends on the process by which interest rates change. For example, if the term structure of interest rates were always flat, immunization would be achieved by the duration strategy. However, if short-term interest rates tended to fluctuate more than long-term interest rates, the average duration of the assets might have to be increased.[1]

Much empirical work is concerned with testing the performance of a particular immunization strategy in the face of a series of real or hypothetical changes in the term structure of interest rates. This is a three-step process:

1. For each period to be analyzed, use the then-current term structure to find the holding-period return that would be achieved if the term structure behaved as anticipated throughout the holding period. In other words, find the target return.
2. Find the actual holding period return associated with the strategy and the realized prices and interest rates during the holding period.
3. Compare the actual and target returns.

What does not seem to have been given adequate consideration in the past is that both the target or achievable holding-period return and the characteristics of the portfolio to be held depend on the definition of "anticipated" as well as on the initial term structure. This paper investigates those problems.

To provide example cases, we consider some of the implications of three alternative definitions of the *anticipated term structure of interest rates*. Their brief forms are

1. *Lutzian.* If the anticipated structures come to be, the forward rates implicit in the initial term structure of interest rates will prove to be perfect forecasters of all later spot and foward interest rates during the holding period.
2. *Rolling yield curve.* The anticipated situation is one in which each year's relationship between term to maturity and yield to maturity for newly issued bonds selling at par is the same as the initial relationship, i.e., the yield curve as a function of *number of years to maturity* remains unchanged.
3. *Fixed yield.* In the anticipated situation, the yield to maturity of each bond remains the same as it was at the beginning of the holding period, i.e., yields to each *date of maturity* remain unchanged.

Differences among these three definitions of *anticipated* may be illustrated by examining anticipated par-bond yield curves, anticipated implicit forward rate curves, and anticipated single-year returns implied by the observed yield curve of August 17, 1981. The yields used to construct the curve were those for U.S. Treasury bonds and notes that were due in a little less than one year or were quoted at or above par. They were found from the mean of bid and ask quotations certified to the Treasury Department by the Federal Reserve Bank of New York as reported the next day in *The Wall Street Journal*. The nominal yields, which are compounded semiannually, have been restated as effective rates (rates compounded annually). The implications of this yield curve were found using the formulas given in Section III.

Figure 1 shows the current par-bond yield curve and the anticipated curves for 1, 3, and 6 years after the quotation date. It is easy to see that the yield curves implied by the rolling yield curve and by the fixed-yield anticipations follow directly from their definitions. Since yields declined as maturity increased, the latter's curves fall more and more below the former's as time passes.

The observed yield curve and the principle of value additivity imply a set of forward rates which decline even more rapidly than the yield curve as the applicable date increases. If Lutzian anticipations are correct, these forward rates will be stationary; and, as time passes, each will become the short-term spot rate of interest. Since a bond yield is a weighted average of the implicit forward rates, an initially declining forward-rate curve and Lutzian anticipations imply lower and lower future par-bond yield curves.

Figure 2 shows the initial forward rate curve and the forward rate curves that will be implied if the anticipated yield curves shown in Figure 1 should actually be observed. Again, the curves that are implied by rolling-yield-curve anticipations are all the same. In this case, the position of the foward rate curves implied by fixed-yield anticipations rises with respect to maturity date but falls with respect to years to maturity as time passes. The Lutzian anticipated forward rates are stationary with respect to dates and therefore, in this case, their position, when plotted against number of years to maturity, declines rapidly.

For the investor, perhaps the most important question is how much the portfolio will actually earn each year. Even if anticipations are met, the answer will usually depend on what securities are actually held. Figure 3 shows the anticipated year-to-year returns for individual securities for years beginning in 1981, 1982, 1984, and 1987. The anticipated return depends on how much the price of a par bond must rise or fall during the year if the subsequent year's anticipated yield curve is to be correct. Again, the rolling-yield-curve definition of *anticipated* implies the same schedule of single-year returns year after

Figure 1. Anticipated Par Bond Yield Curves from
August 17, 1981 Prices.

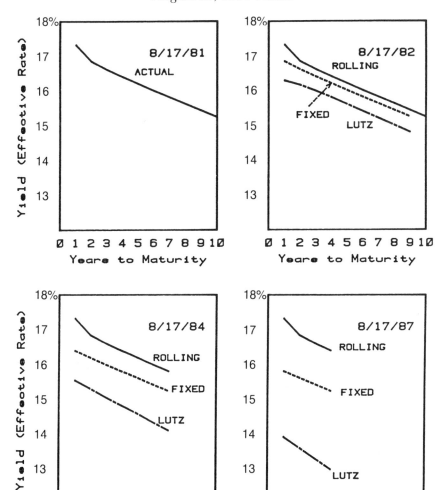

year. The fixed-yield definition implies that prices are not expected to
change. Hence, the fixed-yield anticipated annual-return curves are the
same as the fixed-yield anticipated yield curves. The Lutzian definition
implies that, in any year in which anticipations are met, all securities
will have equal returns. In this case, the Lutzian anticipated returns

Figure 2.   Anticipated Forward Rate Curves from
August 17, 1981 Prices.

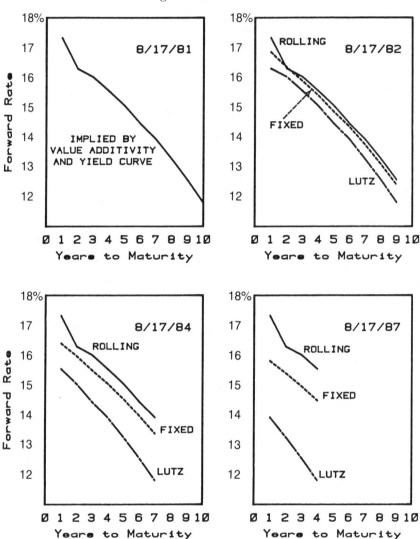

are highest of all in the first year but fall rapidly thereafter. Under
fixed-yield anticipations, the shorter-term anticipated returns tend to
be "eaten up" by the passage of time. Hence, in the case at hand, the
schedule falls, but the fall is less rapid than that of the Lutzian schedule.

From this example, it should be no surprise that, particularly in recent years, the three definitions of *anticipated* sometimes imply substantially different future values of the portfolio. Moreover, except for the Lutzian definition, the anticipated future value may also depend on the investor's intended strategy. Therefore, both *definition* and *strategy* must be taken into account in the estimation of target values. In most

Figure 3.   Anticipated Returns for Single Years from August 17, 1981 Prices.

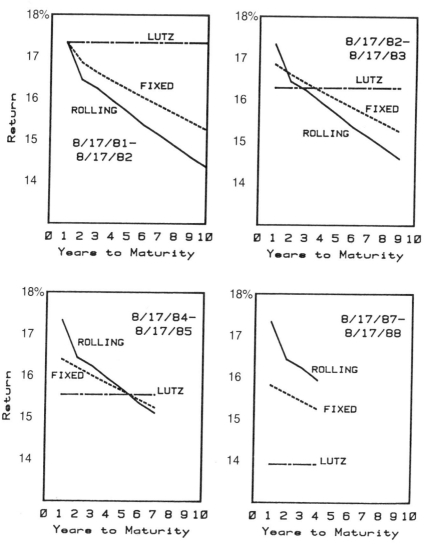

cases, this process requires examination of the intended composition of the portfolio for each year from now until the liability is due.

The *Lutzian* definition is natural under the simplest cases analyzed by Friedrich Lutz [8], which assumed either certainty or that each year's forward interest rate is an unbiased estimator of the future spot rate for that year, negligible transaction costs, and indifference to risk. It is also the easiest to analyze because, as we just noted, during any interval in which anticipations are met under this definition, securities of all maturities have equal realized returns. Hence, under the Lutzian definition, the target holding-period return may be found without considering the particular assets in the immunized portfolio. The Lutzian definition provides a simple definition of market equilibrium.

The *rolling-yield-curve* definition of *anticipated* is natural for many practitioners in the money and bond markets. They tend to describe the state of the market in terms of promised yields of bonds selling at par. Some of its implications have been discussed for many years. It forms a natural point of departure for analyzing scenarios about the course of the bond market as in, e.g., a series of pamphlets by M. L. Leibowitz [7a,7b]. Moreover, if the simplest Lutzian assumptions are modified to allow for the bias that would result because of the effect of some form of liquidity premium on the quoted spot rate, a rolling yield curve may be consistent with market equilibrium.

The *fixed-yield* definition of *anticipated* has intuitive appeal for several reasons. During an interval in which anticipations are met, each security's realized rate of return is exactly the same as its promised yield. Hence, each bond's anticipated future price may be calculated without reference to any other bond. Because of the latter property, the fixed-yield definition is particularly convenient for analyzing holding-period returns for bonds whose promised yields (yields to maturity or to call) differ for reasons other than maturity or duration, e.g., risk of default, callability, or marketability. In recent years, the fixed-yield definition has been used in Fisher and Lorie's study of returns on stocks and bonds [3], in the associated *CRSP Government Bond File* [2], and by Ayres and Barry [1]. The fixed-yield definition is also implicit whenever one assumes that the quoted yields on bonds of the same maturity but differing coupons are directly comparable, as in most analysis of "yield spreads."

All of these definitions are probably oversimplifications of what most serious students and investors actually anticipate. For example, Lutz's article [8] went on to the analysis of the effects of transaction costs and of various types of uncertainty. Ayres and Barry [1] suggested that empirical study of ex post returns could not disprove the fixed-yield hypothesis. That may well be the case because unanticipated fluctuations may swamp the differences in anticipated returns that are associated with different definitions of *anticipated*.

Particular analytical models of the processes that generate the term structure of interest rates might well imply other definitions of *anticipated*.

While *anticipated* is definitional, one's preference is likely to depend on which definition corresponds to a set of unbiased forecasts of future interest rates or bond prices. Given the present state of empirical evaluation, it is difficult to reject conclusively any of these or a number of more complex hypotheses. The primary reason for the difficulty is that many empirical studies—and not just the early ones—have made crucial assumptions that were invalid. Too many have assumed that a series of yields on actual bonds, which pay interest periodically, could be applied to hypothetical zero coupon notes of the same maturities in order to estimate forward interest rates. That is an invalid procedure for *all but* short-term bonds. Too many have simply assumed that transaction costs could be neglected, which is always troublesome. Hence most such studies are of doubtful validity.

The valid studies contradict the Lutzian assumption that forward interest rates provide unbiased estimates of future spot rates. There appears to be a liquidity premium [5,6,10]. When long-term rates are higher than short-term rates, the existence of liquidity premiums provides the rolling-yield-curve definition of *anticipated* with at least qualitative justification as an equilibrium theory. As we shall see below, if forward rates are equal to one another and the expected spot rate is equal to the current spot rate after deducting the liquidity premium from the "full" forward rate), fulfillment of expectations is also consistent with the rolling-yield-curve definition of *anticipated*. Moreover, in such a case, forward rates tend to level off rapidly; and fulfillment of anticipations also implies nearly equal returns during the coming year for all bonds that mature at least two years from now, which is also an implication of the Lutzian definition.[2] In addition, a theoretical analysis of the stochastic processes that generate future forward and spot rates by Charles Nelson [11] suggests that if errors in the forecasts implied by forward rates are positively correlated, a positive liquidity premium does not imply that the expected holding-period return from long-term bonds held to maturity need be higher than the expected return from a portfolio that always consisted of short-term securities. In other words, Nelson showed that a liquidity premium need not imply liquidity preference. Unfortunately, Nelson's accompanying empirical study is not valid.[3]

Nelson's and later theoretical work also suggest that under uncertainty, yield curves that are always flat are not compatible with competitive equilibrium in bond prices. But that was obvious from Rich's discussion [13] of the paper in which Redington introduced the concept of immunization of portfolios [12]. For example, an investor might want to meet a liability due t years from now. If he knew that yield curves were always flat, he could be certain of meeting his obligation with a portfolio whose initial market value was the same as the present value of the liability, initially by investing one-half in a note due in one year and the other half in zero coupon bonds due 2t − 1 years from now. If interest rates did not change, the obligation would be met exactly. If interest rates either rose or fell, the present values of both the obligation and the portfolio would change by nearly the same amounts. However, there is a second-order effect. If yields fell, the rise in the present value of the portfolio would be somewhat greater than that of the obligation. If yields rose, the present value of the portfolio would fall by less than that of the obligation. If immunization were maintained, each change in interest rates would bring further profit. But that would not be an equilibrium situation. Arbitragers would sell additional t-year notes and buy one-year and (2t − 1)-year notes in such large quantities that the yield curve would soon have an appropriate hump.

Empirical study of immunization suggests strongly that, for achieving a given future value, following a duration strategy to immunize a portfolio is substantially less risky than holding a single issue of coupon bonds to maturity at the time horizon. However, returns tend to be slightly less than those suggested by the Lutzian definition of *anticipated* (cf. Fisher and Weil [4]).

Organization

It should be apparent by now that we assume that the reader is familiar with the general idea of portfolio immunization. In Section II, we outline briefly the mechanics of selecting an immunized portfolio and keeping it immunized throughout a planned holding period of several years.

For Section III, we develop some formulas that point out the relationship between par-bond yield curves and forward-rate curves. We present computational formulas for finding Macaulay's duration that are simpler than, but logically equivalent to, his original formulas ([9], pp. 48–50) and a new formula that is valid for transactions taking place between interest-payment dates. Finally, we find the set of returns in the current period that is implied by the current yield curve and the rolling-yield-curve definition of *anticipated*.

In Section IV, we conduct the actual analysis of the effects of anticipations on target holding period returns. Unless the yield curve is flat, each definition of *anticipated* implies

1. A unique set of returns during each year (including the current year) for par bonds with each maturity date
2. Unique sets of sensitivities of later interest rates, yearly returns, and bond prices to unanticipated changes in interest rates.

From the first implication, we deduce that, even with a portfolio chosen without regard for anticipations, e.g., by following either a maturity strategy or a duration strategy, alternative anticipations will imply different target returns. Analyses of actual and hypothetical yield curves show that these differences may be substantial.

From the second implication, one may infer further that *immunization* as usually stated is not a precise concept. Both the anticipated future interest rates and the hazard or hazards being immunized against must be stated in order to define the criteria for portfolio choice. For each of the three definitions of *anticipated* discussed here, a duration strategy *is* also an immunization strategy. But, in each case, a different hazard is being immunized against. Altering either the choice of hazard or form of anticipations (but not both in an offsetting manner) substantially complicates the finding of both the composition of the immunized portfolios and the target holding-period return.[4]

II. THE IMMUNIZATION PROCESS

Suppose that at time 0 you had a liability of L dollars due at time t, where t is an integral number of years after time 0. At 0, bonds of all integral maturity dates are available. They are coupon bonds that pay interest only once a "year" and sell at par.

Initially, suppose further that the term structure of interest rates were always "flat," i.e., that par bonds of all maturities bore the same interst rate. Let the spot rate at 0 on a single-payment note due at t be s(t). Then the present value at 0 of the liability, under any definition of *anticipated* of this paper, is

$$V_t = L \, v(t) = L \, [1 + s(t)]^{-t} \tag{1}$$

where v(t) is the present value at 0 of \$1 due at t.[5]

Obviously, if you could be sure that interest rates would remain at s(t) at all times between 0 and t, you could meet your obligation in a variety of ways, e.g., by investing in any bonds that were handy at time 0, reinvesting each year's interest payment and principal from maturing bonds as they were received, and finally liquidating the portfolio for L dollars at time t.

However, if interest rates were subject to fluctuation, the value of your assets would almost certainly depend on the particular strategy that you had used to select bonds and on the actual course of interest rates. With most strategies, you might either gain or lose: sometimes by time t your asset would be worth more than L, but other times they would be worth less. All such strategies are risky by definition.

Nevertheless, there may be some strategies such that a portfolio which is worth V_t at time 0 will be worth at least L at time t, with probability 1.0. Those strategies, if followed, make the portfolio "immune" to fluctuations in interest rates. A portfolio chosen by applying such a strategy is said to be *immunized*. Under the restrictive assumptions of this section, immunization will almost always be feasible.[6] However, when the assumption of flat yield curves is dropped, we will introduce a more precise definition of immunization.

If t = 1 year, the immunization strategy is fairly obvious: buy one-year bonds. Then the appropriate lump sum will be received at time t.

If t = 2 years, the appropriate strategy is neither obvious nor unique. Immunization requires that the average duration of the assets be exactly two years initially. A simple and adequate strategy (so long as yields are less than 61 percent per annum) is the following "laddered" one: Divide the investment V_t between two-year and three-year bonds so that the weighted average duration of the portfolio is exactly two years. Their durations, and thus the actual division, depend on the interest rate. If interest rates are near zero, almost all of the investment should be in the two-year bonds. As the rate rises, part of the portfolio must be shifted into three-year bonds. For example, at a yield of $y = s = 10$ percent, two- and three-year bonds have durations of 1.909 and 2.736 years, respectively. Hence a portfolio of $0.89V_t$ two-year bonds and $0.11V_t$ three-year bonds has a duration of exactly two years. However, at $y = s = 20$ percent, the respective durations are 1.833 and 2.528 years; and the appropriate fraction of three-year bonds rises to 0.24. If s were greater than 61 percent, three-year par bonds would have a duration of less than 2.000 years, and longer term bonds would be needed.

After a year has passed, interest will be received. If interest rates are still the same, the duration of the entire portfolio, *including cash*, will now be one year. However, the cash must be reinvested, forcing an increase in the portfolio's duration. Hence, further changes must be made.[7] The appropriate adjustment is to hold only one-year bonds.

If t = 3 years and y = s = 10 percent, the initial portfolio worth V_t, might consist of $0.648V_t$ in three-year bonds and $0.352V_t$ in four-year bonds since the duration of a four-year par bond would be 3.487 years. If at time 1, y = s = 10 percent, the portfolio would contain $0.100V_t$ in cash, $0.648V_t$ in what are now two-year bonds, and $0.352V_t$ in three-year bonds.[8] Duration would now be 2.000 years; but, again, cash must be reinvested. An appropriate course is to follow the strategy suggested for a two-year holding-period. If the interest rate no longer equals 10 percent, total wealth will differ, but the strategy remains the same: adjust the portfolio so as to hold an appropriate mixture to two- and three-year bonds. Et cetera.

To summarize: Immunization with a particular time horizon t requires at least the following steps:

1. Select the initial portfolio.
2. Each time cash is received either as interest or as repayment of principal, reallocate the portfolio so that it will remain immunized.

The strategies just outlined meet Redington's [12] and the Fisher and Weil [4] definitions of immunization, i.e., the derivative of the current market value of the portfolio with respect to its yield is equal to the derivative of the present value of L, and the market value of the portfolio is equal to the present value of L.

In general, however, the present value of L cannot be defined until the immunization strategy has been found. We, therefore, propose an alternative definition of *immunization*.

Notation:

L_t = liability due at time t.

W_h = market value of portfolio at time h.

$TA_j(t)$ = amount of one (future value) accumulated over the period j through t under the anticipated behavior of interest rates and the strategy that are being considered.

Recall that the elasticity of a variable z with respect to a variable x is defined as

$$\left(\frac{dz}{dx}\right)\left(\frac{x}{z}\right) = \frac{d(\ln z)}{d(\ln x)} .$$

Then, at time $t - j$, a portfolio is immunized with respect to a lump-sum liability L_t due at time t if

1. The future value at time t of assets held at $t - j$, which is the product $[W_{t-j}][TA_j(t)]$, is equal to L_t.
2. The sum of the elasticities of W_{t-j} and $TA_j(t)$ with respect to the hazard that is being immunized against is equal to zero.

These are first-order conditions, they imply that the derivative of the net future value with respect to the relevant hazard is equal to zero.

Second-order conditions for immunization would require that the net future value be minimized by applying the immunization strategy. Both Redington's [12] and the Fisher and Weil [4] analyses suggest that this second-derivative condition is met easily whenever the first-order conditions are met and the only liability is a single lump sum due at time t. However, the analysis becomes much more difficult when liabilities are due at a variety of dates.

As we shall see, under the fixed-yield definition of *anticipated* and a proportional shift in $1 +$ yield, condition 2 is met by setting Macaulay's duration of the portfolio equal to $t - j$.

Under both the Lutzian and rolling-yield-curve definitions of anticipations, however, realizing anticipations implies that yields on particular bonds *will* change. In such cases, Macaulay's durations must be calculated at "horizon yields," which are the yields anticipated for the date at which the next adjustment of the composition of the portfolio will be made—one year hence in the simple case treated here. Some circumstances, e.g., a substantial change in the level of interest rates or the opportunity to make an advantageous purchase or sale, may make more frequent reallocation desirable. However, such decisions will, in fact, have to take account of the transaction costs involved.

III. SOME COMPUTATIONAL FORMULAS

The problem of finding target returns for immunized portfolios is interesting only when the yield curve is not flat. In order to examine the implications of the alternative definitions of *anticipated*, we must be able to convert par-bond yield curves to forward-rate curves and vice versa. We must also be able to state the duration of any bond that might be included in the portfolio. Finally, we must find the returns for each year under each definition of *anticipated*.

The formulas we need are not readily available. Some are scattered through the literature. Others are brand new. Therefore, we present them here.

Yield Curves and Forward-Rate Curves

Many textbooks show the relationships between forward rates and "bond" prices for "bonds" that pay interest only on their maturity dates. If such bonds were readily available, immunization would not be a topic of much practical interest because liabilities could easily be matched by assets. However, until recently, such bonds have been available in the United States only for maturities of less than one year.

The general relationship between a yield curve and a forward-rate curve may be inferred from Lutz [8] or Fisher and Weil [4]. For the purposes of this paper, which are primarily expository, we make the following simplifying assumptions:

1. Marketable securities consist of coupon "bonds" as defined further below.
2. Bonds are traded only in a spot-cash market.
3. Time is measured in years and has only integer values, 0 (now), 1, 2, . . . , t, . . . , k, ...
4. A bond that matures at time k pays interest at times 1, 2, . . . , k and also pays its par value at k.
5. At any time j there exist bonds maturing at each future time k that sell at par (100 percent or 1.00). These bonds have coupon rates $C_{j*}(k)$.
6. Bonds that sell at other prices because their coupons differ from $C_{j*}(k)$ may also exist.
7. There are no taxes, transaction costs, or risks of default.
8. Payments are made according to the original schedule, i.e., bonds may not be called for early redemption by either issuers or holders.
9. Forward interest rates and bond yields may be computed by assuming that the principle of value additivity holds, i.e., that the market value of a "portfolio" of future payments is equal to the sum of the market values of each payment.

We employ the following additional notation:

Let $P_j(C,k)$ = spot price at time j of a bond with a coupon rate of C which is due at time k,

$v_j(k)$ = present value (at time j) of \$1 due at time k,

$s_j(k)$ = the spot interest rate or promised return as an annual rate, compounded annually, for a single payment of \$1 due at time k, as of time j,

$r_j(k)$ = the forward rate applicable to the period $k - 1$ to k as of time j,

$a_j(k)$ = $\sum\limits_{i=j+1}^{k} v_j(i)$, the present value (as of time j) of an annuity of \$1 per annum payable at time $j + 1$ through time k,

D = duration in years.

N.B. When the subscript j is equal to 0, it will usually be omitted, e.g.,

$$P(C,k) = P_0(C,k) .$$

Inferring Forward-Rate Curves

Suppose that at time j a lump sum due at time k has the same present value as another lump sum due at time $k - 1$. Then by definition, the *forward interest rate* for the period $k - 1$ to k is

$$r_j(k) = \frac{\text{lump}(k) - \text{lump}(k - 1)}{\text{lump}(k - 1)} \tag{2}$$

or

$$r_j(k) = \frac{\text{lump}(k)}{\text{lump}(k - 1)} - 1 . \tag{3}$$

In a consistent system, this relationship can be defined in terms of present value:

$$\text{lump}(k) \, v_j(k) = \text{lump}(k - 1) \, v_j(k - 1) . \tag{4}$$

Rearranging terms and subtracting one from each side of equation (4)

$$\frac{\text{lump}(k)}{\text{lump}(k - 1)} - 1 = \frac{v_j(k - 1)}{v_j(k)} - 1 . \tag{5}$$

Substituting from equation (3),

$$r_j(k) = \frac{v_j(k - 1)}{v_j(k)} - 1 . \tag{6}^9$$

To find the set of forward rates, $r(1), r(2), \ldots, r(t), \ldots r(k)$, from the par-bond yield curve $C^*(1), C^*(2), \ldots, C^*(t), \ldots, C^*(k)$, note that the price of any bond with annual coupon C and a face value of \$1 is

$$P(C,k) = v(k) + C \, a(k) . \tag{7}$$

If the bond sells for par,

$$1.00 = v(k) + C^*(k) \, a(k) , \tag{8}$$

or since $a(k) = a(k - 1) + v(k)$ and $a(0) = 0$,

$$1.00 = v(k) + C^*(k) [a(k - 1) + v(k)] . \tag{9}$$

Collecting terms,

$$v(k) [1 + C^*(k)] = 1 - C^*(k) a(k - 1) \tag{10}$$

Thus we have the recursive formula

$$v(k) = \frac{1 - C^*(k) a(k - 1)}{1 + C^*(k)}, \tag{11}$$

and $r(k)$ may be found from equation (6).

Par-Bond Yield Curve

The par-bond yield for each maturity may be found by solving equation (8) for $C^*(k)$, i.e.,

$$C_{j*}(k) = \frac{1 - v_j(k)}{a_j(k)} . \tag{12}$$

In slightly different form, this relationship between the yield of a par bond and forward interest rates was first stated by Lutz [8, p. 37] as

$$C^*(k) = \frac{[1 + s(1)][1 + r(2)]\cdots[1 + r(k)] - 1}{\begin{array}{l}[1+r(2)][1+r(3)]\cdots[1+r(k)] + \\ {}[1+r(3)]\cdots[1+r(k)] +\cdots+ [1+r(k)] + 1\end{array}} \tag{13}$$

Equation (12) may be found from equation (13) by multiplying the numerator and the denominator by $v(k)$.

Duration

Frederick R. Macaulay [9, p. 48] actually presented two definitions of *duration*. His *verbal definition* implies that, for a bond whose current price is P and which matures at t,

$$D'(t) = \frac{tv(t) + C \sum_{k=1}^{t} kv(k)}{P} . \tag{14}$$

Let the promised yield on such a bond be y. Then, by Macaulay's *algebraic formula*,

$$D(t) = \frac{t(1 + y)^{-t} + C \sum_{k=1}^{t} k(1 + y)^{-k}}{P} . \tag{15}$$

Unless the spot rate s(1) and all forward rates for years 2 through t are exactly equal to y (i.e., unless the current yield curve is flat), equations (14) and (15) are not equivalent (cf. Fisher and Weil [4]). Hence D′ and D will differ. However, for individual bonds, the differences are likely to be small. We may therefore use equation (15) as the definition because it is more convenient. From it we may derive either Macaulay's computational formulas or the following logically equivalent ones, which are more convenient than his.

$$D(t) = \frac{1 + y}{y} - \frac{1 + y + t(C - y)}{C(1 + y)^t - (C - y)}. \tag{16}$$

Equation (16) holds if $y > 0$. If $y = 0$,

$$D(t) = t\left[1 - \left(\frac{1}{2}\right)\frac{t - 1}{t + 1/C}\right]. \tag{17}^{[10]}$$

For par bonds, $C = y = C^*(t)$. Then equation (16) becomes

$$D^*(t) = \frac{1 + C^*(t)}{C^*(t)}\{1 - [1 + C^*(t)]^{-t}\} \tag{18}$$

Bonds with Frequent Interest Payments   In actual markets, bonds generally pay interest more often than once a year. Let C and y now stand for the annual nominal rate and annual yield, each compounded as often as interest in actually paid. For example, most bonds issued in the United States pay interest semiannually. For such bonds

$$D = \frac{1}{y} + \frac{1}{2} - \frac{[1 + y/2 + t(C - y)]}{[C(1 + y/2)^{2t} - (C - y)]} \tag{19}$$

if 2t is an integer. More generally, if interest is paid m times a year,

$$D = \frac{1}{y} + \frac{1}{m} - \frac{1 + y/m + t(C - y)}{C(1 + y/m)^{mt} - (C - y)} \tag{20}$$

if mt is an integer. Note that as the making of payments approaches continuity, the limiting value of duration is

$$D^0 = \frac{1}{y} - \frac{1 + t(C - y)}{Ce^{yt} - (C - y)}. \tag{21}$$

In all of these cases y is a nominal yield. The effective yield is $(1 + y/m)^m - 1$, which approaches $e^y - 1$ as payment becomes nearly continuous.

Bonds Between Interest Payments.   The above formulas for duration are correct only for bonds that have no interest accrued. Attempts to use them between interest-payment dates overstate duration. Figure 4 shows actual duration as a function of time to maturity for a 10 percent bond with annual coupons and a yield of 10.00 percent. If yield is constant, then day by day, as interest accrues, all present values increase at identical rates given by the yield as each payment comes closer. Hence, each day, duration falls by one day. However, when interest is finally paid at the end of each year, what had been the nearest payment drops out of the calculation and duration rises again.

Let f be the time (in years) until the next interest payment and N be the total number of payments to be made. Equation (20) may be generalized to

$$D = \frac{1}{y} + f - \frac{(1 + y/m) + (C - y)N/m}{C(1 + y/m)^N - (C - y)} \qquad (22)^{11}$$

Anticipated Returns for the Current Period

Maintaining an immunized portfolio requires reallocation among assets each time interest (or principal) is received. In Section IV we will sometimes find target holding-period returns from a series of single-period, anticipated returns. Therefore, we present the appropriate formulas here.

Let

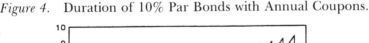

$$RA\left(\left\{\begin{matrix} L \\ R \\ F \end{matrix}\right\}, h, k\right)$$

be the return anticipated during year h on a par bond that matures at

Figure 4.   Duration of 10% Par Bonds with Annual Coupons.

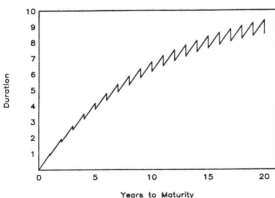

k under the Lutzian (L), rolling-yield-curve (R), or fixed-yield (F) definition of *anticipated*.

Lutzian Returns. A well-known implication of the Lutzian definition of *anticipations* is that, in any period in which expectations are met, all securities, including par and nonpar bonds, have the same realized return. Hence, the Lutzian definition implies that the Lutzian anticipated return is

$$RA(L, h, k) = r(h) \ . \tag{23}$$

Note that RA (L, h, k) is independent of the maturity date k.

Fixed-Yield Returns. Since the fixed-yield definition asserts that *anticipated* means no change in a security's yield to maturity, each year's anticipated return is the same as the yield to maturity at time 0. Such a definition implies that each security has its own anticipated return. Thus, the fixed-yield yearly return is

$$RA(F, h, k) = C_0^*(k) \tag{24}$$

Note that RA(F, h, k) is independent of h but does depend on the value of k.

Rolling-Yield-Curve Returns. The rolling-yield-curve definition of *anticipated* implies that as each security approaches maturity, it rolls along the yield curve—that its yield rolls down an upward-sloping yield curve or rolls up an "inverted" yield curve.

During any period, the realized return RR on a security that pays interest at the end of the period is equal to the sum of its "current yield" and the percentage change in its price, i.e.,

$$RR(h, k) = \frac{C + P_h(C, k) - P_{h-1}(C, k)}{P_{h-1}(C, k)} \tag{25}$$

Under the Lutzian and fixed-yield definitions, for any given yield curve, the anticipated return is independent of a specific bond's coupon rate C. However, under the rolling-yield definition, the anticipated return for a period does depend on C, i.e., on what the interest rate was at the time the bond was acquired if it was bought at par. The effect is very small for reasonable differences between $C(t)$ and $C^*(t)$. For simplicity we shall assume that at the beginning of a period only par bonds are held, i.e., we take

$$RA(R,x,k) = RA(R, 1, k - x + 1) \ . \tag{26}$$

Then,

$$RA(R, 1, k) = C_0^*(k) + P_1(C_0^*, k) - 1 \ . \tag{27}$$

In this case P_1 is an anticipated price, not an actual price. However, just as there are two definitions of Macaulay's duration for a coupon bond [equations (14) and (15)], there are two definitions of $P_1(C^*, k)$ under the rolling-yield-curve definition of *anticipated*.

First, one may assume that prices of all coupon bonds—par and nonpar—are consistent with the set of forward rates. From equation (7),

$$PA_j'(C^*, k) = v_j(k) + C^*(k) \, a_j(k) \ . \tag{28}$$

The rolling-yield-curve definition of anticipated implies

$$v_1(k) = v_0(k - 1) \ ,$$

$$a_1(k) = a_0(k - 1) \ ,$$

and

$$C_1^*(k) = C_0^*(k - 1) \ . \tag{29}$$

Hence, the first version of the anticipated price is

$$PA_1'(C_0^*, k) = v_0(k - 1) + C_0^*(k)a_0(k - 1) \ . \tag{30}$$

Second, one may assume that all bonds with the same maturity date will have the same yield. Then the standard formula for the price of a bond applies:

$$P(C, k) = \frac{C}{y} + \left(1 - \frac{C}{y}\right) (1 + y)^{-k} \ . \tag{31}$$

Under the rolling-yield-curve anticipations, if we substitute $C_0^*(k)$ for C in equation (31), according to equation (29), we must substitute $C_0^*(k - 1)$ for y in solving for $PA_1(C^*, k)$. Thus

$$PA_1(C_0^*, k) = \frac{C^*(k)}{C^*(k - 1)} + \left[1 - \frac{C^*(k)}{C^*(k - 1)}\right]$$
$$[1 + C^*(k - 1)]^{-(k-1)} \ . \tag{32}$$

The first variant implies that

$$RA'(R, 1, k) = \frac{[1 - v(k)]^2}{a(k)} + v(k)r(k) \ . \tag{33}^{12}$$

If we substitute PA_1 from equation (32) in equation (27) and simplify, we find that the second variant implies that

$$RA(R, 1, k) = C^*(k) \left[1 + \frac{1}{C^*(k-1)} \right]$$
$$+ \left(1 - \frac{C^*(k)}{C^*(k-1)} \right) [1 + C^*(k-1)]^{-(k-1)} - 1 \quad (34)$$

For examples in this paper, the magnitude of the difference between RA' and RA tends to increase with k. But the differences are very small. The maximum difference of about 2 basis points was associated with a difference of about 0.02 points between PA' and PA. We shall use RA(R) rather than RA'(R) for simplicity just as we use duration D rather than duration D'.

Comparison of Lutzian and Rolling-Yield-Curve Year-by-Year Anticipated Returns.   We have noted that under the Lutzian definition of anticipations, each year's return is also that year's forward rate. Hence the series of anticipated returns on any instrument is $s(1)$, $r(2)$, $r(3)$, $\ldots$, $r(k)$. If the rolling-yield-curve definition applied to yields of zero coupon bonds instead of yields of par bonds (so that $s_1(k) = s_0(k-1)$ rather than equation (29) supplied the working definition), the series of anticipated one-year returns would depend on k and would be reversed: $r(k)$, $r(k-1)$, $\ldots$, $r(2)$, $s(1)$. Finally, if the fixed-yield definition applied to zero coupon bonds, the annual returns would be simply $s(k)$, $s(k)$, $\ldots$, $s(k)$, $s(k)$. In these series

$$s(k) = \sqrt[k]{[1 + s(1)][1 + r(2)] \cdots [1 + r(k)]} - 1, \quad (35)$$

i.e., $1 + s(k)$ is the geometric mean of the applicable values of $1 + r(j)$.

When we deal with coupon bonds that now sell at par (and assume implicitly that bonds are traded for new, par coupon bonds with the same total market value each year), the sequence, as we have seen, is much more complicated. The value of $1 + C_0^*(k)$ may still be thought of as an average of $1 + r_0(j)$; but it is a weighted average, and the relative weights of the early years' forward rates rise with C^*. The sequence of $1 + RA(R, 1, j)$ is also a complicated set of averages of $1 + r_0(j)$.[13]

IV.   CALCULATION OF TARGET HOLDING-PERIOD RETURNS FOR IMMUNIZED PORTFOLIOS

In this section we shall use the formulas presented in Section III to find target future values of one dollar (or, equivalently, target holding-period returns) in general and for each of the illustrative definitions of *anticipated.* In general, we will find that the target future value of one depends on both the investor's anticipations and on the strategy that he uses.

Let

$$TA_j \left(t, \left\{ \begin{matrix} L \\ R \\ F \end{matrix} \right\}, \left\{ \begin{matrix} M \\ D \\ I \end{matrix} \right\} \right)$$

refer to the target future value or target amount (TA) of one for a portfolio in which

- The investment is made at time j and held until time t.
- According to the Lutzian (L), rolling-yield-curve (R), or fixed-yield (F) definition of *anticipated.*
- Using a maturity (M), duration (D), or truly immunizing (I) strategy.

Under the "maturity" strategy, the portfolio consists entirely of the coupon bond that currently sells at par, pays interest at the end of each year, and matures at time t.

Thus, under the maturity strategy,

$$TA(t,x,M) = \prod_{k=1}^{t} [1 + RA(x,1,k)] .$$

That is,

$$TA(t,L,M) = \prod [1 + r(k)] = \frac{1}{v(t)} ,$$

$$TA(t,F,M) = [1 + C^*(t)]^t ,$$

$$TA(t,R,M) = \prod [1 + RA(R,1,k)] .$$

But note that, although the maturity strategy is far less risky than some strategies, such as always holding Treasury bills or always holding long-term bonds, it nevertheless has more risk than one would like to bear.

Under a duration strategy, the portfolio is chosen so that, at the schedule of yields that are anticipated for the next date that the portfolio will have to be rebalanced, the current value of Macaulay's duration for the portfolio is equal to the time until the liability is due.[14] Under the simplifying assumptions of this paper, portfolios need to be rebalanced only when interest is received at the end of each year. Typically, if it is possible to follow the duration strategy at all, there are a large number of portfolios that will qualify as immunized according to the duration strategy. For simplicity, in the examples we will use Bierwag's "bullet" portfolios. If there is a single security with the appropriate duration, it will constitute the entire portfolio. Otherwise, the portfolio will be divided between the security with the next shorter and next longer durations. If we were testing the duration strategy rather than merely illustrating it, we would also try a number of other methods for meeting the duration criterion.

Whether the duration strategy (or any other) actually immunizes the portfolio, in the sense that the target amount is sure to be achieved, depends on what anticipations of future interest rates the investor actually holds and whether the departures from anticipations are or are not of the form that is assumed implicitly by employing a particular strategy—just as type-A influenza vaccine is likely to work much better against type A virus than against type-B virus, and vice versa.

For example, consider a liability due two years hence. We noted in Section II that such a liability would be immunized with a portfolio that initially held a mixture of two-year and three-year bonds. One year from now, the longer bonds will be sold, and the proceeds, along with the interest just received, will be used to buy what then will be one-year bonds. If, at that time, one-year and two-year interest rates are both higher than anticipated, the gain from higher-than-anticipated interest income in year 2 will be offset by the loss incurred in selling the two-year bonds at the end of year 1. If both interest rates fall, the loss of interest income will be offset by the capital gain. In either case, the target might be achieved. However, if the rates depart from anticipations in opposite directions, the gains or losses will be reinforcing. Unless the departures from anticipations of "long-term" and "short-term" interest rates are closely and appropriately associated, a duration strategy might be riskier than a maturity strategy.

Formal Definition of the Immunization Problem

We are now in a position to characterize the immunization problem in more formal terms. Suppose that at time j we had assets worth W_j and planned an investment strategy that had anticipated portfolio returns

$$PRA(h), \qquad h = j + 1, \ldots, t ,$$

where

$$PRA(h) = \sum_k w(h,k) \, RA(x,h,k) ,$$

in which

$$w(h,k) = \text{fraction of } W_h \text{ invested in bonds}$$

$$\text{that mature at } k$$

and

$$\sum_k w(h,k) = 1 .$$

Then the target would be

$$W_j TA_j(t) = W_j \prod_{h=j+1}^{t} [1 + PRA(h)] . \qquad (36)$$

Suppose that, immediately after the portfolio has been purchased, there were an unanticipated shift in the term structure of interest rates. If the elasticity of W_j with respect to the unanticipated change were equal in magnitude but opposite in sign to the elasticity of $TA_j(t)$, then the logarithm of the product would not change and, therefore, the portfolio would be immunized—at least for small changes. Both the elasticity of W_j and of $[1 + PRA(h)]$ may depend on the composition of the portfolio as well as on the form of the departure from anticipations of the term structure of interest rates.

Since $PRA(h)$ is a weighted average of RA's and $TA_j(t)$ is a product, the elasticity of $TA_j(t)$ does depend on the specific securities to be held with the possible exception of the case where the shift is such that all $\ln (1 + RA)$ change by identical amounts. Then, we must see whether the elasticity of price of each security is given by its duration.

If both conditions are true, then it is fairly simple to find $TA_j(t)$. If not, then we have a problem that appears to be soluble only by numerical methods.

Special Cases

Let us examine the cases in which the duration strategy provides portfolios that are immunized against some particular hazard. First, note that all $\ln (1 + RA)$ change by indentical amounts if all $(1 + RA)$ are multiplied by $1 + \Delta$. Hence, the first criterion will be met if there are proportional changes in $1 + RA$.

Lutzian. Under the Lutzian definition of *anticipated*,

$$RA_j(L,h,k) = r(h) \qquad \text{for all } k .$$

Therefore, a proportional shift in $1 + RA$ means a proportional shift in $1 + r$. From equation (35), we see that a proportional shift in $(1 + r)$, in turn, implies a proportional shift in $(1 + s)$; and from equation (1), that implies that changes in $\ln [1/v_0(k)]$ will be proportional to k.

Thus, it appears that a portfolio which has the proper duration according to equation (14) (D') is immunized with respect to proportional changes in $1 + r$. This corresponds to the case proved for large as well as small changes by Fisher and Weil [4].

Fixed Yield.   Under the fixed-yield definition,

$$RA_j(F,h,k) = C_j^*(k) .$$

Hence, under the fixed-yield definition of *anticipated*, the duration strategy corresponds to immunization against a proportional shift in $1 + C^*$.

Rolling-Yield Curve.   Under the rolling-yield-curve definition, $RA'(R,h,k)$ is a nonlinear function of the whole par-bond yield curve for maturities $1, 2, \ldots, k - h + 1$; and $RA(R,h,k)$ depends on $C^*(k - h)$ and $C^*(k - h - 1)$. Hence we may define a proportional change only in terms of $1 + RA'(C,1,k)$ or $1 + RA(C,1,k)$ for $k \leq t$. Then, it seems to us on preliminary analysis that a portfolio with a duration (calculated on the basis of yields that are anticipated one year from now) that is equal to $t - j$ is immunized with respect to proportional changes in $1 + RA$.

As soon as we know that a particular strategy is appropriate, we may calculate the target amount of one (future value) $TA_j(t)$ by projecting the appropriate curve $(C^*, r, \text{or } RA)$ to $j = t - 1$ and setting $TA_{t-1}(t) = 1 + C_{t-1}^*(t)$. Then, stepping back to $j = t - 2$, we construct the appropriate portfolio for year $t - 1$, find $PRA(t - 1)$ under the definition of *anticipated* that we are using, and compute

$$TA_{t-2}(t) = [1 + PRA(t - 1)] TA_{t-1}(t) .$$

We continue stepping back until we have found $TA_0(t)$ for the definition and strategy in question.

We have already examined TA's under maturity strategies. Moreover, we have noted, that since under Lutzian anticipations,

$$RA(L,h,k) = r(h)$$

and is, therefore, independent of the securities actually held. Hence, the Lutzian TA's are independent of the strategy that is planned. In the other cases, to apply a duration strategy, we must plan on what the composition of the portfolio for each period is to be if anticipations are correct. To do so, we must compute each security's duration at the

subsequent period's anticipated yield and select the appropriate portfolio in the manner discussed in Section II. From the projected RA's
of the securities to be held and the year-by-year planned composition
of the portfolio, we may find TA in a straightforward manner.

While we assume that duration strategies under each definition of
anticipated all lead to portfolio immunization, it is important to remember
that

1. For each definition, portfolio returns are computed under a
   unique set of anticipated yields (recall Figure 1).
2. Each definition assumes a different *process* by which realizations
   depart from anticipations.

Hence, a portfolio that is immunized under a particular definition of
anticipated and for a particular process of changes in interest rates is
very unlikely to be immunized under another definition or another
process of change. Changing the definition means moving from one
set of anticipations to another, thereby altering TA. Changing processes
alters the nature of the hazard against which the portfolio is immunized.
In any case, portfolio composition will be altered. In all but the Lutzian
case, TA will also change, To see why, we turn to a discussion of the
general case.

General Case

Suppose we wanted simultaneously to select an immunized portfolio
of coupon bonds and to estimate its target anticipated compound
amount of one, $TA_j(t)$. For formal discussion we introduce the following
notation.

For a portfolio held to meet a liability due at time t, let w(h,k,t) be
the fraction of the planned portfolio at time h that will be invested in
the security maturing at time k, e.g., w(1987, 1993, 1991) stands for
the fraction of the portfolio for 1987 that will be invested in bonds that
mature in 1993, given that the liability is due in 1991.

Then we must consider several elasticities, which are derivatives of
logarithms of the following variables with respect to the logarithm of
"$1 + \Delta$," the hazard being immunized against:

$1 + RA(x,h,k)$, 1 + anticipated security return [this elasticity will be
   denoted by $\alpha(x,h,k)$].
$1 + PRA(x,h,t)$, 1 + anticipated portfolio return;
$TA(j,t)$, anticipated future value, i.e., 1 + anticipated holding-period
   return.

$PA_{j+1}(k)$ as of time j, anticipated security price [this elasticity will be denoted by $\beta(j,k)$].
W_j using PA_{j+1}, anticipated value of portfolio.

As noted above, the portfolio is chosen according to the constraint

$$\sum_k w(h,k,t) = 1 \ . \tag{37}$$

Since portfolio returns are a weighted average of security returns,

$$\frac{d \ln [1 + PRA(x,h,t)]}{d \ln (1 + \Delta)} = \sum_k w(h,k)\alpha(x,h,k) \ . \tag{38}$$

Since TA is a product,

$$\frac{d \ln [TA(j,t)]}{d \ln (1 + \Delta)} = \frac{\displaystyle\sum_{h=j+1}^{t} d \ln [1 + PRA(x,h,t)]}{d \ln (1 + \Delta)} \ . \tag{39}$$

From the alternative definition of elasticity given in Section II, we note

$$\frac{1 + \Delta}{W_j} \frac{dW_j}{d(1 + \Delta)} = \sum_k w(j,k) \, \beta(j,k) \ . \tag{40}$$

With the sign reversed, the elasticity $\beta(j,k)$ may be considered a "horizon duration" of the security *for the particular hazard being immunized against.*

If $TA(j,t)$ is consistent with the planned strategy, then a portfolio is immunized with respect to anticipated returns and the hazard being immunized against if and only if weighted average horizon duration, equation (40), is equal to the elasticity of $TA(j,t)$ with respect to that hazard.

One could attempt to immunize against other hazards either in addition to or instead of proportional shifts in (1 + interest rate), as suggested in the papers by Brennan & Schwartz, Ingersoll, and Vanderhoff in this volume. In doing so, it is important to consider effects on both TA and W (or, as Vanderhoof has done, effects on the liability), not merely the effects on W. However, it may not be feasible to immunize against all hazards simultaneously.

Example. Recall that, under rolling-yield-curve anticipations, a duration strategy immunizes against proportional changes in 1 + RA. Suppose, however, we wish to change policy and immunize against proportional changes in 1 + C*. How should the portfolio and plans for future portfolios be changed?

Recall that the hazard is measured by a proportionality factor $1 + \Delta$ and that the elasticity of any arbitrary function is equal to

$$\frac{d \ln F}{d \ln (1 + \Delta)}$$

or

$$\frac{dF/d \ln (1 + \Delta)}{F}$$

and that, for small Δ,

$$n (1 + \Delta) = \Delta .$$

Before the change in policy, each security's α was equal to 1.0 and each security's β was equal to the negative of its duration. For the new hazard, β's will still be equal to the negative of duration [which may change slightly because it will be appropriate to use equation (15) instead of (14)]. However, α's must change unless the yield curve is flat.[15] It may be shown that for a par bond maturing at time $k + 1$,

$\alpha(R, 1, k + 1)$

$$= \frac{1 + C^*(k+1) + [1 - C^*(k+1)/C^*(k)]\{1/C^*(k) + [k + 1/C^*(k)][1 + C^*(k)]^{-k}\}}{C^*(k+1) [1 + 1/C^*(k)] - [1 - C^*(k+1)/C^*(k)][1 + C^*(k)]^{-k}}$$

(41)

The elasticity differs from unity by

$\alpha(R, 1, k + 1) - 1$

$$= \frac{[1 - C^*(k+1)/C^*(k)]\{1 + 1/C^*(k) + [1 + k + 1/C^*(k)][1 + C^*(k)]^{-k}\}}{C^*(k+1)[1 + 1/C^*(k)] - [1 - C^*(k+1)/C^*(k)][1 + C^*(k)]^{-k}}$$

(42)

The formulas hold only for $C^* > 0$. The denominator of equations (41) and (42) is positive so long as $RA > -100$ percent. All elements in the braced expression in the numerator of equation (42) are positive. Hence, for a proportional shift in $1 + C^*$ and rolling-yield-curve anticipations, $\alpha(R,1,k)$, the elasticity of $1 + RA$, is less than one for yield curves that rise with increasing maturity and greater than one for falling yield curves. Thus, the change of hazard being immunized against requires that the duration of the portfolio be increased if the term structure falls with increasing maturity and requires reducing duration if the term structure is a rising one (a portion of the "change" comes about automatically through the change in the formula for calculating duration [equation (15) instead of (14)]). Changing the hazard may also result in changing the target return.

Similarly, one might hold Lutzian anticipations and decide to change the hazard being immunized against from forward rates to yields. Since the value of RA(L,h,k) depends only on r(h), we need to know the elasticity of 1 + r with respect to 1 + C*. An analytical computation is not tractable because r(h) is a function of C*(1), . . . , C*(h). However, our numeric results suggest that the relationship is elastic when yield curves rise with maturity and inelastic when yield curves fall. Moreover the departure of the elasticity from unity is several times larger for Lutzian anticipations than for rolling-yield-curce anticipations. It would appear that immunizing against proportional shifts in 1 + r is a rather different policy from immunizing against a proportional shift in 1 + C* if one has Lutzian anticipations

Calculations

To date, we have applied the computations described in this section only for the maturity and the duration strategies. Hence, even for the limited number of yield curves examined in this paper, our conclusions about the magnitude of the effect of the definition of *anticipated* on target values for holding-period returns are only tentative.

Results: Maturity Strategy. The results of applying our analysis under the maturity strategy to five different yield curves are shown in Table 1. For panel A, we used actual yields on U.S. Treasury bonds and notes that were quoted at or above par on December 31, 1980. The usual annual bond yields (compounded semiannually) were converted to effective rates (rates compounded annually), and the effective rates were used to estimate the other numbers in the table for holding periods of 1 through 10 years. The curve for the end of 1980 was a falling yield curve. Note that TA(10,L,M) = 3.3068, which is equivalent to an effective rate of 12.70 percent; but TA(10,R,M) = 3.3546, which is equivalent to 12.87 percent, a difference (from unrounded figures) of 16 basis points. Note also that r(2), . . . , r(10) are in narrow range from 12.42 to 12.67 percent.

For panel B, we smoothed the forward rates by setting them all to 12.50 percent. The effect on the estimated yield curve was negligible. Again, for horizons of two or more years, TA(t,R,M) exceeds TA(t,L,M). This time TA(10,R,M) exceeds TA(10,L,M) by the equivalent of 18

Table 1. Anticipated Amounts of One Under Three Assumptions and the Maturity Strategy.

				Anticipated Amount of One		
Due Date t (1)	Par-Bond Yield C*(t) (2)	Forward Rate r(t) (3)	Rolling-Yield-Curve Anticipated Return RA'(R,l,t) (4)	Lutzian TA(t,L,N) (5)	Rolling-Yield TA(t,R,M) (6)	Fixed-Yield TA(t,F,M) (7)

A. Actual Yield Curve, December 31, 1980

(In Percent)

1	14.27	14.27	14.27	1.1427	1.1427	1.1427
2	13.40	12.42	12.64	1.2846	1.2871	1.2860
3	13.18	12.65	12.82	1.4472	1.4521	1.4498
4	13.04	12.51	12.71	1.6282	1.6367	1.6328
5	12.94	12.40	12.64	1.8300	1.8436	1.8375
6	12.88	12.45	12.67	2.0578	2.0772	2.0687
7	12.84	12.47	12.68	2.3145	2.3406	2.3294
8	12.82	12.59	12.73	2.6058	2.6386	2.6248
9	12.81	12.67	12.76	2.9360	2.9753	2.9589
10	12.80	12.63	12.75	3.3068	3.3546	3.3350

B. Curve for December 31, 1980 with Forward Rates Smoothed

(In Percent)

1	14.27	14.27	14.27	1.1427	1.1427	1.1427
2	13.44	12.50	12.71	1.2855	1.2879	1.2868
3	13.16	12.50	12.70	1.4462	1.4515	1.4491
4	13.02	12.50	12.70	1.6270	1.6359	1.6318
5	12.94	12.50	12.70	1.8304	1.8437	1.8377
6	12.89	12.50	12.70	2.0592	2.0778	2.0696
7	12.85	12.50	12.70	2.3166	2.3417	2.3309
8	12.82	12.50	12.70	2.6062	2.6390	2.6252
9	12.80	12.50	12.70	2.9319	2.9741	2.9567
10	12.78	12.50	12.70	3.2984	3.3518	3.3303

C. Similar, Sharply Rising Forward Rate

(In Percent)

1	10.73	10.73	10.73	1.1073	1.1073	1.1073
2	11.56	12.50	12.32	1.2457	1.2437	1.2446
3	11.84	12.50	12.31	1.4014	1.3968	1.3989
4	11.98	12.50	12.31	1.5766	1.5687	1.5722
5	12.06	12.50	12.31	1.7737	1.7618	1.7669
6	12.11	12.50	12.31	1.9954	1.9786	1.9857
7	12.15	12.50	12.31	2.2448	2.2220	2.2315
8	12.18	12.50	12.31	2.5254	2.4955	2.5076
9	12.20	12.50	12.30	2.8411	2.8025	2.8178
10	12.22	12.50	12.30	3.1962	3.1474	3.1662

(continued)

Table 1.   (Continued)

Due Date t (1)	Par-Bond Yield C*(t) (2)	Forward Rate r(t) (3)	Rolling-Yield-Curve Anticipated Return RA'(R,l,t) (4)	Anticipated Amount of One		
				Lutzian TA(t,L,N) (5)	Rolling-Yield TA(t,R,M) (6)	Fixed-Yield TA(t,F,M) (7)

D. Humped, March 17, 1981

(In Percent)

1	13.49	13.49	13.49	1.1349	1.1349	1.1349
2	13.59	13.70	13.68	1.2904	1.2901	1.2903
3	13.57	13.52	13.54	1.4649	1.4648	1.4648
4	13.52	13.33	13.40	1.6601	1.6611	1.6607
5	13.36	12.48	12.89	1.8673	1.8752	1.8720
6	13.26	12.53	12.91	2.1013	2.1173	2.1109
7	13.20	12.64	12.96	2.3669	2.3918	2.3819
8	13.14	12.44	12.88	2.6613	2.6998	2.6849
9	13.08	12.23	12.79	2.9868	3.0453	3.0232
10	13.04	12.36	12.84	3.3559	3.4362	3.4066

E. Actual, August 17, 1981

(In Percent)

1	17.33	17.33	17.33	1.1733	1.1733	1.1733
2	16.85	16.29	16.44	1.3645	1.3662	1.3654
3	16.61	16.01	16.23	1.5829	1.5879	1.5857
4	16.40	15.55	15.93	1.8290	1.8410	1.8357
5	16.20	15.04	15.65	2.1040	2.1290	2.1185
6	16.00	14.44	15.35	2.4078	2.4559	2.4364
7	15.81	13.91	15.12	2.7427	2.8271	2.7940
8	15.62	13.25	14.86	3.1060	3.2471	3.1935
9	15.43	12.55	14.61	3.4957	3.7213	3.6380
10	15.24	11.80	14.34	3.9084	4.2558	4.1308

basis points. The difference in effective rates arises from the fact that, although both definitions of *anticipated* imply a return of 14.27 percent in one of the 10 years in the holding period, the returns for the other years would be 12.50 percent under the Lutzian anticipations but about 12.70 percent under the rolling-yield-curve anticipations. Panel C illustrates the reverse relationship that is implied by a rising yield curve. For this example, we kept the forward rates at 12.50 percent, but we set s(1) 177 basis points below r(2), viz., at 10.73 percent, instead of 177 basis points above it. The par-bond yield curve is the exact mirror image of the curve for panel B. Now, TA(10,L,M) is equivalent to an effective rate of 12.32% and TA(10,R,M) to 12.15 percent. The magnitude of the difference is about the same—17 basis points—but the sign has changed.

In these three examples, TA(t,F,M) lies between TA(t,R,M) and TA(t,L,M) and is generally closer to the former for $t \geq 2$.

Panel D is for the moderately humped yield curve of March 17, 1981. Like other typical humped yield curves, its peak par-bond yield was for a rather short maturity. In this case, the par-bond yield falls substantially from $C^*(3)$ through $C^*(10)$. Consequently, TA(t,R,M) exceeds TA(t,L,M) for holding periods longer than about three years. In this case, however, the fixed-yield definition of *anticipated* produces the lowest target holding-period return for horizons in the neighborhood of the point where TA(t,R,M) and TA(t,L,M) cross. We must warn that these are not general results for humped yield curves. If the peak yield is at a longer horizon (as in November 1981) or if the yield declined less rapidly as the horizon lengthened, TA(t,L,M) might exceed TA(t,R,M) for all $t > 1$.

In panels A, B, and C, the forward rate curves level off at $k = 2$, and in panel D by about $k = 3$. Panel E is for the yield curve of August 17, 1981. Many of its implications were shown in Figures 1 to 3. Yields declined sharply from $C^*(1)$ to $C^*(2)$ and then nearly linearly through $C^*(10)$. Hence, $r(k)$ was a declining function of k over the entire range examined.

In this case, both $r(k)$ and RA(R, 1, k) also decline substantially for successive future dates. Qualitatively, the target amounts of one are like those of panels A and B, viz.,

$$TA(t, R, M) > TA(t, F, M) > TA(t, L, M) \qquad (43)$$

for $t > 1$.

In addition to interpreting differences among TA's as differences in effective interest rates, we may also look at them relative to the "interest on interest" that the portfolio must earn to achieve its promised yield of $C_3^*(t)$ on the bond. Interest on interest is the difference between the holding-period returns accumulated at a given nominal rate under compound interest and under simple interest. Interest on interest is relevant because it represents the difference between the total return and the amount that the actual issuer of the bond has promised to pay. Its value is

$$II_{(t)} = TA(t) - [1 + tC_3^*(t)] . \qquad (44)$$

For example, in panel A, $II(10) = 1.055$. Since TA(10,R,M) $-$ TA(10,L,M) $= 0.0478$, the difference is about 0.045 times $II(10)$. Also in panel A, TA(5,R,M) $-$ TA(5,L,M) = 0.0136, which is smaller than the difference for 10 years. However, II(5) is only 0.1905. Hence, the difference for 5 years is 0.071 times II(5).

It appears that $\mid$ TA(t,R,M) $-$ TA(t,L,M) $\mid$ increases as either t or the general level of interest rates increases. The same conclusion appears to follow when the difference is converted to a difference in effective rate of return. However, the ratio of the magnitude of the difference to II(t) seems to be affected in the opposite manner.

Results: Duration Strategy. Table 2 presents estimated values of TA for the duration strategy in those cases from which computations have

Table 2. Anticipated Amounts of One Under Three Assumptions and a Duration Strategy

Due Date t (1)	Par-Bond Yield C*(t) (2)	Anticipated Amount of One		
		Lutzian TA(t,L,D) (3)	Rolling-Yield TA(t,R,D) (4)	Fixed-Yield TA(t,M,D) (5)
B. Curve for December 31, 1980 with Forward Rates Smoothed				
1	14.27%	1.1427	1.143	1.1427
2	13.44	1.2855	1.288[a]	—
3	13.16	1.4462	1.451[a]	—
4	13.02	1.6270	1.636[a]	—
5	12.94	1.8304	1.844[a]	—
6	12.89	2.0592	2.078[a]	—
7	12.85	2.3166	2.342[a]	—
8	12.82	2.6062	2.639[a]	—
9	12.80	2.9319	2.974[a]	—
10	12.78	3.2984	3.352[a]	—
E. Actual, August 17, 1981				
1	17.33%	1.1733	1.1733	1.1733
2	16.85	1.3645	1.3657	1.3648
3	16.61	1.5829	1.5848	1.5833
4	16.40	1.8290	1.8306	1.8282
5	16.20	2.1040	2.1033	2.1007
6	16.00	2.4078	[b]	[b]
7	15.81	2.7427	[b]	[b]
8	15.62	3.1060	[c]	[c]
9	15.43	3.4957	[c]	[c]
10	15.24	3.9084	[c]	[c]

Notes:
[a] Estimated from asymptotic yield (AC)
[b] Strategy requires holding bonds with more than 10 years to maturity
[c] Strategy is not feasible with nonnegative holdings of par bonds

been completed. Since TA is independent of strategy for Lutzian anticipations, $TA(t,L,M) = TA(t,L,D)$.[16]

In panel E, since the yield curve falls, reducing risk by moving from the maturity strategy to the duration strategy has the effect of reducing TA for both rolling-yield-curve and fixed-yield anticipations. As a result, in panel E,

$$TA(t,L,D) \simeq TA(t,R,D) \simeq TA(t,F,D) .$$

Now, we have a truly interesting result. *Sometimes*, the form on one's anicipations of future interest rates will affect the target holding-period return for a portfolio that is immunized by following the duration strategy, but, *other times*, it will not. And here *sometimes* refers to actual quoted yield curves from the recent past.

Results: Immunization Strategy. First recall that, with Lutzian anticipations, the choice of strategy does not affect TA. Hence,

$$TA(t,L,D) = TA(t,L,I) . \tag{45}$$

Moreover, if the portfolio is immunized for the hazard of proportional changes in $1 + C^*$, the duration strategy is also the immunization strategy for fixed-yield anticipations. However, without performing the full-scale calculations, there is little that we can say about difference in target values for rolling-yield-curve anticipations.

V. CONCLUSIONS

In this paper, we have examined the problem of immunizing portfolios under a variety of assumptions about the nature of the future interest rates that may be anticipated on the basis of the current term structure of interest rates for par bonds. We have noted that Lutzian, rolling-yield-curve, and fixed-yield anticipations may provide very different "forecasts" of future interest rates.

The compound amount of one (and long-term holding-period return) may be inferred from the par-bond yield curve only under Lutzian assumptions unless the investor's strategy is specified in detail. As a result, we found it necessary to redefine *immunization*. In order to find a target amount of one (future value), both the definition of *anticipated* and the strategy (or, better, the hazard to be immunized against) must be specified. Then, immunization against a particular hazard will be attained if, for each year between now and the due date of the liability, the planned portfolio is such that the weighted average elasticity of security prices in the portfolio is equal to the sum of the elasticities of (one plus anticipated portfolio return) for that year and through the remaining years that the portfolio is to be held.

We noted that, under some conditions, a duration strategy is an immunization strategy. However, the hazard immunized against depends on the type of anticipations the investor holds; and immuniation against other hazards, which may have been considered equivalent in the past, may be very imperfect.

We have not found any simple relationship between the form of the yield curve and the differences in target values that are implied by various strategies or definitions of *anticipations*. We can only note that an examination of a limited number of yield curves that are based on recent price quotations shows that the differences can sometimes be substantial.[17]

To sum up, there are still many interesting problems connected with the idea of immunization of portfolios.

ACKNOWLEDGMENTS

The authors wish to thank George R. Morrison and Alfred Weinberger for their incisive comments on earlier drafts of this paper.

DISCLAIMER

NOTES

1. Changes in yield are reflected by opposite changes in price. If "small" changes in short-term and long-term yields (compounded continuously) are equal, price changes will be proportional to Macaulay's duration. However, if short-term and long-term yields move in the same direction but short-term yields move more, price changes will tend to be less than proportional to duration. Moreover, the magnitude of the departure from proportionality will itself be an increasing function of duration. Hence, under the stated condition, immunized portfolios should have longer Macaulay's durations than those implied by the assumption of parallel shifts in yield curves.

2. However, the return under the rolling-yield-curve definition will be between the spot rate and the forward rate, while the return under the unmodified Lutzian definition will be at the current spot rate. (See also note 13.)

3. Nelson's theoretical result is the reason that we use the term *Lutzian anticipations* rather than the more common term *expectations hypothesis*. His result may be summarized as follows:

Let R(j) = actual interest rate on one-period loans during time j,
   r(j) = the Lutzian forward interest rate on such loans that is implied by the yield curve at time zero,
   u(j) = R(j) − r(j).

As usually stated, the expectations hypothesis is that u(j) is a random variable whose expectation is zero, i.e., that r(j) is an unbiased forecaster of R(j) for j ≥ 2 [R(1) is always equal to r(1)].

Let
$$P[R(t)] = [1 + R(1)] [1 + R(2)] \cdots [1 + R(t)],$$
$$p[r(t)] = [1 + r(1)] [1 + r(2)] \cdots [1 + r(t)].$$

Then the expectations hypothesis is that

$$E \{P[R(t)]\} = p[r(t)] . \tag{1a}$$

However, Nelson showed that, for equation (1a) to hold under the assumption stated above, there is an additional necessary condition: the covariance of u(h) and u(j) must be zero for all h ≠ j, i.e., the errors of forward rates as forecasts of future spot rates must be uncorrelated. Empirically, both long-term and short-term interest rates tend to move in the same direction; and the whole term structure is likely to remain high or low for periods of several years or even longer. Hence, there appears to be positive correlation among the forecast errors. In that case,

$$E \{P[R(t)]\} > p[r(t)] , \qquad t \ge 3 . \tag{1b}$$

The exact relationship depends on the covariance of u(j) and u(k) for j = 2, . . . , t − 1; k = j + 1, . . . , t, and also on r(j) for j = 2, . . . , t.

Equation (1) may hold even in the presence of positive covariance if the expectation of u is less than zero by an amount that just offsets the bias due to serial covariance. If r's, as forecasters of R's, have upward bias, one may say that there is a "liquidity premium." However, Nelson's analysis shows that such liquidity premiums do not imply liquidity preference on the part of investors.

Thus, even the assumptions that all investors have the same time horizon and are maximizers of expected terminal wealth do not imply Lutzian anticipations in the presence of correlated forecast errors.

Nelson went on to see whether actual liquidity premiums were equal to those implied by the covariance of forecast errors. However, he treated estimates of yields of long-term coupon bonds as if they were yields of zero coupon bonds, which is an invalid procedure. Whether there is liquidity preference in the bond market is still unknown.

4. The hazards that we discuss as examples in this paper are all in the form of proportional changes in a set of (1 + interest rate). Bierwag, Kaufman, and Toevs [1a] have recently proposed a hazard that may be easier to analyze and which appears to be consistent with market equilibrium. They propose the hypothesis that the unanticipated change in each single-payment bond is linear function of the realized hazard. If that

hypothesis is correct, then it follows that the unanticipated price change of any default-free bond or portfolio of such bonds is also a linear function of the hazard. See also Fisher [2b].

5. Note, however, that when the term structure is not flat, *present value* may become an ill-defined concept.

6. Traditional immunization—by holding a variety of assets—will not be feasible if t is greater than the duration of longest-duration bond. However, immunization might still be achieved by increasing relatively short-term liabilities. One appropriate method would be short-term borrowing with the proceeds invested in long-duration bonds. Another method would be to buy long-term bonds in the futures market. Both methods introduce complexities that we will not deal with here.

If the assumption of parallel shifts of yield curves is dropped, the feasibility of immunization also depends on the correlation among changes in long-term and short-term rates.

7. The initial portfolio may be broken into interest and principal payments due at times 1, 2, and 3. Between 0 and 1, each time until payment—and hence duration—declines at the uniform rate of 1 day per diem, so long as interest rates remain the same. At time 1, interest is received in cash. Therefore, the duration of the first interest payment can no longer decline. Thus, unless the rest of the portfolio is reallocated, portfolio duration will be more than 364 days at time 1 + 1/365.

8. The respective fractions of the portfolio are 0.0909, 0.5891, and 0.3200.

9. Note that equation 3.5 is far less awkward than the common textbook formula $r_j(k) = [1 + s_j(k)]^k/[1 + s_j(k - 1)]^{k-1} - 1$. "Forward" rates are implied by value additivity. They carry no direct implications about expectations. See McCullogh [10]. However, value additivity may have its own empirically testable implications.

10. We have derived equation (16) directly from Macaulay [9, p. 48], directly from equation (15), and from the known alternative definition of duration as an elasticity (cf. Fisher [2a]). Equation (17) was derived algebraically and compared with Macaulay's formula.

A convenient formula restated from Macaulay [9, p. 49] for the duration of an annuity with rents due at times 1, . . . , t is

$$D_a = \frac{1 + y}{y} - \frac{t}{(1 + y)^t - 1} . \qquad (17a)$$

11. Equation (22) was derived by noting that the difference between the duration at time 0 and time 1/m − f (with 0 ≤ f < 1/m) is 1/m − f and that at time 0, N = mt.

12. From equations (27) and (28),

$$PA_1'(C^*,k) = C^*(k) \, a(k - 1) + v(k - 1) ,$$

$$RA'(R, 1, k) = C^*(k)[1 + a(k - 1)] + v(k - 1) - 1 .$$

But

$$a(k - 1) = a(k) - v(k)$$

and

$$v(k - 1) = v(k)[1 + r(k)] .$$

Recalling equation (12),

$$C^*(k) = \frac{1 - v(k)}{a(k)}$$

and substituting into the second equation of this footnote,

$$RA'(R,1,k) = \frac{1 - v(k)}{a(k)} [1 - v(k) + a(k)] + v(k)[1 + r(a)] - 1$$

$$= \frac{[1 - v(k)]^2}{a(k)} + 1 - v(k) + v(k) + v(k) \, r(k) - 1 .$$

Canceling offsetting terms yields equation (33).

13. Under some conditions we can simplify the calculations through use of an asymptotic yield which may be dubbed "the long-term interest rate." Suppose the series of $r_0(k)$'s leveled off so that for $k > z$, $r(k) = r(z)$. Then the series of $s(k)$'s, $C^*(k)$'s, and $RA(R,1,k)$'s would all approach limiting values asymptotically. It is well known that $s_0(j)$ approaches $r_0(z)$ as k increases without bound. However, $C^*(k)$ and $RA(R,1,k)$ approach a different asymptote, the long-term interest rate, which we find as follows: from equation (12),

$$C^*(k) = \frac{1 - v(k)}{a(k)} .$$

For $k \geq z$,

$$C^*(k) = \frac{1 - v(z) \, [1 + r(z)]^{-(k-z)}}{a(z) + v(z) \sum\limits_{h=z+1}^{k} [1 + r(z)]^{-(h-z)}}$$

But, as k increases without bound,

$$[1 + r(z)]^{-(k-z)} \to 0 .$$

and

$$\sum_{h=z+1}^{k} [1 + r(z)]^{-(h-z)} \to \frac{1}{r(z)}$$

Hence,

$$C^*(k) \to \frac{r_0(z)}{r_0(z) \, a_0(z) + v_0(z)} = AC , \qquad (35a)$$

where AC is the asymptotic par-bond yield. Moreover, $RA(R,1,j)$ and $RA'(R,1,j)$ also approach AC because, if C^* approaches AC, $C^*(k - 1) - C^*(k)$ approaches 0. Indeed, when the asymptotic conditions apply, $RA'(R,1,k)$ approaches AC even more rapidly than $C^*(k)$ does. The process is so rapid that the ratio in equation (35a) may be taken as a good estimate of $RA'(R,1,z)$ whether asymptotic conditions hold or not.

As we shall see, when the asymptotic conditions exist, this approximation can be of great convenience under Rolling-Yield-Curve anticipations. For portfolios that consist entirely of securities that mature at or after time z, the single-year anticipated return of the portfolio may be estimated with negligible error without knowing the portfolio's exact composition, thereby simplifying the estimation of the target holding-period return.

The accuracy of the approximation may be found for $k \geq z$ by subtracting equation (35a) from equation (33) and performing some algebraic manipulation. We find

$$RA'(R,1,k) - AC = \frac{v(k)}{a(k)} \left[\frac{1}{a(k) \, r(k) + v(r)} + a(k) \, r(k) + v(k) - 2 \right] \qquad (35b)$$

$$= \frac{v(k)}{a(k)} \left[\frac{AC}{r(k)} + \frac{r(k)}{AC} - 2 \right] \qquad (35c)$$

The bracketed term is likely to be small, and the ratio of $v(k)$ to $a(k)$ must be less than $1/k$ for positive interest rates.

When the asymptotic conditions do apply, AC may be called the *long-term interest rate*, because if it exists, AC is the yield on a perpetual annuity. We may also note that for "smoothly" rising yield curves, $r(z) > AC > C_0^*(z)$, and for smoothly falling curves, $r(z) < AC < C_0^*(z)$.

14. This is equivalent to setting the "horizon duration" of the assets equal to the horizon duration of the liability. See Leibowitz [7b].

15. For simplicity of notation, let

$$c = C^*(k + 1), \qquad y = C^*(k) .$$

Note that

$$1 + RA = c + \frac{c}{y} + \left(1 - \frac{c}{y}\right)(1 + y)^{-k}$$

Then,

$$\frac{d(1 + RA)}{d(1 + \Delta)} = 1 + c + \frac{1}{y} - \frac{c}{y^2} + k\left(1 - \frac{c}{y}\right)(1 + y)^{-k} + \left(\frac{1}{y} + \frac{c}{y^2}\right)(1 + y)^{-k}$$

Collecting terms and substituting the formal notation for the derivative and for $(1 + RA)$ provide the numerator and denominator of equation (41).

16. Moreover, the form of the duration strategy that we use requires holding bonds that mature either at the due date of the liability (for $j = t - 1$) or no earlier than the due date (for $j < t - 1$). In panels B and C, RA(R,1,k) differs from AC by less than 2 basis points for $k \geq 2$. Therefore, in those panels, we may estimate TA(t,R,D) by TA(t,R,M).

Further, although TA(t,F,D) has not been calculated as yet, lengthening the maturity of the portfolio in order to apply the duration strategy under fixed-yield anticipations makes TA(t,F,D) < TA(t,F,M) for panel B and TA(t,F,D) > TA(t,F,M) for panel C (cf. panel E).

17. These observations suggest that the empirical findings in several of the papers in this volume, as well as in other articles, need further careful scrutiny. In addition, the attempts to immunize against two hazards simultaneously as in the papers by Brennan and Schwartz and by Ingersoll might be developed further via the methods suggested here.

ADDENDUM

We are pleased to see that the *CRSP Government Bond File* is being used to test immunization strategies. Fisher compiled the file with that use as his original motivation. Leibowitz's firm supplied most of the quotations. However, we suspect that many of the tests reported in the papers in this conference have neglected an important point that must be kept in mind whenever one selects securities for a portfolio—real or hypothetical. That factor is *suitability*.

For much research on the stock market, this factor may be ignored because, if prices are in equilibrium and transaction costs may be ignored, many stocks that might tend to be excluded from a portfolio for tax reasons will still be included because of their contribution to diversification.

But, if bonds have low risk in nominal terms, inclusion of bonds that have the wrong tax position will tend to reduce after-tax return by far more than might be justified by their contribution to diversification.

There are two kinds of special tax status to worry about (besides things like "flower-bond" status, which affects both maturity date and taxes). The first is explicit tax exemption or partial tax exemption. All Treasury securities for which data appear in the *CRSP Government Bond File* and which were issued before 1940 were at least partially tax exempt. Interest on bonds issued up to 1917 and on nearly all short-term and intermediate-term issues during the 1930s (1929–February 1941 for Treasury bills) was wholly tax exempt. Such bonds had much appeal to investors who were in high tax brackets but very little attraction for tax-exempt pension funds, etc. Some of the tax-exempt bonds remained outstanding until the early 1960s.

Second, many nominally taxable securities also have partial exemption from Federal income taxes: all of those that sell for less than par and have at least a year to maturity (six months for most of the period covered by the CRSP file). The differential taxation of capital gains and "net interest" implies that tests which are conducted without explicit tax allowances should confine themselves to taxable instruments that are selling at or above par. We suspect that failure to make that restriction will do more harm than failing to exclude flower bonds and bonds that are callable within say 5–10 years. At times these restrictions may result in an empty set. That is a practical problem which should also be investigated.

We could make other comments, but they would be about relatively minor problems.

REFERENCES

1. Ayres, Herbert F., and John Y. Barry, 1979, "Dynamics of the Government Yield Curve" or "The Equilibrium Yield Curve for Government Securities," *Financial Analysts Journal* (May–June), 31–39.
2. Bierwag, G. O., George Kaufman, and Alden Toevs, 1981, "Single Factor Duration Models in a General Equilibrium Framework," Paper presented to the American Finance Association, December 29. (Forthcoming in the *Journal of Finance*.)
3. Fisher, Lawrence (compiler), 1981, *CRSP Monthly File for U.S. Treasury Securities since December 1925*, 1981 edition. Chicago: Center for Research in Security Prices, University of Chicago (magnetic tape).
4. ———, 1966, "An Algorithm for Finding Exact Rates of Return," *Journal of Business*, Vol. 39, No. 1, Part II (January), 111–118.

5. ———, 1981, "Discussion of 'Single Factor Duration Models in a General Equilibrium Framework' by Bierwag, Kaufman, and Toevs," Remarks presented to the American Finance Association, December 29. (Forthcoming in the *Journal of Finance*.)

6. Fisher, Lawrence and James H. Lorie, 1977, *A Half Century of Returns on Stocks and Bonds*, Graduate School of Business, University of Chicago.

7. Fisher, Lawrence and Roman L. Weil, 1971, "Coping with Risk of Interest Rate Fluctuations," *Journal of Business*, Vol. 44, No. 4 (October), 408–431. (Reprinted in *Pros & Cons of Immunization*, edited by Martin L. Leibowitz, Salomon Brothers Inc, 1980.)

8. Hamburger, Michael, and Elliott N. Pratt, 1975, "The Expectations Hypothesis and the Efficiency of the Treasury Bill Market," *Review of Economics and Statistics*, Vol. 57, No. 2 (May), 190–199.

9. Kessel, Reuben A., 1965, *The Cyclical Behavior of the Term Structure of Interest Rates* (NBER Occasional Paper Number 91), National Bureau of Economic Research, New York.

10. Leibowitz, Martin L., 1979, *Total Return Management*, Salomon Brothers Inc., New York.

11. ———, 1980, Bond Immunization: A Procedure for Realizing Target Levels of Return; Bond Immunization—Part II: Portfolio Rebalancing; Bond Immunization Part III: The Yield Curve Case. Reprinted in *Pros & Cons of Immunization*, edited by Martin L. Leibowitz, Salomon Brothers Inc.

12. Lutz, Friedrich A., 1940, "The Structure of Interest Rates," *Quarterly Journal of Economics*, Vol. 55, No. 1 (November), 36–63.

13. Macaulay, Frederick R., 1938, *Some Theoretical Problems Suggested by the Movements of Interest Rates, Bond Yields and Stock Prices in the United States since 1856*. National Bureau of Economic Research, New York. (Partially reprinted in *Pros & Cons of Immunization*, edited by Martin L. Leibowitz, Salomon Brothers Inc., 1980.)

14. McCulloch, J. Huston, 1975, "An Estimate of the Liquidity Premium," *Journal of Political Economy*, Vol. 83, No. 1 (February), 95–119.

15. Nelson, Charles R., 1972, "Estimation of Term Premiums From Average Yield Differentials in the Term Structure of Interest Rates," *Econometrica*, Vol. 40, No. 2 (March), 277–287.

16. Redington, F. M., 1952, "Review of the Principles of Life-Office Valuations," *Journal of the Institute of Actuaries*, Vol. 78, No. 3, 286–340. (Reprinted in *Pros & Cons of Immunization*, edited by Martin L. Leibowitz, Salomon Bothers Inc., 1980.)

17. Rich, C. D., 1952, "Review of the Principles of Life-Office Valuations, Abstract of the Discussion," *Journal of the Institute of Actuaries*, Vol. 78, No. 3, 319–320. (Reprinted in *Pros & Cons of Immunization*, edited by Martin L. Leibowitz, Salomon Brothers Inc., 1980.)

RETURN MAXIMIZATION FOR IMMUNIZED PORTFOLIOS

H. Gifford Fong and Oldrich Vasicek

I. INTRODUCTION

Immunization has been originally conceived as a technique to protect the value of an investment portfolio at the end of a fixed horizon against parallel shifts of interest rates [5,7,10]. Since these pioneering works, the development of immunization theory and practice went in a number of different directions. These can perhaps be classified into the following three major areas:

1. Generalizations of the objectives of immunization
2. Measurement and minimization of risk with respect to nonparallel interest rate changes
3. Maximization of return on immunized portfolios

In the first area of extensions of the basic immunization strategy, the most significant development has been overcoming the limitations of a fixed horizon. Marshall and Yawitz [9] demonstrate that under the assumption of parallel rate changes, a lower bound exists on the value of an investment portfolio at any point in time, although this lower bound may be below the value realized if interest rates did not change. Fong and Vasicek [6] and Bierwag, Kaufman, and Toevs [2] address the case of immunization with respect to multiple liabilities. Multiple liability immunization involves an investment strategy that guarantees meeting a specified schedule of future liabilities regardless of any parallel interest rate shifts. The amount of initial investment necessary for multiple liability immunization is equal to the present value of the liability stream under the initial interest rate structure. The Fong and Vasicek paper provides necessary and sufficient conditions for multiple liability immunization. This work extends the theory further to the general case of arbitrary cash flows (liabilities as well as contributions).

The second area of recent extensions of immunization theory is concerned with relaxing the assumption of parallel changes in interest rates. Most of the works in this area postulate alternative models of interest rate behavior and derive modified definitions of duration corresponding to the assumed interest rate process (see Bierwag [1]; Cox, Ingersoll, and Ross [4]). A limitation of this approach is that immunity is achieved only against the assumed type of rate changes. A different way of dealing with nonparallel rate changes was taken in Fong and Vasicek [6]. They establish a measure of immunization risk against an arbitrary interest rate change, which can be then minimized subject to the duration condition and other constraints to obtain an optimally immunized portfolio. The risk measure is based on second-order conditions for the yield-curve change (first-order conditions define the duration). While duration measures the mean time to payment on a portfolio, the proposed risk measure represents the time-to-payment variance around the liability dates and, therefore, the exposure of the portfolio to relative changes of rates of different maturities.

The third direction of recent interest has been merging immunization with elements of active bond investment strategies. The classical objective of immunization has been risk protection, with little consideration of possible returns. Liebowitz and Weinberger [8] proposed a scheme called contingent immunization, which provides a degree of flexibility in pursuing active strategies while ensuring a certain minimum return in the case of parallel rate shifts. In this approach, immunization serves as a fallback strategy if the actively managed portfolio does not grow at a certain rate.

This paper explores the risk/return trade-off for immunized port-folios using a very different approach. The strategy proposed here maintains the duration of the portfolio at all times equal to the horizon length (or, in the multiple-liability case, keeps the generalized immunization conditions satisfied). Thus, the portfolio stays fully immunized in the classical sense. Instead of minimizing the immunization risk against nonparallel rate changes, however, a tradeoff between risk and return is considered. The immunization risk measure, which represents the portfolio vulnerability to arbitrary rate changes, can be relaxed if the compensation in terms of expected return warrants it. Specifically, the strategy maximizes a *lower bound* on the portfolio return. The lower bound is defined as a confidence interval on the realized return for a given probability level. The optimal portfolio has therefore the following characteristics:

1. Complete immunity against parallel rate shifts. The target rate of return is guaranteed as long as rates of various maturities change by the same amount.
2. The level of immunization risk against arbitrary nonparallel rate changes is measured and minimized in trade-off with expected return.
3. Maximization of the expected portfolio return is included in the objective function together with risk consideration by maximizing a lower bound on return. The lower bound is calculated as a confidence bound with respect to arbitrary interest rate changes.

This paper is organized as follows: Section II describes the risk measure in a single-horizon case. The next section reviews immunization conditions in the general case with multiple liabilities. Section IV derives the confidence intervals used in optimization of the risk/return trade-off. Section V describes the structure of the optimization model.

II. IMMUNIZATION RISK

Assume that an initial investment of I_0 is immunized at time $t_0 = 0$ with respect to a given horizon H against parallel rate changes. Let C_1, $C_2, \ldots, C_m$ be the payments on the investment portfolio, due at times $s_1, s_2, \ldots, s_m$. Denote by $P_0(t)$ the present value of a unit payment at time t, $t \geq 0$, under current interest rates (the discount function). Then

$$I_0 = \sum_{j=1}^{m} C_j P_0(s_j) , \qquad (1)$$

and the immunity is obtained when the portfolio duration

$$D = \sum_{j=1}^{m} \frac{s_j C_j P_0(s_j)}{I_0} \qquad (2)$$

is equal to the horizon length, $D = H$. The target value of the investment at the horizon date is

$$I_H = \frac{I_0}{P_0(H)} . \tag{3}$$

This is the end-of-horizon value of the portfolio if the interest rate structure does not change (which means, specifically, no change in the forward rates). As is known from immunization theory (cf. Fisher and Weil [5]), the target investment value I_H is a lower bound on the end-of-horizon value of the portfolio if rates of all maturities change by the same amount (parallel shift). If rates of different maturities change by different amounts, then I_H is not necessarily a lower bound on the investment value. Specifically, if short rates move down relative to long rates (an adverse twist of the yield curve), the terminal value of the portfolio will be below the target value. In order to establish the riskiness of a given portfolio, we wish to analyze the change in the value of the portfolio at the end of the horizon for a given nonparallel rate change.

Denote by ΔI_H the change in the end-of-horizon investment value corresponding to a given rate change. As has been shown in Fong and Vasicek [6], an expansion of the terminal value function into first three terms of a Taylor's series yields the equation

$$\frac{\Delta I_H}{I_H} = -M^2 \Delta_S \tag{4}$$

where

$$M^2 = \sum_{j=1}^{m} \frac{(s_j - H)^2 C_j P_0(s_j)}{I_0} , \tag{5}$$

$$\Delta_S = \frac{1}{2} \left[\frac{d(\Delta i)}{dt} - (\Delta i)^2 \right]_{t=H} . \tag{6}$$

In the expression (6), $\Delta i(t)$ denotes the change in the forward rates.

Analyzing the structure of equation (4), we see that the relative change in the end-of-horizon value of an immunized portfolio factors into the product of two terms. The first term, M^2, depends solely on the structure of the investment portfolio, while the second term, Δ_S, is a function of the interest rate movement only. The portfolio manager has no control over this second term, which measures, in effect, the twist of the yield curve. For an adverse yield curve twist ($\Delta_S > 0$), the realized return will be under the target level.

The portfolio manager, however, can determine the portfolio composition, and therefore the multiplier M^2. The exposure of the portfolio to a given rate change is proportional to M^2. Portfolios with a low M^2

have a low exposure to interest rate movement, and portfolios with high M^2 have a high exposure. For this reason, M^2 is a measure of *immunization risk*. An optimally immunized portfolio is a portfolio with a minimum exposure to interest rate changes. It is obtained by minimizing the risk measure M^2 subject to the duration condition $D = H$ and any portfolio constraints.

To gain an insight into the significance of the risk measure M^2, note the similarity in form of M^2 to the definition of duration [equation (2)]. While duration is a weighted average of time to payments on the portfolio, the weights being the present values of the payments, M^2 is a similarly weighted time-to-payment *variance* around the horizon date. If the portfolio payments occur close to the horizon date, such as for a deep-discount bond with duration equal to the horizon length, M^2 is low. If the payments are very distant in time from the horizon date, as with a "barbell" portfolio, M^2 is high.

It is not difficult to see why a barbell portfolio should be more risky than a portfolio of low coupon bonds maturing close to the horizon date. Assuming that the durations of both portfolios match the length of the horizon, both portfolios are immune to parallel rate shifts. If interest rates of all maturities decline, the lower reinvestment rate on portfolio payments during the horizon is compensated for by a capital appreciation of the portion of the portfolio still outstanding at the end of the horizon. In the case of interest rate increase, higher reinvestment rates make up for the capital loss. The situation is different for nonparallel rate changes, such as a yield curve twist. Suppose, for instance, the short rates decline while long rates go up. Both portfolios would realize a decline of the end-of-horizon value below the target, since they experience a capital loss in addition to lower reinvestment rates. This decline, however, would be substantially higher for the barbell portfolio for two reasons. One, the portion of barbell portfolio that is still outstanding at the horizon date is much longer than for the other portfolio; so the same rate increase will result in much steeper capital depreciation. Second, the lower reinvestment rates are experienced on the barbell portfolio for longer time intervals than on the portfolio of deep discount bonds, so that the opportunity loss is much greater. As follows from equation (4), the effect of the same adverse yield twist would in fact affect any portfolio proportionally to its M^2.

Note that the risk measure M^2 is always nonnegative. It attains its lowest possible value of zero if and only if the portfolio consists of a single discount bond with maturity equal to the length of the horizon. This is indeed the perfectly immunized portfolio, since no interest rate change affects its end-of-horizon value. Any other portfolio is to some extent vulnerable to an adverse interest rate movement. The immunization risk M^2 in effect measures how much a given portfolio differs from this ideally immunized portfolio consisting of the single discount bond.

III. MULTIPLE LIABILITY IMMUNIZATION

Immunization with respect to a single horizon is applicable to situations where the objective of the investment is to preserve the value of the investment at the horizon date. This may be the case when a single given liability is payable at the horizon date, or a target investment value at that date is to be attained. More often, however, there would be a number of liabilities to be paid from the investment funds, and no single horizon would correspond to the schedule of liabilities. We will call a portfolio *immunized with respect to a given liability stream* if there are enough funds to pay all of the liabilities when due even if interest rates change by an arbitrary parallel shift.

Fong and Vasicek [6] give necessary and sufficient conditions for multiple liability immunization. Suppose that the liability stream consists of n liabilities $A_1, A_2, \ldots, A_n$, payable at times $t_1, t_2, \ldots, t_n$. The initial investment at time $t_0 = 0$ that is necessary for meeting these liabilities in the case of no interest rate change is

$$I_0 = \sum_{i=1}^{n} A_i P_0(t_i) ,$$

where $P_0(t)$ is the discount function. Consider a portfolio with initial value I_0, characterized by payments $C_1, C_2, \ldots, C_m$ to be received at times $s_1, s_2, \ldots, s_m$. We have

$$\sum_{j=1}^{m} C_j P_0(s_j) = I_0 . \tag{7}$$

In order that the portfolio is immunized with respect to the liability stream, it is necessary and sufficient that the following conditions hold:

$$\sum_{j=1}^{m} s_j C_j P_0(s_j) = \sum_{i=1}^{n} t_i A_i P_0(t_i) \tag{8}$$

$$\sum_{j=1}^{m} | s_j - s_k | C_j P_0(s_j) \geq \sum_{i=1}^{n} | t_i - s_k | A_i P_0(t_i) \quad \text{for all } k = 1, 2, \ldots, m .$$

$$\tag{9}$$

Equation (8) means very simply that the duration of the portfolio be the same as the duration of the liability stream. This is a necessary requirement, although in itself it is not sufficient. The inequalities in (9) have a different interpretation. The quantity of the left-hand side resembles a mean absolute deviation (MAD) of the portfolio payment dates, each date being weighted by the present value of the payment. The term on the right of the inequality is a similarly weighted MAD for the liability stream. The set of inequalities in (9) then require that the portfolio payments be more dispersed in time than the liabilities, as measured by MAD around each of the points s_k, for $k = 1, 2, \ldots, m$.

To understand why the portfolio payments have to be more spread out in time than the liabilities to assure immunity, think of the single-horizon case. There, immunization was achieved by balancing changes in reinvestment return on portfolio payments maturing prior to the horizon date against changes in the value at the horizon date of the portfolio portion still outstanding. The same "straddling" of each liability by the portfolio payments is necessary in the multiple liability case, which implies that the payments have to be more dispersed in time than the liabilities. That the requirement of broader dispersion in time of the portfolio payments compared to that of the liabilities should mean specifically the inequalities in (9) is by no means obvious. The proof, given in Fong and Vasicek [6], is based on the duality theory of linear programming. In the case of a single liability, the inequalities in (9) are always satisfied, so that the necessary and sufficient conditions reduce to the requirement that the portfolio duration matches the date of the liability.

The above conditions for multiple liability immunization assure immunity against parallel rate shifts only. In the general case of an arbitrary interest rate change, the change in the value of an immunized portfolio at the horizon date is again described by equation (4). The quantity M^2 is now defined by the formula

$$M^2 = \sum_{j=1}^{m} \frac{(s_j - D)^2 C_j P_0(s_j)}{I_0}$$

$$- \sum_{j=1}^{n} \frac{(t_i - D)^2 A_i P_0(t_i)}{I_0}, \tag{10}$$

where D is the duration of the portfolio, equal to the duration of the liability stream in virtue of equation (8),

$$D = \sum_{j=1}^{m} \frac{s_j C_j P_0(s_j)}{I_0} = \sum_{i=1}^{n} \frac{t_i A_i P_0(t_i)}{I_0}. \tag{11}$$

The risk measure M^2 is defined for immunized portfolios only. It is always nonnegative in virtue of the inequalities in (9) (cf. Fong and Vasicek [6]). It attains its extreme value of zero if and only if the portfolio payments coincide exactly in amount and timing with the liabilities.

IV. CONFIDENCE INTERVALS

The risk measure M^2 described in the previous sections can be used to construct approximate *confidence intervals* for the end-of-horizon portfolio value or for the rate of return on investment over the horizon. Unless it is possible to match each liability exactly in amount and timing by the portfolio payments, an immunized portfolio is subject to some risk, measured by M^2, of exposure to nonparallel rate changes. A confidence interval represents an uncertainty band around the target return within which the realized return can be expected with a given probability. We will now show how such confidence intervals can be constructed.

Consider first the single-horizon case with no cash flows. The rate of return R on investment is defined by the equation

$$(1 + R)^H = \frac{I_H}{I_0},$$

where I_H is the portfolio value at the horizon date and I_0 is the initial investment. If, due to a change in interest rates, the terminal value changes by an amount ΔI_H, then the rate of return changes approximately by the amount

$$\Delta R = \frac{1}{H} \frac{\Delta I_H}{I_H}. \tag{12}$$

Substituting from equation (4), the change in the rate of return is approximately

$$\Delta R = -\frac{1}{H} M^2 \Delta_S, \tag{13}$$

where Δ_S is the yield twist defined in equation (6).

Equation (13) represents the effect of a single interest rate change. Since interest rates can move at any time during the horizon, the difference between the realized and target returns over the horizon has to be calculated as the sum

$$\Delta R = -\frac{1}{H} \sum_{t=1}^{H} M_t^2 \Delta_{St}, \tag{14}$$

where Δ_{St} is the yield twist occurring at time t, and M_t^2 is the risk measure of the portfolio at time t. Assuming independence of yield twists over nonoverlapping periods, the variance of the realized rate of return is then given by

$$\sigma_R^2 = \sigma^2 \frac{1}{H^2} \sum_{t=1}^{H} M_t^4, \tag{15}$$

where $\sigma^2 = \sigma^2(\Delta_{St})$ is the variance of the one-period change in the slope of the structure. This variance can be estimated empirically from historical yield changes.

Theoretical considerations, confirmed by empirical measurements, show that the M^2 of an optimally immunized portfolio, periodically rebalanced, decreases in time in approximate proportion to the third power of the remaining horizon length,

$$M_t^2 = M^2 \left(\frac{H-t}{H} \right)^3$$

where M^2 is the initial risk level. Using this relationship in equation (15) produces an expression for the standard deviation of return in the form

$$\sigma_R = \sigma M^2 a_H \tag{16}$$

where $a_H = (7H)^{-1/2}$ is a function of the horizon length only. Confidence intervals for the realized rate of return of the form

$$R = R_{target} \pm k\sigma_R \tag{17}$$

can then easily be established. The notable aspect of the confidence intervals is that their width is proportional to the risk measure M^2. A portfolio with half the value of M^2 than another portfolio can be expected to produce half the dispersion of realized returns around the target value when submitted to a variety of interest rate scenarios than the other portfolio. This has been confirmed by empirical measurement.

An expression identical in form to equation (16) can be derived for the standard deviation of the realized rate of return in the multiple liability case. The quantity a_H will in this case be a function of the dates and relative sizes of the liabilities, in addition to the horizon length. Confidence intervals in the form of equation (17) can then be constructed. Again, the width of the confidence intervals is proportional to M^2 of the immunized portfolio.

V. RETURN MAXIMIZATION

In the strict sense, the objective of immunization is minimization of risk. As far as only parallel rate changes are considered, any portfolio satisfying the appropriate immunization conditions would be acceptable. In the single-horizon case, it is any portfolio with duration equal to the horizon length. In immunization with respect to a stream of liabilities, the immunization conditions are as given in equation (8) and inequalities (9).

In the more realistic case when rates can move in an arbitrary nonparallel fashion, the appropriate measure of risk for immunized portfolios is M^2 as defined in equation (5) or (10). Constructing an optimally immunized portfolio then becomes an optimization problem with the following structure:

Minimize the immunization risk (M^2) subject to

1. Immunization conditions [conditions (8) and (9) in the multiple liability case]
2. Portfolio constraints (such as concentration constraints)

It could be seen that the objective function M^2, as well as the immunization conditions and portfolio concentration constraints, are all linear in the portfolio holdings. Consequently, constructing optimally immunized portfolios can be accomplished by the use of *linear programming* techniques, which are simple and efficient. It is possible to include both minimum and maximum holding requirements on individual securities, as well as on groups of securities (such as quality/issuing sector constraints). Modifications of the structure of the linear programming problem make it possible even to include transaction costs.

In some situations, the objective of immunization as strict risk immunization may be deemed too restrictive. If a substantial increase in the expected return can be accomplished with little effect on immunization risk, the higher yielding portfolio may be preferred in spite of its higher risk. Consider an example in which an optimally immunized portfolio has a target return of 13 percent over the horizon, with a 95 percent confidence interval of ± 0.20 percent. This means that the minimum risk portfolio would have 1 in 40 chance of realized return less than 12.8 percent. Suppose that another portfolio, less well immunized, can produce a target return of 13.3 percent with 95 percent confidence interval of ±0.30 percent. In all but one case out of 40, this portfolio would realize return above 13 percent, compared to 12.8 percent of the minimum risk portfolio. For many investors, this may be a preferred tradeoff.

It is possible to set up the optimization problem in such a way that instead of risk minimization, the risk/return trade-off is being optimized. This can be accomplished by maximizing a *lower bound* on the realized return corresponding to a given confidence level. Since the confidence interval width is proportional to M^2, the objective function can in this case be expressed as

$$\text{Maximize } R_{target} - k\sigma a_H M^2 .$$

This objective function is equivalent to the objective

$$\text{Minimize } M^2 - \lambda R_{target} , \qquad (18)$$

where

$$\lambda = \frac{1}{k\sigma a_H} .$$

It is seen that the objective function (18) represents a trade-off between immunization risk and target return. If the parameter λ is small (corresponding to a high confidence level for the lower bound), the emphasis in the construction of the optimal portfolio is on risk. In the extreme case of $\lambda = 0$, the objective would be strict risk minimization. On the other hand, if λ is high (such as for low confidence levels), the primary concern of the optimization is maximum return. The extreme case $\lambda = \infty$ would correspond to maximization of return subject only to the requirement that the portfolio be immunized against parallel rate shifts. In the single-horizon case, this would mean selecting the highest return portfolio among all portfolios with duration equal to the horizon length.

Since the target return is also a linear function of the portfolio holdings, linear programming techniques can still be used to solve the optimization problem with the objective function as in equation (18). In fact, *parametric linear programming* can be applied to the coefficient λ to determine an *efficient frontier* for immunized portfolios, analogous to those in the mean/variance framework.

REFERENCES

1. Bierwag, G. O., 1978, "Measures of Duration," *Economic Inquiry* (October).
2. Bierwag, G. O., G. G. Kaufman, and A. Toevs, 1979, "Immunization For Multiple Planning Periods," Unpublished paper, Center for Capital Market Research, University of Oregon, October.
3. Bierwag, G. O., G. G. Kaufman, R. Schweitzer, and A. Toevs, 1979, "Risk and Return For Active and Passive Bond Portfolio Management: Theory and Evidence," Unpublished paper, Center for Capital Market Research, University of Oregon, October.
4. Cox, John C., Jonathon E. Ingersoll, Jr., and Stephen A. Ross, 1979, "Duration and the Measurement of Basis Risk," *Journal of Business*, 52.
5. Fisher, Lawrence, and R. Weil, 1971, "Coping with Risk of Interest Rate Fluctuations: Returns to Bondholders from Naive and Optimal Strategies," *Journal of Business*, October.

6. Fong, H. Gifford, and Oldrich Vasicek, 1980, "A Risk Minimizing Strategy for Multiple Liability Immunization," Institute for Quantitative Research in Finance.

7. Macauley, F. R., 1938, "Some Theoretical Problems Suggested by the Movement of Interest Rates, Bond Yields and Stock Prices in the U.S. Since 1856," National Bureau of Economic Research, New York.

8. Liebowitz, Martin L. and Alfred Weinberger, 1981, "Contingent Immunization," Soloman Brothers, January.

9. Marshall, W. and Jess B. Yawitz, 1974, "Lower Bounds on Portfolio Performance: A Generalized Immunization Strategy," Unpublished paper, Graduate school of Business, Washington University, July.

10. Vanderhoof, Irwin T., 1972, "The Interest Rate Assumption and the Maturity Structure of the Assets of a Life Insurance Company," *Transactions of the Society of Actuaries*, 24, June.

DURATION AND THE TERM STRUCTURE OF INTEREST RATE VOLATILITY

David F. Babbel

I. INTRODUCTION

During the past decade academicians, and of late, fund managers have directed an enormous amount of attention toward the resurrected notion called *duration*. First introduced by Macauley in 1938 [14] and Hicks in 1939 [11], and more recently developed by Fisher and Weil [7], Bierwag et al. [1], Cox, Ingersoll, and Ross [6], and others, duration is an index number associated with a particular payment stream at a given moment in time which conveys information about the average maturity of the payment stream (which may differ from the years to maturity of the underlying instrument if multiple cash flows are involved) and the price volatility of the instrument with respect to interest rate fluctuations. One of the more popular uses of duration is in the construction of portfolios whose rates of returns are "immunized" for unanticipated changes in the market rates of interest. The appeal of an immunized fund is that by appropriately arranging the durations

239

of its component parts, prevailing market yields can be "locked in" over the future irrespective of the future course of interest rates. Thus, achieving a desired yield over time does not require correct forecasts of interest rates.

Avoiding the precarious profession of interest rate forecasting may appear to be advantageous, at first blush. However, in order to avoid relying on such forecasts, we require appropriate duration measures. By "appropriate" it is meant that the computed duration of a payment stream accurately conveys what it is supposed to convey. To achieve appropriate durations necessitates accurate forecasts, not of future interest rate levels, but of relative fluctuations in interest rates appertaining to different lengths of time. In other words, if the first-year spot rate of interest were to fluctuate by x percent over an interval of time, then the spot rate applicable to cash flows in year t is likely to fluctuate by $\beta_t x$ percent over the same time interval where β_t is the relative volatility of the latter rate to the former. When relative volatilities are specified over several maturities, we have what will be called the *term structure of interest rate volatility* (TSIRV).

In deriving duration formulae, forecasts of the term structure of interest rate volatility are implicit in the simplifying assumptions employed. For example, different duration measures have been developed for additive, multiplicative, logarithmic and exponential shifts in the term structure, as well as various combinations of these shifting patterns. In these measures, the general functional forms of the shifts are specified while the precise parameters of these functions are sometimes left unspecified and need to be input by the user. The resulting duration measure will be accurate only to the extent that interest rate term structures at successive dates fluctuate relative to each other in the manner assumed within the formulas.

Unfortunately, most duration measures were developed on the basis of mathematical tractability rather than economic realities; moreover, Ingersoll, Skelton, and Weil [13] and Cox, Ingersoll, and Ross [6] have shown that the stochastic processes implicit in some of the duration measures are inconsistent with economic and statistical theory. Accordingly, we have a number of duration measures which are inappropriate for use in the real world, as the TSIRV forecasts implicit in the formulas have little relation to the TSIRV experienced by the market. Even when the precise parameters of the formulae are left unspecified, the underlying functional forms of the stochastic processes may not allow sufficient degrees of freedom to accurately model the forecasted TSIRV.

In the following section, a generalized duration formula will be presented in which forecasts of the TSIRV are made explicit. Whether at blushes of higher order we have gained an advantage by using duration strategies will depend upon the ease of correctly forecasting the TSIRV to that of correctly forecasting interest rate levels. This latter issue will be dealt with in the third section. In the fourth section, the relative volatility measures that were estimated in the third section are employed to generate bond duration measures. The bonds are combined to form five-year immunized funds with a new fund beginning in each month starting in 1952. The performance of these funds, as measured by their achievement of a five-year target yield, is compared to three competing funds, one of which reinvests in six-month Treasury bills, another of which employs the maturity strategy [7] to achieve the targeted yield, and a third that uses the traditional duration measure and Fisher–Weil immunization strategy.

The major results of this paper are as follows. First it is shown that the generalized immunizing duration formula differs from the generalized bond price-interest rate elasticity measure by a multiplicative factor. Second, it is shown that a single bond, while having only one price elasticity measure with respect to changes in the one-year spot rate of interest, may have multiple durations that solve the equation at a given moment in time. Third, it is noted that in the event of multiple solution durations, not all of the duration measures are "immunizing durations" (i.e., producing the target return if interest rates are not shocked and higher returns if a shock occurs); some may be "nonimmunizing durations" (i.e., where the target return is the best that can be achieved, and this only if interest rates are not shocked). Moreover, a particular bond in a given economic environment need not exhibit any immunizing durations whatsoever. However, given an estimated TSIRV and faced with a term structure of interest rates, the immunizing properties of a particular bond can be investigated a priori and the immunizing duration, if any, can be found. If the bond features no immunizing duration, bonds of other coupon levels and/or maturities can be located which have immunizing durations. Fourth, two TSIRV forecasting techniques are tested and the TSIRV, while found to be extremely volatile, is also found to be amenable to reasonably good forecasts. Fifth, the TSIRV measures are incorporated into bond duration estimates using actual U.S. government obligations price quotations; based on these duration measures, bonds are formed into portfolios designed to be five-year immunized funds and compared with other methods of achieving a targeted return. The immunization techniques were found to have the same success rate as the maturity strategy, albeit with much lower dollar value errors in cases where the strategies failed to achieve the targeted returns.[1] A contribution of this paper is in providing a strategy based upon "look ahead" duration measures, wherein the portfolio uses expected duration estimates to immunize against shocks in the term structure six months hence, rather than the usual duration techniques that immunize against instantaneous shocks in the term structure. Finally, other applications of the techniques presented in this paper are discussed.

II. GENERALIZED DURATION FORMULAS

Rather than restricting the TSIRV to some mathematically convenient functional form, the two formulas derived in this section are designed to accomodate any shape of the TSIRV whatsoever. Separate formulas are derived for the immunizing duration of a bond and the price elasticity (with respect to a fluctuation in the one-year spot rate) of a bond. Both of these measures require estimates of the TSIRV. The matter of estimating the TSIRV is dealt with in a subsequent section.

The notation to be used in the derivations is as follows:

R_t = initial spot rate of interest for t years

R_t^* = spot rate of interest for t years after shock in term structure

λ = $[(1 + R_1^*)/(1 + R_1)] - 1$ [lambda represents the percent change in $(1 + R_1)$; thus, $(1 + \lambda)(1 + R_1) = (1 + R_1^*)$]

β_t = $[(1 + R_t^*)/(1 + R_t) - 1] \div [(1 + R_1^*)/(1 + R_1) - 1]$ (β_t represents the percentage change in $(1 + R_t)$ relative to the percentage change in $(1 + R_1)$; thus, $(1 + \beta_t\lambda)(1 + R_t) = (1 + R_t^*)$)

V_t = the value of a bond (including coupons received and earnings on reinvested coupons, if any) at time t

S_t = cash flow occurring at time t

Now the present value of a bond, before a shock in the term structure of interest rates, may be written as:

$$V_0 = \sum_{t=1}^{m} S_t(1 + R_t)^{-t} . \tag{1}$$

The value of the bond after an instantaneous shock in the term structure is given by

$$V_0(\lambda) = \sum_{t=1}^{m} S_t(1 + R_t^*)^{-t} = \sum_{t=1}^{m} S_t(1 + \lambda\beta_t)^{-t}(1 + R_t)^{-t} . \tag{2}$$

The value of the bond (including coupons received and earnings on reinvested coupons) at time q with no change in the term structure would be

$$V_q(0) = V_0(1 + R_q)^q . \tag{3}$$

The value of the fund at time q with an instantaneous change in the term structure would be given by

$$V_q(\lambda) = V_0(\lambda)(1 + \lambda\beta_q)^q(1 + R_q)^q . \tag{4}$$

If immunization over a time horizon of q years is to occur, the accumulated value of the fund at time q must be greater than or equal to what the accumulated value at time q would have been if no shock in the interest rate structure occurred, regardless of the direction of the term structure shift; that is, the value given by equation (4) must be at least as large as that given in equation (3).

$$V_q(\lambda) \geq V_0(1 + R_q)^q . \tag{5}$$

This will hold true if

$$\phi(\lambda) = (1 + \lambda\beta_q)^q V_0(\lambda) - V_0(0) \geq 0 . \tag{6}$$

Formula (6) can be rewritten by substituting for V_0 from equations (1) and (2) and factoring out $S_t(1 + R_t)^{-t}$, yielding

$$\phi(\lambda) = \sum_{t=1}^{m} [(1 + \lambda\beta_q)^q(1 + \lambda\beta_t)^{-t} - 1]S_t(1 + R_t)^{-t} . \tag{7}$$

To analyze the properties of this function, we take its first and second derivatives with respect to the shock in the first year spot rate of interest.

$$\phi'(\lambda) = \sum_{t=1}^{m} [q\beta_q(1 + \lambda\beta_q)^{q-1}(1 + \lambda\beta_t)^{-t}$$

$$- t\beta_t(1 + \lambda\beta_q)^q(1 + \lambda\beta_t)^{-t-1}]S_t(1 + R_t)^{-t} . \tag{8}$$

$$\phi''(\lambda) = \sum_{t=1}^{m} [q(q - 1)\beta_q^2(1 + \lambda\beta_q)^{q-2}(1 + \lambda\beta_t)^{-t}$$

$$- 2q\beta_q t\beta_t(1 + \lambda\beta_q)^{q-1}(1 + \lambda\beta_t)^{-t-1} \tag{9}$$

$$+ t(t + 1)\beta_t^2(1 + \lambda\beta_q)^q(1 + \lambda\beta_t)^{-t-2}]S_t(1 + R_t)^{-t} .$$

If we desire our lowest terminal rate of return to occur where no shock is manifest in the term structure, we set $\phi'(0) = 0$ and solve for the horizon, q, where this result may be achieved. Substituting 0 where lambdas appear,

$$\phi'(0) = \sum_{t=1}^{m} [q\beta_q - t\beta_t]S_t (1 + R_t)^{-t}. \tag{10}$$

Therefore,

$$\sum_{t=1}^{m} q\beta_q S_t(1 + R_t)^{-t} = \sum_{t=1}^{m} t\beta_t S_t(1 + R_t)^{-t} \tag{11}$$

and the q, or immunizing duration, is given by

$$q\beta_q = \frac{\displaystyle\sum_{t=1}^{m} t\beta_t S_t(1 + R_t)^{-t}}{\displaystyle\sum_{t=1}^{m} S_t(1 + R_t)^{-t}},$$

which implies

$$q = \frac{1}{\beta_q} \frac{\displaystyle\sum_{t=1}^{m} t\beta_t S_t(1 + R_t)^{-t}}{\displaystyle\sum_{t=1}^{m} S_t(1 + R_t)^{-t}}. \tag{12}$$

A sufficient condition for the q given in equation (12) to be an immunizing duration is for the second derivative of the ϕ function to be positive after substituting the solution q. However, further examination showed that the second derivative equation (9) cannot always be proved positive. Nonetheless, it is both necessary and sufficient for the quantity given by equation (7) to be nonnegative. Since the sign of the expression cannot be proven unambiguously positive by analytical means, a numerical investigation was undertaken.

Ideally, equation (7) should be nonnegative for a wide range of coupons (S_t), term structures of interest (R_t), term structures of interest rate volatility (β_t), and maturities (m), regardless of the size or direction of the shock to the term structure. Using an iterative procedure to solve for q, the immunizing capability of the solution q of formula (12) was checked through equation (7) for maturities of 2 to 30 years, coupons of 1.25 to 25 percent, term structures of interest and interest volatilities characterized by a myriad of shapes and ranges (both historical and hypothetical),[2] for instantaneous shocks in the first year spot rate ranging from 0.05 percent to 10 percent. The finding in over 90 percent of the cases analyzed was that the duration generated by equation (12) was, in fact, an immunizing (or "minimizing") duration. In other cases, however, the solution q would lead to a nonimmunizing duration, wherein the terminal rate of return would always be lower in the event of a shock in the term structure than in the absence of such a shock.[3] In these cases there were usually multiple solutions to the duration formula for the bond and economic environment in question. The possibility of multiple durations arises because the product $t\beta_t$ is not necessarily an increasing function of t. Hence, in searching for a product $q\beta_q$ that equals the right hand side of equation (12), multiple solution combinations are possible, as shown in Figure 1. In Figure 1, w represents the right-hand side of equation (12). It is possible to find multiple solution q's along the horizontal axis, corresponding to points where w intersects the $t\beta_t$ function. In cases where the first duration measure was a nonimmunizing duration, successive durations were examined until an immunizing duration was found. In a few rare cases, the term structure of interest and interest rate volatility were so perverse that none of the single or multiple durations of a bond were immunizing so that a bond with a different maturity or coupon would need to be selected. This gave little cause for concern, however, because in practice

Figure 1.

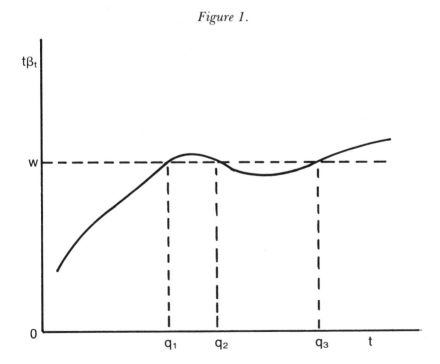

it is easy to check beforehand on the immunizing properties of a given bond in a particular economic environment, and it is easy to form a portfolio of bonds that has the desired duration if no single bond is found possessing such.

The solution q given by equation (12) also serves as a price elasticity measure with respect to changes in the spot rate R_q. However, such price volatility measures are of little use since they cannot be used to assess relative volatilities across bonds, as the price volatility of each bond relates to the volatility of a different R_q. To remedy this situation, if it is assumed that a given TSIRV holds, then the derivatives of the bond prices may all be taken with respect to changes in the first-year spot rate R_1. The emerging price elasticity measures are then comparable across bonds and provide measures of relative volatilities. The price elasticity formula is similar to equation (12) except that the $1/\beta_q$ term is omitted. The derivation is as follows:

$$V = \sum S_t(1 + R_t)^{-t}$$

$$\frac{dV}{d(1 + R_1)} = \sum -tS_t(1 + R_t)^{-t-1} \frac{d(1 + R_t)}{d(1 + R_1)} .$$

Therefore,

$$dV = \sum -tS_t(1 + R_t)^{-t} \frac{d(1 + R_t)}{d(1 + R_1)} \frac{d(1 + R_1)}{(1 + R_t)} \left(\frac{1 + R_1}{1 + R_1}\right) .$$

Recalling the definition of β_t as a relative volatility measure and substituting,

$$dV = [\sum - t\beta_t S_t(1 + R_t)^{-t}] \frac{d(1 + R_1)}{(1 + R_1)} .$$

Dividing both sides by V, or its equivalent expression given by equation (1), results in the price elasticity formula:

$$\frac{dV}{V} = \frac{\sum -t\beta_t S_t(1 + R_t)^{-t}}{\sum S_t(1 + R_t)^{-t}} \cdot \% \Delta(1 + R_1) . \tag{13}$$

Both the duration formula (12) and the price elasticity formula (13) make explicit the inclusion of a TSIRV forecast. In other formulas that have been proposed, this requirement is not always as apparent. The question now becomes one of whether the TSIRV is amenable to accurate forecasting, which is the topic of the next section.

As mentioned earlier, the formulae are advantageous in that they do not restrict the TSIRV to any particular shape. The formulae do not even require that forward interest rates fluctuate in the same direction as the first year spot rate; moreover, they need not fluctuate at all.

In spite of these advantages, there remains one drawback. While the first year spot rate may undergo any kind or size of shock, the relative rates of change in the other spot rates are functionally related by a beta factor to the stochastic shock in the first-year rate. Thus, the formula is deterministic. It is likely that different causes of a shock in the first-year rate may affect longer term spot rates in different ways, even if the first-year rate moves by the same amount in reaction to these causes.

To cope with this possibility, different formula parameters could be specified or estimated, conditional upon the various categories of events that might shock the first-year rate. However, to select an appropriate formula would compound the forecasting problem since the probabilities of the occurrence of the future states of the world would also need to be assessed. It is also conceivable that shocks of similar magnitude in the first-year rates deriving from the same cause, but at different times, may result in different relative shifts in the longer term spot rates. These dissimilar patterns may perhaps be related to a third factor; for example, the stage in the business cycle at the moment of shock. Worse, it may be that dissimilar shifts would occur even if experimentally controlled conditions were approximated, simply because of the stochastic nature of the processes modeled. Finally, shifts in longer term rates relative to one-year rate shocks may be better represented by a nonlinear or multifactor function, where the relative shifts in longer term rates depend upon the magnitude of the one-year interest rate shock and/or the general level of interest rates.

Whether or not these hypothetical problems are binding is an empirical issue which is dealt with in the next section. While further generalization of the formula could accomodate some of these concerns, we have attempted to strike a balance between the completely general and the operational in the formulae presented here. We now proceed to the issue of the forecastability of the TSIRV.

III. TSIRV—EMPIRICAL EVIDENCE

The utilization of formulas (12) and (13) requires forecasts of the TSIRV that will prevail over the time horizon of concern. (In other words, a vector of betas needs to be specified.) It is common to base forecasts upon historical data series and extrapolate into the future from past trends. This approach is justifiable when one has no compelling reason to suspect that the pattern will change appreciably. The tack taken here is to determine whether the TSIRV has exhibited stability over time. If stability at some level is demonstrated over a long period of time characterized by economic and policital diversity, then the forecaster may feel more confident in projecting these relationships to continue into the future.

In order to estimate the betas based on historical information, we first require a series of data on bond prices. From these data the term structure of spot interest rates can be inferred. Finally, by comparing the term structures at successive dates we are provided with measures of spot rate volatilities relative to the variability exhibited in the first year interest rates.

Price Data

Monthly price data for virtually all U.S. government obligations were obtained from the NBER and CRSP government bond data files. The 33-year period for which quotations were obtained began in January, 1947 and ended in January, 1980. Both data series produced similar results; for the version discussed herein, the CRSP data were used to generate the term structures of interest. The data were of reasonably good quality, and only technical adjustments were made to convert the quotation dates into value dates before computing the term structures.

Estimation of Term Structure of Interest

A number of techniques have been devised for estimating the term structure of interest rates [4], [12], [15], [16], [17], [20], [21]. Indeed, after experimenting with four of these methods, including one devised by the author in connection with this project, we opted for the "tax-adjusted" yield curve estimation procedure suggested by McCulloch [17], which uses a cubic spline technique for regression fitting the term structure. The technique was selected because it is efficient and economical. While superior techniques might exist, the McCulloch technique was adequate for our purposes, as the overriding concern was to obtain relative volatility estimates; these appear to be similar regardless of the technique used to generate the term structure. Rather than allow the "tax rate" to fluctuate in search of a best fit, we constrained the rate at 26 percent, which was the globally best fitting rate over the time period considered. This constraint was imposed to avoid introducing into our term structure estimates an element which unnecessarily complicates the volatility structure estimates, as we presume that the effective term structures of interest to an investor or fund eliciting stable tax rates would not always fluctuate over time by the same amounts as the best fitting term structure.

Relative Volatility Estimates

For reasons to be discussed in the applications section, the horizon over which volatilities in the term structure were measured was six months. Because the duration formulas were derived with respect to "instantaneous shocks" to the term structure, the six-month volatilities were converted into their instantaneous equivalents as follows. The word *shock* denotes an unexpected occurrence. Therefore, we measured differences between the actual (or "shocked") term structure at time t and the term structure that at time t − 6 was expected to prevail at time t. Two hypotheses were employed at time t − 6 for generating expected term structures for time t. In the first model it was assumed that the term structure at time t − 6 represented the expected term structure for time t; that is, no changes were expected in the shape or location of the term structure. This hypothesis has its roots in the liquidity preference [11] and preferred habitat [19] hypotheses of the term structure. The second model, founded in the pure expectations hypothesis [18], used the forward rates in the term structure at time t − 6 to infer the implicitly "expected" term structure for time t. (For sake of convenience, these two kinds of shocks will hereafter be dubbed "random walk shock" and "pure expectations shock," respectively.)

Volatility computations consisted of taking the differences between the actual and expected t-period spot rates and then dividing by one plus the t-period expected spot rates. The relative volatility measures, β_t, have been defined as a ratio of the percentage change in $1 + R_t$ to the percentage change in $1 + R_1$:

$$\beta_t = \frac{\% \ \Delta(1 + R_t)}{\% \ \Delta(1 + R_1)}$$

However, a time series of these betas is of little use in predicting the levels of future betas, as the absolute values of the computations range from zero to several hundred and, potentially, infinity (while a reasonable range would be zero to one or thereabouts). An infinite beta could result if, for example, the one-year spot rate does not move and the t-year spot rate moves an infinitessimal amount. Clearly such interest rate movements will have no appreciable impact upon the price of a bond and the use of these betas would result in spurious duration measures. Therefore, the betas were estimated using least-squares techniques where the relative volatilities that potentially impact bond prices most are accorded more weight:

$$\% \ \Delta(1 + R_t) = \hat{\beta}_t \ \% \ \Delta(1 + R_1) + \epsilon$$

Forecasting the TSIRV

Our primary objective in forecasting was to produce accurate forecasts using only information that would be readily available at the time a forecast is made. As the economy has undergone rather substantial structural changes in the past, we did not desire our forecasting model to be unduly dependent on data from the far distant past.

The first forecasting model was simply a five-year moving least-squares estimate of the average beta in the recent past. Data beyond five years in the past were not used at each point in time to forecast the vector of betas to prevail over the next six months, nor were the observations time weighted. The selection of five-year periods for evaluation of past data is somewhat arbitrary, but results from our attempt to balance the need for enough observations to provide statistical credibility while avoiding the shackles of "ancient" history; moreover, five years represents the average length of business cycles, which typically last for four to seven years.

By observing six-month differences for beta estimation, we are limited to two independent observations per year and 12 per five-year period. This would represent an inefficient use of our data, which are available on a monthly basis. To increase the sample size, overlapping samples are taken; six-month differences are taken every month. This increases the sample size (by a factor of 6) to 60 observations on which to base each beta estimate. However, the overlapping periods produce auto-correlation in the residuals, which will give rise to downward biased estimates of the standard errors. To remedy this situation, we used a generalized least-squares regression technique especially designed for this problem by Hansen [9] and used by Hansen and Hodrick [10], Hakkio [8] and Bilson [2] in applications characterized by a similar overlapping data sampling horizon. The method as it applies to our particular measurement problem is described in detail by Chow [5].

Applying the aforementioned forecasting technique to our data resulted in two series of beta vector estimates for each month, beginning in 1952 and ending in 1980. One series was generated by application of the "random walk" definition of *shocks*, while the other series followed from the "pure expectations shock" definition.

In Figures 2 to 4, examples are given of the estimated TSIRV at various dates in the past. These figures, as well as Table 1 and all other figures presented in this paper, are based on the random-walk-shocks definition. (At this point we should mention that application of the pure-expectations-shocks definition produced lower, more stable betas that were more easily predicted.) The figures show that longer term

Figure 2. Relative Interest Rate Volatility—January 1960.

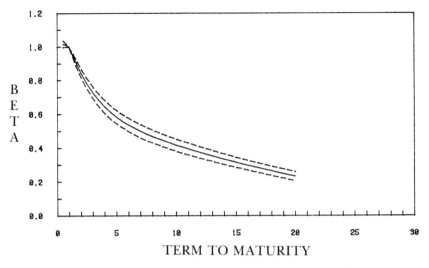

Dash lines—Plus or minus one SE.

Figure 3. Relative Interest Rate Volatility—January 1970.

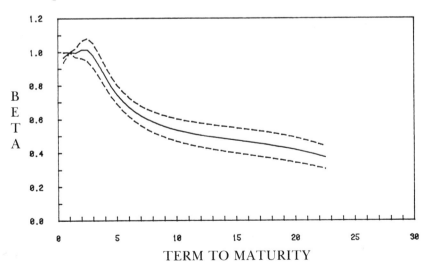

Dash lines—Plus or minus one SE.

251

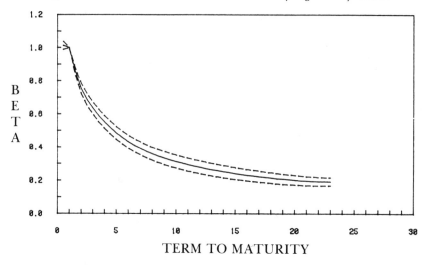

Figure 4. Relative Interest Rate Volatility—January 1980.

Dash lines—Plus or minus one SE.

Table 1. Comparison of Forecast Errors*

	Least Squares			ARIMA		
Beta	Mean error	Mean squared error	Mean absolute error	Mean error	Mean squared error	Mean absolute error
2	.00182	.01548	.09523	-.00061	.00200	.02677
3	.00074	.02454	.11944	-.00073	.00274	.03233
4	.00192	.02360	.11656	-.00085	.00272	.03252
5	.00380	.02271	.11287	-.00113	.00255	.03070
6	.00559	.02331	.11207	-.00101	.00251	.03039
7	.00728	.02398	.11308	-.00088	.00247	.03044
8	.00898	.02425	.11391	-.00079	.00238	.03025
9	.01049	.02418	.11424	-.00081	.00227	.03007
10	.01179	.02382	.11378	-.00088	.00215	.02977
11	.01304	.02341	.11327	-.00091	.00205	.02953
12	.01427	.02294	.11233	-.00090	.00198	.02923
13	.01556	.02248	.11111	-.00084	.00195	.02904

Note: Forecast error is defined as the difference between actual one year averages and forecast value.

spot rates have usually fluctuated by a smaller amount than shorter term spot rates, although in the same direction, when the one-year spot rate of interest was shocked. As shown by the standard errors (indicated by the dashed lines), these relationships have neither been completely deterministic nor stationary over time. In Figures 5 to 7, time series plots of selected individual beta forecasts, along with their respective standard errors, are given. The beta refers to the degree to which the 2-, 6-, and 10-year spot rates fluctuate relative to movements in the one-year spot rate. The figures indicate a downward trend in betas and a slight improvement in standard errors in recent years.

The second forecasting model used was the autoregressive integrated moving average (ARIMA) technique of Box and Jenkins [3]. The model was applied to a 60-month time series of 12-month least-squares betas to generate future beta forecasts.[4] Statistical testing indicated that the underlying stochastic process, after taking first differences of the original time series, was a first-order moving average (see Figure 11). Examples of the forecasts are provided in Figures 8 to 10 for β_2, β_6, and β_{10}, where the forecasted values are given by the broken lines and the actual 12-month least-squares values are given by the solid lines. The volatility of the actual beta time series is more evident in these

Figure 5. Beta 2.

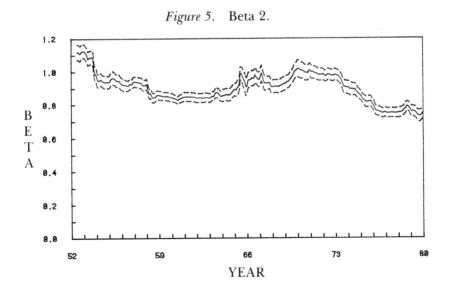

YEAR

Dash lines—Plus or minus one SE.

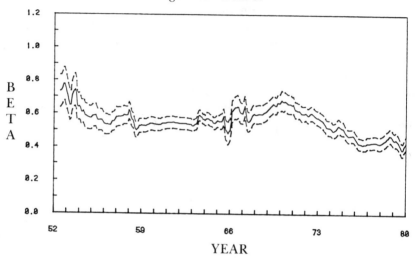

Figure 6. Beta 6.

Dash lines—Plus or minus one SE.

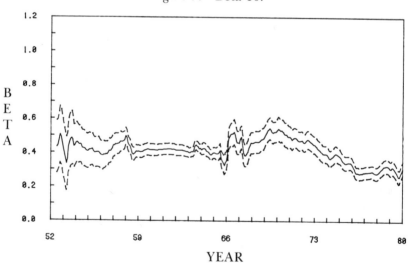

Figure 7. Beta 10.

Dash lines—Plus or minus one SE.

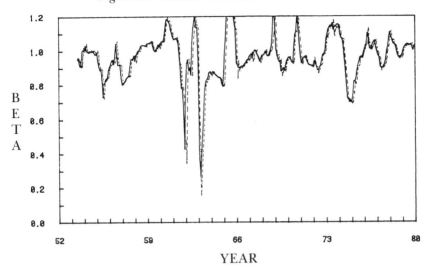

Figure 8. ARIMA Forecasts of Beta 2.

Solid line—Actual One Year Averages.
Broken line—ARIMA Forecasts.

Figure 9. ARIMA Forecasts of Beta 6.

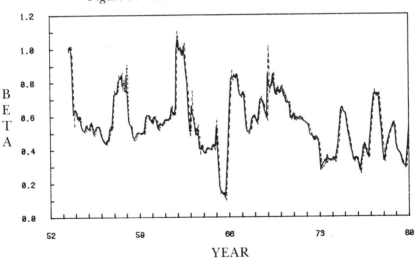

Solid line—Actual One Year Averages.
Broken line—ARIMA Forecasts.

255

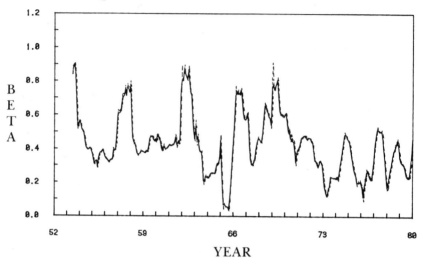

Figure 10. ARIMA Forecasts of Beta 10.

YEAR

Solid line—Actual One Year Averages.
Broken line—ARIMA Forecasts.

Figure 11. Correlogram for Beta 2 after First Difference.

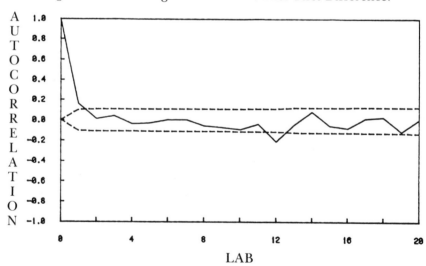

LAB

Dash lines—95X Confidence Interval.

256

figures, although the ARIMA model generally tracks the actual beta series reasonably well, but with a one-month lag. Thus, the ARIMA method is not very effective in forecasting turns in directions, but the forecasts "recover" rapidly.

A comparison of the forecast errors of the two forecasting models is given in Table 1. The mean squared errors associated with the least-squares technique were on the order of ten times larger than those associated with the ARIMA forecasts. However, during periods of large, sudden movements in the actual beta series, the GLS forecasts often closer to the actual beta values than the ARIMA forecasts. Nonetheless, the ARIMA technique usually produces more accurate forecasts than the GLS approach. Whether or not the more accurate forecasting technique is preferred to the generalized least-squares technique remains to be seen.[5]

Before proceeding to the application section, a final note is in order regarding the tests of the TSIRV forecasting models. It will be recalled that the "actual beta values" with which the forecasted beta values were compared are actually least-squares estimates based on 12 six-month observations covering a period of 17 months. There is a five-month data overlap between the forecasting data (which covers 66 months) and the realized data so that the forecasts are not completely independent of the averaged actual betas. Accordingly, the tests of the forecasting models used here are not pure tests.

To remedy this situation, the sampling period used in generating forecasts could have been shortened by five months, or the averaged actual betas could have been based on observations beginning five months later. (Presently, the first actual beta to be used in the averaging is that occurring at $t + 1$, one month after the final one used in the forecasting process; however, the beta is computed by comparing interest rates at $t + 1$ and $t - 5$.) A third alternative would be to simply use the realized beta six months later as the actual beta rather than use a least-squares proxy based on 12 observations.

None of these alternatives were attractive. The first alternative would mean that a forecasting model would ignore five months of recent data that are publicly available, truly an inefficient use of data. The second approach would give averaged "actual" betas that occur, on average, further into the future than the six-month horizon of concern. The third alternative, because of the small numerator-denominator problem (and resulting wildly volatile betas), would tend to divert ones focus to unimportant movements in the beta series. Thus, the impure tests of the forecasting model were performed.

IV. APPLICATION

Objective

The TSIRV estimation procedures and associated duration measures have several uses. Our objective in developing them was to create an immunized investment fund that could compete favorably with the guaranteed investment contracts (GICs) currently offered by life insurance companies. The GIC provides a guaranteed terminal rate of return over a prespecified time interval. Our immunized fund alternative to the GIC has several possible advantages: first, it avoids any default risk by utilizing only government obligations; second, it avoids the fees charged by insurance companies; third, unlike the GIC where premature fund withdrawal is assessed a severe interest penalty, the manager of the immunized fund maintains full control and may withdraw funds at any moment in order to take advantage of new market conditions; fourth, under a GIC, the best one can achieve is the target rate of return whereas under a properly immunized fund the target rate of return is the worst that should be achieved. Thus, if a higher or equal return is available at a lower or equal risk through an immunized fund, the increased flexibility of such a fund would render it dominant over a competing GIC.

Techniques

A five-year period was selected as the horizon over which to invest. The target yield for all funds beginning on any given date is the five-year spot rate of interest, R_5, associated with the term structure applicable to that date. As both callable and noncallable bonds were used in computing the term structure of interest at each date, the implied available yields will be slightly higher than those attainable through only noncallable bonds. Thus, the target yield was reduced by 0.05 percent to reflect attainable yields via noncallable instruments.

The procedures used in setting up and managing our immunized funds are briefly summarized below. To initiate a fund, two bonds were selected, one with a maturity between 4.5 and 5.0 years, another with a much longer term to maturity, usually around 15 years. If the shorter term bond matured before the fund closing date, it was redeemed and proceeds were invested in the money market for the remainder of the period. Bonds were purchased at the CRSP quoted ask prices and sold at the bid prices when necessary to achieve portfolio rebalancing. Portfolios were rebalanced every six months to equate portfolio duration with remaining time of fund horizon. Only bonds having immunizing durations were considered for purchase, where positive holdings of both bonds resulted in the appropriate portfolio duration. Of the numerous bonds meeting the maturity and duration conditions necessary to be eligible for inclusion in the funds, further selection was performed to weed out the callable bonds and the actively traded flower bonds, while favoring the bonds with higher coupons. Efforts were made to maintain through each five-year period the same bonds that were initially selected for each fund in order to avoid unnecessarily large transaction costs.

Two aspects of the immunized fund construction were not entirely realistic. First, fractional purchases of bonds were permitted in portfolio construction. However, this was necessitated in part because the total initial fund size was only one thousand dollars. Large fund sizes would permit the purchase of bonds in round lots, while achieving the desired portfolio duration. A second aspect that was unrealistic is that coupon payments for both included bonds were assumed to occur in exact six-month intervals beginning six months after the start of a new fund. Bond prices were adjusted to compensate for this arrangement to restore realism. The primary distortion of this technique is that portfolio rebalancing was only necessary on a six-month basis when cash inflows occurred. Transactions costs, however, would be about the same, and the duration measures and term structure estimates were based on the current timing of the coupon payments.

The "look ahead" strategies were motivated by two observations: (1) If portfolios are rebalanced only when cash inflows (coupon payments) are received, then the only term structures having a bearing upon the funds' terminal rates of return are those that prevail upon the dates of coupon payments. The term structures can move in all kinds of ways on the intervening dates, all with no effect upon the final fund values. (2) Durations of typical coupon paying bonds decline more slowly over time than the commensurate shortening of the fund time horizon, as shown in Figure 12.

Figure 12 shows that the duration of a bond, measured in years, typically declines less rapidly than time if no shocks in the term structure of interest occur. If a portfolio duration is set equal to five years at the start of a fund, then it is likely that the portfolio duration will be too long at the time of coupon payment six months later, as shown by the solid line, which indicates a duration of approximately 4.7 at a time when a duration of 4.5 is needed. Rather than follow the typical approach of adjusting the duration at time 4.5 to 4.5 after it is too late to properly immunize the fund from interest rate shocks (this approach

Figure 12.

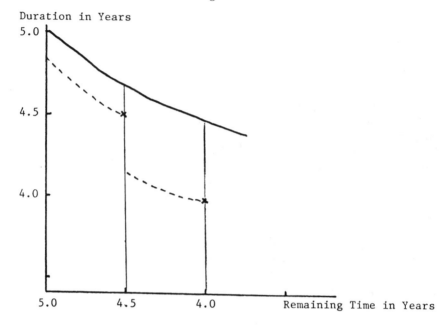

could be dubbed "closing the barn door after the fox has eaten the chickens"), we can set the initial duration of the portfolio at time 5 (to, say, 4.8 years) such that it will be expected to reach the appropriate level of 4.5 at the moment of the first coupon payments. There is really no important reason to have the initial duration of the portfolio set at five years, as it has little bearing on the terminal rate of return and requires greater expected transaction costs at the time of portfolio rebalancing. The look ahead procedure involves computing the durations bonds can be expected to exhibit six months into the future, based upon a six month shorter bond maturity and the interest rates, betas, and prices that are expected to prevail in the absence of shocks to the term structure. Then if the term structure of interest is different from that expected six months down the road, the fund will be prepared for the shock, provided that the beta vector is properly forecast. The optimal initial portfolio duration is given as the solution of a simple algebraic problem.

Tests and Results

Eight versions of the immunization strategies based on the generalized duration measures were tested. Two approaches were taken: the traditional approach of matching today's portfolio duration to the remaining time period of the fund and the "look ahead" approach described above. For each of these approaches, two interpretations of *shocks* were used to compute the betas, the "random walk shocks" and the "pure expectations shocks." For each of these interpretations, both the generalized least-squares five-year moving averages and the ARIMA forecasting techniques were used.

These immunization strategies were compared with the more traditional immunization strategy described by Fisher and Weil [7] and the maturity strategy, wherein a single bond of five years maturity is selected and periodic coupon payments are reinvested in additional of these bonds. Because under each of these strategies our program required (for purposes of comparability) that all funds contained the same short and long-term bonds as those selected under the new immunization strategies, there were also eight versions of both of these strategies, although results were often replicated when bond selection (as opposed to bond weighting) under the new immunization strategies did not change. Finally, a simple strategy of investing in six-month Treasury bills every six months for five years was also tested. Thus, 25 different five-year funds (consisting of eight versions each of the new and traditional duration strategies and the maturity strategy, and one version of the money market strategy) were set up at the beginning of each month and managed throughout their five-year lifetimes in an effort to achieve their target returns.

The bond price data used in the tests began in January, 1947 and ended in January, 1980. As the beta estimations used 60 half-year volatility observations (involving 66 months), the first 25 funds were set up in June of 1952 and the last 25 funds were cashed out in January of 1980. Thus, 25 funds were started on each of 271 months for a total test of 6775 funds.

For this report only the results for 13 of the 25 strategies are available. Testing has been completed for the money market fund, and for the maturity and traditional duration strategies associated with the new immunization strategies based on the random walk and pure expectations definitions of *shocks*, using the five-year generalized least-squares moving average beta forecasts for both the look ahead and non look ahead strategies. (The other 12 strategies, which are all associated with the ARIMA beta forecasts, have not yet been tested.) The results of the completed tests are summarized in Table 2.

Several results are noteworthy. First, the maturity strategies as well as both the old and new immunization strategies, whether look ahead or not, far outperformed the money market strategy in terms of average rate of return and number of times the target rates of return were not

Table 2.   Performance Comparisons

	Failures	Semi–Standard Error	Average Return
NO LOOK AHEAD			
Maturity Strategy	23	.0163	4.837
Old Duration Strategy	22	.0012	4.835
New Duration Strategy*	30	.0015	4.831
Money Market Strategy	129		4.450
LOOK AHEAD			
Maturity Strategy	27	.0098	4.843
Old Duration Strategy	27	.0015	4.849
New Duration Strategy*	27	.0016	4.820

Note: New Duration Strategy relied on "Random Walk Shocks" definition and upon beta forecasts generated by the generalized least squares five year moving average technique. It is notable that almost all of the failures of the immunizing strategies occurred in the 1950's.

achieved. Second, of the 12 non-money-market strategies, all tended to fail to achieve their target yields roughly 10 percent of the time. However, when failures occurred, the immunization strategies (old and new) failed in magnitude by about 10 times less than the maturity strategies in most cases, and by 50 times less in one case, as measured by the "semi-root mean square error" of returns.[6] The strategy that generated the failures of smallest magnitude was the look ahead generalized duration strategy where betas were defined in terms of the shocks from pure expectations. Perhaps more important is that the old, simple immunization strategies did as well as, or slightly better than, the newer immunization strategies, with the one exception mentioned above. However, only the four least promising of the eight new immunizing strategies have been studied, and more accurate TSIRV forecasting may improve the performance of funds using the generalized duration formulas, whereas the only avenue for improved performance in the maturity and traditional duration strategies lies with better bond selection, as the weightings and durations/maturities are fixed. Note that all of the variation in performance exhibited in the old duration and maturity strategies associated with the look ahead and non look ahead duration approaches is due to different bond selection.

The surprisingly good performance of the maturity strategies is due to a secular rising trend in interest rates over the period of time studied, alleviating much of the coupon reinvestment problem inherent in the maturity strategy. Had the long term trend in interest rates been reversed, the immunization strategies would have exhibited much higher success rates relative to the maturity strategies.

V. FURTHER APPLICATIONS

The duration techniques described in this paper may be used by pension fund managers who wish to take some investment risk in stocks or other assets, but wish to couple these risks with a long-term risk-free asset. Another potential use is in constructing futures straddles, where knowledge of the relative volatilities of instruments of different duration is paramount to the reduction of risks and achievement of the desired tax benefits. As the tax courts have taken a dim view of straddles where there is little or no apparent risk, straddles are more and more tending toward instruments of varied maturity dates, and a knowledge of relative volatilities given by the generalized price elasticity formula is important. The TSIRV estimates could also prove important for speculators, who, having forecasted the direction of future movements in the interest rate, would like to capitalize on these forecasts by achieving the greatest price movements in bonds. A knowledge of the relative price elasticities of the bonds is fundamental to such a strategy.

ACKNOWLEDGMENTS

This study was commissioned by Johnson & Higgins of California. The results reported in this paper were achieved through the joint efforts of Roy Bertoldo, Don Weiss, David Dodd, and the author. Helpful suggestions from George Kaufman, Barr Rosenberg, Jeffrey Skelton, and James Wilcox are gratefully acknowledged. Special thanks are given to Eugene Chow, who provided considerable statistical assistance.

NOTES

1. At this point research is still in progress and only the results of the duration strategies that rely on the less accurate TSIRV forecasting techniques are used.

2. The historical shapes examined were taken from the government security yield curves and volatility curves computed by the author on a monthly basis beginning in 1947 and ending in 1980. The hypothetical shapes were designed to be as perverse as could be imagined so that the robustness of the formula could be assessed.

3. In none of the cases for which experimentation was done did q turn out to be merely an inflection point; rather, it was either a minimum or a maximum. However, the numerical analyses performed were not exhaustive, so the possibility of an inflection point cannot be ruled out.

4. ARIMA techniques applied to series of actual single-month past beta values, as opposed to series of least-quares estimated betas over 12 months, were so volatile as to provide no predictive value. As indicated earlier, the least-squares technique has the desirable property of giving more weight to those betas that were associated with larger interest rate fluctuations (and hence more impact on bond prices).

5. The actual beta values fluctuate to such a large extent that accurate forecasts of these values will also exhibit extreme volatility over time. This means that duration measures based on the accurately estimated vector of betas will also fluctuate wildly. In an immunized fund, volatile duration measures will lead to high transaction costs as fund managers make efforts to keep the portfolio in proper balance. At some degree of accuracy these extra transaction costs may outweigh the advantage of more accurate duration measures.

6. The "semi-root mean square error" was computed by squaring the differences between the target and actual rates of return, in percent, when the actual rate of return failed to reach the target, and summing over all failures. The resulting sum was divided by the number of failures, and the square root was taken of this quotient.

REFERENCES

1. Bierwag, G. O., G. G. Kaufman, and C. Khang, 1978, "Duration and Bond Portfolio Analysis: An Overview," *Journal of Financial and Quantitative Analysis*, (November), 671–681.

2. Bilson, J. F. O., forthcoming, "The 'Speculative Efficiency' Hypothesis," *Journal of Business*.

3. Box, G. E. P. and G. M. Jenkins, 1976, *Time Series Analysis: Forecasting and Control*, Holden-Day.

4. Carleton, W. T. and I. A. Cooper, 1976, "Estimation and Uses of the Term Structure of Interest Rates," *Journal of Finance* (December) 1067 +.

5. Chow, E., 1981, *Term Structure of Interest Rate Volatility*, M.B.A. Thesis, University of California at Berkeley.

6. Cox, J. C., J. E. Ingersoll, Jr., and S. A. Ross, 1979, "Duration and the Measurement of Basic Risk," *Journal of Business* (January) 51–61.

7. Fisher, L. and R. L. Weil, 1971, "Coping with the Risk of Interest Rate Fluctuations: Returns of Bondholders from Naive and Optimal Strategies," *Journal of Business* (October), 408–431.

8. Hakkio, C. S., 1980, "Expectations and the Forward Exchange Rate," NBER Working Paper No. 439 (January).

9. Hansen, L. P., 1980, "Large Sample Properties of Generalized Method of Moments Estimators," Working Paper No. 56–79–80, Carnegie Mellon University (March).

10. Hansen, L. P. and R. J. Hodrick, 1980, "Forward Exchange Rates as Optimal Predictors of Future Spot Rates: An Econometric Analysis," *Journal of Political Economy* (October), 829–853.

11. Hicks, J. R., 1939 (1946), *Value and Capital*, Oxford Press.

12. Houglet, M., 1980, *Estimating the Term Structure of Interest Rates for Non Homogeneous Bonds*, Ph.D. Dissertation, University of California at Berkeley.

13. Ingersoll, J. E., Jr., J. Skelton, and R. L. Weil, 1978, "Duration Forty Years Later," *Journal of Financial and Quantitative Analysis* (November), 627–650.

14. Macaulay, F. R., 1938, *Some Theoretical Problems Suggested by the Movements of Interest Rates, Bond Yields, and Stock Prices in the United States since 1856*, Columbia University Press.

15. McCulloch, J. H., 1971, "Measuring the Term Structure of Interest Rates," *Journal of Business* (January), 19–31.
16. ———, 1975, "The Tax-Adjusted Yield Curve," *Journal of Finance* (June), 811–830.
17. ———, 1976, "Tax-Adjusted Yield Curve Estimation—Revised," NBER.
18. Meiselman, D., 1962, *The Term Structure of Interest Rates*, Prentice-Hall.
19. Modigliani, F. and R. M. Sutch, 1966, "Innovations in Interest Rate Policy," *American Economic Review Papers and Proceedings* (May), 178–197.
20. Schaefer, S. M., 1981, "Measuring a Tax Specific Term Structure of Interest Rates in the Market for British Government Securities," *Economic Journal* (June), 415–438.
21. Williams, J. B., 1938, *The Theory of Investment Value*, Harvard University Press.

PART IV

IMMUNIZATION IN PRACTICE
PANEL DISCUSSION

IMMUNIZATION AT
SMITH BARNEY

Peter E. Christensen

INTRODUCTION

First of all, I would like to thank the organizer and moderator of the seminar, Dr. George Kaufman, for extending an invitation to me to appear here today to present Smith Barney's three approaches to the immunization of bond portfolios.[1]

For the past two years I have continually found myself beginning a speech by saying that these are especially turbulent times and that we, as bond investors, must adapt in new ways to today's highly volatile markets. At Smith Barney we have been particularly energetic in pioneering new quantitively based portfolio management products suited to these volatile markets. As we all know, the buy and hold strategies of the past are not always prudent in today's turbulent markets. Nevertheless we do not yet have enough quantitive bond analysis tools to support our growing needs in these new markets. It has been our objective at Smith Barney to serve these growing needs and growing markets.

I will confine my comments to three areas. The first is a brief history of immunization at Smith Barney. The second is the market need for various types of immunization strategies, and the third is a brief description of the three immunization products we currently offer to our clients (with brief reference to two additional strategies we will release later in the year).

Brief History

Smith Barney has been the leading investment banking firm in the development and implementation of the bond immunization strategy. Our firm was the first to apply immunization to the management of pension assets. We subscribed the first U.S. client to the strategy in 1978, held the first Conference for Practitioners on Immunization and Duration in Tarrytown, New York in 1978, and have since developed two new and totally different immunization strategies for release to our clients.

In short, Smith Barney's involvement with and commitment to immunization, in its many forms, continues to expand and adapt to changes in market needs. The firm will continue to develop new funding structures using the immunization concept to meet new market needs.

Market Need for Immunization

Bonds were originally bought as "safe" instruments for investable funds. The original purpose of owning them was for their "certainty of income."

As we all know today, that certainty of income has been totally overwhelmed by the "erosion in principal" that has occurred due to hostile and volatile markets.

In spite of this sad circumstance for bonds, through the use of bond immunization to lock in a fixed rate of return, asset managers can recapture the original distinctiveness and merit of owning bonds; they can recapture that certainty of income without jeopardizing a portfolio to paralytic losses in principal values over a set planning horizon. As a result, in these turbulent markets, mangers may still buy "stability of return"—not with laddered purchases or maturity matching techniques, but with immunization.

Immunization has been used by many of our clients as a "core" to their bond portfolios, one that will appreciate at a fixed assured rate. In other instances, insurance company clients of Smith Barney are using it to fund some of their fixed obligations, such as their GIC liabilities. Since insurance companies seek to lock in a price today for a dollar in the future, this approach not only makes sense but is compelling.

Other clients of the firm like the hedging aspects of immunization, yet they would prefer greater freedom to actively manage an immunized bond portfolio. For their use, we offer "active immunization," which is a strategy that provides a minimum (or floor) return, yet allows the manager to actively manage his or her portfolio for higher expected returns. In volatile markets, full downside risk protection is a very useful safety feature for plan sponsors.

Finally, in an environment of high yields, many plan sponsors find the yields on their bond portfolios much higher than the actuarially assumed rate assigned to their retirement plans. Because of low investment return assumptions and highly risky volatile markets, plan sponsors are finding to their dismay that their unfunded pension liabilities and pension contribution levels are rising faster than forecasted. To address these very real pension problems, we have developed and offer to our clients the "dedicated pension strategy."

Thus, in turbulent markets, there are genuine needs for "stable returns," for which we at Smith Barney offer "bond immunization"; there are needs for a minimum (or floor) return, for which we offer active immunization; and there are needs for strategies to help reduce the unfunded liabilities and costs of a retirement plan, for which we offer the "dedicated" approach.

Smith Barney's Three Immunization Products

This brings me to the third and final area of my address: Smith Barney's three immunization products. These three products, I might add, will soon be supplemented by two more.

Before explaining in detail the specifics of our product offerings, I would like to mention that we offer immunization as a research service to our institutional clients, either investment managers or plan sponsors. As such, we advise in one manner or another over 30 immunized portfolios that currently range from two and one-half to eight years in duration.

These statistics bring up an interesting point. Since Smith Barney was the first to apply immunization to the management of pension assets, we naturally have the longest track record on the Street with actual portfolios. Our results are as follows: over 90% of our portfolios are either on or *ahead* of target and less than 10 percent are *below* target. No portfolio is more than 17 basis points below target as of our last valuation.

These numbers, I might add, are not a pure test of the strategy since most of our portfolios are made up of corporate bonds. From what I read in the financial press however, these results are similar to Salomon Brothers' as published in *Pension & Investments*. They found using data from 1958 to the present, that they achieved their target 96 percent of the time, give or take 8 basis points.

We at Smith Barney have come up with similar results in propriety tests using our own data.

This research, other earlier research, and our own wide ranging experience with over 30 portfolios have given us a comfort level high enough to market this duration matched product for the many different applications discussed a few moments ago. I might also add that I am developing along with Sylvan Feldstein, a municipal bond analyst in our department, an application of bond immunization to a municipal bond portfolio. The other immunization-related strategy that we have under development at this time is the "stripping" of U.S. Treasury bonds into a series of zero coupon bonds for re-sale in the secondary markets as instruments with locked-in rates.

In contrast to the strategies we have under development the second immunization product that we currently market is *active immunization*. With active immunization, we have blended active management together with immunization, allowed greater discretion for the active manager, and provided an immunization stop-out if asset values decline enough that they reach the minimum level associated with a "base" or "floor" return.

With active immunization, we are effectively *controlling* interest rate risk and providing protection to the client, yet allowing a wide range of active management discretion.

As such, this risk controlled approach is used as an asset management strategy with downside protection (much like a call option) rather than as a strategy to offset to a fixed liability.

Finally, we offer the dedicated, or cashflow matching, strategy. With this variety of immunization strategy, we are straying off the topic of duration, however. Therefore, I will keep my remarks brief. With the dedicated strategy, we merely specify a schedule of retired lives liabilities to be funded, then structure a bond portfolio so that the cashflow from the portfolio will match closely the schedule of cash requirements specified by the actuary.

In the process of creating this cashflow match, surplus funds are reduced to a negligable proportion of the fund causing reinvestment risk to be virtually eliminated. We can thereby lock in an immunized rate for the period of years implied by the funding schedule.

No claims are made at Smith Barney that our present forms of immunization are perfect or even the full answer to our funding problems. Certainly no claim is made that our target rates are guaranteed; however, these strategies do permit, to the best of our limited abilities, *risk minimization* in both *funding* and *intermediary functions*.

SUMMARY

In summary, I have discussed with you today the history of bond immunization at Smith Barney starting with the first pension accounts and the Tarrytown conference we sponsored in 1978. Then we discussed the market need for risk control and stable returns. Finally, we discussed the three immunization products that we offer at Smith Barney: those being the duration based bond immunization, active immunization, and the dedicated strategy.

To conclude, I would like to leave you with one thought: though we currently live amidst the turbulence and uncertainty of volatile markets, we still can, with our immunized products, put most of the *fixed* back into fixed income investment.

NOTE

1. The author delivered the preceeding address while an officer of Smith Barney. He is currently a Vice President in the Fixed Income Research Department at The First Boston Corporation offering similar client services to those described herein.

COMMENTS

H. Gifford Fong

Let me start off by sharing some observations concerning immunization in practice. This is an area of fixed income portfolio management which has evolved quite rapidly in practice and, in doing so, has taken a number of interesting turns. For example, the original use in the classical sense was to assure a predetermined return over some specified horizon. This could be used by an investment manager to compete against a guaranteed investment contract (GIC) issued by an insurance company—or so it would appear in theory.

The first major hurdle was to extend the classical theory of immunization to handle parallel as well as nonparallel changes in interest rates. This was at first handled by frequent rebalancing to keep duration equal to the time left to the horizon. Subsequent work explicitly defined the conditions necessary for immunization under all types of interest changes.

Whereas the investment manager must conform to a fairly rigorous set of requirements to insure immunization effectiveness, some insurance companies have quoted rates at times in excess of what can be achieved with high quality, relatively default free securities. Furthermore, although there may be fine print specifying restrictions on reinvestment and principal withdrawal, the market place appears to be exclusively rate sensitive. The net effect is the immunized portfolio promised return to be consistently lower than the highest GIC rates and hence not always competitive. Some of the discrepancy can be explained by the tax advantage enjoyed by insurance companies in underwriting such contracts, use of private placements or the desire to raise capital at rates lower than the prevailing short-term borrowing rates. Whatever the reason, the one period immunized portfolios as an alternative to a GIC has not been as effective as expected.

Where immunized portfolios do have the advantage is in further extensions to the one-period ("bullet") form. Multiperiod strategies where a series of cash inflows and/or outflows can be accommodated allowing customized portfolio construction is a very promising approach. A pension fund with a schedule of retired lives liabilities can be effectively immunized for as long as 30 years. As new liabilities are identified with the passage of time, these can also be integrated into the same portfoilio. An alternative to multiperiod immunization is the so-called cash-flow matching or dedicated portfolio. This is a technique which tries to match the cash-inflow characteristics of a portfolio (coupon payments and maturities) with the schedule of cash outflows (liabilities). In the special situation where there are sufficient default-free pure discount instruments such that the maturities of the securities can be perfectly matched with the necessary outflows, both the multiperiod immunization process and cash-flow matching will produce the same portfolio. However, in the more general case of selecting from coupon-paying securities, important differences can exist. The key performance criteria in this situation is the amount of money necessary to fund the liabilities. Using a return maximization approach available with multiperiod immunization, we have observed anywhere from a 25- to 75-basis-point advantage per year over a cash-flow matching procedure. Ironically, while this return differential appears compelling, by virtue of the ease of understanding of the cash-flow matching approach it is occasionally chosen over the multiperiod immunization capability. This leads to the unfortunate and unnecessary selection of a nonoptimal strategy.

Return maximization has already been described in a previous paper and represents a state of the art refinement which can produce significantly higher returns at a modest increase in risk. Finally, the ability to define and measure immunization risk is itself very important since it can permit a systematic comparison of alternative portfolios in a two-dimensional risk return space and can provide the basis for optimization analysis.

Finally, let me describe a new strategy which is another example of an extension to the basic one-period immunization approach. This combines the ability to be assured of a specified return over a given horizon with the potential of achieving higher returns through active management. Assume a pension plan sponsor has determined a desired minimum return on the total portfolio of 8 percent per year. Assume further, a five-year immunization strategy can achieve a 14 percent return. Based on the need for a minimum of 8 percent and the available 14 percent from an immunized portfolio, an allocation between active and immunized components of the portfolio can be achieved. As long as the active component does not experience a result less than a worst-case scenario, the minimum return on the total portfolio can be achieved. In our example, if the worst-case scenario is a 5 percent return per year over the five years, then a 50/50 allocation between immunization and active management will provide at least an 8 percent yearly return with the potential for superior performance from the part of the portfolio allocated to the active strategy. The active portion can be managed consistent with any other actively managed portfolio. The immunized portfolio can take advantage of the extensions discussed above including return maximization and multiperiod capability. The net result is to achieve a minimum return while retaining the potential for enhanced return through active management.

In summary, the application of immunization has taken on a number of new dimensions which has expanded its effectiveness in fixed income portfolio management as well as its role.

COMMENTS

Michael Jozsa

In beginning, I would like to state my agreement with Jim Hoag's comments regarding the use of duration versus multiple-factor models. As Mr. Hoag and others suggested, the additional benefit of the more complex and expensive multiple-factor models appears to be insignificant in comparison to the relatively simple duration model. Indeed, as we know from Fisher and Weil's work, a naive strategy of matching maturities to the horizon date effectively removes most of the holding period risk anyway.

While I would not advocate a maturity strategy (except in the case of a computer failure), my point is that we may be splitting hairs in an effort to improve on the preciseness of duration, particularly for all government portfolios. I personally doubt the significance of improving the predictive value from ±18 basis points to ±7 basis points. I have no doubt, however, that immunization does offer fund sponsors an important alternative bond strategy not previously available to them. Knowing (within a minimal range of tolerance) the future return of the immunization portfolio, fund sponsors should be better able to plan asset allocations as well as avoid the degree of disappointment they are experiencing today.

Five years ago, for example, yields ranging from 8 percent on long-term Treasury issues to 9 percent for high-quality corporates were available, and to many implied similar returns. However, realized returns over that period ending December 31, 1980 were only about 5 percent using published results of the median managed fixed income account as the return proxy. This, of course, equates to a 300- to 400-basis-point shortfall versus expected return. On the other hand, a target return of 7.60 percent using a five-year immunization strategy was available at the end of 1980. In this context, a ± 18-basis-point range of return seems livable.

From a practitioner's point of view, the distinction between the testing decribed here and the application of immunization strategies in a live competitive environment, should be pointed out. This distinction relates to the testing of duration and multiple-factor models within the constraints of all government portfolios versus the broadening application of immunization to include corporate issues. Motivating the use of corporates (and addressing a frequent criticism of immunization as a minimal return strategy) is the need or desire for higher returns while maintaining interest rate immunity. It is in this environment that my firm and I feel multifactor models are both necessary and cost effective. Efforts such as those of Barr Rosenberg and others to quantify specific risks such as default, callability, industry, and quality rating should continue.

BOND IMMUNIZATION IN PRACTICE

Thomas J. Steffanci

From a pension plan perspective, bond immunization has been an operable strategy for only a few years. Immunization, as a concept, has been used for almost 30 years in Great Britain in the insurance industry to help keep the sensitivity of assets and liabilities in balance. The substantial increase in bond market volatility in recent years and a reexamination and extension of the concept of duration have produced more interest in immunization as a bond strategy for corporate pension plans.

But why should pension plans be interested in bond immunization? The simple answer is that through immunization, especially in its multiperiod form, pension plans have an opportunity to (1) reduce pension costs, (2) reduce unfunded vested liabilities, (3) decrease cost of capital, and (4) increase pension benefits without increasing contributions. These are reasons enough. The above benefits can be achieved through upward adjustment of actuarial interest rate assumptions to more adequately reflect assured rates of return over long-term time periods. By properly matching the duration of a portfolio of fixed income securities to the duration of a known or expected liability stream, pension plans can achieve much the same insulation from interest rate movements that other financial intermediaries can. For a corporate pension plan, bond immunization can provide an identifiable link between assets and liabilities.

In the good old days, during the 1950s and early 1960s, bonds were principally utilized by pension plans to fund the benefit liabilities to those employees who had retired. Along with stability of principal value, the coupon payments provided a measure of "certainty" to the firm's ability to meet known future obligations. Furthermore, up until the mid-1960s, corporate pension plans formally divided benefit obligations into those due to retirees and those due to active employees. Equity investments tended to be thought of as higher return/risk vehicles dedicated to the payment of active live benefit obligations. Because of the deferred nature of these liabilities, more variability of return could be tolerated. The bond portion of plan assets, with its certain cash-flow stream and relatively stable capital value, was assigned to pay off retired lives benefits.

The stock market environment of the early and mid-1960s began to change this linkage between assets and liabilities. Strong and sustained increases in equity values and academic studies supporting the notion that equity returns over a long period of time could be assumed to produce 9 percent per year, compounded, fundamentally altered the liability management of pension plans. Asset allocation began to be directed more toward equities, and plan sponsors were counseled by investment managers to combine their benefit obligations into one pool to be funded with common stock. The newfound "certainty" of generous and consistent returns from equities made it less attractive to use relatively low coupon bonds to pay retired lives benefit obligations. Unfortunately, the 1969–1970 and 1973–1974 stock market experiences disrupted the confidence of the 1960s. Smarting from the dramatic plunge in equity values in those time periods, pension plan sponsors found that their plans became underfunded, and pension costs began to rise rapidly. From 1975 to 1977, in an effort to reduce volatility and add more "certainty" to investment returns, plan sponsors reallocated assets away from stocks and back toward bonds. But that change in asset mix was not accompanied by the return of bonds to their former role as the funding vehicle for retired lives benefit obligations. Indeed, most pension plans got away from separating benefit obligations years before. Instead, bonds were looked upon not only as assets that reduced volatility in a pension plan, or as sources of steady income, but vehicles which were expected to generate capital appreciation. Given the demise of stocks in the 1969–1970 and 1973–1974 periods, bonds became successors to equities in the performance derby. As a consequence, "active bond management" took on new meaning as market timing and interest rate anticipation became the dominant management style of most investment organizations.

The unanticipated inflation of the past three years and erratic monetary policy have produced unprecedented bond market volatility and depression of bond prices. Active bond management in most cases has not been able to generate the types of returns that we expected back in the mid-1970s. As a result, pension plan sponsors are questioning whether bonds have any role to play at all in their investment programs. The analytical reexamination and extension of the concept of duration in conferences such as this have allowed investment practitioners to more fully utilize techniques to re-establish the role of bonds in a pension plan.

The acceptance of immunization techniques on the part of pension plan sponsors has increased substantially over the past few years. But because interest rates have risen dramatically since 1976, bond durations have fallen and are now relatively short from a historical perspective. The problem that has arisen because of this can be particularly acute, namely, requiring immunization for a longer period of time than the duration of the longest bond. One solution proposed recently by Irwin Vanderhoff in *Pensions and Investment Age* (June, 1981) is the use of well-chosen equities as immunizng vehicles. Stocks with very high dividend growth-rate predictability, can have a duration approximating the inverse of the dividend yield. By combining equities with, say, 5 to 6 percent dividend yields with bonds, it may be possible to extend the portfolio duration. However, while dividend increases are "fairly" assured, preliminary testing suggests that assurance is not high enough. What is necessary is to find an investment vehicle that can be combined with equities to eliminate the dividend growth rate uncertainty, but it is not clear how we proceed from here. Simple options are short-lived, and the problem is to find a long-run answer.

Another solution, that offers more promise is the use of financial futures.[1] The computation of duration for a portfolio of bonds and futures is simplied by using

$$D = \frac{(1 + r)}{P} \frac{dP}{d(1 + r)}, \tag{1}$$

where r is the interest rate, P is the value of the portfolio, and D is duration. Since futures have a present value of zero, they do not add to the value of the portfolio, but since they do make a contribution to $dP/d(1 + r)$, they dramatically change the duration of the portfolio. For example, we can write the total value of the portfolio as

$$\frac{dP}{d(1 + r)} = \frac{dB}{d(1 + r)} + \alpha \frac{dF}{d(1 + r)}, \qquad (2)$$

where B is the value of the bonds, F is the value of futures, and α is the proportion of futures to bonds. Assuming the futures contracts are written against the same bonds, we can write

$$\frac{dB}{d(1 + r)} = \frac{dF}{d(1 + r)}.$$

Now,

$$*D = \frac{1 + r}{B} \left(\frac{dB}{d(1 + r)} + \alpha \frac{dF}{d(1 + r)} \right). \qquad (3)$$

Simplifying,

$$*D = \frac{1 + r}{B} \frac{dB}{d(1 + r)} (1 + \alpha) \qquad (4)$$

Then,

$$*D = (1 + \alpha) \qquad \text{(duration of bonds)}. \qquad (5)$$

Thus, by purchasing bonds, and buying the same number of futures contracts, (i.e., $\alpha = 1$), we can double the duration of the portfolio. Rebalancing is done periodically in the usual manner of changing the duration of the bonds as well as the number of futures contracts.

Intuitively, the concept is quite straightforward. If interest rates go down, bond prices rise, and profits are also made on the futures contracts, so that the new future value computed at the lower interest rates remains unchanged. If interest rates rise, bond prices fall, and losses are incurred on futures holdings. Nevertheless, the future value of the portfolio at the new interest rates again remains the same. Preliminary simulations done for a 14-year duration were extremely successful. All of the resulting future values during the simulation period were above 99.6 percent of the initial expected value calculated in the first year. These small errors were found even with annual rebalancing and 200 basis points annual movements in interest rates.

As a final thought on immunization in practice, many pension plan sponsors are beginning to think of immunization as a more formal part of the asset allocation decision. I would say, after 10 years in the investment business, that it is axiomatic that stocks have more appeal to pension plans than bonds. Even apart from their superior long-run expected return characteristics, stocks are more easily understood, traded in auction markets, and represent outright ownership. Immunization techniques actually allow pension plans to assume greater equity-related risk with more precision and the confidence that extraordinary losses in the stock market will not necessarily lead to increases in contributions. Bond immunization, with its assurance of return, offers an ideal "anchor to windward" in highly volatile financial market environments.

NOTE

1. My thanks to Ronald V. Hanoian at Trust Company of the West for the development of this analysis.

COMMENTS

James S. Ward

At Manufacturers Hanover Trust Company, we are fortunate to have a dedicated effort devoted to this particular bond strategy. We started over two years ago with only one immunization design and currently have three different immunization products and about $1 billion under management. This represents a testament to the popularity and potential of the immunization technique. I will briefly cover today the three different types of applications we employ. The first is immunization from the point of view of an asset allocation decision. In other words, immunization considered as a risk-free asset, over a defined investment time horizon. We call it the *lump sum* design. This design allows a plan sponsor to increase or decrease his or her risk exposure by allocating more or less funds to the immunized portion of the pension fund. The second product is one that involves a coordinated effort between the actuary and the investment officer. We call it the *dedicated bond portfolio*. It deals with a specified segment of a pension plan and can present many positive benefits to the plan sponsor. Last, I will describe our newest immunization product, risk-controlled active bond management which is a linkup of active bond management with immunization.

287

I. LUMP SUM DESIGN

Active/Passive Strategy

We regard this immunization strategy as one falling in between passive bond management and active bond management strategies. Although immunization has a passive strategy label, we believe that it does not have to be a passive technique. Most passive strategies will work in only one interest rate environment. We manage immunization portfolios much the same way we manage all other portfolios at our Bank. When opportunities arise to swap into corporate bonds of A ratings or better, we do so to improve the targeted rate of return. We prefer to start our portfolios with high-quality securities and then, as spreads widen, to swap from the higher quality securities into the lower quality securities. This should add about 25 to 50 basis points to the targeted rate of return that we have promised at the outset.

Practical Applications

We regard this model as an investment strategy to be used along with equities and long-term bonds. We realize that a pension fund's liabilities lie well beyond the 10-year limit of this immunization model. The traditional ways of meeting these long-term time horizons, however, have become so highly volatile since 1958, that investment returns have varied widely from year to year.

We believe that immunization can remove some of that volatility by providing the investment manager with a predictable rate of return for a portion of the fund. We feel that investment managers will benefit by knowing that at least a portion of their pension fund is going to earn a specific rate for whatever time is selected. We have said to our clients that we will actively manage a portion of their portfolios, and immunize the balance. As an active bond manager, we should do better than, or at least as well as, the immunized portfolio, which is basically a riskless portfolio. There is, of course, another way of locking up a rate of return, and that is the GIC What makes the immunized portfolio a more attractive vehicle than the GIC is the flexibility of immunization and the fact that the pension plan owns real securities. One can sell an immunized portfolio at any time and, if interest rates have fallen, take the profit into the fund. If rates rose, of course, the portfolio would suffer a market loss. In either case the plan sponsor or investment manager always retains control of the portfolio and has the option to terminate the arrangement, which he or she would not have with a GIC.

Historical Simulations

Would Immunization have worked had it been used back over the last 20 years? Extreme market volatility in the bond market has been in evidence since 1958; so we decided that we would run our own simulations and used actual market prices supplied by Salomon Brothers. Some 210 simulations of five-year periods from 1958 through 1979 were produced. Each month was considered that start of a five-year period. The results showed that immunization really would have worked throughout what was probably the worst bond market in history. We discovered that in nearly all the simulations, the actual realized rate came within 3 percent of the targeted rate. In other words, if the target has been 10 percent, one could expect to come within 30 basis points of 10 percent. These same tests were also conducted for 10-year periods going back to 1958 and the results were nearly the same. Immunization is a very robust system. It does work despite all the twists in the yield curve that took place since 1958.

II. THE DEDICATED BOND PORTFOLIO: A MEANS OF HEDGING ACTUARIAL LIABILITIES AT TODAY'S HIGH INTEREST RATES

The title tells the whole story. The rationale behind this title is that it represents a particular bond portfolio program that is designed for a specified portion of a pension plan, more specifically, that portion of the pension plan where the liabilities do not have to be inflation adjusted and are fixed as far as magnitude and timing in the future. The second part of the title talks about a means of hedging actuarial liabilities at today's high interest rates. Based on the actuary's schedule of liabilities, fixed income assets can be selected at today's high interest rates to hedge the liabilities as far out as 40 years. The benefit to the plan, of course, is that if the future liabilities are funded at today's rate, which is far above the actuarial interest rate assumption of most pension plans, a significant reduction in pension costs could occur.

Coordination Between Actuary and Investment Officer

Dedicated portfolio designs require a coordination between the actuary and the investment officer, which has rarely been witnessed in everyday portfolio practice. The best person to estimate the plan benefits is the actuary. He furnishes a schedule of conservatively estimated cash disbursements to the plan. He tells us what their magnitude would be and when those outflows would have to occur. We as investment officers are assigned the task of coming up with an asset mix which is determined by examining the liability schedule furnished by the actuary. Moreover, we could give him an idea of what type of rate of return, or the minimum rate of return on a portfolio, that could be locked in, given current rates in the capital market.

The Matched Portfolio

The *matched portfolio* design locks in a fixed rate of return and is set up so that the cash flow from maturing assets and income exactly matches the disbursements of liabilities estimated by the actuary.

All one tries to do in a matched portfolio is produce a cash flow stream from assets through income and maturities that exactly matches the liability outflow estimated by the actuary.

For example, rather than assuming a 6 percent actuarial interest assumption, one can promise in a nearly risk free manner, a rate of return in today's market of 14.5 percent. As far as the funding effect of this strategy, an actuary would assume that $9,500,000 in assets would have to be needed at a 6 percent rate of return assumption to fund $16 million of liabilities. However, by going through the matching process itself, one could purchase Treasury and high-quality instruments in the marketplace for less than $7 million leaving a reduction of almost $2,500,000. The actuary has the discretion of setting a separate valuation at the target rate of 14.50 percent or of arriving at a blended rate, recognizing the better investment experience that would be generated through the immunization process.

III.   ACTIVE RISK-CONTROLLED MANAGEMENT SYSTEM (ARMS)

Recognizing the volatility of investment returns that has characterized active bond management in recent years, Manufacturers Hanover Trust Company has introduced a new bond investment technique (ARMS) that links *active bond management* to *immunization*. By combining the two very dissimilar strategies in a unique manner, the strengths of both are employed to produce, on one hand, nearly unlimited upside performance potential and, on the other, nominal downside risk.

We begin this strategy by providing a sponsor with a minimum targeted realized rate of return for a specific period of years. Usually the target will be 100 basis points below what the target would have been for a pure immunized portfolio. The minimum target rate will be the lowest rate the portfolio could earn over the specified time period within the standard deviation associated with immunization. Providing we successfully manage the portfolio using the traditional active management techniques, the return of the fund over the time period will be in excess of the minimum target return, and at no point will it become necessary to employ immunization during the life of the program.

This new strategy offers much greater flexibility to the plan sponsor than either of the component strategies used alone. For example, in the case of a successful investment program the plan sponsor can, at any time, elect to voluntarily abandon the active strategy and lock up what may be a much higher rate for the remaining years of the program than the minimum rate set at the outset.

THE ROLE OF IMMUNIZATION
IN BOND MANAGEMENT

Ray B. Zemon

Interest in immunization among investment practitioners is not surprising in light of the well-publicized reassessments of fixed income securities currently being undertaken by many traditional bond market participants. As with equities in the mid-1970s, this reassessment follows a period of disappointing performance from the class of securities being evaluated. For some, the "reassessment" will take the form of selling what has done poorly to buy what has done well; history suggests capital markets will appropriately reward those who apply this strategy. However, the natural reluctance to follow this course should not obscure the fact that an increased understanding of the nature of fixed income markets and the portfolio strategies applied to those markets has resulted from our recent experiences. This new understanding has already begun to affect the way bonds are being deployed in an overall portfolio structure.

Traditionally, investors have included bonds in their portfolios in order to achieve a predictable total rate of return on a portion of their assets. It was generally accepted that any amalgamation of bonds would generate a reasonably stable return, at least when measured over a three to five-year period. This period was often associated with an interest rate cycle, a notion which implied that the bulk of interest rate movements result from temporal forces that were self-correcting over an entire cycle. As a result, fixed income portfolio strategies were designed to exploit opportunities that arose from the cyclical fluctuations in interest rates; little, if any, emphasis was placed on providing stable returns should interest rate movements depart from a cyclical pattern.

Sharply higher and extremely volatile interest rates during the last few years have dramatized the necessity of secular bond market stability in order for most fixed income portfolio strategies to deliver predictable returns. Disappointing performance by bond portfolios during the late 1970s and early 1980s is the rule rather than the exception. Some market oracles cite this poor historic performance and continuing market volatility as evidence that bonds no longer can be used to provide predictable returns. Others have suggested that the evidence is not sufficient to support this conclusion. It *is* possible to develop a portfolio strategy designed to produce return stability internally, without relying on a stable interest rate environment. It is for this purpose that investment practitioners have been drawn to immunization.

Seldom have practitioners in need of a new tool been as fortunate as those who wish to apply immunization techniques. Immunization has been a subject of serious academic inquiry for over 10 years. A wealth of literature exists on the topic. From a practitioner's viewpoint, present knowledge can be characterized by two observations:

1. Immunization techniques are imperfect. The results which can be obtained by applying immunization techniques in the real world are less satisfactory than those that are "obtained" in the theoretical world in which immunization techniques are developed.
2. The reasons why actual results deviate from theoretical results are known. As such, judgments about how the real world differs from the theoretical world can be incorporated into an immunization program, improving the level of success.

The manner in which these observations guide an immunizer is highlighted below.

It is well known that immunization techniques would be successful if the real world were characterized by flat yield curves and parallel yield shifts. In this case, the yield to maturity of the initial portfolio would be the minimum return achieved from correctly applying an immunization strategy. The assumption of a flat yield curve implies that the portfolio can be rebalanced without reducing yield to maturity. If yield curves are not flat but exhibit parallel shifts, immunization can still be successful, although the minimum return will not be the yield of the initial portfolio. This occurs because the yield of the portfolio will be reduced (positively sloped curve) or increased (negatively sloped curve) at each rebalancing. Parallel shifts insure that the impact of rebalancing is known at the start of the immunization program, allowing the minimum return to be known in advance.

In the real world, the future shapes of the yield curve are uncertain. As such, an unambiguous minimum return cannot be established at the start of an immunization program. In practice, this dilemma is resolved in one of two ways.

Most frequently, nonparallel yield curve shifts are viewed as exogenous to the immunization process. Simply stated, the techniques applied to achieve immunization are not designed to accommodate the prospect of nonparallel shifts. As a result, the total return that will be achieved by following such a procedure takes on an element of variability, a "risk" associated with an immunization strategy.

The justification for this approach is that the variability associated with ignoring nonparallel shifts is not significant. Historic simulations for a five-year immunization program suggest that the actual returns are typically within 25 basis points of the return attainable under parallel shifts. Undoubtedly there are many situations in which the potential for return variability of 25 or even 50 basis points would be more than acceptable.

Alternatively, the immunization program can be designed to accommodate the prospect of nonparallel shifts. Immunization techniques exist that are designed to accommodate specific shifts in the shape of the yield curve. Thus a portfolio manager may adapt an immunization strategy to his *forecast* of the future shapes of the yield curve. To the extent that these forecasts are more accurate than an assumption of parallel shifts, disparity in returns due to nonparallel yield curve shifts will be reduced.

It should be clear that immunization, when applied to actual investment problems, cannot be viewed as a set of mechanical procedures which, if followed correctly, will produce a known result. The relative success of an immunization program will depend on how well the techniques employed match the interest rate environment in which they are applied. This will depend on the quality of the portfolio manager's judgments in implementing the immunization process. In practice, these judgments need not be limited to minimizing immunization risk. More often than not, it is appropriate to encourage the portfolio manager to accept risk in order to enhance expected return. In this context, the immunization process can be used to construct a system of controls designed to monitor the level of risk accepted in seeking increased return.

From a practitioner's perspective, the impact of immunization technology on fixed income portfolio management has been quite favorable. Whether applied in a passive context or as a frame of reference for more active strategies, immunization goes a long way toward assuring return stability for a bond portfolio over a period of years. This is not to say that immunization as it exists today is the final word on bond portfolio management. Work should continue on developing immunization procedures for interest rate environments that more closely approximate the real world. We practitioners look to our academic colleagues for progress in this area, offering assurance that further advances are needed and will be applied.

PART V

SUMMARY OF CONFERENCE

SUMMARY

Richard R. West

First, let me say what a distinct pleasure it is to be a part of this gathering. Some years ago, as dean of the University of Oregon's College of Business Administration, I witnessed and, to a much lesser degree, participated in the creation of the Center for Capital Market Research. Since then, I have followed the progress of the Center, first in pioneering research on a variety of municipal finance problems and, more recently, in expanding our understanding of duration and bond immunization. And now here we are, at this idyllic setting in southern Oregon, participating in what would seem to be the Center's swan song. Would that it were otherwise; but if this is as it must be, how pleased I am to be in attendance.

Beyond being pleased, however, I am highly flattered to be here. Professors Kaufman and Bierwag know that after spending nearly a decade as a dean, I am no longer able to pass myself off as a bona fide researcher. Nevertheless, they have assumed, perhaps imprudently, that I would still be able to read the papers, to participate in the discussions, and to make a few semi-intelligent comments. Now if I can only avoid embarrassing the two of them, as well as myself.

At the start of this morning's session, Professor Sharpe sent me the following brief note:

299

Here is my proposed summary of Thursday's meeting:

1. Duration assumes that the sensitivity of the return of a zero coupon bond of maturity t to the first principal component of the return-generating process is proportional to t. The evidence suggests that it may well be.
2. Immunization assumes that this principal component explains all of the covariance matrix associated with the return-generating process. The evidence shows that it does not.

As I might have expected, Sharpe said much of what is called for in a few, well-chosen words. Indeed, after reading his note, I considered pleading no contest. Having received air fare and expenses from the Center, however, I felt compelled to put together a few additional observations, even at the risk of adding little to, or even detracting from, his simple, yet highly perceptive statement.

In view of the time we have devoted to empirical issues and the assumptions underlying various deviation measures, it might seem logical for me to turn directly to these subjects, as Sharpe did. I would prefer, however, to begin by asking you to return to two questions that have come up several times during the conference: First, does the basic premise of the immunization literature involve a minimax investment strategy? And second, if it does, is this premise really meaningful in a world in which investors are thought to make choices between alternative combinations of risk and return? Unquestionably, the mathematics of the immunization literature involve a minimax strategy—one in which an investor seeks the maximization of a utility function having as an argument net worth at a single point in the future and exhibiting zero risk tolerance. As Sharpe observed in his comments on the paper by Bierwag, Kaufman, and Toevs, Immunization seeks to find "one point on an efficient frontier in risk return space (the point appropriate for someone with a zero risk tolerance) and ignores the task of finding other points"[3].

But so what? Does it follow from this that the immunization concept is too restrictive to have any real applicability or implications for a world in which trade-offs between risk and return are the stuff which derives portfolio decisions? If one assumes that those focusing on immunizing techniques are totally consumed by them, i.e., base all of their investment decisions on the desire to immunize, the answer is obviously in the affirmative. Alternately, however, if one recognizes that an investor might have a need to immunize some portion of his portfolio, while also making a variety of risk and return trade-offs, the answer is less obvious. On numerous occasions over the past day and a half, the practitioners among us have tended to focus on immunization within very constrained circumstances. They have not asserted that one ought to try to apply it to one's total portfolio. To the contrary, several of them have talked about using it to deal with a limited part of the larger problem of selecting a portfolio of securities, trading off risk and return, etc. The fact that individual academic papers often fail to put immunization's potential relevance into the broader context of investment planning should not lead readers to conclude that the underlying mathematics imply anything global about an investor's taste for risk.

Please don't misunderstand. I can sympathize with those who perceive the setting of the immunization literature as unnecessarily limiting. Indeed, on the basis of what I have heard at this conference, it seems safe to predict that the academics will increasingly focus on the more general subject of the elasticity of capital values for so-called fixed income securities, leaving basis risk immunization as but one possible approach to dealing with one particular aspect of risk and return. Nevertheless, it is an important approach, if only because understanding it better should improve our ability to describe and analyze the pros and cons of bond portfolio strategies that seek deliberately to diverge from immunizing basis risk. In this regard, I noted with interest the comments of Fong and Vasicek [2] on the subject of "merging immunization with elements of active bond investment strategies." Similar ideas have also recently been suggested by Bierwag, Kaufman, and Toevs [1].

All this having been said, I suspect that more than a few academics, including some at this conference, will continue to find themselves concerned about, if not preoccupied with, basis risk immunization per se. The reason for my suspicion is simple and, I suppose, somwhat cynical: there is a ready market for immunization research. Many practitioners who have pursued active bond strategies over the last two decades have been badly "burned." They want to know more about immunization and they are prepared to pay handsomely for advice, not to mention computer programs. Hence, even if academics may question some aspects of the preoccupation with basis risk immunization and want to pursue strategies for "constrained immunization," many of them can be expected to give the market what it wants.

How long the market will continue to demand immunization products is a matter for conjecture. My own feeling is that a 250- to 300-basis-point rally in the long sector of the market would do wonders for active bond management, just as a bull market in stocks brings out the boys who would pick winners. In the meantime, however, as we heard this morning, many pension funds have gotten very gun shy and are looking for ways to lock in some specific rate of return for some specific period. But even this may not be enough. Let's face it; immunization strategies draw their raison d'etre from the existance of incomplete markets. With the development of zero coupon bonds and other vehicles designed to provide people with single payments many years into the future, it may be that basis risk immunization strategies may become passe.

Lest I be viewed as the complete cynic, let me add that the results of this conference suggest that both academics and practitioners can be expected, over time, to broaden their research efforts into the general area of bond riskiness, even if the market for investment products seems to have a fixation (dare I say an *irrational* fixation?) on basis risk immunization.

While it would be pretentious for me to try to predict precisely how these efforts will develop, the results of this conference suggest some likely directions. Based on the various papers that have been presented, there seems to be a fairly broad concensus among the academics that a theoretically sound measure of the elasticity of capital calls for a plausible model of the behavior of interest rates or, if you will, of bond prices, over time. Because all of the relatively simple duration models suffer from the fact that they are inconsistent with equilibrium bond pricing relationships, it seems likely that more complex, equilibrium models, such as the one presented by Brennan and Schwartz, will continue to be developed.

At the same time, however, these models will always find themselves being challenged by the simpler, less theoretically sound formulations. Professor Kaufman has observed on numerous occasions that the issue is ultimately one of empiricism. And, as Professor Sharpe said yesterday, "The relevant question concerns the minimum number of factors that can describe most of the variation in the bond pricing function and their identification" [3]. A number of our speakers have told us that for a very important class of debt instruments—namely, U.S. government securities—the relatively simple, nonequilibrium models seem to be able to describe a fairly significant part of price variation—and they do so at very low cost. So, while ever more elegant models are being built, the older, less formal ones will continue to wait in the lists, and they will be joined from time to time by newer, equally simple formulations, such as the one John Ingersoll described earlier in the chapter entitled "Is Immunization Feasible: Evidence from the CRSP Data."

Even if the questions are ultimately empirical ones, and even if the simple models seem to do a fairly good job of dealing with basis risk immunization in government securities, it stands to reason that the equilibrium models should have a secure future; and I don't mean the kind of future that springs from the efforts of those academics who are simply searching for truth and have unlimited computer time and research assistance. Much to the contrary, I mean a future that is based on a general concern for managing risk and return on fixed income securities. Notice that I did not simply say managing basis risk. Clearly, this is important, but it is only part of the picture. This morning we heard from a number of practitioners who talked about so-called immunization products. In general, they were referring to portfolio strategies involving not only government securities, but corporates as well. Indeed, I heard one practitioner mention using immunization concepts to manage portfolios of "junk" bonds. But as Professor Rosenberg so eloquently observed, when you introduce the notion of a default risk, not to mention call feature, etc., the logic of the equilibrium models really comes into its own, as it does when you start talking about strategies designed to identify under and over valued bonds.

Since so much of the papers and comments presented herein have discussed empirical issues, I would be derelict if I did not touch briefly on this general subject. Simply put, the results presented to us make it clear that what body of data you choose to study and how you choose to study it can make a very big difference in what you find. On several occasions I have heard conference participants speculate that using another data source, or changing the way the data were manipulated, would produce significantly different results. While such comments might be dismissed as idle speculation, the fact that existing results seem to be so data dependent gives them some real credibility.

As the final speaker, I would like to take this opportunity to express gratitude to Professors Kaufman and Bierwag for putting together this excellent conference. Like most academics, I find myself invited to many such gatherings and typically decide that staying at home would be the best way to use my time. In this particular instance, however, anyone who declined an invite made a serious error. All of the papers have been first-rate and each of the various discussants has taken his task seriously. Most importantly, the informal conversations have been both stimulating and enjoyable.

REFERENCES

1. Bierwag, G. O., George G. Kaufman, and Alden Toevs, 1980, "Duration Analysis and Active Bond Portfolio Management," Working paper, Center for Capital Market Research, University of Oregon, October.

2. Fong, H. Gifford, and Oldrich Vasicek, 1980, "A Risk Minimizing Strategy for Multiple Liability Immunization," Working paper, September 15.

3. Sharpe, William E. "Comments on Recent Developments in Bond Portfolio Strategies." (Paper in this volume, 1983.)

PART VI

APPENDIXES

SINGLE-FACTOR DURATION MODELS IN A DISCRETE GENERAL EQUILIBRIUM FRAMEWORK

G. O. Bierwag, George G. Kaufman, and
Alden Toevs

Single-factor duration models (SFDMs) for valuing debt securities have gained rapid acceptance by bond practitioners in recent years but slower acceptance by academics. In large measure, the slower academic acceptance reflects the lack of a rigorously developed underlying economic or financial theoretic base. Partially as a result, some SFDMs have undesirable behavioral characteristics. Foremost among these is that they appear to be inconsistent with accepted general equilibrium conditions. This paper has two purposes. The first is to construct explicitly the theoretical underpinnings of the model, and the second is to develop the conditions under which the model does satisfy general equilibrium conditions. This is done in Sections I and II, respectively.

I. THEORY

Duration models did not spring forth full grown from a rigorous and well-defined general equilibrium economic model. Rather, they were developed primarily in piecemeal fashion on an almost ad hoc basis. The term *duration* was coined by Frederick Macaulay in his major review of interest rates and stock prices published in 1938.[1] Macaulay was searching for a more meaningful summary measure of the life of a bond than its term to maturity that incorporated the timing of the bond's flow of coupon payments. The question was how to weight the time periods to each payment (n). After deductively rejecting a weighting of the periods by the future value of each payment, Macaulay chose the present value of each payment. Because "of the insuperable difficulties connected with any attempt to discover the real rates of discount for each half-yearly period in the future," Macaulay chose to use the yield to maturity (i) to discount future payment (S) and defined duration as[2]

$$ D = \frac{\sum_{n=1}^{m} S_n n (1 + i)^{-n}}{\sum_{n=1}^{m} S_n (1 + i)^{-n}} . \tag{1}$$

This specification is now referred to as the *Macaulay duration*. It is important to note that Macaulay developed duration only as a measure that "throws a flood of light on the fluctuations of bond yields on the actual market."[3]

One year after Macaulay, J. R. Hicks independently derived equation (1) by computing the elasticity of capital value with respect to the discount ratio and assuming that the interest rate is the same for all maturities.[4] Like Macaulay, Hicks used duration basically as a volatility measure. In 1945, Paul Samuelson effectively derived equation (1) by examining the effects of changes in interest rates on the present value of net worth of a financial institution and computing the first derivatives of the inflows and outflows with respect to the average interest rate.[5] Unaware of Macaulay's or Hicks's work, he called the term *average time period*, and proceeded to use the statistic to analyze the sensitivity of financial intermediary institutions to interest rate changes. He concluded that "increased interest rates will help any organization whose (weighted) average time period of disbursements is greater than the average time period of its receipts."[6] He did not, however, construct a formal economic model.

In 1952, the British actuary F. M. Redington, apparently unaware of Samuelson's article, used approximately the same methodology to derive equation (1) by solving for "the distribution of the term of the assets in relation to the term of the liabilities . . . [that will] reduce the possibility of loss arising from a change in interest rates."[7] He referred to the statistic as the *mean term*. Redington showed that "the existing business is immune to a general change in the rate of interest" when the mean term of the assets is equal to that of the liabilities and coined the term *immunization*.[8] Other than assuming "a uniform rate of interest whatever the term, and that all funds are invested on fixed-rate securities which are irredeemable or redeemable at a fixed date" and listing some of the practical complications, Redington did not consider further either the underlying assumptions or implications.[9] It is ironic that Redington's article, published in an actuarial journal not widely read by nonactuarials, has received wider recognition than Samuelson's similar and earlier article in the *American Economic Review*.

The first researchers to explicitly concern themselves with the underlying behavioral assumptions of duration analysis were Lawrence Fisher and Roman Weil in their 1971 article "Coping with the Risk of Interest-Rate Fluctuations: Returns to Bondholders from Naive and Optimal Strategies."[10] They explicitly assume the expectations theory of the term structure and that all unexpected interest rate changes— the sole source of uncertainty—will be the same for all terms to maturity, i.e., the changes are additive. Unlike their predecessors, however, they do not assume a flat term structure. Fisher and Weil develop the conditions under which a portfolio of default and option free coupon bonds will realize a return at the end of a given planning period no less than that promised at the time the portfolio was purchased if interest rates change in the assumed pattern, interest is compounded continuously, and investors have single known and fixed investment horizons. The immunization condition involves setting the weighted average of the term to each payment, where the weights are the present values of each payment computed by using one-period zero coupon discount rates, equal to the investor's holding period. They term this *average duration* because of its mathematical similarity to the Macaulay, Hicks, and Redington measures. In a number of subsequent papers, G. O. Bierwag, George G. Kaufman, and Chulsoon Khang assume a number of alternative "reasonable" stochastic processes governing interest rate movements and derive the appropriate statistic, referred to as *immunizing duration*, that when set equal to the investor's planning period, generates returns for the planning period no less than those promised.[11]

At this point, the models were subjected to a number of criticisms. The earliest and most widespread criticism was that duration is useful only when yield curves are flat. This, of course, was explicitly assumed by everyone prior to Fisher and Weil, but it was put to rest with the development of duration measures for a variety of stochastic processes. A second criticism was directed more at the use of SFDMs to achieve immunization than at duration per se. It held that few investors are totally interest rate risk averse and that immunization is only one, and possibly not even a very interesting, point on the risk continuum. However, the emphasis on immunization reflects both computational and practical aspects. Computationally, duration formulas are easiest to derive by solving for the immunization conditions for each assumed stochastic process. Practically, immunization against interest rate risk is of importance to some investors, such as life insurance companies, and to all investors as a means of obtaining the riskless return. Bierwag and Khang develop a formal model to show that immunization is consistent with investors' satisfying minimax conditions.[12] But having derived immunizing durations, these can be used both to value bonds with any degree of interest rate risk exposure and to construct portfolios of coupon bonds that track a desired but not available zero-coupon reference bond. Use of duration analysis in active bond portfolio management has been discussed by Bierwag, Kaufman, and Toevs in a number of papers and will be developed more formally later in this paper.[13] (Valuation of risk sources other than interest rate risk will, of course, entail the need for additional factors in the model describing these sources of uncertainty.)

A third criticism argues that the models are completely deterministic and do not contain an error or residual term. This occurred because the earliest developers either did not assume a stochastic process or assumed only one such process known with certainty. However, once uncertainty and multiple stochastic processes were assumed, the need to identify correctly the true process became obvious. If identified incorrectly, the model contains an error term, which is labeled "stochastic process risk."[14] The assumed stochastic process may be obtained either by fitting single-factor measures to past observations or by choosing a specific single-factor measure on the basis of experience or expectation.

Another criticism concerns the nature of interest rate uncertainty that can be described by a single factor. Changes in all interest rates along the term structure must be perfectly correlated.[15] Thus, stochastic process risk may be incurred even if the stochastic process is identified correctly, but the process does not satisfy this condition.

Ingersoll, Skelton, and Weil and Cox, Ingersoll, and Ross argue that the stochastic processes assumed in traditional SFDMs are inconsistent with general equilibrium conditions.[16] This occurs because these return functions are strictly convex with respect to the magnitude of the interest rate shock so that the larger the shock, the greater the return. It also follows that the larger the coupon rate, the greater the return for a given shock. Thus, opportunities may exist for riskless arbitrage and the highest coupon bonds will dominate all lower coupon bonds. Although this criticism is valid for all of the processes used in the published studies, a general additive stochastic process (GASP) for which the return function is not strictly convex and thus generates implications that are consistent with general equilibrium is developed in the second part of this paper. For stochastic processes that do not have strict convexity properties, a portfolio of coupon bonds has the same characteristics as a zero-coupon bond of the same immunizing duration. Thus, in the absence of transactions costs, the two portfolios are indistinguishable, as are differing compositions of coupon bonds having the same duration.[17] If the desired zero-coupon reference bond is not available, portfolios of coupon bonds may be constructed to track the zero-coupon reference bond perfectly.

In view of these criticisms, why have traditional single-factor duration models been widely adopted and may be expected to continue to receive substantial attention? The answer is because they are cheap to use and their empirical results compare favorably with more sophisticated and rigorously developed models. Nonconsol bonds are by their nature more difficult to value than equities. The passage of time automatically changes the returns on the bonds as the term to maturity decreases, except when term structures are flat. Moreover, because of the differing characteristics of bonds, it is unlikely that the passage of time will affect two alike, even if they had equal terms to maturity. Thus, the covariances of returns between any two bonds or between any one bond and a market portfolio, however defined, are unlikely to be intertemporarily stable. As Brennan and Schwartz have noted:

> The obstacle to estimation of a variance covariance matrix of bond returns from historical data has been that a structure similar to that for common stocks could not reasonably be assumed, and it is unclear what alternative structure should be assumed.[18]

This is a prime reason why single- and multiple-factor CAPM-type models have been significantly less successful for individual bonds or bond portfolios than for equity securities.[19] Improved results have been achieved when, following Brennan and Schwartz, individual points on the term structure rather than individual bonds have been used. Whether these models are superior to SFDMs is an empirical question of cost effectiveness. Preliminary evidence suggests that the SFDM performs well relative to two-factor models as well as to naive maturity matching models in immunizing default and option free coupon bonds for specific and known planning periods.[20]

Thus, it is worthwhile to develop the general SFD bond valuation model further. In particular, it is important to list explicitly the major economic assumptions underlying its development and use:

1. Investors attempt to maximize expected returns for a given level of risk exposure over a known and certain planning period(s).
2. Only default and option-free debt securities (interest rates are the only source of uncertainty).
3. The true stochastic process is known.
4. Changes in all interest rates on the term structure (all returns) are perfectly correlated.
5. The return function generated by the stochastic process is non-convex.

To the extent one or more of the last three assumptions are violated, unexplained return variance (stochastic process risk) results. The model may be written analogous to the one-factor market model as follows:

$$R_{jD_sq} = P_q + \alpha_j + \gamma_j(\,|\,D_s - q\,|\,)r_{K,q} + e_j,\qquad(2)$$

R_{jD_sq} = return relative on bond or portfolio j with duration D_s for period q;

s = assumed stochastic process for all interest rates;

q = number of years to end of investor's planning period;

P_q = risk-free return relative for period q (return on zero coupon bond with maturity q);

D = immunizing duration;

$r_{K,q}$ = excess return relative on zero-coupon reference bond with maturity $K \neq D$, q for planning period q;

α_j = extramarket return relative;

γ_j = proportionality factor (not necessarily constant);

e_j = error term.

All return variables represent expected values. This equation is derived in basically the same form in the second section of this paper.

If the true stochastic process can be summarized in one factor and is identified correctly, then $e_j = 0$. If the market is efficient, then $\alpha_j = 0$. The degree of interest rate risk the investor wishes to assume is directly related to $|\,D_s - q\,|$. If the investor wishes to immunize, then D_s is set equal to q and expected $R_j = P_q$. If the investor wishes to assume interest rate risk, then D_s is set either larger or smaller than q and expected $R_j > P_q$. γ_j depends on the stochastic process and the reference bond selected. If there is no shock—interest rates do not change unexpectedly—the expected return is equal to the riskless return. The model also emphasizes the importance of the investor's planning period and that the expected returns on the same security may differ for different investors having different planning periods.

Equation (2) is likely to be difficult to estimate empirically. For example, the model suggests that the market will reward risk only if investors' q's are either homogeneous or distributed unevenly over all trading periods. If q's were distributed evenly, then one investor's risky portfolio would be another's riskless portfolio. Thus, empirical fits of equation (2) may be more difficult for bonds using ex post data for the market as a whole than it is for equities, where differences in individual planning periods may not be as important.[21] Likewise, the effects on realized returns of misidentifying the stochastic process may not be confined to e_j. Part of the impact may appear in the estimate of γ_j. Nevertheless, the equation is useful to investors in providing a conceptual framework for formulating their strategy if they predict interest rate changes for a reference bond.

Equation (2) suggests a two-step procedure for bond portfolio management in the "real world." First, the investor must choose the bond that, in a world of complete markets including a continuum of zero coupon bonds, provides the desired degree of risk exposure, proportional to $| D_s - q |$. Second, if the selected zero-coupon bond is not available, the investor must construct a portfolio of available bonds that has the same immunizing duration as this reference bond. If the stochastic process has no strict convexity properties and the assumed one-factor stochastic process is correct, the composition of the portfolio is irrelevant. The equations for constructing such portfolios for a discrete SFDM are derived in Section II.

II. GENERAL EQUILIBRIUM CONDITIONS

In a single-factor duration model, there is a single source of interest rate uncertainty that affects the return on each security. As was shown in equation (2), the return on any security can be expressed as a function of the return on any reference security subject only to the same uncertainty. This relationship is technically derived in this section, first for the generally multifactor case for both single and multiple periods and then specialized to the single-factor case. When interest rate uncertainty enters the model in the form of a generalized additive stochastic process, the return relationship is linear and the SFDM has special properties that satisfy general equilibrium conditions and are consistent with a mean-variance framework.

Discount Functions and Future States

Assume that at the beginning of a period of analysis a discount function $P(0,t)$, $t = 1, 2, \ldots$, is observed. This function gives the present value of \$1 to be paid or received at time t. Each of the flows of an income stream can be evaluated with this discount function. At the beginning of the next period, the discount function will be $P_s(1,t)$, where s is an indicator of the state of the economy and is an integer in $[1,K]$. At time $t = 0$, it is uncertain which of the mutually exclusive future states will occur. It is assumed that trading can occur only at integer dates.

Denote the one-period return per dollar on a t-period pure discount bond as

$$R_{ts} = \frac{P_s(1,t)}{P(0,t)}, \qquad t > 1, \qquad s \in [1,K] \, ,$$

and   (3)

$$R_{1s} = \frac{1}{P(0,1)} \, .$$

A matrix of one-period returns may be denoted as

$$R = \{R_{ts}\}, \qquad t = 1, 2, \ldots, T, \qquad s = 1, 2, \ldots, K. \quad (4)$$

if T pure discount bonds are available.

The markets for these securities are complete if the number of pure discount bonds having independent returns is equal to the number of states. Markets are assumed to be complete. In the matrix of one-period returns, we need only to consider K independent pure discount bonds.

If the markets are complete, there exist K Arrow–Debreu securities (contingent claims) that can be formed by portfolios of these pure discount bonds. Let $A = \{\alpha_{st}\}$ be a set of K portfolios, where α_{st} is the proportion invested in a t-period pure discount bond in the sth portfolio, and $\sum_{t=1}^{K} \alpha_{st} = 1$. Then

$$AR = \begin{bmatrix} \theta_1 & & & 0 \\ & \theta_2 & & \\ & & \ddots & \\ 0 & & & \theta_K \end{bmatrix} = \theta \qquad (5)$$

is a diagonal matrix giving the returns on the Arrow-Debreu securities. If the markets are complete, the rank of θ is K; that is, $\theta_s \neq 0$ for any s.

Assume that every investor observes P(0,t) as the current discount function. If P(0,t) is consistent with competitive conditions in which there are no opportunities for profitable and riskless arbitrage, $0 < \theta_s < \infty$, for all s. The Hicksian forward price for a pure discount bond can be defined as P(1,t) = P(0,t)/P(0,1). Each of the forward prices is a function of the observed current discount function.[22]

In discrete models of competitive equilibrium in complete markets, a weighted combination of the returns (prices) on a security over the various states can be regarded as an expectation of the future returns (prices) given particular patterns of subjective probabilities and utility functions among investors.[23] This is true in this model. In addition, under risk neutrality and common investor subjective probabilities, the expected future price of a t-period security is equal to the current forward price P(1,t).

If markets are complete the returns on any security can be expressed as a linear combination of the first K reference securities. That is, we can write

$$R_{\tau s} = \sum_{t=1}^{K} \beta_{t\tau} R_{ts} \qquad \text{for } \tau = 1, 2, 3, \ldots \qquad (6)$$

for any pure discount bond of maturity τ, where $\beta_{t\tau}$ is the proportion invested in the tth reference security. If τ is an integer in [1,K], then $\beta_{\tau\tau} = 1$ and $\beta_{t\tau} = 0$ for $t \neq \tau$. In this last case, equation (6) is an identity. Equation (6), otherwise, is an implication of an arbitrage model; it states that the one-period returns on any security can be expressed relative to the exogeneously determined returns on the reference securities. Subtracting R_{1s} from both sides of equation (6), we can write

$$R_{\tau s} - R_{1s} = \sum_{t=2}^{K} \beta_{t\tau}(R_{ts} - R_{1s}) , \qquad (7)$$

where only $K - 1$ terms remain on the right-hand side. The expression on the left-hand side is the excess one-period return on a τ-period security over the certain return on a one-period security.

This analysis can be extended to returns over more than one period. Multiply equation (6) by $1/P_s(1,q)$, which is the accumulated return on $1 for $q - 1$ periods if state s occurs one period hence and if all forward prices thereafter are realized.[24] Using equation (3), the excess returns on a τ-period security over q periods are

$$\frac{P_s(1,\tau)}{P_s(1,q)P(0,\tau)} - \frac{1}{P(0,q)} = \sum_{\substack{t=1 \\ t\neq q}}^{K} \beta_{t\tau}\left(\frac{P_s(1,t)}{P_s(1,q)P(0,t)} - \frac{1}{P(0,q)}\right), \quad (8)$$

where $1/P(0,q)$ is the riskless return over q periods. Note that as τ shifts, the set of coefficients $(\beta_{1\tau}, \beta_{2\tau}, \ldots, \beta_{K\tau})$ also shifts and that as q is varied, equation (8) holds as long as the qth reference security is removed from the right-hand side.

Complete competitive markets implies that no profitable riskless opportunities exist. The relationship between $P(0,t)$ and $P_s(1,t)$, for all s and t defines a "stochastic process" that is consistent with complete competitive markets. In a world of uncertainty, the wrong process may be assumed and then an error term must be added to equations (7) and (8) to account for the misidentification.

Duration and Two-State Processes

For two-state processes, two securities are specified as the reference securities. Let these be the one- and K-period pure discount bonds respectively. The matrix of one-period returns can be written as

$$R = \frac{1}{P(0,1)}\begin{bmatrix} 1 & 1 \\ \dfrac{P_1(1,K)}{P(1,K)} & \dfrac{P_2(1,K)}{P(1,K)} \end{bmatrix} = \begin{bmatrix} R_{11} & R_{12} \\ R_{K1} & R_{K2} \end{bmatrix}. \quad (9)$$

The one-period return on any t-period pure discount bond ($t \neq 1$, $t \neq K$) can then be stated as

$$R_{ts} = (1 - \beta_t)R_{1s} + \beta_t R_{Ks} \qquad s = 1, 2; t \neq 1; t \neq K, \quad (10)$$

where β_t and $1 - \beta_t$ are respectively the proportions invested in K-period and one-period bonds. There is consequently a mapping of the maturity of a pure discount bond into a value of the proportion β_t. Moreover, the returns on any portfolio of bonds in this two-state model will be equivalent to the returns on some portfolio of the reference securities. Consider, for example, the portfolio mixture consisting of proportion ϕ_t invested in t-period pure discount bonds and a proportion $(1 - \phi_t)$ invested in (t + 1)-period pure discount bonds. Such a portfolio may be of importance to investors who wish to assume a degree of risk that is between that of a t- and a (t + 1)-period pure discount bond. Because in this model bonds are available only with maturities equal to the integer dates on which trading occurs, this degree of risk can be assumed only by constructing portfolios that are mixtures of the available bonds. Using equation (10), one can show that such a portfolio has the same returns as one in which the proportion $\phi_t\beta_t + (1 - \phi_t)\beta_{t+1}$ is invested in K-period pure discount bonds and the proportion $\phi_t(1 - \beta_t) + (1 - \phi_t)(1 - \beta_{t+1})$ is invested in one-period pure discount bonds. As ϕ_t is varied in the interval [0,1], then the proportion invested in K-period bonds varies between β_{t+1} and β_t. As one considers the returns on all possible portfolios, it is evident that the proportion invested in K-period securities can be regarded as a continuous function of t, with the property that $\beta_K = 1$ and $\beta_1 = 0$. If β_t is a monotonic continuous function of t, as is most likely, one can regard t in this mapping as the duration of the portfolio because it has many of the properties of the traditional durations. Every pure discount bond has a duration equal to its maturity. If the duration of a bond portfolio is an integer it behaves like the corresponding pure discount bond. If the duration of the portfolio is not an integer then there corresponds a β that indicates that the portfolio behaves like some mixture of the two closest integer pure discount bonds. In this model a portfolio is completely specified by the stipulation of its duration. Any two portfolios with the same duration will have exactly the same returns in each state s.

Subtract R_{1s} from both sides of equation (10). Then,

$$R_{ts} - R_{1s} = \beta_t(R_{Ks} - R_{1s}) , \tag{11}$$

which is an excess return equation for the two-state model using the K- and one-period bonds as reference securities. This is analogous to equation (7) for the multistate model. Any desired portfolio can be constructed by choosing an appropriate duration corresponding to β_t. The excess returns on the selected portfolio will then be proportional to the excess return on the K-period reference bond.

If we replace the one-period reference bond with a q-period reference bond, the excess return equation for a q-period planning period can be written as

$$R_{ts}^A - R_{qs}^A = \beta_t(q)(R_{Ks}^A - R_{qs}^A) \tag{12}$$

where $R_{ts}^A = P_s(1,t)/P_s(1,q)P(0,t)$, $R_{qs}^A = 1/P(0,q)$, and $R_{Ks}^A = P_s(1,K)/P(0,K)P_s(1,q)$. Here, the superscript A denotes the accumulated return for q periods, and $\beta_t(q)$ indicates the proportion invested in a K-period bond when the planning period is of length q. We can also write $\beta_t(q) = \gamma_t|t - q|$ as indicated in equation (2). Thus, $\beta_t(q) = 0$ when duration t equals the planning period length. If γ_t is a constant independent of t, then $\beta_t(q)$ is linear in duration.

The shape of the function β_t depends on the stochastic process. In the next section, we consider a one-parameter additive stochastic process and derive the corresponding β_t.

The Generalized Additive Stochastic Process (GASP) for a Two-State Single-Factor Model

For a generalized additive process, one can define the price of a t-period discount bond one period hence as

$$P_s(1,t) = P(1,t) + g_s(t,z_s), \qquad s = 1, 2 \qquad (13)$$

in a two state model. In this expression a random term, $g_s(t,z_s)$ is added to the current forward price in order to determine the price next period. The term z_s is a random variable generated by some probability distribution specific to state s.

One can show that z_1 and z_2 are generated from a single source of uncertainty. If the markets are complete and a competitive equilibrium obtains, then there exist weights w_s independent of the distributions of z_s, such that

$$w_1 P_1(1,t) + w_2 P_2(1,t) = P(1,t), \qquad (14)$$

and the weights are positive and sum to unity. To show this, using equation (5), we note that $A^{-1}e = R\theta^{-1}e = e$, where e is a vector of ones. However, $R\theta^{-1}e = e$ implies, using equation (3) in a two-state model, that $\sum_{s=1}^{2} P_s(1,t)/\theta_s P(0,t) = 1$ and that $\sum_{s=1}^{2} 1/\theta_s P(0,1) = 1$. If we define $w_s = 1/\theta_s P(0,1)$, $s = 1, 2$, then $w_1 + w_2 = 1$, and equation (14) follows. Using equations (13) and (14),

$$w_1 g_1(t,z_1) + w_2 g_2(t,z_2) = \frac{g_1(t,z_1)}{\theta_1 P(0,1)} + \frac{g_2(t,z_2)}{\theta_2 P(0,1)} = 0 \qquad (15)$$

for all t and for all generated values of z_1 and z_2. It is now apparent that the distributions of z_1 and z_2 cannot be independent in order that this result hold. Consistency requires that there exist only one source of uncertainty in the determination of the pair (z_1,z_2). Without loss of generality, assume $z_1 = z_2 = z$. It also follows that g_1 and g_2 cannot be zero for all t because then the system reverts to a one-state certainty model.

One can calculate θ_1 and θ_2 in terms of g_1 and g_2, and since θ_1 and θ_2 must be fixed numbers for complete markets, it will follow that g_1 and g_2 must have particular properties. If R is the matrix of one-period returns as before, it follows that

$$R^{-1}e = \begin{bmatrix} 1 \\ \dfrac{1}{\theta_1} \\ \dfrac{1}{\theta_2} \end{bmatrix}$$

Substitution of g_1 and g_2 into R^{-1}, via equation (13), implies that

$$w_1 = \frac{g_2(t,z)}{g_2(t,z) - g_1(t,z)}$$

and (16)

$$w_2 = \frac{-g_1(t,z)}{g_2(t,z) - g_1(t,z)}$$

are fixed constants that must be independent of all t and z ($z_1 = z_2$) if markets are to be complete. From this condition for complete markets, we see that

$$\frac{g_2(t,z)}{g_1(t,z)} = \frac{-w_1}{w_2} = \frac{-\theta_2}{\theta_1} \tag{17}$$

for all t and z.

Given that the returns from the contingency claims are independent of z, it follows that the proportions invested in the reference securities to produce the returns on any other security are independent of z and s. To show this, we simply substitute equation (13) into (10), using the definitions of R_{ts}, R_{1s}, and R_{Ks}, and solve for the proportion β_t as

$$\beta_t = \frac{P(0,K)}{P(0,t)} \frac{g_s(t,z)}{g_s(K,z)}, \qquad s = 1, 2 . \tag{18}$$

The results in equations (16) and (17) imply that β_t is independent of s and z.

A Special Example of the Generalized Additive Stochastic Process

To illustrate the GASP process, we select a one-parameter example in which it is assumed that $g_1(t,z) = \lambda^t z$ and that $g_2(t,z) = -(\theta_2/\theta_1)\lambda^t z$, where λ is a positive parameter and z has a probability distribution in which $\text{Prob}(z < 0) = 0$. It follows that $g_s(t,z)/g_s(K,z) = \lambda^{t-K}$. Equation

(18) now implies that

$$\beta_t = \frac{P(0,K)}{P(0,t)} \lambda^{t-K}, \qquad t > 1 . \tag{19}$$

One can uniquely identify every portfolio by a measure of duration. Consider the income stream with flows $f_1, f_2, \ldots, f_N$. Its present value is $\sum_1^N f_t P(0,t)$. The one-period return is

$$R_s(f_1, f_2, \ldots, f_N) = \sum_{\tau=1}^N \gamma_\tau \frac{P_s(1,\tau)}{P(0,\tau)} \tag{20}$$

where $\gamma_\tau = f_\tau P(0,\tau)/\sum_1^N f_t P(0,t)$, and $P_s(1,1) = 1$. Now,

$$\frac{P_s(1,\tau)}{P(0,\tau)} = (1 - \beta_\tau) \frac{1}{P(0,1)} + \beta_\tau \frac{P_s(1,K)}{P(0,K)}, \tag{21}$$

where $\beta_\tau = 0$ when $\tau = 1$, and $\beta_\tau = 1$ when $\tau = K$. Substitution of equation (21) into (20) gives

$R_s(f_1, f_2, \ldots, f_N)$

$$= \left[\sum_1^N \gamma_\tau(1 - \beta_\tau) \right] \frac{1}{P(0,1)} + \left[\sum_1^N \gamma_\tau \beta_\tau \right] \frac{P_s(1,K)}{P(0,K)} . \tag{22}$$

Thus, this bond will behave like a bond in which $\sum_1^N \gamma_\tau \beta_\tau$ is invested in the K period and $\sum_1^K \gamma_\tau(1 - \beta_\tau)$ is invested in the one-period bond. From equation (19)

$$\sum_1^N \gamma_\tau \beta_\tau = \sum_2^N \gamma_\tau \frac{P(0,K)}{P(0,\tau)} \lambda^{\tau-K} . \tag{23}$$

If this bond with flows $(f_1, f_2, \ldots, f_N)$ is equivalent to a pure discount bond of maturity D, then equation (19) with $t = D$ is the proportion on the left-hand side of (23), and therefore,

$$\frac{\lambda^D}{P(0,D)} = \sum_2^N \frac{\gamma_\tau \lambda^\tau}{P(0,\tau)} . \tag{24}$$

Thus, equation (24) implicitly defines the duration for this special additive process. If D is not an integer, but $G < D < G + 1$, one can show that the bond with the income stream $(f_1, f_2, \ldots, f_N)$ behaves as a mixture of a G and a $G + 1$ maturity pure discount bond.

Dividing equation (13) by $P(0,t)$ gives us the return equation for every security. If the stochastic process is described by a single parameter and the mean and variance of the distribution of the factor (z) are known, then values of duration correspond uniquely to the mean and variance characteristics of any portfolio. This can be shown as follows. Let the one-period return per dollar invested in a t-period pure discount bond $(t \neq 1)$ be

$$
R_{ts} = \begin{cases} \dfrac{1}{P(0,1)} + \dfrac{\lambda^t z}{P(0,t)} & s = 1 \\[4mm] \dfrac{1}{P(0,1)} - \dfrac{(\theta_2/\theta_1)\lambda^t z}{P(0,t)} & s = 2 . \end{cases} \tag{25}
$$

Let p_1 and p_2 be the respective probabilities of states one and two. Assume $E(z) = \mu$ and $var(z) = \sigma^2$. Then

$$
E(R_{ts}) = \frac{1}{P(0,1)} + \frac{\lambda^t \mu}{P(0,t)} M, \qquad t \neq 1 , \tag{26}
$$

where $M = p_1 - p_2(\theta_2/\theta_1)$. The variances and covariances of the one-period returns per dollar can be calculated as

$$
var(R_{ts}) = \frac{\lambda^{2t}}{[P(0,t)]^2} L \tag{27}
$$

and

$$
cov(R_{ts}, R_{\tau s}) = \frac{\lambda^{t+\tau}}{P(0,t)P(0,\tau)} L , \tag{28}
$$

where

$$
L = \left[1 + \left(\frac{\theta_2}{\theta_1} \right)^2 \right] \sigma^2 + \mu^2 \left[(1 - M)^2 + \left(M + \frac{\theta_2}{\theta_1} \right)^2 \right] .
$$

The correlation between the returns per dollar is equal to unity, as would be expected in a two-state model with only one source of uncertainty. The relationship between the mean and the standard deviation of the return is linear. Taking the square root of the variance, solving for λ and substituting the result into equation (26) renders

$$
E(R_{ts}) = \frac{1}{P(0,1)} + \frac{\mu M}{\sqrt{L}} \sqrt{var(R_{ts})} , \tag{29}
$$

where $1/P(0,1)$ is the one-period risk-free return and $\mu M/\sqrt{L}$ is the slope of the efficiency frontier.

Both the mean and variance are determined by duration D. Thus, each point on the efficiency locus corresponds to a specific duration value. From equation (26) the expected return of any bond portfolio of duration D is

$$\frac{1}{P(0,1)} + \frac{\lambda^D \mu M}{P(0,D)} \, ,$$

and its variance is

$$\left(\frac{\lambda^D}{P(0,D)} \right)^2 L \, .$$

This model may be extended to multiperiods, but the expressions for means and variances become considerably more complex. Thus, the risk-return frontier is more difficult to derive than for single periods.

ACKNOWLEDGMENT

Reprinted with permission from *The Journal of Finance*, May 1982, pp. 325–338.

NOTES AND REFERENCES

1. Frederick R. Macaulay, *The Movements of Interest Rates, Bond Yields and Stock Prices in the United States Since 1856*, (New York: National Bureau of Economic Research, 1938). A good review of the early research on duration appears in Roman L. Weil, "Macaulay's Duration: An Appreciation," *Journal of Business*, October 1973, pp. 589–592.

2. *Ibid.*, p. 52.

3. *Ibid.*, 50.

4. J. R. Hicks, *Value and Capital*, 2nd ed., (Oxford University Press, 1939), pp. 185–88.

5. Paul A. Samuelson, "The Effect of Interest Rate Increases on the Banking System," *American Economic Review*, March 1945, pp. 16–27.

6. *Ibid.*, p. 19.

7. F. M. Redington, "Review of the Principles of Life-Office Valuations," *Journal of the Institute of Actuaries*, 1952, p. 289, reprinted in Martin L. Leibowitz, ed., *Pros & Cons of Immunization*, (New York: Salomon Brothers, 1980), pp. 286–340.

8. *Ibid.*, p. 289.

9. *Ibid.*, pp. 289–90.

10. Lawrence Fisher and Roman L. Weil, "Coping with the Risk of Interest-Rate Fluctuations: Returns to Bondholders from Naive and Optimal Strategies," *Journal of Business*, October 1971, pp. 408–31.

11. G. O. Bierwag, "Immunization, Duration and the Term Structure of Interest Rates," *Journal of Financial and Quantitative Analysis*, Dec. 1977, pp. 725–42; G. O. Bierwag and George G. Kaufman, "Coping with the Risk of Interest-Rate Fluctuations: A Note," *Journal of Business*, July 1977, pp. 364–70; and Chulsoon Khang, "Bond Immunization when Short-Term Rates fluctuate More than Long-Term Rates," *Journal of Financial and Quantitative Analysis*, December 1979, pp. 1085–1089. See also I. A. Cooper, "Asset Values, Interest-Rate Changes and Duration," *Journal of Financial and Quantitative Analysis*, December 1977, pp. 701–723.

12. G. O. Bierwag and Chulsoon Khang, "Immunization Strategy is a Mini-Max Strategy," *Journal of Finance*, May 1979, pp. 389–414.

13. G. O. Bierwag, George G. Kaufman, Robert Schweitzer, and Alden Toevs, "The Art of Risk Management in Bond Portfolios," *Journal of Portfolio Management*, Spring 1981, pp. 27–36 and G. O. Bierwag, George G. Kaufman, and Alden Toevs, "Duration Analysis and Active Bond Portfolio Management," (Unpublished paper, University of Oregon), October 1980. See also Myron A. Grove, "On 'Duration' and the Optimal Maturity Structure of the Balance Sheet," *Bell Journal of Economics and Management Science*, Autumn 1974, pp. 696–709.

14. G. O. Bierwag, George G. Kaufman, and Alden Toevs, "Bond Portfolio Immunization and Stochastic Process Risk," *Journal of Bank Research*, Spring 1983.

15. Ronald Lanstein and William F. Sharpe, "Duration and Security Risk," *Journal of Financial and Quantitative Analysis*, November 1978, pp. 653–668.

16. Jonathan E. Ingersoll, Jr., Jeffrey Skelton, and Roman L. Weil, "Duration Forty Years Later," *Journal of Financial and Quantitative Analysis*, November 1978, pp. 627–650; and John C. Cox, Jonathan E. Ingersoll, Jr., and Stephen A. Ross, "Duration and Measurement of Basis Risk," *Journal of Business*, January 1979, pp. 51–61.

17. G. O. Bierwag and George G. Kaufman, "Bond Portfolio Strategy Simulations: A Critique," *Journal of Financial and Quantitative Analysis*, September 1978, pp. 519–528.

18. Michael J. Brennan and Eduardo S. Schwartz, "Duration, Bond Pricing and Portfolio Management" and G. O. Bierwag, George G. Kaufman, and Alden Toevs, "Duration Analysis in Bond Portfolio Management," both in G. O. Bierwag, George G. Kaufman, and Alden Toevs, eds., *Innovations in Bond Portfolio Management: Duration Analysis and Immunization*, (JAI Press, 1983).

19. Irwin Friend, Randolph Westerfield, and Michael Granito, "New Evidence on the Capital Asset Pricing Model," *Journal of Finance*, June 1978, pp. 903–17; Michael D. Joehnk and James F. Nielsen, "Return and Risk Characteristics of Speculative Grade Bonds," *Quarterly Review of Economics and Business*, Spring 1975, pp. 27–46; John Percival, "Corporate Bonds in a Market Model Context," *Journal of Bank Research*, October 1974, pp. 461–68; and Frank R. Reilly and Michael D. Joehnk, "The Association Between Market Determined Risk Measures for Bonds and Bond Ratings," *Journal of Business Research*, December 1976, pp. 1387–1403.

20. See papers in volume cited in note 18.

21. George G. Kaufman, "Duration, Planning Period, and Tests of the Capital Asset Pricing Model," *Journal of Financial Research*, Spring 1980, pp. 1–9.

22. It would seem reasonable that for some probable s_0, $P_{s_0}(1,t) = P(1,t)$, so that the future prices one period hence will be equal to the forward prices currently observed. However, this result can never obtain in the framework developed here if markets are complete and there is a competitive equilibrium. If s_0 is a state such that $P_{s_0}(1,t) = P(1,t)$, then matrix R will contain a row and a column in which each element is $1/P(0,1)$. It follows that θ_{s_0} will be undefined because the elements of the s_0th row of R^{-1} sum to zero. This implies that $\theta_k (k \neq s_0)$ is undefined, a result inconsistent with complete markets in competitive equilibrium. The discount functions $P_s(1,t)$ consistent with competitive equilibrium must be such as to exclude the possibility that every forward price (rate) can be equal to every future spot price (rate).

23. J. C. Cox, S. A. Ross, and M. Rubenstein, "Option Pricing: A Simplified Approach," *Journal of Financial Economics*, September 1979, pp. 229–63.

24. The accumulated excess return is used because the analysis is undertaken in a discrete multiperiod context.

THE ART OF RISK MANAGEMENT
IN BOND PORTFOLIOS

G. O. Bierwag, George G. Kaufman,

Robert Schweitzer, and Alden Toevs

This paper demonstrates that risk, at least for default-free coupon bonds, is a function of the investor's planning period as well as of the characteristics of the security or portfolio itself. Thus, risk is more complex than is widely believed, and the accurate formulation of general risk measures applicable to all investors at all times is highly unlikely. We go on to demonstrate, however, that passive strategies are available in this area that can effectively reduce or even eliminate interest rate risk for most investors. In the process, we present empirical evidence on the success of such passive hedging strategies as well as of alternative active strategies that attempt to outperform the passive strategies.

Our arguments enlarge and elaborate on previous work on this subject provided by two articles in recent issues of *The Journal of Porfolio Management*. Both of these earlier articles emphasized the importance of the investor's planning period or investment horizon in formulating bond portfolio management policies and in measuring performance.

Seymour Smidt demonstrated that the same bond can have different risk-reward characteristics for different investors.[1] For a given change in interest rates, the greater the difference between the "duration" of a default-free bond (or bond portfolio) and the length of the planning period of the investor, the greater is the change in the return over the investor's planning period. If the duration of the bond were equal to the investor's planning period, the change in interest rates would not reduce the return on the bond from that promised at the time the bond was purchased. Interest rate risk would have been effectively eliminated. Thus, a change in interest rates affects investors in the same bond differently when they have different planning periods. Smidt concludes that "the risk of an asset depends in part on the characteristic of the investor as well as the characteristics of the asset."[2]

Francis Trainer, Jess Yawitz, and William Marshall argue that the risk assumed by an investor in default-free bonds depends on the difference between the maturity of the bond and the investor's planning period.[3] They conclude that "the least risky security is the one whose maturity matches the length of the HP (holding period)."[4]

I.   IMMUNIZATION THEORY

Investors could always realize the yields promised them at the time they purchase their bonds if they were able to purchase default-free zero coupon bonds with maturities equal to their planning periods. But what if zero coupon bonds do not exist for the required planning periods or cannot be constructed through short sales or option strategies? That is, what if markets are incomplete?

In an important article, Lawrence Fisher and Roman Weil have proven that it is possible, under restrictive assumptions, to devise a strategy that protects investors in default-free coupon bonds from unexpected changes in interest rates during the planning period in such a way that the yield realized will never be less than the yield to maturity for that period at the time they purchased the bond.[5] The assumptions restricted the analysis to a one-time change in interest rates of equal magnitude for all maturities across the yield curve as well as zero taxes and transaction costs. In addition, Fisher and Weil used continuous compounding.

Under the Fisher-Weil strategy, the investor must calculate a weighted average of the periods in which the bond (or bond portfolio) is expected to make its coupon and maturity payments and must then select those bonds (or that bond portfolio) for which this weighted average is equal to the investor's planning period. In computing the average, the payment periods are weighted by the proportion of the present value of the corresponding payment to the overall present value of all payments (the price of the bond).

If the yield curve is flat, so that all one-period discount rates are equal, the equation for the weighted average of the payment periods is equal to the statistic developed more than 40 years ago by Frederick Macaulay to measure the average life of a bond.[6] If the yield curve is not flat, the Fisher-Weil and Macaulay measures differ. Nevertheless, because of the similarity of the measures, Fisher and Weil adopted Macaulay's term *duration*. For the flat yield curve, the duration of a bond is defined as

$$D = \frac{\sum_{n=1}^{m} Cn/(1 + i)^n + Am/(1 + i)^m}{\sum_{n=1}^{m} C/(1 + i)^n + A/(1 + i)^m} \tag{1}$$

where C = coupon payment;
A = maturity payment;
i = yield-to-maturity;
n = years to coupon payment;
m = years to maturity.

Fisher and Weil described their strategy for realizing no less than the yield promised for the planning period at the time of purchase as an "immunization" strategy.

Subsequent research by Bierwag, Kaufman, Khang, and others has shown that immunization is possible for default-free coupon bonds under conditions less restrictive than those postulated by Fisher and Weil.[8] Portfolios may be immunized for discrete compounding, for more complex types of unexpected interest rate changes, for more than one unexpected change in interest rates during the planning period, and for multiple planning periods. However, the investor must predict the correct stochastic (random) process generating interest rate changes even though prediction of interest rates themselves is unnecessary. (Expected interest rate changes may be assumed to be already impounded in existing market yields.)

The stochastic generating process describes whether unexpected interest rate changes will affect all maturities equally, short-term maturities more than long term, long term more than short term, and so on. The nature of the stochastic process determines the exact weights in the formula for duration that provides for immunization. This duration is termed the *immunizing duration* (ID).

Although the formulas used to compute IDs become more complex than are given by equation (1), they remain weighted averages of the payment periods with the weights related to the proportional present value of the payments but not necessarily to the proportional present values themselves. Equations for IDs that are consistent with a number of reasonable stochastic processes are shown in the Appendix.[9]

We can illustrate how an immunization strategy works in a simple example of a single bond. Unexpected interest rate changes after the purchase of a bond or bond portfolio have two effects: (1) they affect the prices of bonds, and (2) they affect the interest rate at which the coupons and maturing bonds in the portfolio may be reinvested until the end of the planning period. The two effects work in opposite directions: An unexpected increase in rates, for example, will decrease bond prices but will increase the income from reinvestment during the planning period. Thus, these changes affect the overall return the investor will realize.

For a single bond, the annual realized return for a given planning period of length s that is equal to or shorter than the maturity of the bond is computed as follows:

$$ h_s = \left[\frac{P_{t+s} + \sum_{n=1}^{s} C_n \prod_{q=n+1}^{s} (1 + i_q)}{P_1} \right]^{1/s} - 1 , \qquad (2) $$

where h_s = annual return realized for s periods;

P_{t+s} = sale price at period $t + s$;

P_1 = purchase price at period;

s = length of planning period;

C_n = coupon payment in $t + n$;

i_q = one period interest rates in period $t + q$;

$\prod$ = product of a geometric series.

The equations for a single bond whose maturity is longer than the planning period and for bond portfolios are similar.

An unexpected increase in interest rates after purchase, on the one hand, will reduce the return from that promised at the time of purchase by reducing P_{t+s} in the numerator below its expected or amortized value. On the other hand, it will increase the return above that promised at time of purchase by increasing the income from coupon reinvestment income (the second term in the numerator). The net effect on the total return depends on the relative magnitude of the two individual effects. These magnitudes, in turn, depend on the difference between the length of the immunizing duration of the bond and the length of the particular investor's planning period.

As already noted, when the appropriate immunizing duration of the bond is equal to the investor's planning period, the effects of interest rate changes on the price change and reinvestment components of return are approximately equal in magnitude. As they are opposite in direction, however, the two effects essentially offset each other so that the yield realized for the period cannot fall below the promised yield. The bond investor is immunized. When the length of the planning period and the ID are unequal, the two effects only partially offset each other and the realized return may fall below that promised at the beginning of the planning period.

If the ID exceeds the planning period, the downward price effect of an unexpected interest rate increase will outweigh the upward reinvestment effect, and the realized return will fall below the promised return. If the ID is shorter than the planning period, the reinvestment effect will outweigh the price effect, and unexpected interest rate increases will produce a return greater than that promised.[10] These outcomes would be reversed for unexpected interest rate decreases.

The above relationships are demonstrated numerically in Table 1 for the one bond case. We assume for simplicity that the yield curve is flat at $7\frac{1}{2}$ percent that there are no transactions costs associated with the reinvestment of coupons, and that an investor has a planning period of 10 years. All interest rate changes are assumed to be across the board, so that the yield curve will move up or down by the same amount for every maturity.

If the investor wishes to guarantee a return of at least $7\frac{1}{2}$ percent, the immunization strategy requires that the investor select a default-free coupon bond with an immunizing duration of 10 years as defined by equation (1). Such a bond is approximated by a 5 percent coupon, 15-year bond. If the investor wishes to attempt to better that return, he or she should choose a bond having a longer or shorter duration than the 10-year planning period, depending on his or her prediction of interest rates relative to the market consensus. Of course, the risk of realizing a lower return by following such an active policy is greater than that for the passive immunization strategy.

If interest rates do not change in the 10 years the investor will realize an annual return of $7\frac{1}{2}$ percent regardless of the duration of the bond selected. For example, when the market rate of interest is $7\frac{1}{2}$ percent, the market price of the 5 percent coupon, $100 par value, 15-year bond with an approximate immunizing duration of 10 years is $77.71. Ten years later, at the end of the planning period, the price of

Table 1. Effects of an Unexpected Increase in Interest Rate on
Three Bond Strategies per $100

Given: Flat yield curve = 7½ percent
Coupon bond rate = 5 percent
Planning period   = 10 years

	Maturity (years)		
	10	*15*	*20*
Duration (years)	7.8	10.1	11.6
Beginning bond price	82.63	77.71	74.31
Promised annual return (percent)	7.50	7.50	7.50
A. No change in interest rates:			
Bond price after 10 years	100.00	89.73	82.63
Coupons paid	50.00	50.00	50.00
Reinvestment of coupons semi-annually @ 7½%	22.54	22.54	22.54
Total value of investment	172.54	162.27	155.17
Realized annual return (percent)	7.50	7.50	7.50
B. Immediate increase to 9%:			
Bond price after 10 years	100.00	84.17	73.98
Coupons paid	50.00	50.00	50.00
Reinvestment of coupons semi-annually @ 9%	28.43	28.43	28.43
Total value of investment	178.43	162.60	152.41
Realized annual return (percent)	7.84	7.52	7.32
Loss in bond price	0.00	5.56	8.65
Gain in reinvestment income	5.89	5.89	5.89
Net change	+5.89	+0.33	−2.76

the bond will have risen to $89.73 from the amortization of the discount.
At the end of the period, the investor has also collected $50 in coupons
in 20 equal $2.50 installments. If the coupons are fully reinvested at
the end of each semiannual period at 7½ percent, the interest income
over the period will amount to $22.54. Substituting those numbers in
equation (2) and solving for the annual return yields 7½ percent.

In another case, a 5 percent coupon, 10-year bond would be priced
at $82.63 at the beginning of the period. This bond would have an
initial duration of 7.8 years. Its value at the end of the period is $100.00.
Coupons again would total $50, and their reinvestment income would
produce $22.54 by the end of the 10 years. The annual return for that
bond computed by equation (2) is also 7½ percent. As may be seen
from Table 1, a 7½ percent return is also realized for a 5 percent
coupon 20-year bond if interest rates do not change.

Now, let interest rates rise unexpectedly from 7½ to 9 percent immediately after the purchase of the bonds, and let them stay there for the remainder of the 10-year planning period. The price of the 15-year maturity, 10-year duration bond at the end of the period will be only $84.17, or $5.56 less than before. On the other hand, the reinvestment of the coupons at 9% will yield $28.43, or $5.89 more than before. The two changes approximately offset each other, and the annual return increases slightly to 7.52 percent.[11]

That, however, will not be the case for the other two bonds, including the 10-year bond whose maturity is equal to the planning period but whose ID is only 7.8 years. The price of the 10-year bond will rise from $82.63 to $100.00 as before, but the yield from the reinvestment of the coupons will now be $28.42, rather than $22.54. The total return thus increases to 7.87 percent. If the 5 percent coupon, 20-year maturity, 11.7-year duration bond had been purchased, its price at the end of the 10 years would be $73.98, slightly lower than the purchase price of $74.31. That is also $8.65 less than if interest rates had not changed. The price loss would more than offset the gain in coupon reinvestment income. The total annual return would be only 7.32%.

The ordering of the returns would be reversed if interest rates declined unexpectedly, but the 15-year bond would still generate at least a 7½ percent return. These results would differ if the investor's planning period were shorter (say, 7.8 years) or longer (say, 11.6 years) than 10 years. If it were 7.8 years, the 10-year bond would now be the bond that would guarantee at least the 7½ percent return.

If interest rates do not change unexpectedly, a default-free coupon bond generates a promised return to the end of the planning period that is known to the investor at the time the bond is purchased. Thus, the only risk the investor incurs is the risk that arises from unexpected interest rate changes that may reduce the realized return below the promised return.

It follows from the above analysis that, in a world of uncertainty, an investor can always realize at least the promised yield by purchasing one or more default-free coupon bonds whose appropriate immunizing duration is equal to the planning period. At this point, interest rate risk is effectively zero.[12] For bonds with durations either longer or shorter than the planning period, the risk of receiving less than the promised return is greater than zero and increases with the magnitude of the difference between the duration and the length of the planning period.

We can see from Table 1 that the difference between the realized return and the promised return is greater when the duration declines by 2.3 years from 10.1 to 7.8 years for the 10-year bond than when the duration increases by 1.5 years from 10.1 to 11.6 years for the 20-year bond, although the maturity change is 5 years for both bonds. Nevertheless, the differences in realized returns from the immunized return for these two bonds is proportional to the differences in their duration from the immunized 15-year bond. Thus, the 10-year bond generates a return 32 basis points higher than the 7.52 percent immunized return; this is 60 percent greater than the shortfall of 20 basis points generated by the 20-year bond and is about the same percentage as its duration of 7.8 years is shorter than 10 years as the 11.6-year duration of the 20-year bond is longer than 10 years.

II.   DURATION'S ATTRACTIONS

The determinants of the risk on a default-free bond may be expressed as

$$\text{Risk} = f(\text{PL, ID}) , \tag{3}$$

where PL is the investor's planning period and ID is the appropriate immunizing duration. This formulation verifies Smidt's statement that bond risk depends on the characteristics of both the bond (ID) and the investor (PL). Furthermore, measures of risk computed for a given bond or bond portfolio, a given planning period, and a given stochastic process are not meaningful for investors with different planning periods because the computation of the appropriate immunizing duration depends on the nature of the stochastic process that causes interest rates to change, because bond risk also depends on characteristics of the market and the ability of the investor to identify correctly the actual stochastic process, and, finally, because it is unlikely that all investors will have the same planning period. Consequently, universal risk measures cannot be estimated. At best, we can compute risk measures for a given bond and a given stochastic process for a range of planning periods; investors may choose those that correspond to their own particular situation.[13]

Thus, *risk is related to the difference between the length of an investor's planning period and the bond's duration as Smidt argued, not maturity as Trainer et al. argued.* As we can see in Table 1, equating maturity with the length of the planning period eliminates price risk but it does not eliminate reinvestment risk.

A coupon bond is in fact a series of zero coupon bonds having maturity values equal to the coupon payments and terms to maturity equal to the term of each coupon payment, plus one zero coupon bond having a maturity value equal to the par value of the coupon bond and a term to maturity equal to the maturity of the coupon bond. Because duration is an average of all these payment dates, it is always less than the final maturity of a coupon bond. Therefore, we may view an immunization strategy that matches the ID of a bond to the investor's planning period as a diversification strategy that uses bonds of different terms to maturity on each side of the investor's planning period. Duration matching approximately transforms a coupon bond into a zero coupon bond with a term to maturity (and thus also duration) equal to the planning period.

Duration analysis has important implications for formulating and evaluating bond portfolio strategies. It also improves significantly on traditional maturity analysis for these purposes, although the rules of thumb remain the same.

For example, investors in default-free bonds may pursue either passive or active policies. A passive policy locks in the current market interest rate for the investor's particular planning period. It is a hedging strategy for the investor who prefers not to try to out guess and possibly outperform the market. The optimum long-term passive strategy is a duration matching immunization strategy.

On the other hand, an active strategy attempts to achieve a return greater than the current promised market return for the planning period. To be successful, the investor must predict interest rate changes that are different from those that are expected by the market, that are incorporated in the existing market term structure, and that will be realized if interest rates do not change unexpectedly. The expected return is higher but so also is the risk. As is demonstrated in Table 1, if an investor expects interest rates to be higher than the market does, the appropriate ID of an active portfolio would be one that is shorter than the planning period. The resulting return would be greater than the promised return. Conversely, if the investor expects interest rates to be lower than the market does, the appropriate ID of an active portfolio would be one that is longer than the planning period.

III. EMPIRICAL EVIDENCE

All of this may be fine in theory but does it work in practice? After all, the proof of the pudding is in the eating!

How well do these rules work in the real world? To find out, we simulated alternative strategies for the period 1925 to 1978 using annual interest rate data. Transactions costs and taxes are assumed to be zero for prime corporate bonds.[14] All coupons are assumed to be paid in full and compounded semiannually. A 10-year planning period is assumed. We then constructed eight portfolios of bonds depicting two active strategies, five passive duration matching strategies, and one "yardstick" maturity matching portfolio. The five duration matching immunization strategies reflect five alternative assumptions about the nature of the stochastic process for interest rate changes.

The simplest strategy assumes a flat yield curve and equal interest rate changes for all maturities. The corresponding ID is the Macaulay formulation shown in equation (1) and identified as ID1. The other four immunization strategies assume that the yield curve can have any shape.

The second strategy assumes further that any unexpected interest rate changes affect all maturities equally up or down by an amount λ, where λ represents the magnitude of the change as shown in Figure 1. Thus, the shape, although not the location, of the yield curve remains the same before and immediately after the shock. This strategy is referred to as an additive shock and is identified as ID2. (The ID equations for this and the next two shocks are shown in the Appendix.)

The third strategy assumes that the unexpected interest rate changes cause the rate on each maturity to be changed by an amount that is related to the product of the rate and λ, and is identified as ID3. This is a more complex shock to the term structure and is referred to as a *multiplicative* shock. The shape of the yield curve immediately after the shock relative to the yield curve before the shock depends upon the shape of the initial yield curve. If the initial yield curve was upward sloping, long-term rates would change more than short-term rates. If the initial yield curve was downward sloping, long-term rates would change less than short-term rates.

The final two immunization strategies assume that short-term rates always change by more than long-term rates. The two differ by the proportion that the short-term rates fluctuate more than the long-term rates. This is determined by the value of α in the ID4 equation in the Appendix. The greater α, the greater are changes in short-term rates relative to long-term rates. The relative magnitude of the changes in short- and long-term rates also depends on the slope of the term structure. For a moderately upward sloping structure, an $\alpha = 1$ indicates that the changes in the one-year rate are approximately three times as great as the changes in the 10-year rates; an $\alpha = 0.1$ indicates that the changes in one-year rates are approximately 1.3 times as great. The first strategy is labeled ID4(1.0) and the second ID4(0.1). It can be seen from the equations that, as the value of α approaches 0, ID4 approaches ID3. The five stochastic processes developed here do not exhaust all possibilities, but do appear reasonable.[15]

I. ID1

$$\frac{\Delta \lambda}{\Delta t} = 0:$$

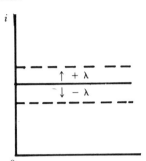

II. ID2

$$\frac{\Delta \lambda}{\Delta t} = 0:$$

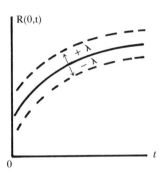

III. ID3

If term structure slopes up,

$$\frac{\Delta \lambda}{\Delta t} > 0.$$

If term structure slopes down,

$$\frac{\Delta \lambda}{\Delta t} < 0.$$

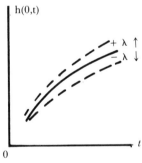

IV. ID4

$$\gamma(t) = \frac{\lambda \ln(1 + \alpha t)}{\alpha t},$$

$$\frac{\Delta |\gamma(t)|}{\Delta t} < 0.$$

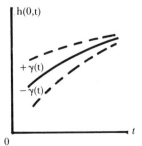

All of the immunization strategies select a portfolio of bonds whose appropriate ID is equal to the 10-year planning period.[16] All portfolios consist of combinations of two bonds, one long and one short. The long bond is a 20-year bond at the beginning of the planning period that is maintained in the portfolio, so that its maturity declines linearly to 10 years. The short bond has an initial maturity of ten years, equal to the length of the planning period and is also maintained in the portfolio throughout the planning period so that its maturity is always equal to the remaining length of the planning period. Dollar amounts of the two bonds are selected so that the initial ID of the portfolio is 10 years.

Because the passage of time does not reduce maturity and duration equally, the portfolio must be restructured at least annually to maintain the ID equal to the remaining length of the planning period.[17] The use of two bonds minimizes the number of bonds in the portfolio that need to be sold to achieve the annual restructuring, and we selected the initial 10- and 20-year bonds to reduce transactions costs. Most of the restructuring may be achieved through additional purchases of the short bond from the proceeds of the coupon payments.

Because duration is an average, there is an infinite number of portfolio compositions that are consistent with a specific value of duration.[18] However, because the relationship between interest rates and bond prices is not linear, all portfolio compositions do not generate the same results.[19] Theory and evidence suggest that the differences are not great if the investor correctly identifies the stochastic process and uses the correct ID.[20] The differences become more important if the stochastic process is not identified correctly and the incorrect ID is used. In these instances, the narrower the maturity spread of the portfolio, the smaller appear to be any returns below those promised. For zero coupon bonds with a maturity equal to the length of the planning period, a true "bullet" portfolio, the promised return is realized regardless of the stochastic process. The portfolio composition tested in this paper represents a "middle ground" barbell. More compressed portfolios may be expected to be better immunized against all possible stochastic processes and less compressed portfolios to be more poorly immunized.

One active policy involves "going short." That is, the portfolio consists of a series of one-year bonds that are successively rolled over each year. The second active policy involves "going long."[21] This portfolio consists of one initial 20-year maturity bond that is maintained in the portfolio so that its maturity declines to 10 years at the end of the 10-year planning period. In both of these active strategies, all coupon payments are used to buy the particular bonds involved in the respective strategy.

The "yardstick" portfolio consists of a single bond having an initial maturity equal to the 10-year planning period. Through time, all coupons in this portfolio are reinvested in bonds having a maturity equal to the remaining length of the planning period. Because, as noted earlier, the duration of a portfolio of coupon bonds is always less than the term to maturity, the maturity matching strategy belongs in the "go short" class. Nevertheless, this strategy is specified separately as a yardstick portfolio, because it has been widely used as an "immunization" strategy, e.g., by Trainer et al., and thus provides a convenient basis against which to evaluate all the other strategies with respect to immunization.

We evaluated the strategies both as passive and as active strategies. On the passive side, we evaluated each of the seven strategies on the basis of how close the yield realized over the planning period is to the associated promised yield. This is measured both by the frequency with which the realized yield is within plus or minus 5 basis points of the promised yield, and also by how often the realized yield is closer to the promised yield than the yield generated by the maturity strategy. As an active strategy, the portfolios are evaluated both by how often the generated realized yield is above the promised yield and how often the realized yield is the higher yield.

In order to examine the strategies under different market conditions, we divided the 1925–1978 period into three approximately equal subperiods according to the movement in interest rates. In the first subperiod 1925–1949, interest rates decline and remained at low levels. In the second subperiod 1940–1963, interest rates began to climb slowly. In the third subperiod 1954–1978, interest rates became more volatile and increased sharply on average. The overlapping dates in the subperiods occur because of the assumed 10-year holding period. The last portfolio in each period is purchased 10 years before the end of the period. Thus, the last planning period began in 1939 in the first subperiod, 1953 in the second, and 1968 in the third. Because the overall period includes a severe depression, numerous recessions; a major world war, two smaller wars, and a severe peacetime inflation, one can expect the results to be robust and applicable to other periods. The results appear in Table 2. In addition to the measures described above, the average promised and realized yields are also shown.

We can readily see that the duration matching immunization strategies generate returns closer to the promised return than the maturity or the other nonimmunization strategies. The ID1, ID2, and ID3 strategies produce very similar results. The results for ID4 differ somewhat, particularly when $\alpha = 1$. For the overall period, immunization strategies

Table 2. Promised and Realized Returns for Alternative Portfolio Strategies: 10-Year Planning Periods 1925–1978

Strategy	Promised (Annual Average)	Realized (Annual Average)	Realized Minus Promised	Return (Percent)				
				Closer to Promised than Maturity Strategy	Within 5 Basis Points of Promised	Greater than Promised	Highest Realized	Lowest Realized
1925–1978[a]								
Immunization[d]								
ID1	3.364	3.286	−.078	86	48	9	0	0
ID2		3.289	−.075	89	48	9	0	0
ID3		3.289	−.075	89	48	9	0	0
ID4 (0.1)		3.270	−.094	82	27	2	0	0
ID4 (1.0)		3.236	−.128	52	34	11	2	0
Maturity		3.329	−.035	—	16	41	0	0
Rollover[b]		2.927	−.437	2	7	48	50	48
Long Bond[b]	→	3.194	−.170	9	7	45	48	52
1925–1949[c]								
Immunization[d]								
ID1	3.697	3.552	−.145	93	13	0	0	0
ID2		3.555	−.142	93	13	0	0	0
ID3		3.555	−.142	93	13	0	0	0
ID4 (0.1)		3.595	−.102	93	20	0	0	0
ID4 (1.0)		3.668	−.029	93	53	27	0	0
Maturity		3.465	−.232	—	0	0	0	0
Rollover[b]		1.801	−1.896	0	0	0	0	100
Long Bond[b]	→	4.749	+1.052	7	0	100	100	0

338

1940–1963[a]

Immunization[d]								
	2.257							
ID1		2.214	-.043	79	50	14	0	0
ID2		2.214	-.043	86	50	14	0	0
ID3		2.214	-.043	86	50	14	0	0
ID4 (0.1)		2.214	-.043	86	50	7	7	0
ID4 (1.0)		2.212	-.045	64	50	7	0	0
Maturity		2.214	-.043	—	36	29	0	0
Rollover		2.074	-.183	7	14	43	50	43
Long Bond[b]	→	1.987	-.270	21	21	36	43	57

1954–1978[a]

Immunization[d]								
	4.064							
ID1		4.026	-.038	87	80	13	0	0
ID2		4.027	-.037	87	80	13	0	0
ID3		4.027	-.037	87	80	13	0	0
ID4 (0.1)		3.930	-.134	67	13	0	0	0
ID4 (1.0)		3.759	-.305	0	0	0	0	0
Maturity		4.234	+.170	—	13	93	0	0
Rollover		4.848	+.784	0	7	100	100	0
Long Bond[b]	→	2.767	-1.297	0	0	0	0	100

Notes:
[a] The last portfolio in each period purchased 10 years before the last year in the period.
[b] Maintained bond with initial maturity of 20 years.
[c] 10-year yield-to-maturity at date of purchase.
[d] Portfolio consists of initial 10- and 20-year bonds.

339

ID1–3 generated returns closer to the promised return than those generated by the maturity strategy about 90 percent of the time. For the individual subperiods, the success of these strategies ranges from 80 to 100 percent. Strategies ID1–3 also produce returns that are within 5 basis points of the promised return considerably more often than do those produced by the maturity strategy. Strategy ID4, with an $\alpha = 1$, which assumes that unexpected changes in short-term rates are much greater than those in long-term rates, immunizes less successfully. Indeed, in the 1954–1978 subperiod, ID4($\alpha = 1$) fails to beat the maturity strategy in any year. In contrast, this strategy immunizes better than the maturity strategy in the 1925–1949 subperiod and generates returns closer to the promised yield more often than do strategies ID1–3. When α is 0.1, the results are somewhere between those of ID4 ($\alpha = 1$) and ID3. In no period, however, are the results in favor of immunization improved over those of ID3.

The relatively poor results of ID4, which is the most intuitively pleasing, may be attributed in part to the use of annual average data. In these data, the greater variability observed in short-term rates for briefer intervals is averaged out. For the entire period, the standard deviation in one-year rates is only 10 percent greater than in 10-year rates and is only 50 percent greater in the most extreme subperiod. In contrast, the differences in variability are considerably greater for monthly observations.

The preliminary evidence in Table 2 suggests that, if the past is any guide to the future, portfolios structured in the basis of the simplest ID to compute—ID1, which requires only readily available promised yield data—have immunized almost as well as the more complex strategies and appear to be the most cost effective. Although the duration matching immunization strategies come closer to realizing the promised returns than does the maturity matching strategy, contrary to theory, they generally produce returns somewhat less than those promised.[22]

As noted earlier, the above results are sensitive to the composition of the portfolios. If the width of the maturity spread in the barbell portfolios were widened to include, say, only 1- and 20-year maturity bonds, all of the duration matching strategies fail in almost every instance to realize returns closer to the promised returns than those realized by the maturity matching strategy. This suggests that the "true" stochastic process may be too complex even in the Durand data to be captured adequately by the IDs tested. On the other hand, the investor can minimize shortfalls from the promised return by compressing the portfolio into a bullet or near bullet portfolio regardless of the stochastic process assumed.[23] Attempts to eliminate interest rate risk by duration matching immunization strategies appear to subject investors to a new "stochastic process risk." Thus, the potential gain from pursuing a duration matching immunization strategy depends on the relative magnitudes of the interest rate and stochastic process risks, and this strategy is desirable only if the latter is perceived to be smaller than the former.

The evidence in Table 2 also indicates that the passive strategies performed less well than the active strategies in maximizing returns if the investor had selected the "correct" active strategy. It is evident that the correct active strategy varied depending on the movement in interest rates during the planning period. Of course, in practice, selecting the correct active strategy requires that the investor accurately predict interest rates.

Because interest rates both increased and decreased in the 1925–1978 period, the "go-short" rollover and "go-long" strategies performed about equally well. In the 1925–1949 period, when promised yields declined sharply on average, the go-long strategy outperformed the promised yield and all other strategies in every year. In 1954–1978, when interest rates increased sharply on average, the rollover strategy outperformed the other strategies 100 percent of the time. In 1940–1963, when interest rates increased slowly from very low levels, the two strategies did about equally well on average. The maturity strategy did poorer than the rollover strategy when interest rates rose and better when rates declined.

Thus, the maturity strategy remains a hedging strategy, but one that is generally inferior to the correct immunization strategies. It is of interest to note that, on average, neither active strategy generated returns greater than the promised yields for the period as a whole or for the middle subperiod.

APPENDIX

Equations for Immunizing Durations for Single Bonds (Annual Discrete Compounding)

I. ID1—Additive shock, flat yield curve $(1 + i_M + \lambda)$

$$ID1 = \frac{\displaystyle\sum_{t=1}^{m} tC(1 + i_m)^{-t} + mA(1 + i_m)^{-m}}{\displaystyle\sum_{t=1}^{m} C(1 + i_m)^{-t} + A(1 + i_m)^{-m}}$$

II. ID2—Additive shock $(1 + h(0,t) + \lambda)$

$ID2 \mid 1 + h(0,ID2) \mid^{-1} =$

$$\frac{\displaystyle\sum_{t=1}^{m} tC(1 + h(0,t))^{-t-1} + mA(1 + h(0,m))^{-m-1}}{\displaystyle\sum_{t=1}^{m} C(1 + h(0,t))^{-t} + A(1 + h(0,m))^{-m}}.$$

III. ID3—Multiplicative shock $(1 + \lambda)(1 + h(0,t))$

$$ID3 = \frac{\displaystyle\sum_{t=1}^{m} tC(1 + h(0,t))^{-t} + mA(1 + h(0,m))^{-m}}{\displaystyle\sum_{t=1}^{m} C(1 + h(0,t))^{-t} + A(1 + h(0,m))^{-m}}$$

IV. ID4—Maturity dependent shock

$$\left(1 + \frac{\lambda \ln (1 + \alpha t)}{\alpha t}\right)(1 + h(0,t))$$

$\ln (1 + \alpha ID4) =$

$$\frac{\displaystyle\sum_{t=1}^{m} \ln (1 + \alpha t)C(1 + h(0,t))^{-t}\ln (1 \, \alpha m)A(1 + h(0,m))^{-m}}{\displaystyle\sum_{t=1}^{m} C(1 + h(0,t))^{-t} + (1 + h(0,m))^{-m}}$$

Key: i_m = yield to maturity,

$h(0,t)$ = zero coupon yield equivalent for period spanning 0 to t,

C = annual coupon payment,

α = indicator of ratio of change in short-term rate to change in long-term rate,

λ = random interest rate shock.

Calculation of the Duration for Portfolios of Bonds

In the formulas below, D_S is the duration of the bond with short maturity, D_L is the duration of the bond with the longer maturity, and D is the duration of a portfolio of the two bonds, where β_s is the proportion invested in the short bond.

I. ID1 and ID3

$$D = \beta_s D_s + (1 - \beta_s)D_L.$$

II. ID2

$$\frac{D}{1 + h(0,D)} = \frac{\beta_s D_s}{1 + h(0,D_s)} + \frac{(1 - \beta_s)D_L}{1 + h(0,D_L)}$$

III. $\ln (1 + \alpha D) = \beta_s \ln (1 + \alpha D_s) + (1 - \beta_s) \ln (1 + \alpha D_L)$.

ACKNOWLEDGMENT

An earlier version of the paper was presented at the Fall Seminar of the Institute for Quantitative Research in Finance in Hot Springs, Virginia, October 28–31, 1979.

Reprinted with permission from *The Journal of Portfolio Management*, Spring 1981, pp. 27–36.

NOTES

1. Seymour Smidt, "Investment horizons and performance measurements," *Journal of Portfolio Management*, Winter 1978, 18–22.

2. Smidt, p. 20.

3. Francis H. Trainer, Jr., Jess B. Yawitz, and William J. Marshall, "Holding period is the key to risk thresholds," *Journal of Portfolio Management*, Winter 1979, 48–54.

4. Trainer, et al., p. 53.

5. Lawrence Fisher and Roman Weil, "Coping with the Risk of Interest-Rate Fluctuations: Returns to Bondholders from Naive and Optimal Strategies," *Journal of Business*, October 1971, 408–431. The promised yield to maturity is defined as the yield to maturity that would exist in the market on a zero coupon bond with the relevant maturity. The theory assumes that the implicit forward rates are unbiased estimates of the expected future rates for the same period.

6. F. R. Macaulay, *Some Theoretical Problems Suggested by the Movements of Interest Rates, Bond Yields, and Stock Prices in the United States Since 1856* (New York: National Bureau of Economic Research, 1938).

7. Duration has been previously discussed in this *Journal* by Richard W. McEnally, "Duration as a practical tool for bank management," *Journal of Portfolio Management*, Summer 1977, 53–57; D. Don Ezra, "Immunization: A new look for actuarial liabilities," *Journal of Portfolio Management*, Winger 1976, 50–53; and Madeline W. Einhorn, "Breaking tradition in bond portfolio investment," *Journal of Portfolio Management*, Spring 1975, 35–43. For a derivation of duration and its relationship to bond price volatility, see Michael H. Hopewell and George G. Kaufman, "Bond Price Volatility and Years to Maturity: A Generalized Respecification," *American Economic Review*, September 1973, 749–753.

8. Reviews of recent developments appear in G. O. Bierwag and George G. Kaufman, "Bond Portfolio Strategy Simulations: A Critique," *Journal of Financial and Quantitative Analysis*, September 1978, 519–525; G. O. Bierwag, George G. Kaufman, and Chulsoon Khang, "Duration and Bond Portfolio Analysis: An Overview," *Journal of Financial and Quantitative Analysis*, November 1978, 671–681; George G. Kaufman, "Measuring Risk and Return for Bonds: A New Approach," *Journal of Bank Research*, Summer 1978, 82–90; G. O. Bierwag, "Immunization, Duration, and the Term Structure of Interest Rates," *Journal of Financial and Quantitative Analysis*, December 1977, 725–741; G. W. Bierwag, George Kaufman, and Alden Toevs, "Management Strategies for Savings and Loan

Associations to Reduce Interest Rate Risk," *Proceedings of Conference on New Sources of Capital for the Savings and Loan Industry* (Federal Home Loan Bank of San Francisco, 1979); G. O. Bierwag, George Kaufman, and Alden Toevs, "Immunizing for Multiple Planning Periods," (Working Paper, University of Oregon, June 1980), and G. O. Bierwag, George Kaufman and Alden Toevs, "The Sensitivity of Immunization to Correctly and Incorrectly Identified Stochastic Processes," (Working Paper, University of Oregon, August 1980).

9. Duration is frequently used also as a proxy for basis risk. Because the change in the price of a bond is determined by the change in all discount rates in the term structure up to the maturity of the bond, the duration to be used must be based on the correct stochastic process causing these rate changes. This will require the same IDs as required for immunization. Thus the Macaulay duration is an accurate measure of basis risk only for flat yield curves.

10. For a single bond whose maturity is less than the planning periods, all the proceeds are assumed to be reinvested in a bond whose maturity is equal to the remaining length of the planning period. Thus, unexpected interest rate changes have no price effect; they affect only reinvestment income.

11. The greater increase in reinvestment income than decrease in price and the resulting slightly higher return realized than promised occurs because changes in bond prices and interest rates are nonlinearly related.

12. Interest rate risk is not precisely zero, as the realized return can be above but not below the promised return. Although the above analysis refers only to default-free bonds, the theory is equally applicable to any security, equity as well as debt. When future cash flows and terminal values are uncertain, probabilities must be assigned to these values and the computed IDs become expected IDs. In order to achieve immunization with these securities, nonsystematic risk must first be eliminated through appropriate diversification. Some preliminary analysis appears in George G. Kaufman, "Duration Planning Period and Tests of the Capital Asset Pricing Model," *Journal of Financial Research*, Spring 1980, 1–9.

13. Some of these arguments were made by Josph Stiglitz lin 1970: "If there are multiperiod bonds, returns will not in general be statistically independent over time; moreover which is the safe security and which is the risky depends on one's horizon, and as the individual grows older, this is likely to change . . . It is not correct to treat the long-term bond as a risky asset and the short-term bond as a safe asset. Since, from different horizons each are safe and from different horizons each are risky, at times each may act 'more' like a safe asset then the other." Joseph E. Stiglitz, "A Consumption-Oriented Theory of the Demand for Financial Assets and the Term Structure of Interests Rates," *Review of Economic Studies* (July 1970), 349.

14. For the sake of expediency and because of the roughness of the data, the yields to maturity are not adjusted to their zero coupon equivalents. To the extent that the Durand data are annual averages, they understate the variance in daily interest rates and bond prices. This may affect the results if the incorrect stochastic process and associated ID are selected and if the individual trading prices fluctuate around the "true" price for that day.

15. Other stochastic processes have been developed in Jonathan E. Ingersoll, Jr., Jeffrey Skelton, and Roman Weil, "Duration Forty Years Later," *Journal of Financial and Quantitative Analysis* (November 1978); John C. Cox, Jonathan Ingersoll Jr., and Stephen Ross, "Duration and Measurement of Basis Risk," *Journal of Business* (January 1979), and Michael J. Brennan and Eduardo S. Schwartz, *Savings Bonds: Theory and Empirical Evidence* (New York: Salomon Brothers Center for the Study of Financial Institutions, New York University 1979).

16. The duration of the portfolio of bonds is a function of the duration of the constituent bonds. See Appendix.

17. The relationship between duration and maturity is discussed in Michael H. Hopewell and George G. Kaufman, "Bond Price Volatility and Term to Maturity: A Generalized Respecification," *American Economic Review*, September 1973, 749–53.

18. Bierwag and Kaufman, "Bond Portfolio Strategy Simulations: A Critique."

19. Because duration is a mean, portfolios having the same duration can have different second (variance) and higher moments.

20. Bierwag, Kaufman and Toevs, "The Sensitivity of Immunization to Correctly and Incorrectly Identified Stochastic Processes."

21. It may be noted that, to the extent the stochastic process is incorrectly identified and an incorrect ID used to immunize a portfolio, the investor has in effect pursued an active rather than passive strategy.

22. The ability of the IDs to generate returns approximating the promised planning period yields is strong evidence that the imputed forward rates contain substantial information about expected future rates as suggested by the expectations theory of the term structures. The slightly lower than promised average returns suggest the possibility of liquidity premiums.

23. Bierwag, Kaufman and Toevs, "Sensitivity of Immunization to Correctly and Incorrectly Identified Stochastic Processes."

OFFICIAL ATTENDEES:
DURATION CONFERENCE, ASHLAND, OREGON

David Babbel
University of California at Berkeley

G. O. Bierwag
University of Oregon

Phelim Boyle
University of British Columbia

Norman Bradley
U.S. National Bank (Portland)

Michael Brennan
University of British Columbia

Krista Chinn
Data Resources, Inc.

Peter Christensen
Smith Barney Harris Upham (New York)

Kurt Dew
Chicago Mercantile Exchange

Edward Dyl
University of Wyoming

Lawrence Fisher
Rutgers University

Chris Foley
Bank of America

Gifford Fong
Gifford Fong Associates (Santa Monica)

Bob Fuhrman
Barr Rosenberg Associates

William Gibson
McGraw Hill (New York)

Charles Haley
University of Washington

Robert Higgins
University of Washington

James Hoag
University of California, Berkeley

Jonathan Ingersoll
University of Chicago

Martin Jones
Harris Bank (Chicago)

Michael Jozsa
Eberstat Asset Management (New York)

George G. Kaufman
Loyola University of Chicago

Terrence Langetieg
University of Southern California

David Wilson
Morgan Stanley

Richard McEnally
University of North Carolina

Jeffrey Nelson
Stanford University

Hugh Richey
Sun Life Assurance

Gordon Roberts
Dalhousie University (Canada)

Richard Roll
University of California, Los Angeles

Barr Rosenberg
Barr Rosenberg Associates and University of California at Berkeley

Harvey Rosenblum
Federal Reserve Bank of Chicago

Stephen Schaefer
Stanford University

Eduardo Schwartz
University of British Columbia

William Sharpe
Stanford University

James Snyder
Northern Trust (Chicago)

Thomas Steffanci
Trust Company of the West (Los Angeles)

Alden Toevs
University of Oregon

Irwin Vanderhoof
Equitable Life Assurance Society (New York)

Oldrich Vasicek
Gifford Fong Associates (Santa Monica)

James Ward
Manufacturers Hanover Trust Co. (New York)

Jeffrey Wernick
National Bank of Detroit

Richard West
Dartmouth College

Paul Wilkinson
Chicago Board of Trade

David Woolford
The First National Bank of Chicago

Young W. Yoon
Equitable Life Assurance Society (New York)

Ray Zemon
Lincoln Income Group (Chicago)

BIOGRAPHICAL SKETCH OF
THE CONTRIBUTORS

David F. Babbel.   Assistant Professor of Business Economics, University of California at Berkeley. B.A. from Brigham Young University, M.B.A. and Ph.D. from the University of Florida. His major fields of interest include international finance, capital markets, and investment strategies.

Michael Brennan.   Albert E. Hall Professor of Finance, University of British Columbia. B.A. from Oxford University, M.B.A. from the University of Pittsburgh, and Ph.D. from the Massachusetts Institute of Technology. He has published widely in the areas of corporate finance, regulation and valuation of financial securities, and currently serves as editor of the *Journal of Finance.*

Peter E. Christensen.   Vice President, Fixed Income Research Department, The First Boston Corporation. B.A. from Cornell University and M.B.A. from New York University. His areas of concern include fixed income strategy and bond immunization. He delivered his address while a Second Vice President, Smith Barney, Harris, Upham & Co. He was previously employed by the Equitable Life Assurance Society of the U.S.

Lawrence Fisher.   Professor, Rutgers University and Consultant, Salomon Brothers. B.A. from Pomona College and M.A. and Ph.D. from the University of Chicago. He previously taught at the University of Chicago and was associated with the Center for Research in Security Prices. He has published widely in security market prices and returns.

H. Gifford Fong.   President, Gifford Fong Associates, B.S., M.B.A., and J.D. all from the University of California at Berkeley. His major interests include the bond market and the development of software for formulating and evaluating portfolio strategies.

Jonathan Ingersoll.   Associate Professor of Finance, University of Chicago. B.S., M.S., and Ph.D. all from the Massachusetts Institute of Technology. He has published widely in the areas of option pricing, contingent claims, and bond valuation.

Michael Jozsa.   Vice President, Eberstadt Asset Management. B.B.A. from Kent State University. His primary responsibility includes portfolio pricing. He was previously employed by the Equitable Life Assurance Society of the U.S.

Terrence Langetieg.   Associate Professor of Finance, University of Southern California. B.A., M.S., and Ph.D. from the University of Wisconsin-Madison. His fields of interest include financial intermediaries, corporate mergers, and portfolio management.

Martin Leibowitz.   Managing Director, Salomon Brothers, Inc. A.B. and M.S. from the University of Chicago and Ph.D. from New York University. He heads the bond portfolio analysis department and has published widely in the areas of bond valuation and portfolio strategies.

Jeffrey Nelson.   Marakon Associates. B.A. from Clairmont Men's College and B.S. and M.S. from Stanford University. He is on leave from the Ph.D. program in finance at Stanford University. His major field of interest is corporate finance.

Stephen Schaefer.   Senior Research Fellow, London Business School. M.A. from Cambridge University and Ph.D. from the University of London. He was formerly Assistant Professor of Finance at Stanford University. His major fields of interest include bond pricing and the effects of taxes on securities markets.

Eduardo Schwartz. Associate Professor, University of British Columbia. B.S. from the University of Chile, M.S. and Ph.D. from the University of British Columbia. He has published widely in the areas of business finance and the pricing of options, bonds, and insurance contracts.

William Sharpe. Timken Professor of Finance, Stanford University. B.A., M.A., and Ph.D. all from the University of California at Los Angeles. He has published widely in the areas of investments and portfolio theory and contributed significantly to the development of the capital asset pricing model. He is a past president of the American Finance Association.

Thomas Steffanci. Senior Vice President, Trust Company of the West. B.A. from Providence College, M.A. from the University of New Hampshire, and Ph.D. from the University of Connecticut. His major area of concern is financial market analysis.

Irwin Vanderhoof. Senior Vice President, Equitable Life Assurance Society of the U.S. B.A. from Worcester Polytechnic Institute. He has made major contributions in the areas of actuarial science and analyzing the problems of financial intermediaries.

Oldrich A. Vasicek. Vice President, Gifford Fong Associates. M.S. from the Czech Technical University of Prague and Ph.D. from Charles University (Prague). His areas of interest include pure and applied probability theory in statistics, quantitative finance, and operations research.

James S. Ward. President, Ward Wissner Capital Management. B.S. and M.B.A. from New York University. He was previously Vice President at the Manufacturers Hanover Trust Company. His major interest is in investment strategies.

Richard West. Dean and Professor of Finance, Amos Tuck School of Business Administration, Dartmouth College. B.A. from Yale University, M.B.A. and Ph.D. from the University of Chicago. He has previously been on the faculty of Cornell University and the University of Oregon. He has published in the areas of securities markets, investment banking, and investment strategy.

Ray Zemon. Executive Vice President, Lincoln Income Group. B.S. from Rensselaer Polytech Institute and M.B.A. from the University of Wisconsin-Madison. He was formerly in the fixed income departments at The First National Bank of Chicago and the Harris Trust and Savings Bank.

BIOGRAPHICAL SKETCH OF
THE EDITORS

G. O. Bierwag.   Professor of Finance and Economics, School of Business Administration, University of Arizona.

Professor Bierwag received his B.A. from the University of Idaho (1958) and Ph.D. in economics from Northwestern University (1962). From 1962 through 1981, he was assistant professor, associate professor and full professor of economics at the University of Oregon. He was visiting professor at the Warwick University (England) in 1968–1969.

Professor Bierwag's teaching and research interests are in econometrics, economic and financial theory, and the mathematics of bond prices. He has published extensively in the *American Economic Review, Journal of Finance, Journal of Finance and Quantitative Analysis* and other professional publications. Professor Bierwag is the author of *The Primary Market for Municipal Debt: Bidding Rules and the Cost of Long-Term Borrowing* (JAI Press, 1981). He is on the board of editors of the *American Economic Review, Journal of Financial and Quantitative Analysis,* and *Journal of Financial Research* and is on the board of directors of the Western Finance Association.

Alden Toevs.   Associate Professor of Economics, University of Oregon.

Professor Toevs received his B.S. from Lewis and Clark College (1971) and Ph.D. in economics from Tulane University (1975). From 1975 through 1978, he taught economics at Louisiana State University and was a graduate fellow at the Massachusetts Institute of Technology in 1976. In 1982, he was a visiting scholar at the Federal Reserve Bank of San Francisco. He has been at the University of Oregon since 1978.

Professor Toevs' teaching and research interests are in microeconomics, financial economics, and econometrics. He has published in the *Journal of Finance, Southern Economic Journal, Journal of Portfolio Management,* and *Journal of Bank Research* and has contributed chapters to a number of books.

George G. Kaufman.   John F. Smith, Jr. Professor of Finance and Economics, School of Business Administration, Loyola University of Chicago.

Professor Kaufman received his B.A. from Oberlin College (1954), M.A. from the University of Michigan (1955), and Ph.D. in economics from the University of Iowa (1962). He was senior economist at the Federal Reserve Bank of Chicago from 1959 to 1970. From 1970 to 1980, he was the John B. Rogers Professor of Banking and Finance and Director of the Center for Capital Market Research in the College of Business Administration at the University of Oregon. He has been a visiting professor at Stanford University (1975–76) and the University of California at Berkeley (1979) and a visiting scholar at the Federal Reserve Bank of San Francisco (1976) and the Office of the Comptroller of the Currency (1978). Professor Kaufman also served as Deputy to the Assistant Secretary for Economic Policy of the U.S. Treasury in 1976.

Professor Kaufman's teaching and research interests are in financial economics, institutions, and markets and he has published extensively in the *American Economic Review, Journal of Finance, Journal of Financial and Quantitative Research* and other professional journals. Professor Kaufman is the author of *Money, the Financial System and the Economy* (third edition, Houghton-Mifflin, 1981) and *The U.S. Financial System: Money, Markets, and Institutions* (Prentice-Hall, Second Edition, 1983). He served on the board of directors of the American Finance Association (1977–80) and as president of the Western Finance Association (1974–75).

Index